Visual (vi) Editor

Syntax:

vi [-options] [command] [filename]

Options:

w n : sets the default window size to n.
R : sets a read-only option of input file.

Special Keys:

Interrupt (Del) : generates an interrupt.
/ : used to specify a string to be searched for in forward direction.
? : like '/' but performs backwards search.
: : prompt for ex command.

Text Insertion:

i [text] **ESC**
a [text] **ESC**
o [text] **ESC**

Text Deletion

x : deletes char. beneath cursor.
X : deletes char. before cursor.
d d : deletes whole line.
D : deletes from cursor to end of line.

To exit editor:

Z Z : editor buffer written to file only if changes were made.
: x : does same as zz.
: q ! : cancels editing session.

UNIX® Programming
Methods and Tools

James F. Peters III
Kansas State University

Harcourt Brace Jovanovich, Publishers
and its subsidiary, Academic Press

San Diego   New York   Chicago   Austin   Washington, D.C.
London   Sydney   Tokyo   Toronto

To Kathie

Cover photo: Werner Kalber, Professional Photographic Services

Copyright © 1988 by Harcourt Brace Jovanovich, Inc.

All rights reserved. No part of this publication may be reproduced or transmitted in any form or by any means, electronic or mechanical, including photocopy, recording, or any information storage and retrieval system, without permission in writing from the publisher.

Requests for permission to make copies of any part of the work should be mailed to: Permissions, Harcourt Brace Jovanovich, Publishers, Orlando, Florida 32887.

ISBN: 0-15-593021-4

Library of Congress Catalog Card Number: 87-81874

Printed in the United States of America

Unix is a registered trademark of AT&T Bell Labs.

NOVA and ECLIPSE are registered trademarks of Data General; PDP and VAX are registered trademarks of Digital Electronic Corporation; Honeywell 6000 is a registered trademark of Honeywell; IBM PC, IBM PC XT, and IBM PC AT are registered trademarks of International Business Machines Corporation; Xenix is a registered trademark of Microsoft; SCO and SCO Xenix System V are registered trademarks of Santa Cruz Operation; Tunis is a registered trademark of the University of Toronto; MULTICS is a registered trademark of the Massachusettes Institute of Technology; Univac 1100 is a registered trademark of Univac; 4.2/4.3BSD is a registered trademark of the University of California Board of Regents.

Preface

Unix has many features that have made it one of the most widely used operating systems. Since it is written almost entirely in C, it is highly portable and thus is commonly found on a wide variety of computers, both large-scale and micro. Its powerful shells and rich selection of system calls make it an ideal tool for system programming. Its sh and csh shells offer a wide spectrum of built-in commands, making Unix readily accessible to non-programmers. Customizing the use of Unix by setting up command procedures (files of Unix commands) is a simple matter. The sh and csh shells have a healthy selection of control structures that make shell programming possible. Finally, Unix inherits from C both elegance and simplicity.

This book constitutes an introduction to shell programming that draws on the techniques and methods of software engineering. It begins with the Bourne shell and concludes with the Joy C shell, and it also gives a complete presentation of stream editing with **sed** and software development with **awk**. It assumes no prior knowledge of Unix. The book includes the following special features:

Experiments   Each chapter contains experiments that are step-by-step developments of ideas, applications of Unix tools, or opportunities for the student to test out what is being discussed. Each experiment represents a mini-tutorial on some feature of Unix.

Early treatment of processes   Chapter 3 offers an in-depth study of Unix processes and also introduces seven ways of executing commands.

Complete procedures   Unix programming tools can be used to fashion new tools in the form of command procedures, and this book emphasizes throughout a variety of procedures that suggest how Unix can be used to create a customized working environment.

Refinements   Most of the procedures explained in this textbook have been designed in stages. The same procedure is returned to several times, to show by example how refinements can be added to produce a procedure that is more useful as well as "robust."

Pre- and post-conditions   Special attention is given to providing the pre- and post-conditions for command procedures. These are put into comments at the beginning of a procedure.

Chapter aims   Each chapter begins with a set of aims, or "roadmaps," that give the student a quick overview of the chapter.

Chapter introductions   Also at the beginning of each chapter is an introduction to that chapter's new symbols and terminology.

Chapter summaries   These summaries have been deliberately written as a fresh look at the ideas in the chapter, not merely a restatement of them, so that students can recognize by reading the summary whether they understand the chapter or not.

Review of commands, symbols, and keywords   Each chapter concludes with a review of the commands, symbols, and keywords that have been presented. These lists will later serve as handy reminders of the chapter material.

Review quizzes   Each chapter has a review quiz that offers the student another way to test his or her understanding of chapter concepts.

Annotated reading lists   An annotated reading list appears at the end of each chapter to direct students' attention to other publications they may want to read in parallel with this book.

Graded exercises   Exercises at the end of each chapter are graded by means of these hourglass symbols:

⧗ for intermediate   ⧖ for advanced

Elementary exercises have no symbol.

Shell Commands Handbook   At the end of the book is a directory of the commands that have been introduced. A knowledge of these commands is crucial, and the handbook is an easy reference for students with questions about any of the commands that have been introduced here.

ACKNOWLEDGMENTS

The development of materials for this book was funded in part by AT&T, which provided a 3B2 computer and software as well as consultants for an experimental System V Unix course; by Santa Cruz Operation, which provided an evaluation copy of its Xenix System V operating system for the IBM PC XT, IBM PC AT, and all major 8086- or 80286-based personal computers; and by St. John's University, which supported this research as part of various course development projects.

I also wish to thank the following for their various suggestions and generous help: John G. Seiler, Tom Schroer, Andy Wilde, Dr. Tom Kirkman, and Ann Lee Bain at St. John's University; Brigid Fuller and Kirk Raymond at the Santa Cruz Operation; Don Zierdon, Dave Massman, Mike Flynn, and Keiler Dreir at At&T; Mike Marrin and Glenn Fugeber at Computerland, St. Cloud, Minn.; Ed Smolensky, director of the

Collegeville Community Credit Union; Ruth and Richard Kellum; Mary Ortiz, Margie and Tim Rapley; Margaret Dumont; Kirk and Kris Peters; Brian and Hungi Peters; Joe Peters; Erik Peters; Dr. Richard Allen at St. Olaf College; Tom Burks at AT&T; Dale Brown, formerly at Academic Press; Ted Buchholz at Holt, Rinehart and Winston; Karl Glander at Mankato State University; and Dave Ranum at the University of Utah.

I am grateful to the following reviewers for their helpful comments and suggestions: Dr. Hamed Sallam, Mankato State University; Henry A. Etlinger, Rochester Institute of Technology; and Frank Burke at AT & T.

I want to pay special tribute to one of my students, John G. Seiler, at St. John's University, who found many neat ways to improve procedures that appear in the book. Both John Seiler and Andy Wilde verified many of the experiments, procedures, and exercises on a variety of different Unix-based systems: Unix System V on an AT&T 3B2, SCO Xenix System V on an IBM PC AT, and Ultrix-11 on a PDP-11/24. Many of my ideas on cross-referencing stem from discussions with Heinz-Jürgen Hess at the Leibniz Archiv, Hannover, West Germany. A number of the experiments and related problems grew out of discussions with Dave Ranum, Karl Glander, and Dr. Sallam.

I also wish to thank the following persons at Harcourt Brace Jovanovich: Jack Thomas, Margie Rogers, Amy Dunn, Kim Svetich, Cheryl Solheid, Stacy Simpson, Lynn Edwards, and especially Richard Bonacci and Meg Van Buren, to whom I owe a great deal for helping to guide the book through its various stages to completion. Finally, my wife, Kathie, and the rest of my family have made this book possible by letting me spend many hours chasing after rainbows cast by Unix when I should have been doing other things.

J. F. P.

Brief Contents

1 Discovering Unix / 1
2 Files and Directories / 45
3 Processes and the Shell / 84
4 Command Procedures / 131
5 Procedure Design / 179
6 Filters and Stream Editing / 236
7 awk Programming Methods / 282
8 The Joy C Shell / 334

Shell Commands Handbook / 396

Appendixes / 427

    Appendix A: Tables / 427
    Appendix B: Guide to Editing with **ed** / 429
    Appendix C: Guide to Editing with **vi** / 431
    Appendix D: C Programs / 432
    Appendix E: Cross-reference of Shell Procedures and Commands / 434

Selected Solutions / 438
Index of Symbols / 443
Index / 444

Contents

Preface / v

1 Discovering Unix / 1

1.0 Aims / 1
1.1 The Unix Landscape / 1
1.2 What is Unix? / 3
1.3 The Shell / 4
    1.3.1 The First Steps with Unix / 4
    1.3.2 Commands and Command Lines / 6
    1.3.3 Customizing Your Terminal with the **stty** Command / 9
    1.3.4 More about the **mail** Command / 11
1.4 A Beginner's Guide to Unix Files / 13
    1.4.1 Directories / 14
    1.4.2 Subdirectories / 16
    1.4.3 Changing Directories with the **cd** Command / 19
    1.4.4 Fishing through Your Directories / 21
    1.4.5 Filenames / 21
    1.4.6 Pathnames / 22
    1.4.7 Your .profile / 23
    1.4.8 Search Paths / 24
    1.4.9 Wildcards / 25
    1.4.10 Copying, Moving and Removing Files / 26
1.5 Redirection of Input and Output / 27
    1.5.1 Creating Files with **cat** and Redirection / 31
    1.5.2 Using the **cat** Command to Concatenate Files / 32

1.6   Pipes / 32
      1.6.1 Pipes and Redirection / 33
      1.6.2 Pipes and Filters / 34
1.7   Summary / 37
1.8   Review of Commands, Symbols and Keywords / 39
      1.8.1 Commands / 39
      1.8.2 Symbols / 39
      1.8.3 Keywords / 40
1.9   Exercises / 41
1.10 Review Quiz / 43
1.11 Further Reading / 43

2 Files and Directories / 45

2.0   Aims / 45
2.1   Introduction to the Unix File System / 45
2.2   Ways to Create Files / 49
      2.2.1 Pipe Fitting with the **tee** Command / 49
      2.2.2 Splitting a File into Smaller Files / 53
      2.2.3 Creating a New File with **ed** / 55
      2.2.4 Creating New Files with **vi** / 56
2.3   Directories / 57
      2.3.1 Inspecting Inumbers / 57
      2.3.2 Analyzing the Bytes Representing Inumbers / 58
      2.3.3 Inumbers Written in hex / 60
      2.3.4 Inodes / 61
      2.3.5 File Permissions and the **chmod** Command / 62
      2.3.6 Special Access Bits / 64
      2.3.7 File Types / 65
      2.3.8 Block and Serial Devices / 65
2.4   Using the **od** Command to Display a Complete File / 66
2.5   Disk Usage / 66
2.6   Finding Files with the **find** Command / 67
2.7   Linking Files with the **ln** Command / 70
2.8   Survey of Selected Unix Directories / 73
      2.8.1 /bin and /usr/bin for Commands / 73
      2.8.2 /usr/man and /usr/doc for Manuals and Documentation / 75
      2.8.3 /lib and /usr/lib for System Libraries / 75
2.9   Summary / 75
2.10 Review of Commands, Symbols and Keywords / 77
      2.10.1 Commands / 77
      2.10.2 Symbols / 78
      2.10.3 Keywords / 78
2.11 Exercises / 79
2.12 Review Quiz / 82
2.13 Further Reading / 83

3 Processes and the Shell / 84

- 3.0 Aims / 84
- 3.1 Introduction to Unix Processes / 84
- 3.2 Ways to Execute Commands / 88
  - 3.2.1 Running a Shell for Multiple Commands / 91
  - 3.2.2 Executing a Command Using **sh** / 93
  - 3.2.3 Using a Dot to Execute a Command / 94
  - 3.2.4 How to Save Time with the Dot Command / 94
  - 3.2.5 Executing a Command with **exec** / 95
  - 3.2.6 Command Substitution with Backward Quotes / 96
  - 3.2.7 Executing Commands Assigned to Variables / 99
- 3.3 Special Variables / 100
  - 3.3.1 Special Command-line Variables / 101
  - 3.3.2 Using Special Variables to Select Actions / 105
  - 3.3.3 Refinement: Adding Arguments / 105
  - 3.3.4 Refinement: Throwing Out the Deadwood / 106
- 3.4 The **set** Command and Standard Shell Variables / 106
  - 3.4.1 What to Do in Case You Ruin Your .profile / 107
  - 3.4.2 The Internal Field Separator (IFS) Characters / 108
  - 3.4.3 The PS1 (primary) and PS2 (secondary) Prompts / 108
  - 3.4.4 The Value of * / 109
  - 3.4.5 Exporting Variables to Child Processes / 110
  - 3.4.6 Calls-by-value / 110
  - 3.4.7 Using the **set** Diagnostic Modes in Debugging / 112
- 3.5 Customizing Your Environment with the **trap** Command / 113
- 3.6 Executing a Command in the Background / 115
- 3.7 The **$?** Exit Status Variable / 116
- 3.8 Batch Processing: Delayed Execution of a Command / 118
- 3.9 Putting a Command to Sleep: Suspended Execution / 119
  - 3.9.1 Refinement: Suspended Printing of a Message / 120
  - 3.9.2 Refinement: Embedded Background Processing / 121
- 3.10 Summary / 122
- 3.11 Review of Commands, Symbols and Keywords / 123
  - 3.11.1 Commands / 123
  - 3.11.2 Symbols / 124
  - 3.11.3 Keywords / 124
- 3.12 Exercises / 125
- 3.13 Review Quiz / 130
- 3.14 Further Reading / 130

4 Command Procedures / 131

- 4.0 Aims / 131
- 4.1 Introduction to Command Procedures / 131

4.2 Control Structures / 133
    4.2.1 Selection Control with a Simple **if** Statement / 134
    4.2.2 Double Alternatives with an **if/then/else** / 139
    4.2.3 Example: Searching Directories / 141
    4.2.4 Selecting Multiple Alternatives with an **elif** / 142
    4.2.5 Multiple Alternatives with the **case** Statement / 143
    4.2.6 Example: Automating File Creation / 145
4.3 Iteration Control Structures / 147
    4.3.1 Indexed Iteration with a **for** Statement / 147
    4.3.2 Conditional Iteration with **while** and **until** / 151
    4.3.3 Example: Housecleaning Procedure / 154
4.4 Evaluating Conditions with the **test** Command / 158
4.5 Arithmetic with the **expr** Command / 160
4.6 Comparing Strings with the **expr** Command / 162
4.7 Evaluation of Shell Variables / 166
4.8 Here Documents / 168
4.9 Recursive Procedures / 170
4.10 Summary / 173
4.11 Review of Commands, Symbols and Keywords / 174
    4.11.1 Commands / 174
    4.11.2 Symbols / 174
    4.11.3 Keywords / 175
4.12 Exercises / 175
4.13 Review Quiz / 177
4.12 Further Reading / 178

5 Procedure Design / 179

5.0 Aims / 179
5.1 Introduction to Procedure Design / 179
5.2 Procedure Design Techniques / 182
    5.2.1 Scaffolding / 183
    5.2.2 Identifying Preconditions and Postconditions / 184
    5.2.3 Invariant Assertions / 184
    5.2.4 Test Data / 185
    5.2.5 Robustness / 185
    5.2.6 Stepwise Refinements / 187
5.3 Deleting Files / 189
5.4 Zapping Unwanted Processes / 194
5.5 Refinement: Adding Options to **zap** / 198
5.6 Scanning Directories / 199
    5.6.1 Scanning a Directory for Subdirectories / 199
    5.6.2 Scanning Directories for Dated Entries / 200
    5.6.3 Scanning All Subdirectories of a Directory / 202

5.7 Hewett and Gosling Method of Bundling Software / 202
    5.7.1 Bundling Software Recursively / 205
    5.7.2 Unbundling into Subdirectories / 208
5.8 Other Scanners / 210
    5.8.1 A Spelling Checker / 210
    5.8.2 Gred, a Single-result Greplike Command / 218
    5.8.3 Using **cal** to Print a Partial Calendar / 219
    5.8.4 A Phone Directory Scanner / 221
    5.8.5 Another Directory Scanner / 222
5.9 Other Files for Your $HOME/bin Directory / 222
5.10 Cross-referencing New Commands / 224
5.11 Summary / 225
5.12 Review of Commands, Symbols and Keywords / 226
    5.12.1 Commands / 226
    5.12.2 Symbols / 226
    5.12.3 Keywords / 227
5.13 Exercises / 227
5.14 Review Quiz / 234
5.15 Further Reading / 235

6 Filters and Stream Editing / 236

6.0 Aims / 236
6.1 Introduction to Filters and Stream Editing / 236
6.2 The **grep** Family / 240
    6.2.1 How to Construct Regular Expressions / 240
    6.2.2 Extended Regular Expressions for **egrep** / 245
6.3 Stream Editing / 248
    6.3.1 Stream Editor Functions / 250
    6.3.2 Multiple Input-line Functions / 253
    6.3.3 Hold and Get functions / 257
6.4 **sed** Equivalents of **grep** Family Commands / 259
6.5 The Kernighan-Mashey Rhyming Dictionary Problem / 261
6.6 Lewis Carroll's Game of Doublets / 265
6.7 Filtering the Output from **cal** / 266
    6.7.1 Printing the Remaining Weeks in the Month / 267
    6.7.2 Filtering out the Remaining Days of the Month / 268
6.8 Summary / 272
6.9 Review of Commands, Symbols and Keywords / 272
    6.9.1 Commands / 272
    6.9.2 Symbols / 273
    6.9.3 Keywords / 273
6.10 Exercises / 274
6.11 Review Quiz / 281
6.12 Further Reading / 281

7 awk Programming Methods / 282

- 7.0 Aims / 282
- 7.1 Introduction to Features of **awk** / 282
- 7.2 Structure of **awk** Programs / 283
- 7.3 Records and Fields / 286
- 7.4 Patterns / 288
  - 7.4.1 BEGIN and END Patterns / 288
  - 7.4.2 Conditionals / 290
  - 7.4.3 Pattern Ranges / 291
  - 7.4.4 Using Shell Arguments Inside **awk** Programs / 291
- 7.5 Variables, Arithmetic, and Assignments / 293
- 7.6 Formatted Output with **printf** / 295
- 7.7 Control Structures / 298
- 7.8 Built-in Functions / 301
- 7.9 Arrays / 304
  - 7.9.1 Associative Arrays / 306
  - 7.9.2 Example: Scanning /usr/dict/words / 307
  - 7.9.3 Example: Bentley Anagram Classes / 308
  - 7.9.4 Random Numbers and Frequency Tables / 313
- 7.10 Interacting with the Shell / 316
- 7.11 Comparison of **awk** and C / 318
- 7.12 **awk** Leads to C / 320
- 7.13 Summary / 323
- 7.14 Review of Symbols and Keywords / 323
  - 7.14.1 Symbols / 323
  - 7.14.2 Keywords / 324
- 7.15 Exercises / 326
- 7.16 Review Quiz / 332
- 7.17 Further Reading / 332

8 The Joy C Shell / 334

- 8.0 Aims / 334
- 8.1 Introduction to the C Shell / 334
- 8.2 Getting Started with the C Shell / 337
  - 8.2.1 Customizing Your Environment with .login and .cshrc / 338
  - 8.2.2 C Shell Escape Characters / 344
  - 8.2.3 A note on **whereis** / 346
  - 8.2.4 Customizing logoff with .logout / 346
  - 8.2.5 Enhanced Version of the .cshrc File / 347
- 8.3 Retrieving Events in Your History / 348
- 8.4 Aliases / 350
  - 8.4.1 Nested Aliases / 351
  - 8.4.2 Alias Arguments / 353
  - 8.4.3 A Word of Caution about Your History and Aliases / 355

- 8.5 C Shell Procedures / 355
  - 8.5.1 Referencing Command-line Arguments with **argv** / 357
  - 8.5.2 Setting Values of C Shell Variables / 360
  - 8.5.3 C Shell Operators / 363
  - 8.5.4 Variables with Numeric Values / 364
  - 8.5.5 Bitwise Operations / 364
  - 8.5.6 C Shell Control Structures / 367
  - 8.5.7 Example: Checking for Empty or Nonexistent Files / 370
- 8.6 New Clothes for Old Procedures / 372
  - 8.6.1 Automating File Creation / 373
  - 8.6.2 Automating the Deletion of Old Files / 374
  - 8.6.3 Anagram Classes Revisited / 375
- 8.7 Redirection in the C Shell / 379
- 8.8 Globbing Filenames / 381
- 8.9 Summary / 386
- 8.10 Review of Commands, Symbols and Keywords / 388
  - 8.10.1 Commands / 388
  - 8.10.2 Symbols and Special Characters / 389
  - 8.10.3 Keywords / 390
- 8.11 Exercises / 391
- 8.12 Review Quiz / 393
- 8.13 Further Reading / 394

Shell Commands Handbook / 396

Appendixes / 427

Appendix A: Tables / 427
Appendix B: Guide to Editing with **ed** / 429
Appendix C: Guide to Editing with **vi** / 431
Appendix D: C Programs / 432
Appendix E: Cross-reference of Shell Procedures and Commands / 434

Selected Solutions / 438
Index of Symbols / 443
Index / 444

1 Discovering Unix

*Intelligence . . . is the faculty of
making artificial objects,
especially tools to make tools, and
of varying the fabrication
indefinitely.*
—Henri Bergson, 1907

1.0 AIMS

- Give an overview of the various versions of Unix
- Distinguish between the Unix kernel and shell
- Start using Unix
- Introduce various commands
- Give a brief tour of the Unix file system
- Show various forms of communication between persons logged onto a Unix system
- Show how program input and output can be redirected
- Introduce pipes, pipelines, and filters

1.1 THE UNIX LANDSCAPE

An *operating system* is a program which serves as an interface between computer resources and computer users. An operating system is used to control the use of computer resources. In effect, an operating system is a resource manager. Unix is an operating system designed to permit time sharing on a computer system. A *time-share* system makes it possible for more than one user to carry out various processes on the same computer at the same time.

Unix was developed by Ken Thompson and Dennis Ritchie at Bell Labs during the late 1960s and early 1970s. The first production-level Unix system was run on a PDP-11/20 in 1971. It now runs on a variety of different computer systems. These include various PDP-11 and VAX-11 computer systems from the Digital Computer Corporation. Unix also runs on an Interdata 7/32 and 8/32, Amdahl 470, Honeywell 6000, Data General Nova and Eclipse, HP 2100, Harris /7, Univac 1100 series, Amdahl 5800 series, and IBM S/370. Finally, Unix also runs on a variety of microprocessors like the IBM PC/AT, IBM PC/XT, and the AT&T UNIX PC. Unix is so portable largely because it is written almost entirely in the programming language C. This makes it possible to install Unix fairly easily on various systems.

There are many versions of Unix which stem from the 5th edition (Unix V5) released in 1973. It is the 7th edition of Unix (Unix V7) released in 1978 by the Bell Labs Unix Support Group (USG) which has been the dominant influence in the development of other versions of Unix. Before 1982, Unix was used internally by Bell Labs and various universities. Bell Labs released the first external version of Unix with its System III in 1982. This was followed a year later by Unix System V (System IV was never released!).

Paralleling the development of USG Unix by Bell Labs was the work done on a separate version of Unix by Bill Joy and Ozalp Babaoglu starting in 1978 at the University of California at Berkeley. Joy and Babaoglu made substantial additions to the 7th edition of Unix using a VAX-11 computer system. These additions included a provision for virtual memory, which made it possible to develop very large programs. Each of the Berkeley Unix editions is called BSD (Berkeley Software Distribution) Unix. The most popular of these is 4.2BSD and 4.3BSD Unix.

The first version of Unix for microcomputers was released by the Microsoft Corporation in 1984 and was called Xenix. MS Xenix was derived from System III and has been dubbed Xenix-3 by Marc Rochkind (1985). In 1985, the Santa Cruz Operation released its powerful Xenix System V, which we call Xenix-5 and which is derived from Unix System V. For example, both Xenix-3 and Xenix-5 run on the IBM PC/AT. Finally, Andrew S. Tanenbaum's MINIX (1987) is based on Unix V7 and runs on an IBM PC. MINIX has 12,165 lines mostly written in C.

Variants of Unix have also been developed. Perhaps the most prominent of these variants is Tunis (*Toronto UNIversity System*) developed at the University of Toronto in 1979 by Patrick Cardozo and Mark Mendell. Unlike Unix, Tunis is written entirely in the Concurrent Euclid programming language, which is also a product of the University of Toronto. (Concurrent Euclid closely resembles Modula-2.) Tunis was made compatible with Unix in 1980.

Obviously, there are many different *and* competing versions of Unix. The front-runners are System V, 8th edition Unix (called Unix Time-Sharing System, Eighth Edition [version 8]), which is being developed by the AT&T Bell Laboratories Research group, and 4.2BSD and the newly released 4.3BSD Unix. For someone new to the Unix world, this may all seem bewildering. Fortunately, IEEE (Institute for Electrical and Electronic Engineers) has just released a proposed standard for an operating system called POSIX which is based on Unix (IEEE, 1986).

It is helpful to tack up on your wall somewhere close by a chart showing how all the major versions of Unix fit together in time and in relation to each other. A very good example of such a Unix time chart is given by Peterson and Silberschatz (1985). Unfortunately, their chart predates the advent of Xenix-3 and Xenix-5 and omits mention of Tunis. To help you obtain a comprehensive view of the Unix

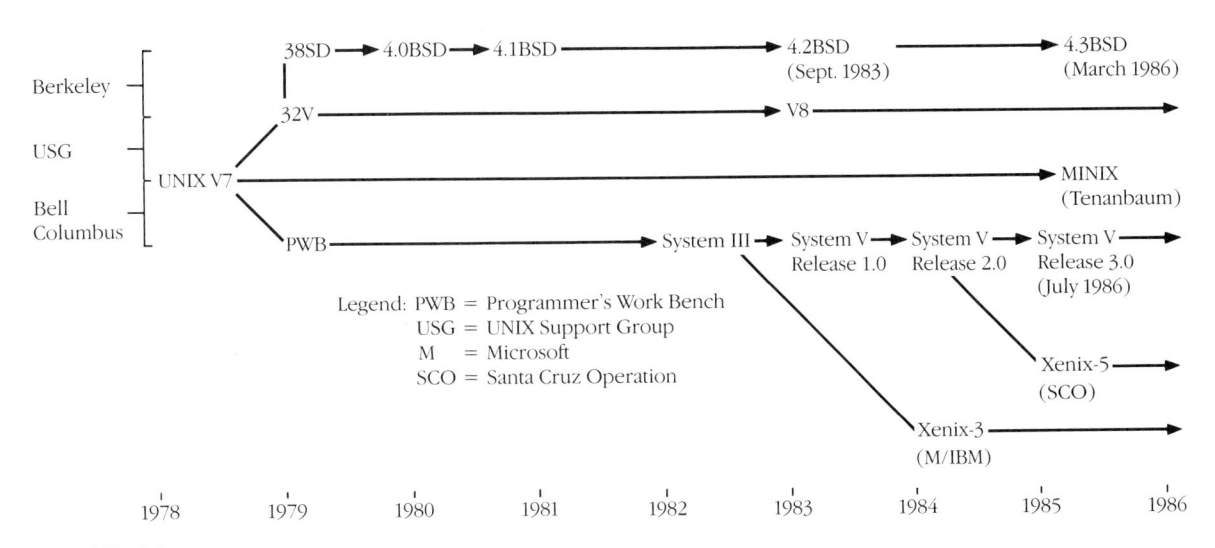

FIGURE 1.1
Unix Time Chart

landscape, an updated Unix time chart is given in Figure 1.1. A Unix standard has been proposed by the /usr/group. Details about /usr/group proposals are given in IEEE, 1986.

1.2 WHAT IS UNIX?

Unix is an operating system that supports general-purpose, time-shared use of a computer system. In other words, Unix is a multiuser system. In Unix terminology, it is the *kernel* (also called the operating system nucleus) that is the program in charge of the Unix system. The origins of Unix can be traced back to the Multics operating system at M.I.T. Multics stands for Multiplexed Information and Computing Service. Dennis Ritchie was part of the Multics development team before he joined Bell Labs. In fact, Unix is not an acronym but rather a pun on the word Multics. The name Unix was intended to indicate that while Multics attempts to do many things, Unix tries to do one thing well. Even so, the following features of Unix are carry-overs from Multics:

1. organization of the Unix file system
2. using a command processor (or shell) as a user process
3. use of a process per command
4. Multics line editing characters # and @

Unix also borrows the *fork* operation from the UC Berkeley GENIE (XCS-940) operating system. A fork is a Unix system call that creates a new process that is a clone of an existing one (the clone process inherits the user-data and system-data belonging to the old process).

Since Unix is a pun and not an acronym like IBM and VAX, we follow the more recent practice begun by Kernighan and Mashey (1982) of writing Unix instead of UNIX. (The name Unix was suggested by Brian Kernighan.)

The Unix kernel provides the following services:

1. **scheduling** the use of the central processing unit
2. **managing** the use of main memory (finding places in memory to put programs, data, and documents)
3. **file-handling** (swapping of files between main memory and various auxiliary storage units like magnetic disks, diskettes, and tapes)
4. **terminal-handling** (managing the streams of characters to and from various terminals)

Unix can also be viewed more broadly as a kernel plus a collection of other programs which are used to communicate with the kernel. For example, surrounding the kernel is another program called a *shell,* that provides an interface to the Unix kernel.

1.3 THE SHELL

The Unix shell is a *command programming language* that is used to interact with the kernel. The shell interprets commands and arguments entered at a terminal or read from a file. The name of the shell for the AT&T Bell versions of Unix (V7 and System V, for example) is 'sh.' Since sh is just a program outside the kernel, other shells are possible. For example, three shells are available in Xenix-3; three in Xenix-5. The best way to learn about a shell is to use it. To do this, you first need to log onto your Unix system. We show you how to do that next.

1.3.1 The First Steps with Unix

A terminal connected to a Unix system will display the following prompt:

```
login:
```

In response, you type

```
login: <type your username> <return>
password: <type your password> <return>
$
```

The <return> at the end of each line you type is crucial.

Be sure to type <return> at the end of each line you type. This tells the shell to start doing something with what you have typed. If you are using an IBM PC, use the <enter> key instead. If you make a typing mistake, don't worry. The shell will catch your mistake and let you know. You then need to type in your username and password again.

If you have typed your username and password correctly, the system will respond with a welcome message and shell prompt (the dollar sign or $). The system uses the name and password you have given your system administrator to determine if you have logged in properly.

The default sh shell prompt is a dollar sign ($). For instance, we can respond to the shell prompt using the **who** shell command to see who else is using the system:

```
$ who
susu         tty03           Jan 1 10:17
bwk          tty07           Jan 1 11:20
you          tty09           Jan 1 11:23
karl         tty49           Jan 1 09:18
```

This says three other persons besides you are currently on the system (on New Year's day!). You can also type

```
$ who am i
you            tty07             Jan 1 11:23
```

to view your own status (which keyboard you are using, when you logged on). The words **am i** are used as arguments to specialize the use of the who command. The implementation of the who command varies widely on various Unix systems. For example, the System V version of the who command has ten options that can be used when this command is executed. These options allow you to vary the information produced by who. You might want to check on the last time your system clock was set (usually after a system crash) by typing

```
$ who -t
       .         old time Dec 30 22:35
       .         new time Jan  1 10:15
```

The capabilities of a shell command tend to vary widely on various Unix systems. Unix V7 (the 7th edition), for instance, provides no options for the who command.

By contrast, Xenix-5 outdoes System V by providing 13 options, including a -q option to get a "quick" who listing like the following one:

```
$ who -q
# users=5
```

You will need to check Part 1 of your *Unix Programmer's Manual* to learn what options (if any) are available for the shell commands on your system. You will find that your manual has at least five parts and each of the shell commands has a (1) suffix like who (1) on p. 181 of the V7 Unix Manual (1983).

Before we look deeper into the shell, we will stop the word-train long enough to tell you how to log onto your Unix system and some other commands to help you get acquainted with your system.

1.3.2 Commands and Command Lines

The line

```
$ who am i
```

is an example of a *command line*. Each command line provides one or more commands and zero or more arguments (like **am i** used by the who command). A shell command identifies a program for the kernel to execute. It's the shell's job to interpret your command lines (find out what you are requesting). Here is a short list of Unix commands you might want to try after you have logged in:

A more complete list of shell commands is given in the Shell Commands Handbook at the end of this book (these commands are cross-referenced with shell procedures given in this book in Appendix E). Commands entered by you from a terminal keyboard are interpreted by the shell as requests to run corresponding hidden programs. Try this with the date command:

Some Unix Commands

COMMAND	EXPLANATION
cat	display file
date	gives date and time
ls	lists names of files in your directory
mail	send mail to someone
mesg	print or deny messages
who	see who's on the system
write	talk to someone on the system

```
$ date
Wed Jan 29 10:37:22 CST 1986
$
```

The shell prints the $-prompt after it finishes with the command you gave. In this case, the date command results in plenty of information about the date and time. The above output says the date command was run on a Unix system which is CST (Central Standard Time) at 10:37:22 A.M. in hours, minutes, and seconds. After you have logged in, you might also be curious about who else is logged on the system. You can satisfy your curiosity by typing the who command again:

```
$ who
phil        tty04       Mar 2 09:15
you         tty06       Mar 3 08:01
```

The who command prints out the following information about each user logged on the system:

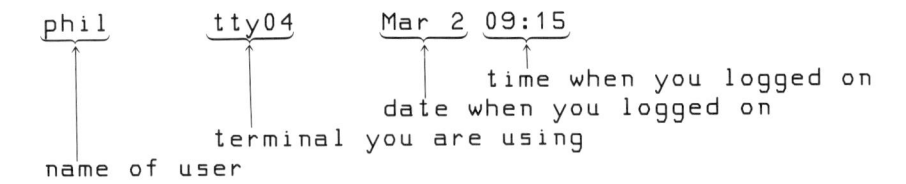

```
phil        tty04       Mar 2  09:15
 ↑            ↑           ↑     ↑
 |            |           |     time when you logged on
 |            |           date when you logged on
 |            terminal you are using
 name of user
```

A 24-hour clock is used on a Unix system, so we know Phil has been logged on for 23 hours! You may want to check if Phil is still awake by using the **write** command as follows:

```
$ write phil
Phil, are you awake? (over)
```

If Phil is awake, he may respond by also using the write command.

To let the other person know you are ready for a response, type some form of (over) each time you have finished "speaking." Since it gets tiresome typing (over) every time, you might try (o) instead. To signal the end of a writing session, you might try typing (ov&o) or just (oo) for "over and out" to let the other person know you are hanging up. To end the write session, type

```
control d
```

THE SHELL

Messages written by Phil will appear on your screen. Here is a complete sample write-session:

Sample Write Session

YOUR SCREEN	PHIL'S SCREEN
| ```
$ write phil
Phil, are you awake? (ov)



Message from phil ... <beep!>
Yes (o)
Did you sleep last night? (ov)



No (o)
Oh, well.  I sent you a
nice program in the mail
yesterday. (ov)






Thx.  I'll check it out
after I get some sleep. (oo)
(end of message)
Pleasant dreams....  Bye
(oo)
ctrl-d
$
``` | ```
$
Message from you ... <beep!>
Phil, are you awake? (ov)
write you
Yes (o)



Did you sleep last night? (ov)
No (o)




Oh, well.  I sent you a
nice program in the mail
yesterday. (ov)
Thx.  I'll check it out
after I get some sleep. (oo)
ctrl-d
$




$ Pleasant dreams....  Bye
(oo)
(end of message)
``` |

If you decide you do not want to be interrupted by messages, then type

```
$ mesg n
$
```

Now, for example, if Phil tries to write to you, here is what he sees:

8 CHAPTER 1 / DISCOVERING UNIX

```
$ write you
permission denied.
$
```

Now nobody on the system can write to you. If you later decide you want to let others write to you, then type

```
$ mesg y <return>
$
```

To find out the current mesg- state, type mesg by itself as follows:

```
$ mesg <return>
is y
$
```

It may happen that you are the only one on the system now (or you want to write to someone—Shelly, for example—on the system who blocked on-line messages with the mesg command). In that case, you can use the mail command to send a letter to that person in the following way:

```
$ mail shelly
Shelly, thanks for sending me a copy of the proposed
/usr/group Standard. Tom
ctrl-d
(end of message)
$
```

About mail:
1. Type **ctrl-d** (short for control d) to tell Unix you have reached the end of your message and exit from mail.
2. Type **delete** to abort mail, not send the note you started. (This puts your unfinished letter into a dead.letter file.)

It is helpful to get to know your keyboard, especially if you make typing mistakes.

1.3.3 Customizing Your Terminal with the stty Command

You can find out what settings your terminal has by typing

```
$ stty -a
speed 9600 baud; erase = #; kill = @; ...
$
```

Try using the erase character (# by default) when you make typos. Here is an example:

```
$ met#sg
is y
$
```

which is the same as

```
$ mesg
is y
$
```

If you want to erase an entire botched line, use an @:

```
$ notok!!!!!!!!!!!@
$
```

You can tell the shell to ignore the settings for special purpose characters with a backslash as follows:

```
$ write susu
susu, have you got a \# of butter? (ov)
Message from susu ...
No! See you \@ 10:15 am. (oo)
(end of message)
...
$
```

You can use the stty command to customize your terminal. For example, try

```
$ stty erase '^h'
$ stty kill ~
$ met^hsg
is n
$ metsg~
$
```

Now the backspace and ~ keys can be used to correct your typos. The backspace tends to be a better choice for an erase character because it "whites out" your typos. For a less messy kill character, try a control-u ('^u').

The single quotes in '^u' or '^h' are used to tell the shell that the up-arrow (^) is just a prefix to the letter h. The '^' by itself will be interpreted by the shell as what is known as a pipe operator (explained later in this chapter). The single quotes prevent a misinterpretation of the up-arrow.

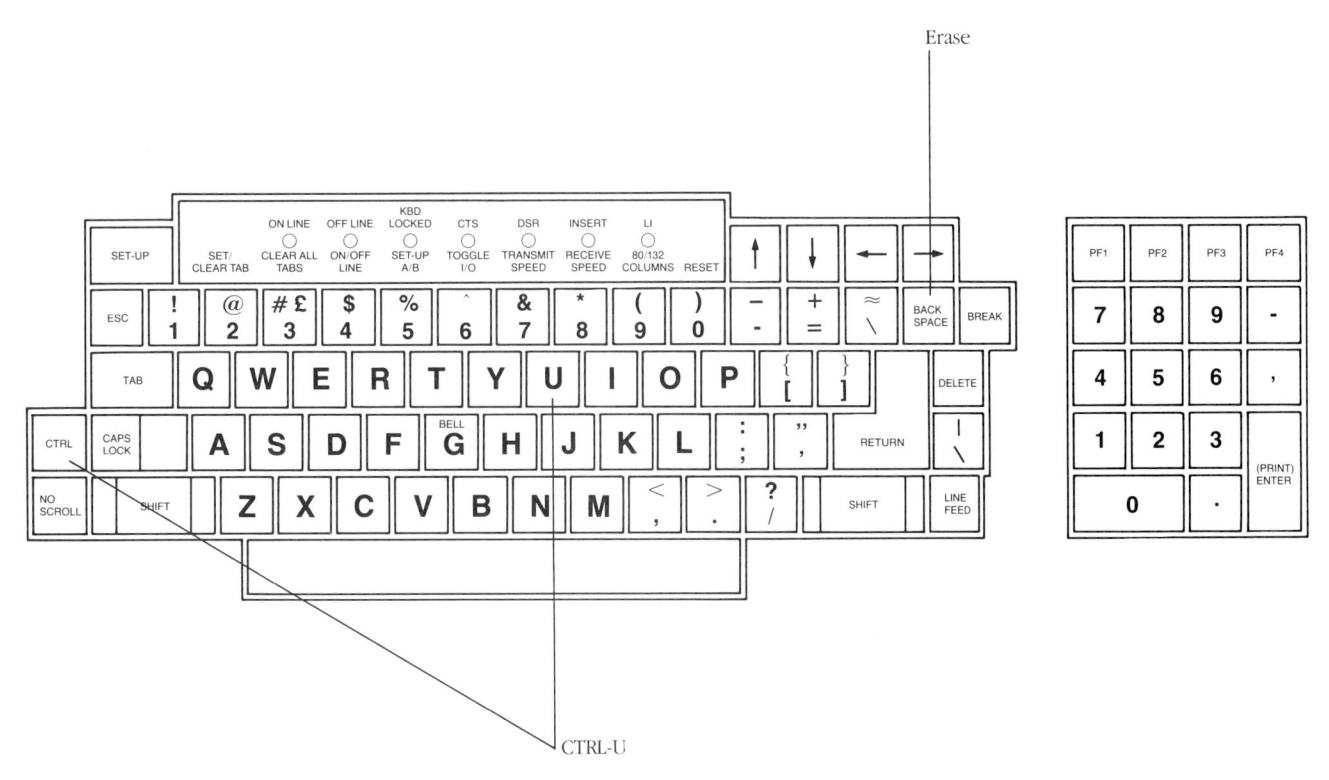

FIGURE 1.2
VT100 Keyboard

The results of the above two lines are shown graphically in Figure 1.2 with a sketch of a vt100 keyboard.

Throughout the rest of this book we will assume that a backspace is used as the erase character. Later, you will see how the #-sign can be used in command line comments.

1.3.4 More about the mail Command

To see if you have any mail, type

```
$ mail     [Type return to see first mail message.]
From shelly Wed Jan 1 12:48:47 1986
Happy New Year!
?
```

You need to type <return> to see the next message:

```
? <return>
From Tom Tue Dec 31 09:02:15 1985
```

THE SHELL

```
Have you got a copy of vol. 2 of the Programmer's
Manual I can borrow? Tom.
?
```

If you type a ? after the ?-prompt, you can get a list of mail options available to you:

```
? ?
<newline>         go on to next message
+                 same as <new-line>
d                 delete message and go on to next
                  message
p                 print message again
-                 go back to previous message
s [files]         save message in named files
w [files]         save message without header in named
                  files
q                 quit
m [persons]       mail message to named persons
!command          escape to shell to do command
? q
Held 2 messages in /usr/spool/mail/you
$
```

Here is an experiment you might try to get used to mail:

☐ EXPERIMENT

```
$ mail you
Sample message: mail is a tool.
ctrl-d
$ mail you
Another sample message: use your toolkit.
ctrl-d
$ mail
From you Wed Jan 1 14:00:56 1986
Sample message: mail is a tool.
?
```

This experiment is possible because you can mail letters to yourself. Instead of learning to use mail by burdening an unsuspecting friend with a trial-and-error session, first try to mail options on letters you have mailed to yourself. Can you tell what the following lines do?

☐ CONTINUATION OF EXPERIMENT

```
? w copy
? m susu
```

```
? -
? <new-line>
? q
```

A remarkable thing happened when you typed

```
? w copy
```

You just created a file which is used to hold a copy of the message you just read. A beginner's guide to Unix files is given in the next section.

1.4 A BEGINNER'S GUIDE TO UNIX FILES

From outward appearances, a *file* is a named piece of information. Examples of named files are **who, date,** and each of the other commands we have used so far. Each Unix command names a file which is executable by the kernel. For example, the file named **who** contains the instructions needed by the kernel to print a list of users on the system.

Here is a list of commands that are helpful in working with files:
You can judge a file by what it contains. The copy file created by

```
? w copy
```

contains a message. You can see what is in this new copy file by typing

```
$ cat copy
Sample message: mail is a tool.
$
```

It is possible to run two or more commands with the same command line by separating the commands with a semicolon (;). For example, try typing

Some File Management Commands

COMMAND	EXPLANATION
cd	change directory
cp	copy a file
file	determine file type
ls	list directory of files
mkdir	make a directory
mv	move a file
pwd	print working directory
rm	remove a file
rmdir	remove a directory

```
$ date; cat copy
Fri Jan 3 16:30:47 CST 1986
Sample message: mail is a tool.
$
```

or

```
$ date; who; cat copy
Fri Jan 3 16:32:23 CST 1986
you       tty07           Jan 3 9:30:10 CST 1986
Sample message: mail is a tool.
$
```

Notice that you get the shell prompt back after the multiple commands have been run. You can tell how Unix classifies this file by typing

```
$ file copy
copy: ascii text
```

The **file** command is used to determine the file type of the named file (copy, in this case). For example, the copy file is a file of characters. The copy file is not executable (it contains no commands).

The word ascii is an acronym for American Standard Code for Information Interchange. The ascii coding system is used by most Unix systems. Ascii codes are used by Unix in place of each of the keyboard characters you type. An ascii table is given in Appendix A. Also, ascii(7) in Part 7 of the *Unix Programmer's Manual* gives a map of the ascii character set.

Each time you create a file, its name is put into a directory.

1.4.1 Directories

A *directory* is a file used to hold filenames and information (called *inumbers*) used to locate files. When you log in, there is a directory associated with your terminal. It is called the *home directory,* or the *login directory.* You can see the name of your home directory by typing

```
$ pwd
/usr/you
$
```

You can see what is in your home directory by typing

```
$ ls /usr/you
copy
$
```

This says you own a file called copy. The names of the files associated with your terminal are maintained by Unix in your working directory. Whatever directory you are working in is called your working or *current directory*. Your home directory is your working directory when you first log in. A dot by itself (.) is another name for your working directory. You can verify this by typing

```
$ ls .
copy
$
```

The **ls** command has many options, even in the 7th edition where ls has 11 options (Sytem V has 12 options, Xenix-5 has 23 options). More is not necessarily better. The System V options are probably all you will ever need (or remember!). The -l and -t ls options, shown below, are two of the most useful ones.
Try typing

```
$ ls -l copy
ls -l copy
-rw-r--r--      1 you group      32 Jan 2 14:23 copy
$
```

The command line

```
ls -l copy
```

tells the shell we want the /usr/you entry for just the copy file. (This may be all you have in your directory right now!) A graphical interpretation of the parts of the long form of directory listing is given in Figure 1.3. To see your complete working directory in its long form, type

```
$ ls -l
-rwxr-xr-x      1 you group      69 Dec 26 17:49 411
```

Capsule View of Two ls Options

OPTION	DESCRIPTION
-l	list directory in long format
-t	sort by time of last modification

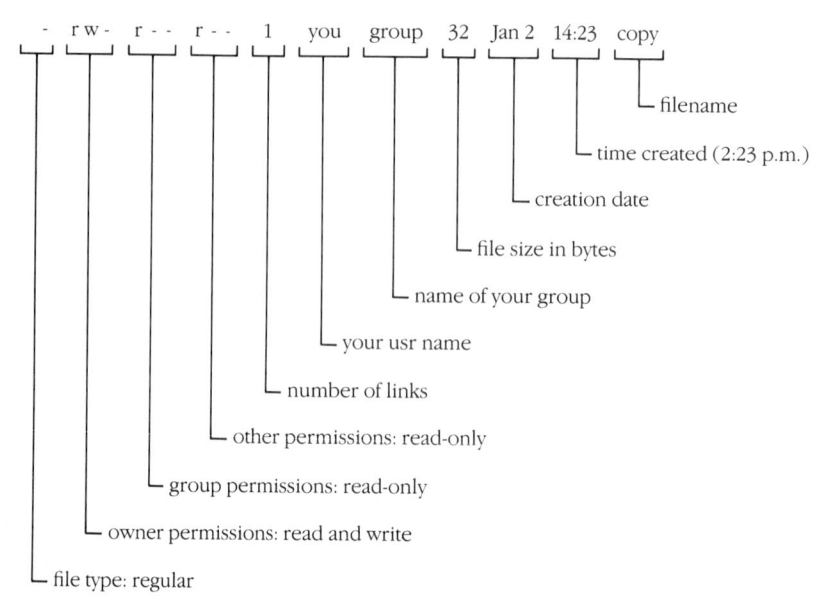

```
             - rw- r-- r--   1   you   group   32  Jan 2  14:23  copy
```
- filename
- time created (2:23 p.m.)
- creation date
- file size in bytes
- name of your group
- your usr name
- number of links
- other permissions: read-only
- group permissions: read-only
- owner permissions: read and write
- file type: regular

FIGURE 1.3
Parts of a Directory Listing

```
-rw-r--r--     1 you group      32 Jan  2 14:23 copy
drwxr-xr-x     1 you group     289 Dec 27 18:36 lib
-rwxr-xr-x     1 you group     277 Dec 30 18:33 peel
```

Notice the leading **d** on the lib directory listing. This says that lib is a subdirectory of this directory.

1.4.2 Subdirectories

You see what's in lib by typing

```
$ ls -l /usr/you/lib
drwxr-xr-x     4 you group      88 Dec 22 11:24 cs
-rw-r--r--     1 you group     419 Dec 18 11:11 index
-rw-r--r--     1 you group     544 Dec 26 17:56 phonebk
drwxr-xr-x     2 you group     112 Dec 30 12:55 tools
```

This says that the lib subdirectory itself has its own subdirectories (cs and tools).

A *subdirectory* is a directory which has a parent (a directory containing the name of the subdirectory). For example, /usr is the name of the parent directory for your home directory.

To see what is in one of these subdirectories, type

```
$ ls -l /usr/you/lib/tools
```

or you can type

```
$ ls -l lib/tools
```

and the shell will affix /usr/you to the front of this filename. You can use the same technique to refer to any filename in your current directory. For example, you can type

```
$ ls lib
cs
index
phonebk
tools
$
```

and the shell will affix /usr/you to the front of lib for you. Notice that the -l option for the ls command prints your directory entries in sorted order according to name (digits appear before letters in the ascii table, so, for example, 411 appears before the rest of the entries in the above /usr/you directory listing). You can use the -t option to print out your directory listing in sorted order by time (either the short form or long form of ls). Try typing

```
$ ls -t lib
tools
index
phonebk
cs
```

or you can combine these two ls command options as follows:

```
$ ls -lt lib
drwxr-xr-x   2 you group   112 Dec 30 12:55 tools
-rw-r--r--   1 you group   419 Dec 28 11:11 index
-rw-r--r--   1 you group   544 Dec 26 17:56 phonebk
drwxr-xr-x   4 you group    88 Dec 22 11:24 cs
```

Your home directory is actually a subdirectory of another directory, namely, the /usr directory. You can peek inside your /usr directory by typing

```
$ ls /usr
adm
bin
dict
games
lib
man
news
```

```
phil
spool
sys
susu
tmp
you
$
```

The /usr directory contains the names of all users on your system. This says phil, susu, and you are the only users with accounts on this system (thousands of usernames are possible). The /usr directory also contains the names of subdirectories used by its parent. The parent of /usr is called the root directory (its name is /). You can list the root directory by typing

```
$ ls /
bin
boot
core
dev
etc
lib
  .
  .
  .
usr
$
```

To see what shell commands are available on your system, try typing

```
$ ls /usr/bin
admin
at
awk
  .
  .
  .
$
```

You will also find a treasure-trove of commands in your /bin directory. No matter what directory you are currently in, the name of the parent of your current directory is given by two dots.

> Two dots (..) is the name of the parent of the current directory you are in. If you are in your home directory, then .. is another name for /usr, for example.

18 CHAPTER 1 / DISCOVERING UNIX

You can verify this by first typing

```
$ ls ..
```

and then typing

```
$ ls /usr
```

while you are in your home directory.

1.4.3 Changing Directories with the cd Command

You can change directories (move up and down the directory tree) using the **cd** command. For example, try typing

```
$ cd ..          # move up to parent of .
$ pwd            # where am i?
/usr
$ cd ..          # move up to parent of .
$ pwd            # where am i?
/
$
```

Notice that four of the above command lines have comments.

Command line comments:
Characters to the right of a **#** are ignored by the shell (they are taken as command line comments).

The /usr/you directory is called your home directory. It is very simple to change back to your home directory—no matter what directory you are in.

To change back to your home directory, type

```
$ cd
```

To move down into subdirectories of your home directory, you might want to try the real thing by creating some subdirectories. You can do this with the **mkdir** command. Try typing

```
$ mkdir lib              # creates lib subdirectory
$ mkdir lib/tools        # creates subdirectory of lib
$ mkdir cs               # creates cs subdirectory
$ mkdir bin              # creates bin subdirectory
$ mkdir exp              # creates exp subdirectory
$ mkdir exp/sorts        # creates subdirectory of exp
```

Now try the file command again on any one of these new files:

```
$ file lib/tools
lib/tools:     directory
```

Later you will find the file command very helpful in shell programs where you need to know if a file is a directory. As a result of creating these subdirectories, we have built the directory tree shown in Figure 1.4.

If you want to remove a subdirectory (it must be empty!), use the **rmdir** command:

```
$ rmdir lib/exp                          #wrong!
rmdir: lib/exp is not empty
```

Notice that your lib/exp subdirectory is not empty! You can verify this by typing

```
$ ls lib/exp
sorts
$
```

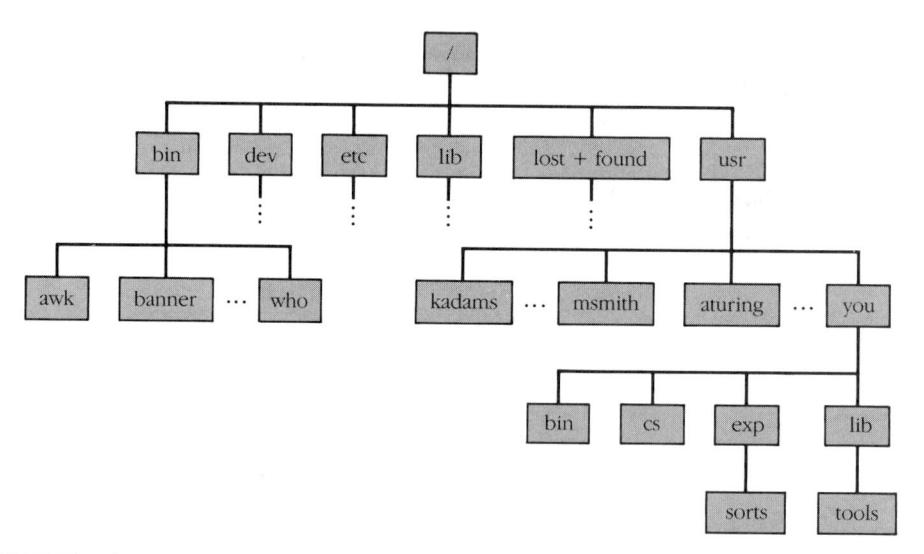

FIGURE 1.4
Directory Tree

CHAPTER 1 / DISCOVERING UNIX

The lib/exp subdirectory has its own subdirectory, namely, sorts. Assuming the sorts subdirectory is empty, you must remove it first (clean out your lib/exp subdirectory, in other words) before you can remove your lib/exp directory. Try

```
$ rmdir lib/exp/sorts
$ rmdir lib/exp                    # now it works
```

1.4.4 Fishing through your Directories

Now you are in a position to dip into the incredible amount of information available in a typical Unix system. This is true even though you have not created any files of your own yet. You might want to spend a few minutes now exploring the various subdirectories of the root. You might be surprised by how much you find. If your system has games, stop off in the games directory for a while. You can run these games without leaving your home directory. Try typing

```
$ ls -C /usr/games
arithmetic    back      bj      chess    craps    hangman
ocelot        rogue     ...
$
```

To start playing one of these games, try

```
$ /usr/games/hangman
guesses:    word:   .......   errors: 0/7
guess: t
guesses:    t word:  ...t...  errors:   0/7
   .
   .
   .
ctrl-d
$
```

To stop the execution of a running program, hit the **del** (delete) key. You can also terminate a running program with a **ctrl-d** (hold down 2 keys: control and d key). A break key will probably also work, if your keyboard has one. We stopped the execution of the hangman program by pressing the delete key. This gives you back the shell prompt.

1.4.5 Filenames

Every file has a name associated with it. A filename like copy, which we have been using, is a human name (one we picked). In 7th edition Unix and System V, filenames are limited to 14 characters which can be any of the characters on your keyboard. Berkeley 4.2BSD and 4.3BSD have virtually no limit on the number of characters in a filename. Filenames should be chosen with care. You may find the following rules helpful:

1. Keep filenames short (pl is better than PrintLine)
2. Limit yourself to lowercase letters (Unix is case sensitive, so the name Freq is not the same as freq) and the period '.' in choosing filenames. Notice that all shell commands are made of lowercase letters only. You will find the period useful if you want to have filenames like try.1 (notice that try1 is easier to type, simpler, and takes less storage—it has one less character than try.1).
3. Choose descriptive filenames. A name like copy is better than c or stuff, for example.

Notice also that the proposed Unix standard from IEEE (1986, p. 21) puts only two restrictions on the characters that can be used in filenames. Names can consist of 1 to {NAME__MAX} characters and all characters except a null (octal 0) and slash (/) can be used. A filename is also referred to as a pathname component.

1.4.6 Pathnames

Another name for every file in the Unix system is its *pathname*. A pathname consists of all the directory names (starting with the root /) prepended to the name of a file in a directory or the name of a directory.

> Keynote:
> A directory is a file. A complete filename for any directory is a sequence of directory names in the path to a directory.

For example,

```
/usr/you/lib/tools
```

is the pathname of the tools subdirectory. The pathname for the copy file in your home directory is

```
/usr/you/copy
```

A *pathname* is a complete filename. A path is written as a sequence of directory names in the path leading from the root / to the name of the file at the end of the path.

It is common for a Unix system administrator to set up a .profile in the home directory for each user. Among other things, the .profile gives you a way to tell the shell what path to use in looking for commands you want to execute. This gives you a way to customize your programming environment.

1.4.7 Your .profile

Each time you log on, the shell will carry out any commands *and* make the settings for the variables you specified in your .profile (if you have one). You can see what is in your **.**profile by typing

```
$ cat .profile          # to see your path variable
date                    # prints date when you login
$HOME=/usr/you
PATH=:/bin:/usr/bin:/usr/games:.
MAIL=/usr/spool/mail/`logname`
TERM=...
export HOME PATH MAIL TERM
$
```

This sample **.**profile tells the shell to do the following things each time you log in:

1. execute the date command
2. set the values of the HOME, PATH, MAIL, and TERM variables

In general, a variable is given a value by typing

```
$ <variable name>=<setting>
```

You need to use a $-sign prefix on a variable name, to *access* the value of a variable (its setting). Try using the **echo** command to see the value of a variable after it has been set. Here is an example:

```
$ music=tumti-tumti-tumti-tum-tum!
$ echo $music
tumti-tumti-tumti-tum-tum!
$
```

If you type

```
$ echo music
music
$
```

just the variable name will be printed.

> | | |
> |---|---|
> | **$HOME:** | default argument for cd (this tells the shell to change directory to your $HOME directory, if you type cd by itself. |
> | **$MAIL:** | where shell keeps your mail. You can look at this file by typing |
> | | `$ cat /usr/spool/mail/you`
`$` |
> | | (You don't have any mail, apparently.) |
> | **$PATH:** | this variable is used to define the path to be followed by the shell in looking for commands typed by you. This variable defines a *search path* for the shell. |
> | **$TERM:** | tells the shell the type of terminal you are using. |

A variable with a $-prefix indicates the value of the variable.

Now try this by experimenting with the **.profile** variables. For example, try typing

```
$ echo $HOME            # print value of HOME
/usr/you
$ ls $HOME              # print home directory
bin
copy
exp
lib
tools
$ cd tools              # change directory
$ cd $HOME              # same cd
$ pwd
/usr/you
$
```

The shell variables at the top of the page are given settings by this sample .profile.

1.4.8 Search Paths

Take a minute to look closely at the definition of $PATH in the sample .profile in Section 1.4.7. It is the $PATH variable in your .profile that tells the shell where to look for a command. If you type

```
$ wumpus                # assume wumpus does not exist
wumpus: not found
```

the shell follows a search path *like* the following one:

```
shell then looks in /bin
  shell then looks in /usr/bin
    shell then looks in /usr/games
      shell then looks in . (your current directory)
        stop! --search failure results in error message
```

The search path defined by the $PATH variable in the sample .profile tells the shell to conclude its search in the current directory.

Recall that the **.** is the name of your current directory. The **.** can be different from your home directory.

Using an editor, you can modify the search path used by the shell. For example, if you want the shell to look in your home directory and your own bin directory *before* it looks in the /bin or /usr/bin directory, you can use

```
PATH=:$HOME:$HOME/bin:/usr/bin:/usr/games:.
```

There is a danger in this form of PATH. It is possible for you to create a file with the *same* name as a system command file. For example, suppose you have created a file called test in your home directory (we show you how to do this in Section 1.5.1). There is also a Unix command file called test in /bin (the system bin directory). The /bin/test command can be used in a variety of ways to check the nature of a file. For example, to test whether a file exists and is a directory file, type

```
$ test -d bin
```

Notice that if you already have a file called test in your home directory, Unix will will fail to find /bin/test. To avoid this problem, use the following alternative form of PATH:

```
PATH=:/bin:/usr/bin:$HOME/bin:$HOME:.
```

Now the shell will check your /bin directory first in looking for commands.

1.4.9 Wildcards

A *wildcard* specifies an ambiguous filename. Wildcards are used to specify groups of files. Here are some examples:

```
$ ls /*                      # files belonging to root
.....................
$ ls /usr/*                  # files belonging to /usr/
```

```
. . . . . . . . . . . . . . . . . . .
$ ls /usr/bin/*           # files belonging to /usr/bin/
. . . . . . . . . . . . . . . . . . .
$ ls *                    # files belonging to .
```

This is an extremely powerful tool for getting a quick overview of your file system.

1.4.10 Copying, Moving, and Removing Files

A copy of a file can be made using the **cp** command. Try typing

```
$ cp copy xerox           # creates xerox file in .
$ cp copy lib/test        # creates test file in lib/
$ cp lib/test mirror      # creates mirror file in .
$ cp lib/test lib/tools   # creates test file in
                            lib/tools
```

You have just created four new files. You can verify this by typing

```
$ cat lib/tools/test
Sample message: mail is a tool.
```

Try this with the other new files we just created. Moving a file is another story which is subtle.

Try typing

```
$ mv copy lib             # moves copy to lib
```

Now verify that copy is no longer in your current directory:

```
$ ls .                    # copy is gone
bin
exp
lib
mirror
xerox
$ ls lib                  # copy is now in lib
copy
cs
tools
$
```

The *mv* command is used to move a file. When a file is mv'd (moved), the original is purged from its directory and a copy of the original file is put into a newly named file. A file cannot be moved to itself.

It is almost too easy to remove files using the **rm** command. To remove copy from your lib subdirectory, type

```
$ rm lib/copy          # removes copy
$ rm mirror            # removes mirror
$ rm xerox             # removes xerox
```

Wildcards can be used with the cp, mv, *and* rm commands, but it is dangerous to use wildcards with rm. For example,

```
$ rm *                 # cleans your .
$ rm lib/*             # cleans your lib
$ rm c*                # removes files with c prefix
$ rm c*y               # remove all c*y files
```

The last command line would remove files having names like the following ones:

```
copy cry creemy creepy
```

The cat command has other uses besides displaying the contents of a file on your screen. It can be used to create new files. In addition, the cat command can be used to concatenate files together using what is known as *redirection*.

1.5 REDIRECTION OF INPUT AND OUTPUT

The shell treats your terminal as another file on the Unix system. It automatically opens three files which are used in connection with terminal input/output:

> file 0—the standard input file used when you are entering characters at a keyboard
> file 1—the standard output file used in connection with characters printed on your screen
> file 2—the standard error output file used for error messages resulting from mistaken command lines

Unix sets up these three files for every Unix command which is issued by you. A graphical interpretation of this idea in terms of

```
$ who
```

is given in Figure 1.5.

You can tell the shell to change the file to be used for either input or output before it executes a program. You can do this in the following ways:

```
$ cat copy >xerox      #puts copy in new xerox file
$ who >persons         #puts list into new persons file
```

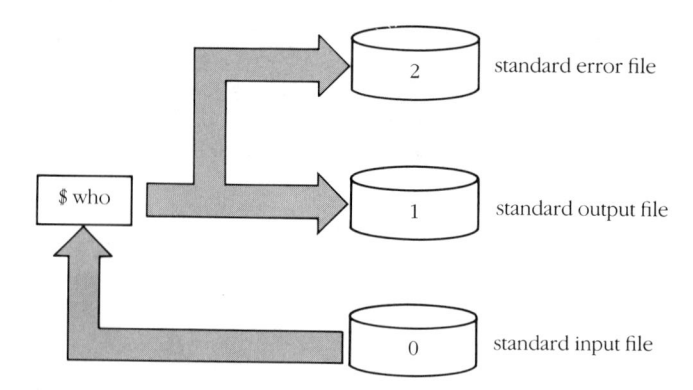

FIGURE 1.5
Files Set Up for Each Command

```
$ cat <persons              #prints contents of persons file
$ cat <persons > list       #sets up new list file
$ ls >names                 #sets up names file
```

The syntax (where you put blanks) for these command lines is critical on some systems. To be safe, put no blank after either

> (to redirect the standard output)

or

< (to redirect the standard input)

Each of the above command lines specifies different uses of the standard input and output (0 and 1) files. In fact, each of the above command lines can be rewritten to express this idea explicitly as follows:

Equivalent Command Lines

SHORT FORM	LONG FORM
cat copy >xerox	cat copy 1>xerox
who >persons	who 1>persons
cat <persons	cat 0<persons
cat <persons >list	cat 0<persons 1>list
ls >names	ls 1>names

The command line

```
$ cat <persons >list
```

28 CHAPTER 1 / DISCOVERING UNIX

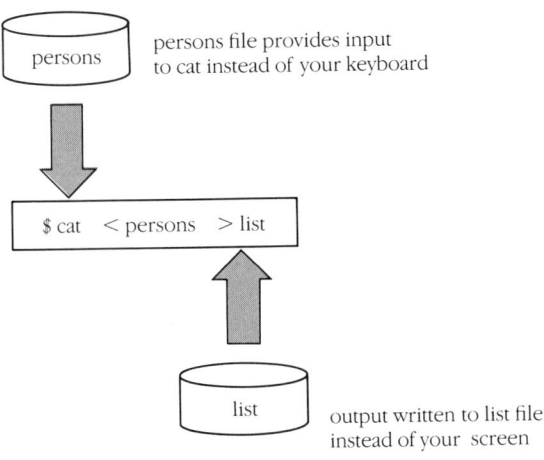

FIGURE 1.6
Redirection Standard Input/Output

is a bit tricky, since it redirects *both* the standard input (from the persons file instead of your keyboard) and the standard output (to the list file instead of your screen). What this command line does is illustrated graphically in Figure 1.6.

You can also use a double arrow (>>) to append the redirected output to a named file. Here are some examples:

```
$ ls >>list              # appends file names to list
$ cat <copy >>persons    # appends copy to persons file
```

For example, if we type

```
$ ls
copy
xerox
persons
list
```

which prints a copy of the filenames in your directory, then

```
$ ls >>copy
```

appends a copy of your directory in the copy file (the one with a copy of the message taken from your mailbox). You can verify this by typing

```
$ cat copy
Sample message: mail is a tool.
copy
xerox
persons
```

```
list
$
```

If you ask the shell to do something unreasonable (something it doesn't "know" about), it will print an error message. Try, for example, the following sequence:

```
$ cat copy -ok
Sample message: mail is a tool.
cat: cannot open -ok
$
```

This time the standard error file is used to print the error message on your screen:

```
cat: cannot open -ok
```

The shell attempted to open a nonexistent file named -ok. You can redirect error messages (squirrel them away in a safe place and prevent their appearance on your screen) using the following technique:

```
$ command 2>problems          #redirect errors to
                                problems
```

This technique can be used with the above command line:

```
$ cat copy -ok 2>problems
```

This puts the error message produced by the shell into your problems file. You can verify this by typing

```
$ cat problems
cat: cannot open -ok
```

Here is a summary of these ideas about redirection:

REDIRECTION	MEANING
>	redirect standard output example: $ ls >list
<	redirect standard input example: $ cat <list
>>	append redirected standard output: $ ls >>list

BSD Unix handles the redirection of standard error slightly differently and it has many more ways to handle redirection thanks to its noclobber option. If you are curious about BSD Unix redirection methods, see Section 8.7 of Chapter 8.

Redirection combined with the **cat** command gives us a straightforward way to create new files.

1.5.1 Creating Files with cat and Redirection

It is possible to use redirection with the cat command to redirect the output from cat to a named file. Here is an example:

```
$ cat >toolkit
tool            good example
-----------------------------------------------------
sort       Dale Shelly, ""Painless Programming,''
           Digital Review. Vol. 2, No. 10 (July, 1985), 103.
<,>,>>     Brian W. Kernighan, John R. Mashey, "The
           Unix Programming Environment,'' IEEE Selected
           Reprints in Software. Los Angeles, CA: IEEE
           Computer Society, 1982. Pp. 255-266,
           esp. 258.
ctrl-d
$
```

Now try

```
$ ls
copy
list
names
persons
toolkit
$
```

You now have a file called toolkit listed in your directory. You can use redirection to mail a copy of this file to a friend in the following way:

```
$ mail shelly <toolkit
```

This puts a copy of the toolkit file in Shelly's mailbox. You can use >> redirection to append more information to your toolkit file in this way:

```
$ cat >>toolkit
cat        S. R. Bourne, The UNIX System. Reading,
           MA: Addison-Wesley Publishing Co., 1983.
ctrl-d
$
```

You may be surprised at what comes up on your screen when you type

```
$ cat toolkit
```

after you have finished the above session. If you find that the toolkit file has typing errors, you will have to use your favorite editor to fix the errors. Information on how to use the **ed** and **vi** editors is given in Appendixes B and D.

1.5.2 Using the cat Command to Concatenate Files

The cat command can be used with redirection to concatenate ("glue") two or more files together in a new file *or* to append two or more files to an old file. We can do this in the following way with files already in "our" directory:

```
$ cat copy persons >boxM      # copies copy, persons to
                                boxM
$ cat copy copy copy >boxN    # 3 copies of copy in boxN
```

You can append one file to another file in the following way:

```
$ cat names >>copy            # append names to copy file
$ cat persons names >>yes     # append 2 files to yes
```

Besides redirection, you can use what are known as pipes to connect the output from one program to the input of another program.

1.6 PIPES

A *pipe* connects the standard output from one program to the standard input of another program. The vertical line | is the pipe operator symbol. Commands connected together by a pipe form a *pipeline*. We will illustrate the use of pipes with the two printing commands, **pr** and **lpr**.

For example, instead of using

```
$ ls -l >temp                 # copy directory to temp
$ pr <temp                    # print temp
```

▦ Two Printing Commands

pr	print files (listing will be separated into pages, each headed with a page number, date, time, and filename)
lpr	put file into printer queue (see lpr(1))

we can pipe the output from ls -l to pr as follows:

```
$ ls -l | pr
```

This pipeline is illustrated graphically in Figure 1.7. You can have more than one pipe in the same command line. Instead of using

```
$ ls -l | pr >temp
$ lpr <temp                    # put temp in print queue
```

try using two pipes:

```
$ ls -l | pr | lpr
```

You can also combine the use of redirection *and* pipes.

1.6.1 Pipes and Redirection

Pipes and redirection can be used together on the same command line. For example, try

```
$ date | cat - copy >message
$
```

The dash argument (-) tells the shell to take input from its standard input as well as from a file. In this case, the cat command takes its input from the pipe as well as from the copy file. The output from the pipe is redirected to the message file, which you should verify. A graphical interpretation of this new command line is given in Figure 1.8.

You can group commands together inside parentheses and pipe the output from the grouped commands. Here is an example:

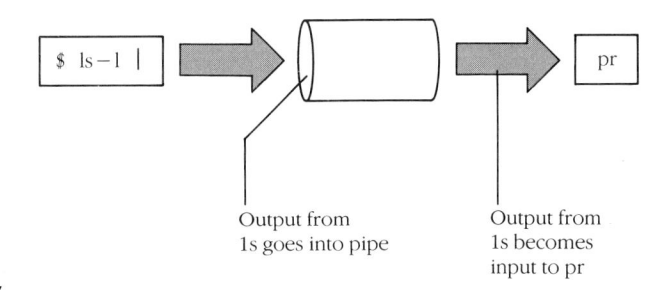

```
$ (date;who) | cat - /usr/spool/mail/you >pobox
$
```

[Diagram: `$ ls-l |` → Output from ls goes into pipe → `pr` ; Output from ls becomes input to pr]

FIGURE 1.7
Pipeline

PIPES 33

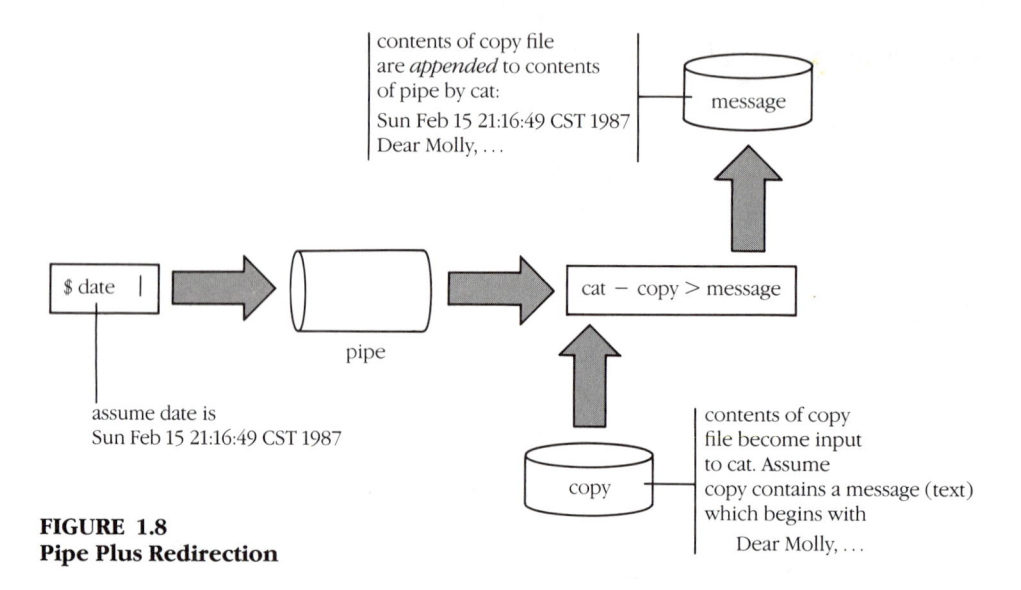

```
                              contents of copy file
                              are appended to contents
                              of pipe by cat:              ┌─────────┐
                              Sun Feb 15 21:16:49 CST 1987 │ message │
                              Dear Molly, ...              └─────────┘
                                                                ▲
                                                                │
  ┌────────┐                ┌──────┐               ┌────────────────────────┐
  │ $ date │ ═══════▶       │ pipe │  ═══════▶     │  cat − copy > message  │
  └────────┘                └──────┘               └────────────────────────┘
       │                                                      ▲
       │                                                      │
  assume date is                                        ┌──────────┐   contents of copy
  Sun Feb 15 21:16:49 CST 1987                          │   copy   │   file become input
                                                        └──────────┘   to cat. Assume
                                                                       copy contains a message (text)
  FIGURE 1.8                                                           which begins with
  Pipe Plus Redirection                                                    Dear Molly, ...
```

This puts together in the pobox file the following things:
 1. date and time
 2. list of who's logged on
 3. list of messages in your /usr/spool/mail/you file

The date goes into the pipe first. ==The cat takes its input from the pipe before it uses your mailbox following the dash==, so the date will end up being in the first line of the pobox file. Then follows the output from who, which is followed by a list of what is in your mailbox. You can verify this by using the cat command on pobox.

Pipes are commonly used with programs called filters.

1.6.2 Pipes and Filters

A *filter* transforms its input in some way. Here are some examples of filters:

▦ Some Filters

FILTER	ACTION
grep	searches input files for lines which match a pattern and writes lines found on standard output
sort	sorts lines of named files and writes result on standard output
wc	counts lines, words, characters of named files and writes counts on the standard output

---

To use these filters, we need to have access to files that can be filtered. We can use the wc command on our copy file as follows:

```
$ cat copy                              # review copy
Sample message: mail is a tool.
$ wc copy                               # filter copy
      1      6     32 copy
$
```

We need a file with multiple lines to put the other two filters through their paces. Try your directory!

```
$ ls | grep .bak | wc -l
      0
$ ls | grep scan | wc -l
      3
$
```

Notice that grep looks for lines containing the indicated pattern; *grep* stands for "global regular expression print." Briefly, a *regular expression* serves as a template which can be used to identify a set of strings (or words) which fit into the template. This is the idea behind wildcards typically used in directory searches on most systems. For example, to list all filenames beginning with the letter c, we can type

```
$ ls c*
c
chop
chkdir
cutw
$
```

Then all names that fit into the c* pattern will be listed. In the above sample pipes (with ls, grep, and wc), **scan** is used as a regular expression (a template to find all words containing **scan**) as in:

```
$ ls scan*
scanb
scane
scanm
$
```

You can count the users on the system using

```
$ who | wc -l                    # counts users
         5
$
```

PIPES 35

(You could put this command line into your .profile to see how many persons are logged on.) You can also try using these filters by creating the following file:

```
$ cat >sample
"We're going through!" The Commander's voice was like
thin ice breaking. He wore his full-dress uniform, with
the heavily braided white cap pulled down rakishly over
one cold grey eye. "We can't make it, sir. It's
spoiling for a hurricane, if you ask me." "I'm not
asking you, Lieutenant Berg," said the Commander.
"Throw on the power lights! Rev her up to 8,500! We're
going through!" The pounding of the cylinders
increased:  ta-pocketa-pocketa-pocketa-pocketa . . .
(James Thurber, "The Secret Life of Walter Mitty,"
1936).
ctrl-d
$
```

Now try

```
$ grep ! sample
"We're going through!" The Commander's voice was like
power lights! Rev her up to 8,500! We're going
through!" The pounding of the cylinders increased:
$
```

Now try piping this output to wc:

```
$ grep ! sample | wc -w >wdc
$
```

which puts into the wdc file a count of the number of words on the lines found. If you use

```
$ grep -v ! sample | wc -w >>wdc
$ cat wdc
    24
    57
$
```

then the *-v* option with grep produces all the lines in the file that do *not* match the pattern (one without a !). The words on these lines are counted and the result is *appended* to the wdc file. A very complete specification of the commands given in this chapter can be found in the *Unix Programmer's Manual* (1983, Volume 1, Ch. 1). A detailed presentation of regular expressions and their use by Unix filters is also given in Chapter 6 of this text.

1.7 SUMMARY

Unix is an operating system that supports general-purpose, time-shared use of a computer system. It is also known as a time-sharing kernel. The *kernel* is a program that is responsible for managing the resources of a computer system. Surrounding the kernel is the shell. A *shell* is a program which provides an interface between users and the kernel. It is a command programming language used to interpret commands taken from command lines typed at a terminal or from a file.

The 7th edition of Unix was introduced to the world in 1978 with a quote about intelligence and tool-making from Henri Bergson. Unix tools are programs that are identified by shell commands. A *tool* is a program which is useful in day-to-day computing tasks. A variety of tools are available in a typical Unix system. One of the secrets of becoming comfortable with Unix (making it work for you) is learning to use its tools. You will see later how it is possible to use these tools to make *new* tools called shell procedures.

Unix provides an efficient file system to manage information. A *file* is a named piece of information. Unix files are organized in terms of a directory system. A *directory* is a file which contains the names of files. A directory can contain the names of other directories called subdirectories. A *subdirectory* is a directory that has a parent. The Unix directory system begins with a first parent called the *root* (its name is /). A child of the root has a name of the form:

```
/child
```

In effect, Unix directories form a tree. The interior nodes of the tree are directories. The leaves of the tree can either be subdirectories or names of other files (a program or a mailbox containing a letter, for example).

The path between the root and a leaf is used by the shell to look for commands that you specify. In fact, the complete name of a file is a sequence of directory names like the following one:

```
/usr/you/lib/tools
```

The leaf in this case is tools, a subdirectory we created in Section 1.4.3. For files in your current directory, you can simply refer to their directory names and the shell will prepend the necessary path to each name you use. For example, if you are in your tools directory which has a file called xref, you can type

```
$ cat xref         # use tools directory name
mkdir              (see Section 1.4.3)
sort               (see Section 1.6.2)
  .
  .
  .
$
```

The name used by the shell to find the cat command will be

```
/usr/you/lib/tools/xref
```

This is called the *pathname* for xref.

Redirection and pipes are two of the most powerful facilities provided by Unix. Program input and output can be *redirected* using

<   (redirect standard input)
>   (redirect standard output)
>>   (append standard output)

For example, you can use

```
$ (date;who) >roster             # redirect date, who
$ cat roster
Sun Jan  5 12:41:14 EDT 1986
bilboe       tty02        Jan 3 11:02
you          tty23        Jan 5 08:30
$
```

The output from date and who will be put into the roster file. Or you can use

```
$ mail kath <message             # redirect input to mail
$
```

A *pipe* connects the standard output from one program to the standard input of another program. The vertical line (|) is used as the pipe operator (this tells the shell to set up a pipe). Commands connected by a pipe form a *pipeline*. This is an extremely useful tool, especially in combination with redirection. For example, try

```
$ grep a /usr/dict/words | wc -l
    12293
$
```

This command line begins with grep, which searches the words file for all words containing the letter 'a'. The standard output from grep is piped to wc, which counts the words in the pipe. The standard output from wc in this example is a line count (each word in the words file is on a separate line). On our Unix system, there are 12,293 words containing the letter 'a'. You can check if your system has a words dictionary by using either the ls or cat command.

You will find it helpful to get acquainted with the *Unix Programmer's Manual*. On many Unix systems there is an on-line copy of this manual. Try typing

```
$ man man            # use man command
     .
     .
     .
$
```

If your system has an on-line copy of the *Programmer's Manual,* this command line will print a copy of Section 1, which gives a complete description of the shell commands. Even if your system does not have an on-line copy of the manual, printed versions are available. For example, Bell Laboratories (1983) offers a revised and expanded version of these manuals in two volumes (see Further Reading [Section 1.11] at the end of this chapter). Morris I. Bolsky (1985) offers a very readable handbook of commonly used Unix commands that is helpful.

1.8 REVIEW OF COMMANDS, SYMBOLS, AND KEYWORDS

This section gives an overview of the commands, symbols, and keywords discussed so far.

1.8.1 Commands

COMMAND	ACTION
cat	concatenates and prints files
cd	changes directory
cp	copies file
date	prints date and time
echo	echoes argument
file	determines file type
grep	(filter) searches for lines in a file having a pattern
hangman	plays hangman game
lpr	puts file in print queue
ls	lists directory
mail	mails letter
man	lists manual
mesg	permits or denies messages
mkdir	makes directory
mv	moves file
pr	paginates and prints file
pwd	prints working directory
rm	removes directory
sort	(filter) sorts file
stty	sets terminal (customize keyboard)
wc	(filter) counts lines, words, and characters in a file
who	lists who is on the system
write	writes an on-line message

1.8.2 Symbols

SYMBOL	USAGE
#-erase	default erase character
#-comment	shell convention that characters to right of # are taken as comment, provided # is not used as erase character
^	old symbol for pipe operator
^-prefix	prefix used to specify control characters like ^h (control h for a backspace)

1.8.2 Symbols (continued)

!-mail	mail command used to escape from the shell
.	name of current directory
..	name of parent directory
/	name of root directory
- (cat)	cat argument
- (mail)	mail command used to backtrack to earlier messages
+ (mail)	mail command used to move ahead in your mail file
@-kill	default kill character used to delete a line you have typed
$-prefix	$ used as prefix of a variable name to access the value of the variable
$-prompt	default sh prompt
*-wildcard	use * to specify a group of filenames
>	operator to redirect standard output
<	operator to redirect standard input
>>	operator to append standard output
|	pipe operator
;	command separator
(...;...)	group commands
0	standard input
1	standard output
2	standard error

1.8.3 Keywords

KEYWORD(S)	EXPLANATION
command	name of a program
command line	line containing commands and possible arguments
comment	characters to right of #, if # is not used as the erase character
directory	file containing filenames
current directory	working directory (its name is .)
home directory	login directory (its name is /usr/you)
parent directory	immediate predecessor of current directory (its name is ..)
root directory	first parent (its name is /)
subdirectory	directory which has a parent
kernel	Unix resource manager

control d	used in a variety of ways:
	   1. to log off, type control d
	   2. to stop a running program
	   3. to exit from such programs as mail

control h	backspace (good erase character)
delete	use to stop a running program
$HOME	home directory name

1.8.3 Keywords (continued)

operating system	program used to manage the resources of a computer system
pathname	complete filename, which is a sequence of directory names in the path from the root to a file (at the leaf)
pipe	connects standard output from a running program to the standard input of another program
pipe operator	|
pipeline	commands connected by a pipe
redirect	change direction of a program's standard input/output
search path	path used by the shell to look for commands
wildcard	ambiguous filename used to specify a group of files

1.9 EXERCISES

1. Print a list of the commands in your /usr/bin and /bin files.
2. Use a pipeline to print a list of files in /* in paginated form.
3. Set up a pipeline to pipe the output from date and who to a rosterfile. Print a copy of the roster. Hint: see summary.
4. Which version of Unix are you using?
5. Use cat with redirection to create a file called message, which contains a message you want to mail to a friend. Then give the command line to mail a copy of the message to John and Susu (use a single command line).
6. Show how to mail a message to yourself.
7. Show how to access the message from Exercise 6 to create new files called xerox1 and xerox2.
8. Show how to concatenate five copies of the message from Exercise 5 in a new file called xerox3.
9. Show how to pipe the output from date and who to cat, which has its output redirected to a file called letter. Hint: use - by itself as a cat argument.
10. What is in / directory?
11. If you are in your home directory, what is its parent?
12. List the contents of the parent of your home directory.
13. If chess is a game in /usr/games on your system, give the command line which will allow you to run chess without being in the games directory.
14. Give a real-world example of a structure resembling the kernel surrounded by the shell.
15. In this example

    ```
    $ stty erase e
    ```

    what is wrong with using 'e' as the erase character? What problems will this create? Give an example.

16. List (with examples) ways to create files.
17. Show how to remove all files
    a. beginning with 't'
    b. beginning with 't' and ending with 'k'
    c. containing the letter 't'
    d. containing the word 'bell'
    e. ending with the word 'bell'
    f. beginning with the word 'bell'
18. Write a command line which scans your current directory for all directory names and prints them. Hint: ^ used as a prefix on a search pattern indicates a pattern found at the beginning of a line.
19. Create the following set of subdirectories of your home directory:
    a. lib
    b. lib/letters
    c. lib/letters/phil
    d. bin
    e. lib/tools
    f. lib/letters/susu
    g. lib/letters/ATT
    h. exp
    Note: give the command line to do this.
20. Give a sketch of the complete directory tree starting with the root resulting from Exercise 19.
21. Using the directory system built in Exercise 19, give the pathnames for each of the following files:
    a. xref in tools
    b. unixref in tools
    c. ATT2 in ATT
    d. scan in exp
    e. commands in tools
    f. susu10 in susu
    g. message in home directory
    h. where in bin
22. Give an example of
    a. a path that ends in a leaf that is a directory
    b. a path with a parent with no children
    c. a path that ends in a leaf that is not a directory (see Exercise 21 for ideas)
23. Add date and who to your .profile. Give a listing of the new version of .profile.
24. Replace the command line with who in the .profile from Exercise 23 with a line that tells the shell to print only the number of users logged on. Precede this command line with a command line that uses the echo command to print the heading

    ```
    number of users:
    ```

    Hint: put the heading inside single quotes to use as an echo argument.
25. Use cat and redirection to create a file called symbols in $HOME/lib/tools containing the symbols dictionary given in Section 1.8.2.

26. Write a command line to print all entries in the symbols file in Exercise 25 containing
    a. the word 'prompt'
    b. the symbol '^'
27. Write a command line which counts the lines in the symbols file from Exercise 25.

1.10 REVIEW QUIZ

Indicate whether each of the following statements is true or false:
1. Unix is an acronym.
2. The shell surrounds the kernel.
3. The default shell prompt is a #-sign.
4. A pathname can consist entirely of directory names.
5. You can use the name of a file in your current directory as an argument for the cat command.
6. Every pathname contains the name of the root given by two periods (. .).
7. Another name for your home directory is the period (.) if you are in a subdirectory of your home directory.
8. The period (.) is always another name for your home directory.
9. The cp and mv commands achieve the same result.
10. If you type

    ```
    $ stty erase e
    ```

    you will not be able to use the grep command.

1.11 FURTHER READING

Bergson, H. L'Evolution creatrice in Henri Bergson Oeuvres, Paris, France: Presses Universitaires de France, 1970.

Bolsky, M. I. The UNIX System User's Handbook. Englewood Cliffs: Prentice, 1985.

Bell Labs, Inc. Unix Programmer's Manual, vol. 1 and 2. New York: Holt, Rinehart and Winston, 1983. This is 7th edition Unix.

IEEE. Draft American National Standard. IEEE Trial-Use Standard Portable Operating System for Computer Environments. New York: The Institute of Electrical and Electronic Engineers, Inc., 1986. See Section 2.3 on definitions of terms.

Kernighan, B. W., and J. R. Mashey. "The Unix Programming Environment" in IEEE Selected Reprints in Software, 255–66. Los Angeles, CA: IEEE, 1982.

MINIX (see Tanenbaum).

Peterson, J. L., and A. Silberschatz. Operating System Concepts. Reading, MA: Addison-Wesley, 1985. See Chapter 14 for an excellent overview of Unix.

Quarterman, J. S., A. Silberschatz, and J. L. Peterson. 4.2BSD and 4.3BSD as Examples of the UNIX System. ACM Computing Surveys, vol. 17, no. 4 (December 1985), 379–418. See especially Section 1.1 on history of Unix, 1.2 on design principles, and 1.3 on processes.

Ritchie, D. M. and K. Thompson. "The UNIX Time-Sharing System" in The Bell System Technical Journal, vol. 57, no. 6 (July–August, 1978), 1899–1929.

Rochkind, M. J. Advanced UNIX Programming. Englewood Cliffs: Prentice, 1985.

SCO Xenix for Intel 8086, 80286, and 80386-based personal computers (also known as Xenix-5). Available from The Santa Cruz Operation, POB 1900, Santa Cruz, CA 95061, telephone (800) 626–UNIX.

SSC. UNIX System V Command Summary. Seattle, WA: Specialized Systems Consultants, 1985.

SSC. UNIX System Command Summary for Berkeley 4.2 & 4.3. Seattle, WA: Specialized Systems Consultants, 1987.

Tanenbaum, A. S. Operating Systems: Design and Implementation. Englewood Cliffs: Prentice, 1987. See p. xvi for descriptions of various versions of MINIX, that can be obtained from Book Distribution Center, Prentice-Hall, Inc., Route 59 at Brook Hill Drive, West Nyack, N.Y. 10995. See pp. 433–686 for MINIX source code (all 12,649 lines!).

Western Electric. Unix System User's Guide, release 5.0. NJ: Bell Laboratories, Inc., 1982.

Xenix-5 (see SCO).

2 Files and Directories

Because directories are themselves files, the naming structure is potentially an arbitrary directed graph . . . A file is named by a sequence of directories separated by "/" leading towards a leaf of the tree.
—*Dennis Ritchie, 1978.*

2.0 AIMS

- Introduce the Unix file system
- Show how to inspect the inumbers for files and the structure of an inode
- Begin using the ln command to give files added links
- Introduce various ways to create files
- Inspect various directories
- Scan octal dumps of both directories and files
- Show how octal numbers are used to represent inumbers
- Show how to use octal numbers to change the access bits for a file
- Show various ways to survey the Unix directory system

2.1 INTRODUCTION TO THE UNIX FILE SYSTEM

A Unix file is a sequence of characters. The Unix kernel does not distinguish between files in terms of their internal organization. Unlike other operating systems, Unix leaves the internal organization of files to users. Unix files are organized hierarchically in directories. This hierarchy begins at the top with the root directory (/) and leads through the offspring of the root (its subdirectories) in a sequence of directories which lead to the leaves. Such a directory tree is shown in Figure 2.1.

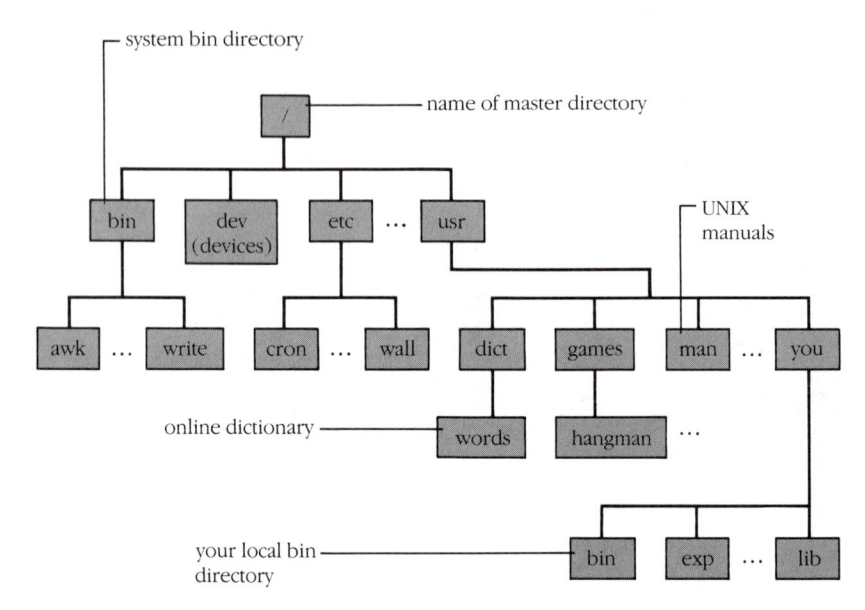

FIGURE 2.1
System Directory Hierarchy

Files get their names from the path traced from the root to a particular file, which can be either an ordinary file like susu10 (letter to susu, which is a text file) or a directory like tools shown in Figure 2.1.

Each entry in a Unix directory has two parts:

1. Filename (up to 14 characters).
2. Inumber (pronounced "eye number"), which identifies the location of information about the named file (its type, its permissions, its size, pointers to the first data blocks of a disk file, and so on) in an inode.

Every file has an inumber and a corresponding inode. "Inumber" is short for "i-node number." A sketch showing the inumber, inode, and corresponding file is shown in Figure 2.2.

You can think of an inumber as the system name for a file. By maintaining an inumber for each file, it is possible for a file to have more than one human name. For example, if the inumber of a file called Texas is 1510, then the following filenames are possible for this file:

DIRECTORY	INUMBER	FILENAME
/usr/you/tools	1510	/usr/you/tools/Texas
/usr/you	1510	longhorn
/usr/you	1510	bigsky

46   CHAPTER 2 / FILES AND DIRECTORIES

```
                    /
                   / \
                 bin ... usr
                          |
                         you
                         / \
                     bigsky ... Texas
```

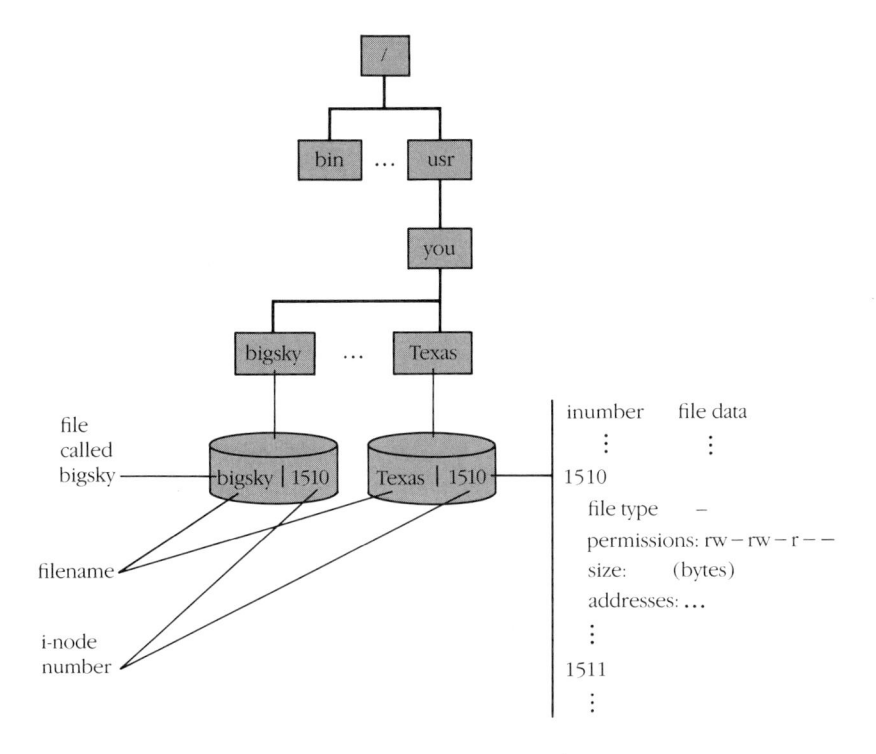

file   inumber   file data
called
bigsky ──── bigsky | 1510   Texas | 1510 ─── 1510
                                               file type   −
filename   permissions: rw−rw−r−−
                                               size: (bytes)
                                               addresses: ...
i-node
number   1511

Note: Since bigsky and Texas have the same i-node
number, these names identify the *same* file.

Legend: 🗄 = file

FIGURE 2.2
File Name, Inumber

Notice that Texas is also called longhorn (in /usr/you) and bigsky (in /usr/you). The names are different but the inumber remains the same, namely, 1510. Unix uses the inumber, not the human name like Texas, so the use of different names for the same file does not cause a problem. Each new name of a file is called a link to the file. The same inumber appears along with each new link to a file. The ln command is used to form a link to a file.

---

ln command to link files:

```
ln OldFileName NewFileName
```

INTRODUCTION TO THE UNIX FILE SYSTEM

Here is an example:

```
$ cat >lib/Texas
Rise with sun in Texas.
ctrl-d
$ ls -l lib/Texas
-rw-r--r--  1  you   unix        67 Jan 9 20:04 Texas
$ ln lib/Texas bigsky               # make link
$ ln lib/Texas longhorn             # make link
$ ls -l lib/Texas
-rw-r--r--  3  you   unix        67 Jan 9 20:04 Texas
$
```

This sample use of ln tells us that Texas now has three links (the original one and the new ones, bigsky and longhorn in your home directory). You can verify this by typing

```
$ ls -l bigsky
-rw-r--r--  2  you   unix        67 Jan 9 20:04 bigsky
```

Now you can use the name "bigsky," for example, instead of "lib/Texas" to access the Texas file. Try the following experiment:

☐ EXPERIMENT 1

```
$ pwd
/usr/you
$ cat bigsky                    # what gets printed?
   .
   .
   .
$ rm bigsky                     # remove the link
$ ls -l lib/Texas               # what gets printed?
   .
   .
   .
$
```

A graphical interpretation of the relationship between a file and its links is shown in Figure 2.3.

In this chapter we look more closely at ways to inspect inumbers for files, the structure of an inode, and shell commands which can be used to inspect the structure of a file. We also give a survey of upper-level Unix system files which are typically available. We start by showing various ways to create files.

```
$ ls - l Texas bigsky longhorn
-rw-r--r--3   you   UNIX   unix   67   Jan 9   20:04   bigsky
-rw-r--r--3   you   UNIX   unix   67   Jan 9   20:04   longhorn
```

The file named Texas has 3 links. The files bigsky and longhorn also identify Texas.

```
-rw-r--r--3   you   unix   67   Jan 9   20:04   Texas
```

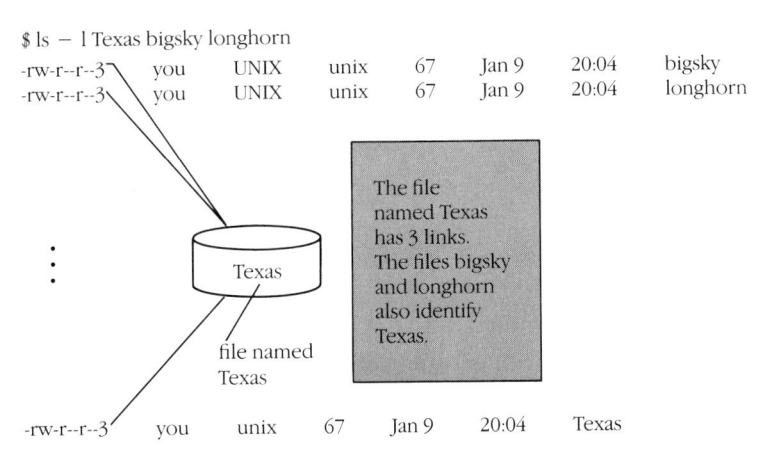

FIGURE 2.3
A File with Three Links

2.2 WAYS TO CREATE FILES

There are a variety of ways to create new files. Here are some examples:

1. redirection of program output (Section 1.5)
2. redirection of keyboard output with cat (Section 1.5.1)
3. concatenating files with redirection (Section 1.5.2)
4. writing (with the w command) from mail (Section 1.3.4)
5. (new) copy input from keyboard to files with tee
6. (new) copy from pipe to files with tee
7. (new) using split to make files where each one is made of a piece of an existing file
8. (new) using ed to create a file
9. (new) using vi to create a file

First we show how to use the tee command to create new files.

2.2.1 Pipe Fitting with the tee Command

The **tee** command has the following syntax:

tee [-i] [-a] [file(s)]
-i option says to ignore interrupts
-a option says to append output to file(s)

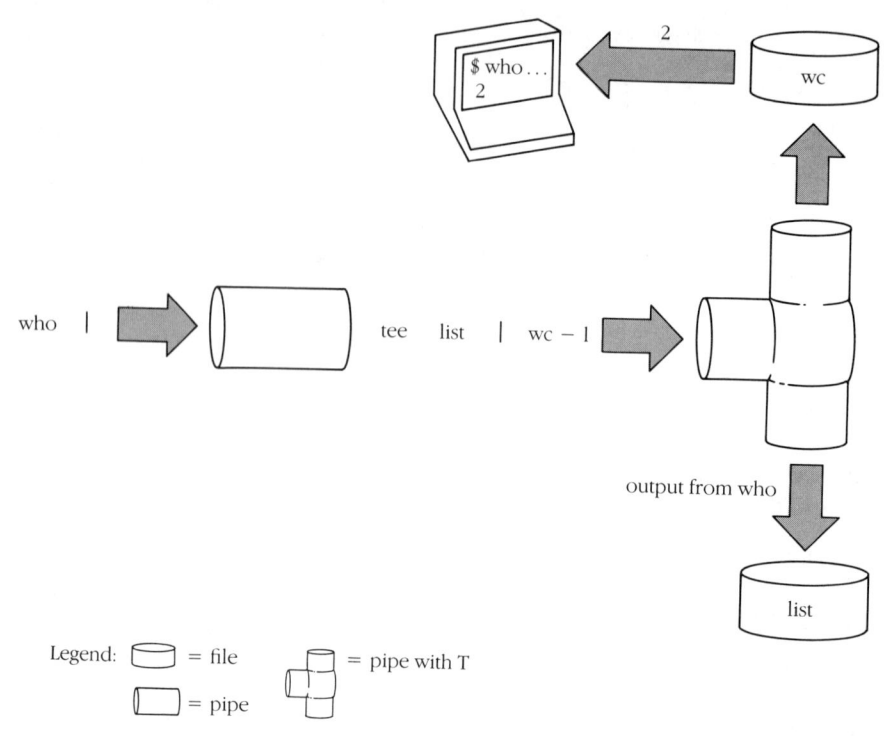

FIGURE 2.4
A Pipe with a T

This is a remarkably powerful and versatile command, which is easy to use. The tee command can be employed with and without a pipe. If it is employed with a pipe, it copies what is in the pipe to one or more named files *and* to its standard output. Here is an example:

```
$ who | tee list | wc -l      # creates list file
    2
$ cat list
jcagney         tty02         Oct 29 08:40
you             tty14         Oct 29 11:15
$
```

In this example, the standard output from who is put into the pipe. The tee command copies the login roster to the new list file and it copies what is in the pipe to the next pipe, which is fed to the wc command. This is illustrated graphically in Figure 2.4.

More than one file can be created with tee. Try typing

```
$ who | tee persons devices times | wc -l
    2
```

CHAPTER 2 / FILES AND DIRECTORIES

```
$ ls
  devices
  persons
  times
     .
     .
     .
$
```

This time tee copied the input from the pipe to persons, devices and times. In effect, we have set up a pipe with multiple outlets as shown in Figure 2.5.

You can append the input from a pipe to existing files using the following technique:

```
$ date | tee persons devices times      # record date
Sat Jan 11 10:05:29 CST 1986
$ who | tee -a persons devices times | wc -l
      15
$ cat persons
Sat Jan 11 10:50:29 CST 1986
susu       tty08     Jan 11 08:48
   .
   .
   .
$
```

This time tee has appended the contents of the pipe to persons, devices, and times. We leave it for an exercise to show how to accomplish the same thing with one command line without the -a option. You can also use tee as a simple way to copy keyboard input to new files. Try typing

```
$ tee Tolkien
Tom went walking on up the Withywindle (Tolkien).
Tom went walking on up the Withywindle (Tolkien).
ctrl-d
$ ls
devices
persons
Tolkien
times
   .
   .
   .
$
```

Notice how the typed quote from Tolkien is echoed on the next line.

WAYS TO CREATE FILES

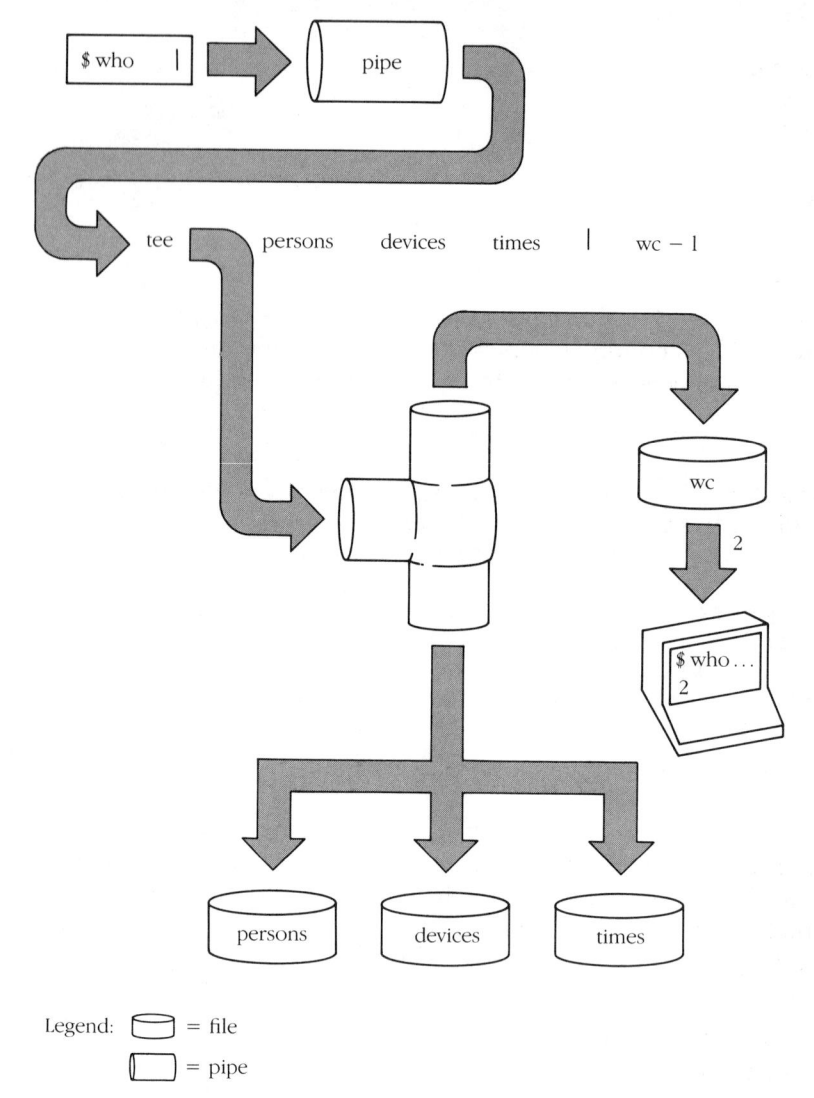

FIGURE 2.5
Multiple Files from Tee

Tee copies its standard input both to named file(s) *and* to its standard output.

You are seeing the standard output from tee in the echoed line in the creation of the Tolkien file. The standard output from tee goes to your screen instead of a pipe. This use of tee offers a simpler way of the doing the same thing as

52 CHAPTER 2 / FILES AND DIRECTORIES

```
$ cat >quote
The shell ....
ctrl-d
$
```

Instead of > and >>, we can use tee with and without the -a option to create and append to files. Here is a challenge for you:

> **CHALLENGE:**
> Write a command line which uses tee to create a new file and which suppresses the standard output to the screen each time a new input line is entered from your keyboard in a command line like
>
> ```
> $ tee idea
> tumtytumtytumtoes!
> tumtytumtytumtoes!
> ```

The echoed line produced by tee in the above challenge is in boldface. We can also create new files using the split command.

2.2.2 Splitting a File into Smaller Files

New files can also be created with the **split** command. This command has the following syntax:

---

split [-n] [file [name]]
-n option specifies n lines per piece
name specifies prefix to use on new files used to hold pieces of split file
file can be -, which specifies that the standard input is to be split.
Note: **x** is the default prefix, **aa** the first suffix on x, **ab** the second suffix on x and so on for the names of the new files. The default value of n is 1000.

A typical on-line dictionary of words will have about 25,000 words. We can split this file into five (possibly six, if it has 25,001 or more words) smaller files by typing

```
$ split -5000 /usr/dict/words lex     # split words
$ ls lex*
lexaa
lexab
lexac
lexad
lexae
$
```

WAYS TO CREATE FILES 53

This splits the words file into five files. The first four files (lexaa, lexab, lexac, lexad) will each have 5,000 lines which are a copy of 5,000 entries in the words file, and the remaining file (lexae) will get the leftover 4,000 or more lines from the /usr/dict/words file. These new files are put into your current directory.

It is also possible to use a — (minus) argument with split. The minus argument specifies that split is to take its input either from a pipe *or* from the keyboard. To see this, try the following experiment:

☐ EXPERIMENT 2A

```
$ cat >phonebk                              # create phonebk file
file
sugarplum    Orlando (305) 226-3375
shelly       Upper Montclair, N.J. (201) 561-9902
     .
     .
     .
$ grep 305 phonebk | split -2 - 305
$ ls 305*
305aa
395bb
     .
     .
     .
$
```

If you run this experiment, you will find that the lines of phonebk containing 305 found by grep get split into a sequence of two line files. Try some variations of this experiment. For example, what happens if you try using the following command line?

☐ EXPERIMENT 2B

```
$ grep 305 phonebk | split -2 - Florida visit
```

When you "run" (type in) Experiment 2, also try varying the size of the split (try -5, instead of -2, for example).

You can also create files by feeding the standard input from a keyboard to split. Try typing

```
$ split -2 - Joyce
riverrun,
past Eve and Adam's,
from swerve of shore to bend of bay,
brings us by a commodius vicus of recirculation ...
```

```
ctrl-d
$ ls Joyce*
Joyceaa
Joyceab
$
```

This splits the lines from the keyboard input into the Joyceaa and Joyceab files. You have just created two new files. You can also use an editor to create new files.

2.2.3 Creating a New File with ed

A new file can be created with **ed** by typing

```
$ ed <filename>            # create new file
```

If the named file you use to invoke ed is a new file, then ed has a w (for write) command which can be used to copy the text created with ed to the new file. First you must use ed to create a text. Here is a sample ed session:

```
$ mkdir exp; cd exp        # set up exp directory
$ ed letter
?letter
P                          get ed prompt
*a                         enter append mode
Kath,
   I left the key under the mat.
            Luv Jim
.                          ends append mode
*w                         write text to file
58
* stop                     unknown command
?
*q                         quit editor
$
```

The boldfaced comments must not be used in an actual ed session. They are given to explain what is happening during this sample editing session. By entering the **w** command in

```
*w
```

we tell ed to create a new file called letter. This takes the edited text and copies it to the named file. You can enter ed without specifying a file and then use the w command to specify the output file. Try

```
$ ed                       # enter ed
P
```

WAYS TO CREATE FILES 55

```
*a
First message: Hello, world!
.
*w startup
*q
$
```

This writes the edited text to a startup file. Notice that if you want to use ed to modify (correct, add to, delete from) an existing file, you should specify the old filename when you invoke ed. More information about ed is given in Appendix B. The vi editor can also be used to create new files and it is simpler to use than ed.

2.2.4 Creating New Files with vi

To create a new file with the **vi** editor, try Experiment 3, which has many features.

☐ EXPERIMENT 3

Type

```
$ vi                                    # enter vi
<i>                                     enter insert mode
The /usr/group
4655 Old Ironside Drive, Suite 200
Santa Clara, CA 95050 USA
<escape>
<shift> <:>
:w network                              create network file
"network" [New File] 4 lines, 69 characters
<shift> <:>
:w >> list                              append to list file
"list" 4 lines, 69 characters
<shift> <:>
:w! places                              writes over places file
"list" 4 lines, 69 characters
<shift> <:>
:w !mail susu                           put text in susu's mail
<shift> <:>
:q!                                     quit editor
You have mail                           message from system
$
```

This experiment shows various ways a newly created text (unnamed in the beginning!) can be written to various files. Notice that

```
:w >>list
```

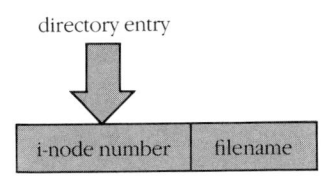

FIGURE 2.6
Directory Entry Format

gives you a way to append your edited text to an old file. Try varying Experiment 3 by using

```
:1,1w >>network          append first line
```

In other words, you can use line numbers x and y in **x,yw** to select the lines to be written (or appended) to a file. More information about vi is given in Appendix C. Unix files are organized with directories.

2.3 DIRECTORIES

Unix directories contain filenames and information which tells how to locate the named files. Directory entries have the format shown in Figure 2.6. You can also inspect the inodes of a directory.

2.3.1 Inspecting Inumbers

The structure of a directory entry used by Unix is given in /usr/include/sys/dir.h. It will have the following form:

```
struct directory {
    int d_inumber;
    char d_name[DIRSIZ];
}
```

This specifies in C a structure having an integer and a string field with up to DIRSIZ characters. DIRSIZ specifies the maximum number of characters a directory name can have. The value of DIRSIZ will vary. System V Unix, for example, allows filenames and directory names to have up to 14 characters. Berkeley Unix allows up to 255 characters for filenames and directory names. For information on the C language struct data type, see Kernighan and Ritchie (1978).

Each Unix directory entry will have this structure. You can inspect the inumbers for filenames in a directory by using the **i** option for the ls command. Try typing

```
$ ls -i yes*
1663 yesaa
```

```
1739 yesab
1742 yesac
$
```

This says 1739 is the inumber for the yesab file. This name is the internal filename used by Unix to locate the inode for a file. You can also use the **od** command to list the inumbers for a file. You can list the inumbers in base 8 (octal) by typing

```
$ oc -c .                        # dump directory listings
0002660 177 003 y e s a a \0 \0 \0 \0 \0 \0 \0 \0 \0
0002700 313 003 y e s a b \0 \0 \0 \0 \0 \0 \0 \0 \0
0002720 316 003 y e s a b \0 \0 \0 \0 \0 \0 \0 \0 \0
          .
          .
          .
$
```

This displays the inumbers in octal (shown in boldface) and the characters used for the filename (the \0's represent unused characters). To see how the pairs of octal numbers are related to the corresponding inumbers listed by ls -i, you need to see how these bytes fit together.

2.3.2 Analyzing the Bytes Representing Inumbers

Octal has eight digits (0 through 7). These octals digits and some other octal numbers rewritten in three different bases are given in the following table:

Octal Numbers in Three Bases

BASE 10	BASE 16 (HEX)	BASE 8 (OCTAL)	BASE 2 (BINARY)
0	0	0	000
1	1	1	001
2	2	2	010
3	3	3	011
4	4	4	100
5	5	5	101
6	6	6	110
7	7	7	111
8	8	10	1000
9	9	11	1001
10	a	12	1010
11	b	13	1011
12	c	14	1100
13	d	15	1101
14	e	16	1110
15	f	17	1111

In other words, every octal digit (0 through 7) can be rewritten as three binary digits. So a number like 177 (octal) can be rewritten in binary as follows:

$$177 \text{ (octal)} = 001\ 111\ 111 \text{ (base 2)}$$

You can rewrite either of these numbers in base 10 by writing out the powers of the base multiplied by the corresponding digits of the number. For example, try

$$\begin{aligned} 177 \text{ (octal)} &= 1 \times 8^2 + 7 \times 8^1 + 7 \times 8^0 \\ &= 64 + 56 + 7 \\ &= 127 \text{ (base 10)} \end{aligned}$$

Try doing the same thing with the above base 2 number to verify that it also equals 127 (base 10). The boldface bytes for the inumber in the following od listing need to be seen in the context of the 16 bits they come from:

```
$ od -c .                                    # character dump
0002660  177 003  y  e  s  a  a  \0 \0 \0 \0 \0 \0 \0 \0 \0
          ↑   ↑
          |   high byte (upper 8 bits out of 16 bits)
       low byte (lower 8 bits out of 16 bits)
          .
          .
          .
$
```

The octal number 177 is actually the low byte and 003 is the high byte in a bitstring with 16 bits. These numbers are shown in context in Figure 2.7.

If you write out the decimal equivalent of the 16 bits shown in Figure 2.7 you will get the corresponding inumber written in decimal which is displayed by ls -i. That is,

```
0 000 011 001 111 111 = 0 x 2^15 +
                        0 x 2^14 + 0 x 2^13 + 0 x 2^12 +
                        0 x 2^11 + 1 x 2^10 + 1 x 2^9 +
                        0 x 2^8 + 0 x 2^7 + 1 x 2^6 +
                        1 x 2^5 + 1 x 2^4 + 1 x 2^3 +
                        1 x 2^2 + 1 x 2^1 + 1 x 2^0
                      = 0 +
                        0 +
                        0 + 1024 + 512 +
                        0 + 0 + 64 +
                        32 + 16 + 8 +
                        4 + 2 + 1
                      = 1663 (base 10)
```

This says the corresponding inumber is 1663 written in base 10. Notice that when the high and low bytes are seen in a 16-bit string, a new octal number can be written to represent all 16 bits. For example,

DIRECTORIES 59

```
    0    0    3    1    7    7
  ┌──┐ ┌──┐ ┌──┐ ┌──┐ ┌──┐ ┌──┐
  │00│ │00│ │00│ │01│ │11│ │11│
  └──┘ └──┘ └──┘ └──┘ └──┘ └──┘
  └──── high byte ────┘└──── low byte ────┘
```

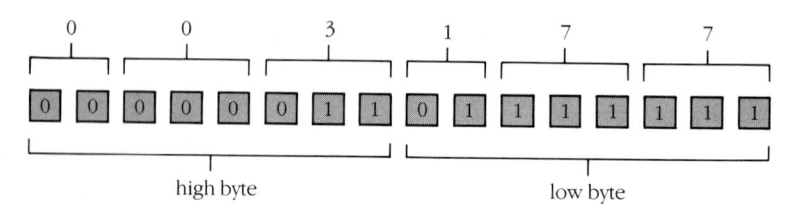

FIGURE 2.7
Sample Bit String

```
0 000 011 001 111 111 = 003177 (octal)
                      = 0 x 8^5 +
                        0 x 8^4 +
                        3 x 8^3 +
                        1 x 8^2 +
                        7 x 8^1 +
                        7 x 8^0
```

Try expanding out the above powers of 8 to verify that you get 1663 (base 10) again. The use of octal by Unix is a carry-over from its beginnings on PDP-11 computers, which are 16-bit machines (their bitstrings are written in octal). An extensive treatment of the use of octal on PDP-11s is given in Chapters 1 and 2 of Peters (1985).

The od command can also be used to display inumbers in hex (short for hexadecimal or base 16), which is convenient for 32-bit machines (VAXes, for example).

2.3.3 Inumbers Written in hex

The od command also has a -x option which gives a hex dump of a directory listing. Here is an example:

```
$ od -x .
0002660 067f 6579 6173 0061 0000 0000 0000 0000
0002700 0bcb 6579 6173 0062 0000 0000 0000 0000
0002720 0bce 6579 6173 0063 0000 0000 0000 0000
     .
     .
     .
$
```

You can unravel the inumbers in this hex dump by picking out the powers of 16 and corresponding decimal equivalents of the hex digits. Try

```
067f (hex) = 0 x 16^3 +
             6 x 16^2 +
             7 x 16^1 +
             15
```

```
              =    0 +
                1536 +
                 112 +
                  15
              = 1663
```

Try using this technique to unravel the inumbers (in base 10) corresponding to the hex numbers given in the above dump. Even if you have trouble reading the octal or hex numbers, you can match addresses between an od -c and an od -d (for decimal) dump to pick out the inumbers. Here is a sample decimal dump:

```
$ od -d .                       # dump directory in base 10
0002660  01663 25977 24947 00097 00000 00000 00000
0002700  01739 25977 24947 00098 00000 00000 00000
0002720  01742 25977 24947 00099 00000 00000 00000
   .
   .
   .
$
```

The od command has other uses besides displaying inumbers for files. Later you will see how this command can be helpful in debugging (it can be used to display hidden characters like newline or \n's in a file). For now, it is the inumber that has center stage. An inumber identifies the location of the inode for a file. It is the inumber that Unix uses to locate the inode, which gives information about a file.

2.3.4 Inodes

You can inspect the structure of the inodes used by Unix by typing

```
$ cat /usr/include/sys/inode.h        # see inode structure
```

Briefly, each inumber identifies an inode which contains the following information about a file:

1. file type (block device, character device, directory, or regular file)
2. access bits (there are 12 of these)
3. number of links to a file
4. size (in bytes or characters) of file
5. thirteen pointers (addresses) to data blocks on disk used by file
6. times of creation, last use, and last change
7. user and group ID for owner of file

The access bits are divided into the following groups of three bits as shown in Figure 2.8.

You can see the settings for the permission bits labeled (in Figure 2.8) owner, group, and other in the long form of a directory listing (use ls -l). There is a chmod command which can be used to change the permission bits in various ways.

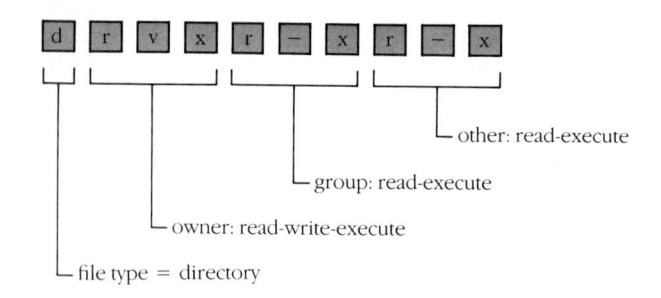

```
d r w x r - x r - x
```
- file type = directory
- owner: read-write-execute
- group: read-execute
- other: read-execute

FIGURE 2.8
Access Bits

2.3.5 File Permissions and the chmod Command

The chmod command has the following syntax:

---

chmod [who] [permission(s)] [file]

who can be u (user), g (group), o (other)

permission can be an absolute octal number or + (add permission) or − (take away permission) with r (read), w (write), or x (execute)

To illustrate the use of the chmod command, we will use the following directory listing for a phonebk file:

```
$ ls -l phonebk                    # show file permissions
-rw-r--r--   2 you      unix      835 Jan 11 09:15 phonebk
```

This says the phonebk file has the following permissions:

```
user:  read (r) and write (w) but not execute (x)
group: read (r) but not write or execute
other: read (r) but not write or execute
```

You can use octal numbers to set (make 1) or unset (make 0) the permission bits. To see how this is done, try rewriting (in your mind) the permission bits in base 2 or binary form:

HUMAN FORM	BINARY FORM
rw-r--r--	110100100

Recall that each of the octal digits represents three binary digits and we can rewrite the binary form of the above permission as follows:

```
110100100  =   6 4 4
```

This is equivalent to writing

```
$ chmod 644 phonebk           # set permission bits!
```

To change the write permission so that other persons in your group can write to this file, use

```
$ chmod 664 phonebk           # set rw for group
$ ls -l phonebk
-rw-rw-r--    2 you      unix    835 Jan 11 09:15 phonebk
```

To select the right octal number to use, try imagining which bits are turned on (equal 1) and which are turned off (equal 0) by an octal number. The octal numbers used to set permissions are called *absolute modes*. Here is a useful table of octal numbers (they are not easy to remember but are easy to figure out from the context):

ABSOLUTE MODE	PERMISSION BITS AFFECTED	
0444	r--r--r--	(read only file)
0644	rw-r--r--	(only you can write to file)
0744	rwxr--r--	(everybody can read file but only you can read, write to, and execute file)
0755	rwxr-xr-x	(everybody can read and execute but only you can write to file)
0764	rwxrw-r--	(you can read, write to, and execute; group can read and write; others can read file)
0100	--x------	(executable only by owner)
0111	--x--x--x	(executable by everybody)

The fourth octal digit on the left of these absolute modes is used to set what are known as the special access bits, which are given in the next section. You can drop this fourth digit if it is zero. For example, you can use

```
$ chmod 765 phonebk           # set permission bits
$ ls -l phonebk
```

DIRECTORIES

```
-rwxrw-r--    2  you    unix  835 Jan 11 09:50 phonebk
$
```

Surprisingly, the literal forms of these permissions are more cumbersome to use than their octal counterparts. For example, the literal equivalent of chmod 765 phonebk is

```
$ chmod +r phonebk              # everybody reads
$ ls -l phonebk                 # check permission bits
-r--r--r--    2  you    unix    835 Jan 11 09:50 phonebk
$ chmod u+wx phonebk            # user writes, executes
$ ls -l phonebk
-rwxr--r--    2  you    unix    835 Jan 11 09:50 phonebk
$ chmod g+w phonebk             # group writes
$ ls -l phonebk
-rwxrw-r--    2  you    unix    835 Jan 11 09:50 phonebk
```

There are three other access bits maintained in the inode for every Unix file. These are called the *special access bits*.

2.3.6 Special Access Bits

The special access bits do not appear in the long form of a directory listing, but are maintained in the inode for a file. Here are the special access bits shown in Figure 2.7 (page 000), which are used as follows:

1. SUID (Set User ID bit)
   The SUID is stored in an inode. It is set for a file containing an executable program; in the 7th edition and System V, this applies only to programs, not to files of commands (shell procedures). You can set this bit by typing

   ```
   $ chmod u+s filename(s)
   ```

2. SGID (Set Group ID bit)
   The SGID is stored in an inode. It is used for group-owned executable files. You can set this bit by typing

   ```
   $ chmod g+s filename(s)
   ```

3. sticky bit: S_ISVTX in /usr/include/sys/inode.h.
   This bit can only be set by your system administrator. When it is set, the system will not swap out an executable file when it stops running. That is, the core image of a file is maintained (it stays in memory) instead of being swapped out to the disk (memory occupied by a program will not be used for another program which is needed and must be brought into core from disk). This is useful for frequently used programs like sh, ed, and vi. You will not have to wait for these programs to be brought into main memory

from disk. If you have a program you use repeatedly, you may want to have its sticky bit set by your system administrator, who will probably resist. If too many files have their sticky bit set, the system will bog down, that is, will not be free to do needed swapping. A *sticky file* is a file which has its sticky bit set.

The ls -l command lists only nine of the twelve access bits (ones for user, group, and other). The leading mode bit listed by ls -l indicates the file type.

2.3.7 File Types

Unix keeps track of four file types. Here are some examples:

```
$ ls -l /dev/swap                       # for block type
brw-------  1 sysinfo sysinfo  1,41 Oct 14 17:10 swap
$ ls -l /dev/tty                        # for character type
crw-rw-rw-  1 bin     bin      1, 0 Oct 14 17:28 tty
$ ls -l                                 # other types
drw-r--r--  1 you     unix       34 Jan 11  9:30 lib
-rw-r--r--  1 you     unix       56 Jan 11 11:34 Tolkien
```

In each case the leading bit indicates the file type used by the corresponding inode. The first two file types are block and serial files for associated devices.

2.3.8 Block and Serial Devices

Every device on a Unix system has a corresponding device file. A terminal is an example of what is known as a serial device (it has character input and output). The 'c' file type is for a character serial device. By contrast, a disk is a block access device. In 7th edition Unix, a *block* is 512 bytes. A *byte* is usually eight bits. In System V and later versions of Berkeley Unix, a block is 1,024 bytes. The advantages of using larger blocks are discussed by McKusick, Joy, Samuel, and Leffler (August, 1985). They focus on the new file system released with 4.2 BSD Unix.

A disk is a block-structured device. Disk input and output are in blocks (as opposed to characters on a terminal). A file associated with a block device is a 'b'-type file. The swap file in /dev is an example.

The file-type bit is **d** for directories and left blank (with a **-**) for regular files. Although file types are possible (for example, program files, command procedures, text files), Unix does not classify other files. This is left up to a file owner. You can use the file command to check the file type "guessed" by this command.

The **file** command attempts to classify a file by checking the first 512 bytes of a file.

DIRECTORIES 65

We return now to another use for the od command in looking at hidden characters in a file.

2.4 USING THE od COMMAND TO DISPLAY A COMPLETE FILE

If the od command is restricted to a single file, then it displays the contents of that file. For example, suppose we start with

```
$ cat >letter
Susu,
     How about coffee at 10am?
                    Tom
ctrl-d
$
```

Now use the od command to inspect this file:

```
$ od -c letter                  # display characters
0000000   S  u  s  u  ,  \n     H  o  w     a  b  o  u
0000020   t     c  o  f  f  e  e     a  t     1  0  a  m
0000040   ?  \n
0000060   T  o  m  \n
$
```

A newline (in boldface) is represented by a **\n** in the octal dump of letter. In debugging programs this can sometimes be useful, since you may have hidden (and did not want) characters in your file which you cannot see by simply listing your file.

There are a couple of ways to check disk usage.

2.5 DISK USAGE

The **du** command has the following syntax:

---

du [-s] [-a] [name]

-s option to show grand total

-a option to show disk usage for each file

You can check the number of blocks used by files in your directory by typing

```
$ du .                  # disk usage for current directory
54             ./bin
6              ./lib/cs/unix
38             ./lib/tools
60             ./lib
62             ./exp
220            .
$
```

This sample output lists the number of blocks used by each directory you own. For instance, this says that the ./bin directory uses 54 blocks. (Notice that ./bin is another way of writing /usr/you/bin or just bin. This notation says that bin is a subdirectory of your current directory. Notice that the dot (.) is taken from the command line used to activate the du.) What would the listing look like if the following command line is typed?

```
$ du $HOME              # guess what gets listed
```

You might also wonder what to type to list the disk usage for *every* directory on your system. You can check the total number of blocks used by your current directory by typing

```
$ du -s .
  220   .
$
```

You can tell how much disk storage is free on a device by typing

```
$ df devicename
```

For example, try entering

```
$ df /dev/root
   (/dev/root ):   6960 blocks      2021 i-nodes
```

To see what storage devices are used on your system, type

```
$ ls /dev
```

If you lose track of a file, you can use the find command to locate a file.

2.6 FINDING FILES WITH THE find COMMAND

The find command has the following syntax:

---

find pathname-lists option expression
option (partial list):
  -name filename specifies file to find
  -atime n true if file accessed in n days
  -ok command executes command
  -print causes display of current pathname
  -type x finds files of type specified by x which can be
      b for block special file
      c for character special file
      d for directory
      f for regular file
  Note: see find(1) for all options.

For example, to print out the current pathname for the phonebk file, type

```
$ find . -name phonebk -print       # finds pathname
./lib/phonebk
./phonebk                            # linked in .
$
```

You can display the paths for files specified with a wildcard. This will include those in your current directory plus those in subdirectories of your current directory. Try

```
$ find . -name 'yes*' -print        # finds yes* files
./book/yes
./yesaa
./yesab
./yesac
$
```

This says you have a filename *yes,* which is a subdirectory book. The other yes* files are in your current directory. To get a listing of all *.h files containing definitions used by Unix on your system *and* which you can inspect, try typing

```
$ find / -name '*.h' -print >temp
```

After you get the $-prompt back, try the following experiment:

☐ EXPERIMENT 4

(Note: your temp and /usr/include/sys/ascii.h will probably be different.)

```
$ head -10 temp
/usr/lib/term/terms.h
/usr/include/sys/ascii.h
/usr/include/sys/a.out.h
        .
        .
        .
$ cat /usr/include/sys/ascii.h
#define A_SUB   26
#define A_ESC   27
        .
        .
        .
```

The find command can be used to clean out your directories. To remove the yes* files accessed in the last two days, for example, try typing

```
$ find . -name 'yes*' -atime +2 -ok rm {} \;
< rm ... ./book/yes >? y
< rm ... ./yesaa >? y
< rm ... ./yesab >? n
< rm ... ./yesac >? n
$
```

The boldfaced letters are the typed responses to the prompts (followed by a ?) printed by the **-ok** find option. The double braces ({ }) are replaced by find with the current pathname. The backslash is called an escape character.

Special use of the backslash:
  The backslash \ is used to remove the special meaning of a character for the shell. By itself, the semicolon (;) is a command separator. If you type \;, this tells the shell to ignore the semicolon. In effect, the \; escapes the semicolon (it will not be interpreted by sh as a command separator).

We just removed two files: book/yes and yesaa (in the current directory). This assumes we have accessed these files in the last two days. If you want to scan all files accessed in the last two days (to see which one to remove with rm), then use

```
$ find . -name '*' -ok rm {} \;
```

In this command line, the **-ok** command is coupled with the rm command to prompt for files you may want removed. Any of the other commands we have used so far can be used with this option. To select files to list, try the following experiment:

☐ EXPERIMENT 5

```
$ find . -name '*' -ok cat {} \;
< cat ... ./lib/letter >? y
       .
       .
       .
< cat ... ./lib/tools/xref >? n
       .
       .
       .
$
```

If you type **y** after a prompt in the above experiment, the indicated file would be printed on your screen by cat. You can find all files with a given type by using

```
$ find . -type d -print
.
./bin
./lib
./lib/cs
./lib/tools
./exp
$
```

This lists all the subdirectories of your current directory as well as their subdirectories. A variation of this command line will allow you to scan the *entire* tree of directories on your Unix system. Can you see how? More details about this command are given in the Shell Commands Handbook following Chapter 8.

We return now to the use of the ln command and what happens to slots in your directory formerly occupied by files with zero links.

2.7 LINKING FILES WITH THE ln COMMAND

The minimum number of links an existing file can have is 1, including a file which is empty but not removed from your directory. For example, we will create the following three empty files:

```
$ tee tumty1 tumty2 tumty3
ctrl-d
$ ls -l tumty*
-rw-r--r--    1 you     unix         0 Jan 12 15:33 tumty1
-rw-r--r--    1 you     unix         0 Jan 12 15:33 tumty2
-rw-r--r--    1 you     unix         0 Jan 12 15:33 tumty3
```

The boldfaced numbers indicate the file sizes, which are zero. Each of these empty files has 1 link, corresponding inumbers, and inodes. We can give other names to the same file by typing

```
$ ln tumty1 LewisC                        # make new link
$ ln tumty1 OhMy                          # add link
$ ln tumty1 sugarplum                     # add link
$ ls -l tumty1 LewisC OhMy sugarplum      # check results
-rw-r--r--   4 you      unix         0 Jan 12 15:33 LewisC
-rw-r--r--   4 you      unix         0 Jan 12 15:33 OhMy
-rw-r--r--   4 you      unix         0 Jan 12 15:33 sugarplum
-rw-r--r--   4 you      unix         0 Jan 12 15:33 tumty1
$
```

If you remove one of the links, then each of the links on the other directory entries with the same inumber is decremented by one. Try the following experiment:

☐ EXPERIMENT 6

```
$ rm LewisC
$ ls -l OhMy sugarplum tumty1
-rw-r--r--   3 you      unix         0 Jan 12 15:33 OhMy
-rw-r--r--   3 you      unix         0 Jan 12 15:33 sugarplum
-rw-r--r--   3 you      unix         0 Jan 12 15:33 tumty1
$
```

It is important to realize that removing the original link to a file does not remove the file itself, if that file has more than one link. To see this, try fleshing out the tumty1 file:

☐ EXPERIMENT 6B

```
$ cat >tumty1
Halley's comet is barely visible this month.
ctrl-d
$ ls -l OhMy sugarplum tumty1
-rw-r--r--   3 you      unix        37 Jan 12 16:26 OhMy
-rw-r--r--   3 you      unix        37 Jan 12 16:26 sugarplum
-rw-r--r--   3 you      unix        37 Jan 12 16:26 tumty1
$
```

Notice that each of these files has the *same* inumber:

```
$ ls -i OhMy sugarplum tumty1
1595 OhMy
1595 sugarplum
1595 tumty1
$
```

LINKING FILES WITH THE ln COMMAND

This says that each of these filenames refers to the same inode, which is another way of saying that each of these filenames identifies the *same* file. If you remove tumty1, you do not destroy the file. Try

```
$ rm tumty1                          # remove original link
$ ls -l OhMy sugarplum
-rw-r--r--   2 you     unix    37 Jan 12 16:29 OhMy
-rw-r--r--   2 you     unix    37 Jan 12 16:29 sugarplum
$
```

In other words, the file whose original name was tumty1 is still accessible. You can verify this by typing

```
$ cat OhMy
Halley's comet is barely visible this month.
$
```

You might wonder what happens to slots in your directory if you remove all of the links to an existing file. To see what happens, try the following variation of Experiments 6a and 6b:

☐ EXPERIMENT 6C

```
$ od -c .
0002700  027 005   O   h   M   y  \0  \0  \0  \0  \0  \0  \0  \0  \0  \0
0002720  351 006   s   u   g   a   r   p   l   u   m  \0  \0  \0  \0  \0
$ rm OhMy sugarplum
$ od -c .
0002700   \0  \0   O   h   M   y  \0  \0  \0  \0  \0  \0  \0  \0  \0  \0
0002720   \0  \0   s   u   g   a   r   p   l   u   m  \0  \0  \0  \0  \0
$
```

In other words, even though all the links are gone and the file has been removed, the directory slots used by these removed files remain. These slots now have zero inumbers (they do not identify an inode). If you create a new file now, one of these old directory slots will be used (but probably *not* with the same inumber). Here is a continuation of Experiment 6c:

☐ EXPERIMENT 6D

```
$ cat >memory                                        # create new file
Visualizing, repetition, and association are the three keys to
memorizing.
ctrl-d
$ od -c .                                            # check directory
0002700  027 005   m   e   m   o   r   y  \0  \0  \0  \0  \0  \0  \0  \0
0002720   \0  \0   s   u   g   a   r   p   l   u   m  \0  \0  \0  \0  \0
$
```

In this sample directory, the new file called memory gets the directory slot originally used by the file called OhMy. The best way to see how this works is to try variations of these experiments on your own Unix system—seeing is believing.

The last thing we will do in this chapter is survey some of the files above your home directory.

2.8 SURVEY OF SELECTED UNIX DIRECTORIES

To get a list of all subdirectories of /usr, for example, you can use the following command line:

```
$ ls -l /usr | grep '^d'       # list subdirectories
drwxr-xr-x   2 bin        bin         80 Oct 14 17:43 adm
drwxr-xr-x   2 bin        bin       1872 Dec 11 17:24 bin
    .
    .
    .
$
```

The grep argument ^d is quoted to prevent the shell from misinterpreting the up-arrow ^ (the old name for a pipe). This is an example of what is known as a regular expression. A *regular expression* provides a template which is used to match actual expressions. For example, '^d' specifies all actual expressions (strings of characters) which begin with a lowercase **d.** The up-arrow is used to indicate that the pattern specified by the regular expression must be matched with the *beginning* of a string. In other words, a regular expression serves as an "expression-getter" (it is used to find strings with a pattern matching the regular expression). The rules for constructing regular expressions are given in Section 6.2.1.

You can also scan your system directories using the find command. Here is a challenge question:

> **CHALLENGE:**
> How does the output from
>
> ```
> $ ls -l | grep '^d'
> ```
>
> differ from the output from the following?
>
> ```
> $ find . -type d -print
> ```

You will want to browse through your system commands directories to become familiar with the programming potential of your system.

2.8.1 /bin and /usr/bin for Commands

Commands available to all Unix users are in the /bin and /usr/bin directories. These directories can be listed like any other directory. You may want to ask your system administrator to run the following command line for you:

```
$ cd /bin; file *
ar:        separate executable
as:        separate executable
at:        separate executable
awk:       separate executable
diff:      separate executable
diff3:     commands text
dircmp:    commands text
  .
  .
  .
$
```

The files which are classified *executable* cannot be inspected. The term *separate* indicates a file on a 16-bit machine, where programs are limited in size to 64k bytes (on a VAX-11/780, for example, this will be different). A file which is classified as a commands text in /usr/bin is readable. You can inspect a commands text (calendar, for example, which may be listable on your system). As a rule, only your system administrator can effectively run the file command on the /bin and /usr/bin directories. If you try this from your home directory, you will probably get a message like the following one:

```
login: you
password:
$ cd /bin; file *
ar:        cannot open for reading
as:        cannot open for reading
at:        cannot open for reading
awk:       cannot open for reading
diff:      cannot open for reading
diff3:     commands text
  .
  .
  .
$
```

Even though the file command will not tell you as much as it would if you were the system administrator, it does tell you which files can be inspected (the ones labeled "commands text"). Try using the file and grep commands together in a single command line which produces a list of only those files that are commands. Try, for instance, the following experiment:

☐ EXPERIMENT 7

```
$ cd /usr/bin; file * | grep commands
```

You may be surprised at the output from Experiment 7. We leave variations of this experiment for exercises.

2.8.2 /usr/man and /usr/doc for Manuals and Documentation

If your system has an on-line set of Unix programming manuals, they will be in /usr/man. You can use

```
$ cd /usr/man; ls -l | grep '^d'
```

to check on the subdirectories of /usr/man, and type

```
$ cd /usr/man; ls | 3
```

to print the contents of this directory in three columns. It is common for a Unix system to have commands named 2, 3, 4, and 5, which are used to print the output in the number of columns identified by the filename. If your system does not have a command named **3,** then try

```
$ cd /usr/man; ls | pr -3 -t -l1 $*
```

The **$*** is a shorthand for *all shell arguments* (the arguments for pr will be taken from the pipe in this example). If you want the output to be printed in five instead of three columns, then change the **-3** to a **-5** in the above command line. Try varying this argument to see what happens.

You will want to peek inside your /usr/doc directory for a look at system documents. Among these, you will probably find the Tutorial Introduction to the Editor useful.

2.8.3 /lib and /usr/lib for System Libraries

The /lib and /usr/lib directories provide a huge pool of information. To get an overview of this information, type

```
$ cd /usr/lib; ls | pr -5 -t -l1 $*   # prints in 5 cols
accept         flip         libcurses        lpmove         style3
   .              .              .               .              .
   .              .              .               .              .
   .              .              .               .              .
$
```

For example, libcurses comes from Berkeley. This file has window and cursor subroutines.

2.9 SUMMARY

A Unix file is a sequence of characters. A hierarchy of directories is used to organize Unix files. This hierarchy begins with the root directory. A filename is derived from the path from the root to a specified file. In effect, each file (including directories themselves) is identified by its place in the directory tree.

Unix directories are used to maintain two pieces of information about each file: its inumber and name. An *inumber* is used by Unix as the internal name of a file. An inumber identifies the location of the inode for a named file. An inode also provides a description of a file (except for the file name)—its size, data blocks, type, time of creation, and other data. The structure of an inumber *and* inode can be listed by you using cat on /usr/include/sys/dir.h (for the inumber) and /usr/include/sys/inode.h (for the inode).

The use of inumbers makes it possible for a file to have more than one name without ambiguity. Each new name for a file gives a new link (directory name plus the *same* inumber) for a file. For example, if secrets is the name of a file, then the following technique can be used to give new names (new links) to this file:

```
$ ln secrets codes            # now file has two names
$ ln secrets encryptions      # now file has three names
```

If the inumber for secrets is 1893, then each of the new names for secrets will have the same inumber. You can verify this by typing

```
$ ls -i secrets codes encryptions
   1893    secrets
   1893    codes
   1893    encryptions
```

There is no ambiguity in giving a file more than one name because the same inumber is used for each new directory entry. This feature has many uses. Chief among these is that the ln command gives us a way to specify files in other directories without having to use the pathnames for these remote files. Here is a typical case:

```
$ ln ./lib/tools/commands/filemgmt mgmt
$ cat mgmt                               # use new name
```

The new name goes into the current directory and can be used instead of the more cumbersome pathname for a remote file.

The Unix file system gains much of its strength from its simplicity. It maintains a minimum amount of information about each file. It is left up to the user to determine the internal organization of each file. The kernel does not do what you have seen the file command do, that is, it does not attempt to classify a file based on what is contained in a file. It does not tamper with a file—it does not add bytes to files you create; it does not attempt to separate a file into logical units called records; it does not distinguish between direct access and serial access files. In a Unix system, a lot is left up to the user.

Mastery of the Unix file system is crucial. This means *you* must be comfortable with shell commands used to create, find, classify, inspect, edit, and maintain files.

This starts with exploring various ways to create files (eight methods have been given so far). It does not take long to create lots of files, both regular files and directories. To maintain control of your part of the file system, it is helpful to be comfortable with the following commands:

FILE MANAGEMENT FUNCTION	COMMAND	PURPOSE
1. storage measurements		
	du	disk usage
	df	space left (free)
2. editing		
	ed	line editor
	vi	visual editor
3. inspection		
	cat	list file
	find	locate file
	ls	list directory
	od	octal dump
	pr	controlled printing
4. access		
	chmod	change permissions
	ln	give file new name

2.10 REVIEW OF COMMANDS, SYMBOLS, AND KEYWORDS

This section reviews the commands, symbols, and keywords introduced in this chapter.

2.10.1 Commands

COMMAND	ACTION
chmod	changes permission(s)
+permission	adds permission
−permission	removes permission
u, g, o	selects user, group, other access bits
r, w, x	specifies read, write, and execute bits
df	prints number of blocks free on your file systems
du	determines number of blocks currently being used in specified directory *and* its subdirectories
-a option	determines number of blocks being used by each file in specified directory
-s option	gives grand total of blocks being used by a specified directory
ed	line editor
find	finds files along specified path
-name	specifies name of file to find

2.10.1 Commands (continued)

COMMAND	ACTION
-atime	specifies time stamp on files to find
-ok command	executes command and prompts for y or n to determine action to take
-print	prints list of files found
-type	determines file type
ln	link file
ls -i	list inumbers for files in your current directory
od	octal dump of directory or file
-c	dumps characters in file *or* directory listing
-d	dumps contents in decimal
-x	dumps contents in hexadecimal
split	splits file
-n	specifies size of split
-	specifies input to split is to be taken either from a keyboard or a pipe
tee	t-shaped pipe, which is used to write to a file and produce standard output
-a	appends to file in tee

2.10.2 Symbols

SYMBOL	INTERPRETATION
-(split)	used to specify input to split is to be taken either from a pipe or from a keyboard
* (ed)	ed prompt
P	turn on ed prompt
.	quit ed append mode
*w	write ed text to a file
*q	quit ed
:	vi command prompt
:w	vi command to copy a vi text to a new file
:w!	vi command to overwrite an old file with a vi text
:w !command	use !command to write vi text
:x,yw >>place	append lines x to y to place
\ (backslash)	escape character (see Section 2.6)
\;	escape semicolon

2.10.3 Keywords

KEYWORD(S)	EXPLANATION
absolute mode	octal numbers used to set access bits
access bits	specify file permissions (12 access bits are maintained in the inode for each file)
binary	base 2
block device	device with block i/o (example: disk)
block file	for a block device (example: /dev/swap)

2.10.3 Keywords (continued)

KEYWORD(S)	EXPLANATION
byte	usually eight bits
high byte	upper eight bits of 16-bit string used on PDP-11 computers
low byte	lower eight bits of 16-bit string
dir entry	inumber + filename
file	sequence of characters (bytes)
file command	attempts to determine file type

file type	four possibilities:
	  b: block
	  c: character
	  d: directory
	  -: regular

hex	short for hexadecimal (base 16)
inode	data structure used to maintain information about a file (to see its structure, cat /usr/include/sys/inode.h)
inumber	internal (behind-the-scenes) name of a file used by Unix (to see its structure, cat /usr/include/sys/dir.h)
link	name of a file (see ln command, Section 2.7)
octal	base 8 (cf. absolute mode, chmod, and od)
serial device	character i/o device like a terminal
special access bits	access bits maintained in inode for a file (these are not printed by ls -l)
SUID	Set User id bit (set for executable programs)
SGID	Set Group id bit (set for group executable programs)
sticky bit	prevents swapping, if set
sticky file	file with sticky bit set (ed, vi, and sh are examples)
tee	copies input to files(s) and standard output (used for pipe-fitting)
-a	appends rather than overwrites file(s)

2.11 EXERCISES

1. How does a directory differ from a regular file?
2. If an inumber were four bytes, what would be the maximum number of inodes that would be possible on a Unix system?
3. If a directory lists 5,000 filenames with identical inumbers, how many inodes do these directory entries identify?
4. Create a file named terms in your $HOME/lib subdirectory. Then give the command line which can be used to identify the location of your $HOME/lib/terms file.

The next eleven exercises use the following file:

```
$ cat >keillor
When the Allis-Chalmers got away from him one day and
he had to jump free, Alfred didn't run after it but
```

```
stood and watched as the tractor went around and around
in wider and wider circles, discing and harrowing . . .
forty acres of spring wheat until it stopped, out of
gas, then said to Edna, "Look at that. She done almost
as good a job as if I'd been on her myself" (G.
Keillor, 1982).
```

5. Show how to append the following line to the keillor file without using an editor:

    Garrison Keillor, Happy to Be Here, p. 204.

6. Give the command line which uses tee to create the keillor file directly from keyboard input.

7. Show how to use the tee command to append the line given in Exercise 5 to the keillor file.

8. Show how to use grep, tee, and wc with multiple pipes to do the following things:
    a. find lines in the keillor file containing **ing**;
    b. put lines found in new copy file
    c. count the words in the lines found
    d. put the count in a counts file
    e. print the word count

9. Put the command line from Exercise 8 into a file called tab and make the file executable. You have just created a file called a *command procedure,* which contains commands. When a command procedure is executable, the commands inside the procedure are read by the shell just the way they would be if you had typed them in from a keyboard. Execute tab.

    Hint: use chmod to make the file executable.

10. Replace the filename keillor used in the command line in the tab file in Exercise 9 with $*. Now give the command line to run tab to find the -ing words in /usr/dict/words.

11. Give the command line to split the keillor file into a sequence of one-line files with the prefix **happy.**

12. (Refinement) Modify the command line for Exercise 8 so that the standard output from count is *appended* to the new copy file instead of the counts file and prints the lines found by grep.

13. (Refinement) Using the command structures from Exercise 12, add the following features:
    a. file command as well as grep, tee, and wc
    b. find all commands text files in /usr/bin
    c. put list of files found in /usr/you/commands
    d. append count to /usr/you/commands
    e. also prints count

    Use cat to show the contents of /usr/you/commands (note: **you** represents your name and /usr/you = $HOME).

14. (Refinement) Rewrite the command for Exercise 13 using $HOME instead of /usr/you/commands. Give a sample run.

15. (Refinement) Put the command from Exercise 14 into a file named fc and
    a. replace /usr/bin with $*
    b. use tee to *append* lines found to $HOME/commands
    c. make fc executable

Give sample runs with
d. fc /usr/bin
e. fc /bin

In each case, give a listing of $HOME/commands after you have activated fc.

16. Give a command line which uses tee to create a new file and which suppresses the standard output to the screen each time a new input line is entered from your keyboard (see the challenge in Section 2.2.1). Give a sample run.

17. Create a phonebk file in ./lib with the following entries:
    E. W. Dijkstra   UTexas   unlisted
    Bilboe Baggins   Orlando, FL   (305) 746-2788
    R. C. Holt   UToronto   unlisted
    A. Ralston   SUNY   (212) 366-9101
    R. Pattis   SUNY   (212) 367-1221

18. Give the command line to do the following:
    a. find entries in ./lib/phonebk from Exercise 17 having an area code you choose
    b. split entries found into a sequence of files with a prefix which is the same as the area code you use in your search.

19. Give the command line to concatenate the files produced by Exercise 18 using
    a. a wildcard to specify the files to be concatenated
    b. a new file you have created called FL to hold the concatenated files

20. Implement Experiment 1 in Section 2.1 and explain the results.

21. Implement Experiments 2a and 2b in Section 2.2.2 using the ./lib/phonebk file from Exercise 17 and explain the results from both experiments. (In explaining the results from Experiment 2b, show what new files are created and why.)

22. Show how to use ed to append the following entry to the ./lib/phonebk file from Exercise 14:
    Abigail G.   NY   (201) 345-7712

23. Implement Experiment 3 in Section 2.2.4 and use ls and cat to verify your results.

24. Give the computations necessary to convert the following inumbers written in octal to their base 10 equivalents:

```
$ od -c
0002700    526  114  y  e  s  a  a  \0 \0 \0 \0 \0 \0 \0 \0 \0
0002720    373  007  y  e  s  a  b  \0 \0 \0 \0 \0 \0 \0 \0 \0
```

Hint: see Section 2.3.2.

25. Give the decimal equivalent of the following inumbers which are written in hex:

```
$ od -x
0002700    0aaa 6579 6173 0064 0000 0000 0000 0000
0002720    076e 6579 6173 0065 0000 0000 0000 0000
```

26. Write the command line which can be used to list the disk usage for all files you own.

27. Write the command line which lists all directories in
    a. /;
    b. /usr;
    c. /usr/bin;

d. /etc;
e. /usr/include/sys
f.
28. Write the command line which lists all files of type commands texts in each of the directories in parts a. through f. of Exercise 27.
29. Write a command line which does the following things:
   a. finds all files with a specified prefix
   b. gives you the option of removing each of the files that is found
   Give a sample run.
   Hint: see examples in Section 2.6.
30. Write a command line which does the following things:
   a. finds all files in your current directory and its subdirectories
   b. allows you to compute a word count for selected files
31. Implement Experiments 6a and 6b in Section 2.7. Use the ls command to probe the results of these experiments. Explain what you find.
32. Implement Experiments 6c and 6d in Section 2.7. Again, use the ls and od commands to probe the results of these experiments and explain what you find.
33. Give a response to the challenge in Section 2.8.
34. Implement Experiment 7 in Section 2.8.1 and explain what you find.
35. Use the technique shown in Section 2.8.2 to create new commands called 2, 3, 4, and 5. Make these files executable and give sample runs of these new commands using ls on the directories discussed in Section 2.8.2.
36. Give a listing of commands text in one of the directories above your home directory.
37. Write a command line which can be used to create a file called list into which we can insert a list of commands texts in /usr/bin *and* /bin.
38. If lib is a subdirectory of your home directory, give four different ways to specify this subdirectory from your home directory (you can assume HOME has been defined for your login directory).
39. Identify the files specified by
   a. ../*
   b. /usr/../lib*
   c. /usr/you/ch*
   d. ./lib
   e. .
   f. /../../lib

2.12 REVIEW QUIZ

Indicate whether the following statements are true or false:
1. /bin and ./bin specify the same subdirectory.
2. The following command line always lists what is in your login directory:

   ```
   $ /bin/ls
   ```

3. Every directory name has an inumber.
4. *Inumber* is short for "illicit number."

5. Every Unix file has an inode.
6. Directories are files.
7. A file of type separate executable can be listed by cat.
8. A directory is an example of a regular file.
9. The following command line prints the output from ls in the indicated directory in five columns:

```
$ cd /usr/bin; ls -l | pr -5 -t -l1 $*
```

10. One command line can have more than one tee.

2.13 FURTHER READING

Foxley, E. Unix for Super-Users. Workingham, England: Addison-Wesley, 1985. Chapter 3 gives a tour of the Unix file system.

Keillor, G. Happy to Be Here. New York: Atheneum, 1982.

Kernighan, B. The Unix Programming Environment. Englewood Cliffs: Prentice, 1984. See Chapter 2 on the Unix file system, especially Sections 2.4–2.6.

Kernighan, B., and J. R. Mashey. "The Unix Programming Environment" IEEE Selected Reprints in Software. Los Angeles: IEEE, 1982. See pp. 255–57 on the Unix file system.

Kernighan, B., and D. M. Ritchie. The C Programming Language. Englewood Cliffs: Prentice, 1978. See Chapter 6 on structures. See also Stroustrup (1986).

Lampson, B. W., M. Paul, and H. J. Siegert, eds. Distributed Systems: Architecture and Implementation. New York: Springer-Verlag, 1981. See Section 9.4 on human-oriented filenames and pathnames.

Lions, J. A Commentary on the Unix Operating System. New South Wales, Australia: Department of Computer Science, University of New South Wales, 1977. See Chapter 19 on file directories and directory files.

McKusick, W. K., W. N. Joy, S. J. Leffler, and R. S. Fabry. "A Fast File System," ACM Transactions on Computer Systems, vol. 2, no. 3 (August, 1984), 181–98. See especially pp. 182–84 on the old and the new file system.

Nichols, E. A., S. C. Bailin, and J. C. Nichols. Unix Survival Guide. New York: Holt, Rinehart and Winston, 1987. See Chapter 6 on directories.

Peters, J. F. The Digital Way: Macro-11 Assembly Language Programming (PDP-11). Englewood Cliffs: Prentice, 1985. See Chapters 1 and 2, especially Sections 2.2 and 2.3.

Ritchie, D. "The Unix Time-Sharing System: A Retrospective" in The Bell System Technical Journal, vol. 57, no. 6 (July–August, 1978), pp. 1947–69. See especially pp. 1953–54 on the Unix file system.

Stroustrup, B. The C++ Programming Language. Reading, MA: Addison-Wesley, 1986. See Section 2.3.8 on structures.

3 Processes and the Shell

The shell is substantially more powerful than might be inferred from simple examples.... It is a programming language in its own right.
—Brian W. Kernighan and John R. Mashey, 1982.

A good shell, such as the Unix shell, allows the user interface to be tailored to a given user's requirements to a certain extent.
—Eric Foxley, 1985.

Angling is an art, either by practice or by long observation or both.
—Isaak Walton and Charles Cotton, 1847.

3.0 AIMS

- Track actions by the shell which lead to the creation of processes
- Introduce various ways to execute commands
- Distinguish between foreground and background processing
- Begin using both background processing and suspended execution of commands
- Introduce special shell variables
- Show various ways to customize your programming environment
- Introduce the use of the export command in calls by value
- Show various uses of the set command, including the set diagnostic modes
- Begin developing simple command procedures

3.1 INTRODUCTION TO UNIX PROCESSES

It is essential to have an understanding of what goes on behind the scenes when you activate a command. This chapter deals mostly with tracking what happens when the shell begins interpreting a command line. There are many ways to look behind the scenes whenever the shell starts processing command lines. This is helpful in gaining control of and building your skills with the built-in set of commands.

The shell begins interpreting a command line when it detects a newline. A newline serves as a signal to the shell that you have finished typing in a command line. The shell interprets the characters from the beginning of a command line up to the first blank (or tab or newline) as the *command verb*. In effect, a command line has the following syntax

```
$  <command-verb> <' '><arg 1> ... <' '><arg k><\n>
```

where $<'\ '>$ is a blank or tab (or newline \n, if there are no arguments). Here are the steps followed by the shell when you login:

1. The login shell starts running when you log in; the shell immediately initiates the execution of your .profile, if you have one.
2. Prompt with a **$**.
3. Wait for standard input from your terminal or specified file.
4. Obtain command-verb from command line.
5. Search for command in directories defined by your PATH variable.
6. Issue a 'not found' message if the command is not found. Otherwise, the following things happen:
    a. If a command identifies an executable binary file, the kernel establishes a process relative to the named program. Otherwise if the verb identifies an executable file,
    b. The kernel starts a copy of the shell running on behalf of the current shell and the new shell takes its input from the named file. Each new shell is a new process. The new shell repeats steps 4 through 6 for the lines of the named file.
7. While the kernel is managing a new process, the shell which initiated the process waits for a reply from the kernel. If there are no problems, the shell created on behalf of the login shell (and any other child processes) will die and the login shell will start running again.
8. When the login shell starts running again, it issues the **$** prompt and the above steps are repeated until you log off.

Most of the commands in Part 1 of the Unix Programmer's Manual name executable binary files (sh and cd are examples). In such cases, the kernel takes over when these commands are issued.

A file of commands is called a *command procedure*. A new shell starts running (this is a new process) to take charge of a named command procedure. One or more of the lines of a command procedure can also identify command procedures. Each time a command procedure is identified, another copy of the shell starts running. Another process is created (spawned) on behalf of the shell that is running. Again, the new shell takes care of the newly found command procedure. Unless you specify otherwise, the login shell waits for the new shell process created on its behalf to stop running. In other words, nothing else happens until the processing of the command line you typed in has been completed. You will see later that it is not necessary to wait (you can run a process in the background).

Each time a new shell starts running, a process is created. Ritchie and Thompson (1978) define a *process* as an execution environment. In an execution environment, the kernel sets up the necessary bookkeeping for a process (a copy of the executable image is kept in memory, which is write-protected, and special instruction, data, and system segments are set up for a process).

It is important to understand the difference between a file which is an *executable* program and a program which is *in execution* (is running). An *executable program* is a file containing instructions and data used to initialize the instructions. By contrast, a program *in execution* is a process which has, in addition to its instructions and user data, system data which are set up by the kernel whenever a process begins. These system data include a copy of such information as your current directory and CPU time accumulated by a process. You can think of each new process as the environment *in which* a program executes.

A *process* is an environment in which a program executes. (Rochkind, 1985)

In the proposed Unix standard, a *process* is identified with "an address space and single thread of control that executes within that address space, and its required system resources" (IEEE, 22). Every process is created by the kernel on behalf of a currently executing process. Initially, when you log in and the shell starts running, it is the login shell which is the current process.

Each process has its own id number (this is labelled the PID for Process IDentity number). You can see the PID for your login shell (usually sh) by typing

```
$ ps
   PID TTY  TIME COMMAND
    34  02  0:12 sh
   309  02  0:84 ps
$
```

Notice that the kernel creates a process for the program named by the **ps** command. Its PID is 309 in this sample run. The PID of the login shell is 34 (the process created for your login shell will probably be different *and* this changes each time you log in). Also notice that the process created for ps was done by the kernel *on behalf of sh,* which is the current process when you type in the ps command.

In effect, the login shell has the relationship of a parent to a new shell created to take charge of a command procedure. Each time the kernel detects a new command procedure, a new process is created—a copy of the sh shell is started running on behalf of the current shell. The new shell takes charge of the new command procedure, which triggers the creation of yet another process. When the processes created on behalf of the current shell die, this means the current shell also dies and the parent process of the dying shell revives. The parent process reenters its execution environment. We can illustrate this with the following command procedures:

```
$ cat act0
echo '*'; act1; ps
$ cat act1
echo '**'; ps; act2
$ cat act2
echo '***'; ps; act3
$ cat act3
echo '****'; ps
```

Each of these command procedures contains two kinds of commands:

1. Commands which identify executable binary programs (echo and ps). The kernel will create a new process on behalf of the shell that encounters these commands; these command procedures each contain the following:
2. A command that identifies a command procedure:

```
act1 in act0
act2 in act1
act3 in act2
```

To run act0, we can use the chmod command to make act0, act1, act2, and act3 executable:

```
$ chmod +x act0 act1 act2 act3    # make files executable
```

If we run act0, this leads to a succession of births followed by a succession of dying processes and revived parent processes until we get back to the first parent process, the running copy of sh that activated act0. A sample run of act0 is given in Figure 3.1.

Telling the shell to activate act0 results in the creation of a copy of sh which starts running (its PID in Figure 3.1 is 353). After the kernel processes the echo command in the act0 file, then the kernel starts a second copy of the shell running to take charge of act1. This pattern is repeated with a new printed message, and a new copy of sh (the login shell) starts running to handle act2. While the new shell is running, the other copies of sh are in a wait state. This pattern repeats itself again (a third copy of the shell starts running to handle act3). This is shown graphically in Figure 3.2.

Making copies of the login shell is possible because the shell is just another program. You can trace the revival of act2 *after* the act3 process dies by adding the ps command to the act2 file. Similarly, you can trace the revival of the act1 process when act2 dies by appending a ps command to the act1 file. You will have a chance to work through these changes in Exercise 12.7.

Finally, notice in Figure 3.1 that each time the ps command is detected by a running shell, a new process is created. Keep in mind that ps identifies a program. A process is created for *each* program that is processed by the kernel. Initially, for ex-

```
$ act0
*
    PID  TTY  TIME  COMMAND
     34   02  0:14  sh  ─────────────── login shell process
    353   02  0:00  sh  ─────────────── act0 shell process
    355   02  0:04  ps  ─────────────── process for ps
**
    PID  TTY  TIME  COMMAND
     34   02  0:14  sh
    353   02  0:00  sh
    356   02  0:00  sh  ─────────────── act1 shell process
    358   02  0:04  ps
***
    PID  TTY  TIME  COMMAND
     34   02  0:14  sh
    353   02  0:00  sh
    356   02  0:00  sh
    359   02  0:00  sh  ─────────────── act2 shell process
    361   02  0:04  ps
****
    PID  TTY  TIME  COMMAND
     34   02  0:14  sh
    353   02  0:00  sh
    356   02  0:00  sh
    359   02  0:00  sh
    362   02  0:00  sh  ─────────────── act3 shell process
    364   02  0:04  ps
*
    PID  TTY  TIME  COMMAND
     34   02  0:14  sh
    353   02  0:00  sh  ─────────────── revived act0 shell process
    366   02  0:04  ps
```

FIGURE 3.1
Succession of Processes

ample, the PID for ps is 355 (for the shell running act0). The PID for ps is 358 for the shell running act1, and so on.

In this chapter we look more closely at ways to execute commands, ways to run processes in the background and ways to customize your working environment further. First, we look at various ways to execute commands and track processes that have been initiated. When all is said and done, what Walton and Cotton say about fishing applies to shell programming: *the best way to learn about the shell is to use it*. A good way to read this chapter is to pause from time to time and type in some of the suggested commandlines and files to check out the inner workings of Unix. Chapter experiments are good places to do this.

3.2 WAYS TO EXECUTE COMMANDS

There are many ways to execute a command. Here is a preliminary list of ways to do this:

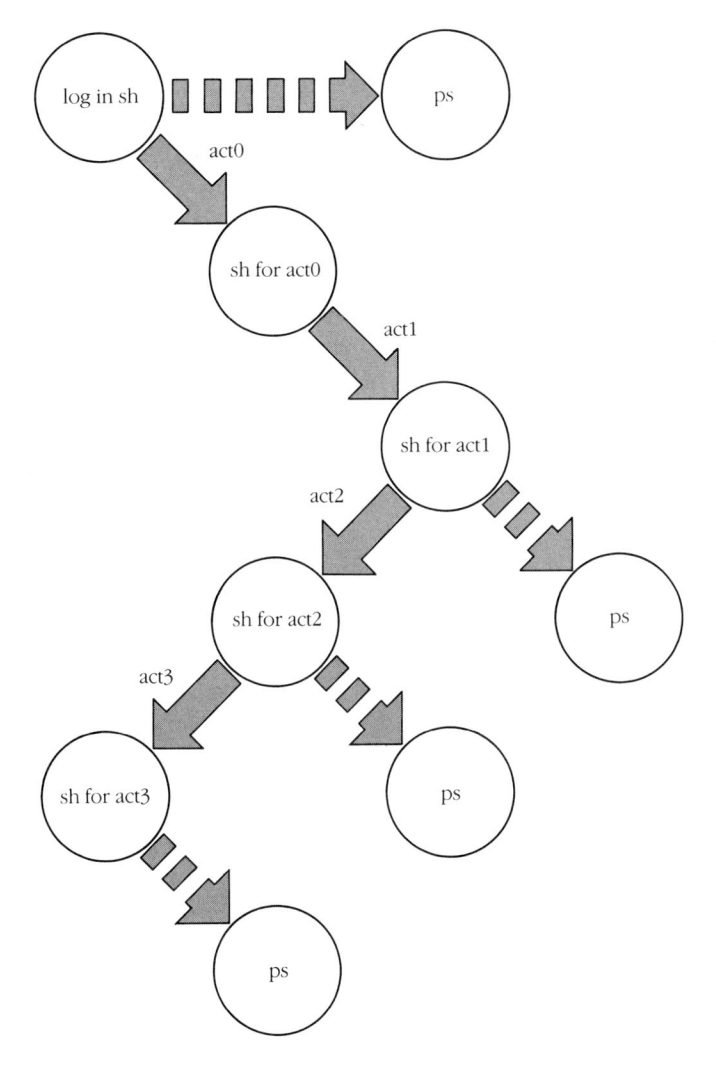

**FIGURE 3.2
Succession of Copies of sh**

1. If a command is already executable, type

   ```
   $ <command>
   $ date                          # example
   ```

2. If a command names a command procedure which is not executable, then type

   ```
   $ chmod +x <command>
   $ <command>
   ```

```
   $ cat >welcome                    # build example
   echo "Hello, world!'              # command in welcome file
   ctrl-d
   $ chmod +x welcome                # make it executable
   $ welcome                         # execute command
   Hello, world!
   $
```

3. To execute more than one command on the same line, type

   ```
   $ cd /usr/bin; ls                 # example
   ```

4. (new) Start a new shell running for multiple commands on the same line by typing

   ```
   $ (cd /usr/bin; ls)               # special example!
   ```

5. (new) If a command names a non-executable file, type

   ```
   $ sh <command>
   ```

6. (new) Make the execution of a command *part of the current process* by typing

   ```
   $ . <command>
   $ . .profile                      # executes .profile
   ```

7. (new) Execute a command as part of another command by enclosing a command inside backward quotes. Try typing

   ```
   $ echo ' working directory: ' `pwd`
   working directory: /usr/you
   $
   ```

   (This technique has a variety of uses.)

8. (new) Execute a new command in place of a current process by typing

   ```
   $ cat >act20                      # build example
   ps
   exec welcome                      # execute welcome
   ps
   ctrl-d
   $
   $ sh act 20                       # execute
   act20
        PID TTY TIME COMMAND
        719 02  9:30 sh
   ```

```
         639 02   9:31 sh
         332 02   9:31 ps
   Hello, world!                              output from exec
   $
```

The exec command is tricky to use. Can you guess what happens if you type the following line?

```
   $ . act20
```

9. (new) Assign an executable command name to a variable and execute the variable by using $-prefix (the value of the variable!). Try

```
   $ yes=welcome              # give yes a value
   $ $yes                     # execute yes
   Hello, world!
   $
```

You will see how this last method of executing a command can be used in combination with the read command inside shell procedures. In the following sections we examine in more detail each of these new methods of executing commands.

3.2.1 Running a Shell for Multiple Commands

There is a subtle difference between

```
$ cd /usr/bin; ls | 5
adb    ar    as    asm    ...
$ pwd
/usr/bin           your current directory has changed!
$
```

and

```
$ (cd /usr/bin; ls | 5)
adb    ar    as    asm    ...
$ pwd
/usr/you           your current directory is the same
```

In the first example, the multiple commands are run by your login shell, so the cd command changes the directory used by your login shell. By enclosing the same multiple commands inside parentheses, the kernel spawns a new shell to take care of the commands inside the parentheses. This means the cd command will affect the new shell (the child created on behalf of the current shell), but the cd command will have no affect on the current shell (it is in a wait state while the new shell takes care of the commands inside the parentheses). You can see this by trying the following experiment.

☐ EXPERIMENT 1A

```
$ (cd /usr/bin; pwd)
/usr/bin
$ pwd
/usr/you
```

You current shell will be in a wait state while the new shell finishes with the commands inside the parentheses. You can see this more clearly by using the ps command as follows:

☐ EXPERIMENT 1B

```
$ ps; (ps; cd /usr/bin; pwd); pwd
```

You may be surprised at the results of this experiment. This experiment suggests the possibility of leaving the current shell intact (its variables and its directory) to do something in another directory without affecting your current shell. You can see this by experimenting with a variable in two different shells:

☐ EXPERIMENT 2

```
$ x=5; (echo $x; x=1000; echo $x); echo $x
5
1000
5
$
```

This experiment shows that changes to x in the new shell do *not* change the value

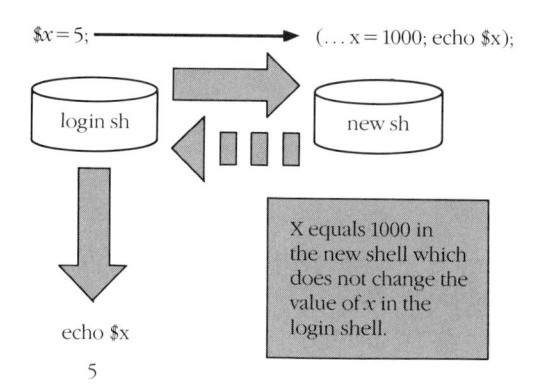

FIGURE 3.3
Commands inside Parentheses

CHAPTER 3 / PROCESSES AND THE SHELL

of x maintained by the parent shell. The difference between two ways of executing multiple commands on the same line is illustrated graphically in Figure 3.3

3.2.2 Executing a Command Using sh

The sh command can be used to execute procedures whose x- permission bits have not been set. Here is an example:

```
$ cat >act20
echo 'PID of current process = ' $$
sh welcome
echo 'PID of current process = ' $$
```

The command procedure called act20 uses a new variable, $$.

The PID of the process currently running is stored in **$$**.

We can use this variable to track which shell is being used to run a command. If you echo the value of $$ before you use sh to execute act20, you will find that a different process is running act20. Try this experiment.

☐ EXPERIMENT 3

```
$ cat welcome
echo 'Hello, world! with process id no. = ' $$
$ echo $$; sh act20; echo $ $
```

Experiment 3 draws on your knowledge of what the kernel does *each* time the current shell finds a command which is the name of a command procedure.

Unless you specify otherwise, the kernel starts a new shell running each time the current shell finds a command which identifies a command procedure. Each new shell which is running is a new process.

Knowing this, how many different PIDs will be printed by Experiment 3? Actually, four PIDs will be printed by this experiment. Two of these PIDs will be the same. Which ones?

You will find that you can use sh to execute command procedures regardless of whether they are executable or not. However, you cannot use sh to execute the built-in commands like date in the following command line:

```
$ sh date
date: date: cannot open
```

It is also possible to use the dot command to execute a command as part of the current process.

3.2.3 Using a Dot to Execute a Command

Instead of telling the kernel to start a new shell running when a command is executed, a dot can be used in the following way:

```
$ echo $$              # show PID of current process
93
$ . welcome            # execute command
Hello, world! with PID of current process = 93
$
```

The dot command tells the kernel to use the current shell to execute welcome instead of spawning a new process (a new copy of sh). This contrasts sharply with what the kernel does if you use sh to run welcome:

```
$ echo $$; sh welcome     # spawns new process
93
Hello, world! with PID of current process = 779
$
```

You cannot use the dot command to execute the built-in commands. Try

```
$ . date
date: not found
```

You can also save time with the dot command.

3.2.4 How to Save Time with the Dot Command

If you change your .profile, these changes will not be "known" to the login shell. Recall that each time you log in, your .profile is run by the sh shell. The settings for PATH and TERM used by your login shell are set up by your .profile. By running your .profile, the values assigned to variables in your .profile are the values used by your login shell. You can also revise your .profile. To make the login shell run in terms of your new .profile, you have two choices:

1. Change .profile, log off, log on again (to make the login shell run your .profile again), or
2. change .profile and use

    ```
    $ . .profile
    ```

    to run your .profile.

The second way of running your .profile should be done while your login shell is running. You can also run your .profile with the sh command as follows:

```
$ sh .profile              # quite different!
```

This second way of running your .profile causes a copy of your current shell to run your .profile. So it is the new shell, not the current one, that is affected by the changes in .profile. To see this, try the following experiment.

☐ EXPERIMENT 4

```
$ cat >>.profile              # add to your .profile
UnixUses=zillions             # new variable
ctrl-d
$ sh .profile; echo $UnixUses
                                          ?????
$ . .profile; echo $UnixUses
                                          ?????
```

Because the kernel does not start a new shell running when you use a dot command inside a procedure, the shell will continue processing inside the procedure after the dotted command stops running. You can force a running shell to ignore the rest of a command procedure *after* a command (inside a procedure) has been run by using the exec command.

3.2.5 Executing a Command with exec

If you use an exec command, this will overwrite the current process (obliterate it). Here is a command procedure that illustrates this idea:

```
$ cat >blastoff                    # create new procedure
echo 'PID of process running now is ' $$
exec welcome                       # execute welcome
echo 'PID now is ' $$
ctrl-d
$ sh blastoff
PID of process running now is 163
```

```
Hello, world! with process id no. = 163
$ sh act20                              # from section 3.2.2
PID of process running now is 739
Hello, world! with PID of current process = 739
$
```

Notice that

```
echo 'PID now is ' $$
```

is not executed. The exec command causes the shell running blastoff to be overwritten by welcome. So the process with the PID = 739 is gone; the welcome process takes the place of the running shell. This causes a disaster if you run the exec command in the foreground (while the login shell is running). Here is what happens:

```
$ exec welcome                          # overwrites login sh
Hello, world! with PID of current process = 93


login:
```

This logs you off. The best place to run exec is inside a command procedure where it is desirable to exit from the procedure *immediately* after running the exec command. When you use exec inside a procedure, you get back the login shell. Unlike the dot command, the exec command can be used to execute any command. Try the following experiment to get closer to what the exec and dot commands do.

☐ EXPERIMENT 5

```
$ . welcome; echo 'Back again...'; exec welcome
```

It is also possible to use backward single quotes to execute a command.

3.2.6 Command Substitution with Backward Quotes

There are two systems of quoting with single quotes, one that we have already used repeatedly and a second one that is "new" (it was implicitly used in the .profile in Section 1.4.7):

1. Forward (righthand) single quotes to enclose the parts of an argument as in

    ```
    $ echo 'If this is winter, can spring be far
    behind?'
    ```

2. Backward (lefthand) single quotes to enclose a command to be executed as part of another command:

```
$ echo 'The date' `date` 'says it is winter.'
The date Tue Jan 21 19:13:46 CST 1986 says it is winter.
$
```

In the second example, notice how the date command appears to run "inside" the echo command. What actually happens is this:

A '`<command>`' (command inside backward quotes) makes the *output* from a command part of a command line. This is known as *command substitution*.

Double quotes can be used to enclose expressions with single quotes *and* take away the special meaning of single quotes. Try

```
$ echo 'The date' `date` "says it's winter."
```

The " allows **it's** to be printed. Can you guess what happens if you use the following command line?

```
$ echo 'The date' `date` 'says it's winter.' #careful!
```

You can assign the output from a command run with backward quotes to a variable. Here is an example:

```
$ now=`date`                    # assign date to now
$ echo $now                     # check value of now
Tue Jan 21 19:18:20 CST 1986
```

Can you guess what gets assigned to list by the following command line?

```
$ list=`ls`                     # hint: this is massive!
```

A great deal can be done *inside* backward quotes. Here is a more bizarre example of this:

```
$ count=`wc -w $HOME/welcome | cut -c6-7`
$ echo $count
11
$
```

In this example, the output from

```
`wc -w $HOME/welcome | cut -c6-7`
```

```
$ wc - w  $HOME/welcome
_ _ _ _ _ 1 1      words
          └┬┘
           └──── cut out 6th and 7th characters
1  2  3  4  5  6  7


$ wc - w  $HOME/welcome | cut.- c6 - 7
11
```

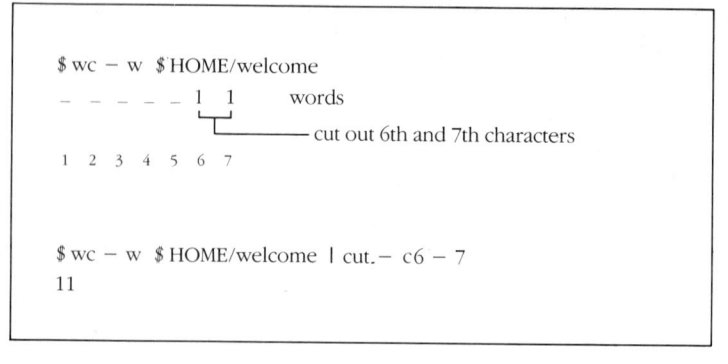

FIGURE 3.4
Use of Cut Command

is assigned to the count variable. Notice that the normal output from wc -w has the following format:

<blank><blank><blank><blank><blank><digit><digit> ...
                                      │   │
                                      │   └─ 7th character
                                      └─ 6th character

The output from the above command line "cuts" out digits for numbers printed by wc -w. This is illustrated graphically in Figure 3.4.

Command substitution will prove to be a very handy tool in later procedures. The following experiment demonstrates a practical use of this idea.

☐ EXPERIMENT 6

1. Set up a mailing list with

   ```
   $ cat >team
   susu
   wpayton
   jjones
   ctrl-d
   $
   ```

2. Then send a message (a copy of a procedure, for example) to the people on your team:

   ```
   $ mail `cat team` <welcome
   ```

98   CHAPTER 3 / PROCESSES AND THE SHELL

This experiment works because the output from 'cat team' goes to mail, so the people listed in the team file get a copy of welcome. Notice that you can also mail a copy of your mailing list to your team with

```
$ mail `cat team` <team
```

By clever reconstruction of the team file (turn it into a new command procedure), the above command line can be simplified. This simplification is left for an exercise.

Finally, it is possible to assign a command-string to a variable and give the shell the value of the variable to execute the command in the original command-string.

3.2.7 Executing Commands Assigned to Variables

We can assign a command-string to a variable, then use the value of the variable to tell the shell to interpret the command- string. Try

```
$ then=date                         # assign command
$ $date
Tue Jan 21 08:31 1986
$
```

The shell also provides a read command which can be used to assign values to variables. In the following example, we use the System V \c option with echo command to inhibit a carriage return and line feed (this does the same thing as the Berkeley Unix -n option with the echo command). The \c or -n option is helpful whenever we want to enter a value on the same line with an echo'd prompt like the one shown next:

```
$ echo 'Enter command: \c'; read action; $action
Enter command: date
Tue Jan 21 09:50 1086
$
```

The boldfaced **date** is assigned to the action-variable by read. It is **date** which is the value of action, so

```
$ $action
```

is just another way of entering

```
$ date
```

The usefulness of this new way of executing commands will be more apparent after we show how to reference command procedure arguments *inside* a procedure using special variables.

3.3 SPECIAL VARIABLES

A fairly extensive set of special variables is maintained by the shell. A summary of these special shell variables is given in the following table.

Special Shell Variables

TYPE	VARIABLES	USAGE
1. command-line	$#	number of arguments
	$*	shell arguments
	$0	command-verb
	$1...$9	individual arguments
	"$*"	"$1...$9"
	"$@"	"$1"..."$9"
2. names	*	names in current directory
3. process	$$	PID of current process running
	$!	PID of last background process
4. status	$—	set diagnostic status

The arguments in a command line have special features (and restrictions), as shown in the following table.

Features of Command-line Arguments

FEATURE	EXAMPLE
1. arguments are arbitrary strings	$ cat 2 BlueSky
2. arguments are separated by spaces (not commas)	$ cat x y (not cat x, y)
3. arguments containing spaces are quoted	$ grep 'x y' temp (not $ grep x y temp grep: can't open y

4. arguments are not enclosed by parentheses	$ grep x y temp (not
	$ grep (x y) temp
	syntax error: '(' unexpected

In the following sections we examine each of these special shell variables in detail.

3.3.1 Special Command-line Variables

There are special variables available for inspecting the parts of a command line:

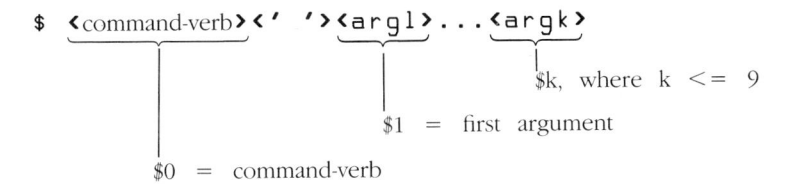

$ <command-verb><' '><arg1>...<argk>

- $0 = command-verb
- $1 = first argument
- $k, where k <= 9

You can print all the arguments in a command line by using **$***. The number of arguments in a command line is stored in **$#**. Here is an example:

```
$ cat >window                   # set up procedure
echo '$# = ' $# ' with '        # print number
echo 'command-verb = ' $0       # prints name
echo 'arguments = ' $*          # prints arguments
ctrl-d
$
```

Then this window procedure can be run with various arguments as follows:

```
$ sh window                     # run without arguments
$# = 0 with
command-verb = window
arguments =
$
```

Now we can execute window with arguments as follows:

```
$ sh window tumty tumty tumtoes!    # run with arguments
$# = 3 with
command-verb = window
arguments = tumty tumty tumtoes!
$
```

You can give these variables default values by using the set command and command substitution as follows:

```
$ set `date`         # for default values of $*, etc.
$ echo $*
Wed Jan 22 08:31 CST 1986
$ echo $0
-sh                            sh was the command verb used
```

SPECIAL VARIABLES   **101**

```
$ echo $1
Wed
$
```

You can make a mammoth assignment to $* with

```
$ set `ls`          # assign current dir names to $*
$ echo $*
Bergson C act0 act1 ...
$
```

Even though there are probably more than nine arguments assigned to $* by set 'ls', these can only be inspected individually with

```
$1, $2, $3, $4, ... ,$9
```

If you type $10, for example, you will get Bergsonl (or the argument assigned to $1 with a 1 tacked on). To examine the 10th or higher argument, the shift command can be used in the following way:

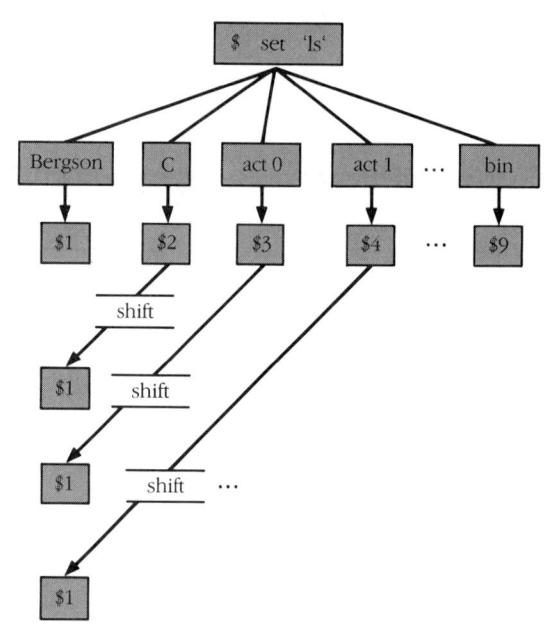

```
$ echo $1; shift; echo $1; shift; echo $1    # 2 shifts
Bergson
C
```

FIGURE 3.5
Shifting Values to $1

```
act0
$
```

In other words, you can use the shift command to shift arguments to the left by one. This idea is illustrated graphically in Figure 3.5.

Two other special variables you should know about are

1. `"$*"` for "$1 $2 ... "
2. `"$@"` for "$1" "$2" ...

There is a subtle difference between these two special variables. A "**$***" represents a single word made up of all the arguments (all the names in your directory taken as one name in the above example). By contrast, "**$@**" represents not one word but all the individual arguments for the current shell. This will become clearer in the next chapter. A summary of the details of these special command-line variables is given in the following table.

Special Command Variables

SPECIAL VARIABLE	VALUE
$#	number of arguments to shell
$0	command-verb
$1	first argument (if there is one)
$2 ... $9	next eight arguments (if there are any)
$*	all arguments (uninterpreted)
"$*"	all arguments interpreted as one word
"$@"	all arguments but not joined together

The special command variable "$@" is both subtle and very useful. To see how this variable can be used, suppose we want to print a copy of the first line of every file in your current directory. We can use "$@" in combination with 'ls -t' to pick out the names of these files inside a **for** loop. To see how this can be done try the following experiment.

☐ EXPERIMENT WITH "$@" VARIABLE

Use an editor to install the lines of the following file (call it lexicon, for example). You can also use your cat command to append to a new file called lexicon in the following way:

```
$ cat >lexicon
# procedure to print first line of selected files
```

```
for name in "$@"
  do
    echo $name ' \c'              # print filename
    head -1 $name                 # print first line
  done
$
```

Now execute your lexicon file in the following way:

```
$ sh lexicon `ls`
```

(*sample* output from lexicon)

```
bin u.blake  To see a world in a Grain of Sand
bun # Hewett-Gosling bundling method
bunch # bunch single letters together
caldm # prints all mos from current mo to end of yr
catch # print lines with more than 1 field
cksp # check spelling
         .
         .
         .
```

In other words, the output from the **ls** command becomes the command line arguments by typing

```
$ sh lexicon `ls`
```

Then each filename in this command line is selected by the following command line:

```
for name in "$@"
```

The **for** command will continue to execute as long as there is an argument left to assign to the name variable. In other words, this sets up an iteration. Inside this **for** loop, it is just a matter of printing each $name value and selecting the first line of the named file by using

```
echo $name ' \c'
head -1 $name
```

More examples of how the for command can be used are given in Chapter 4. Notice that if you get into the habit of inserting an explanatory comment (using a # sign) at the beginning of each new file you set up, then you can use a procedure modelled after lexicon to print an annotated index for all the files in each of your directories. You should find this helpful later when you have many files. The following sections illustrate the use of some of these variables.

3.3.2 Using Special Variables to Select Actions

A common problem in shell programming is selecting various parts of the standard output for inspection and for use in some application. We can write a command procedure that uses the special variables to select the fields we want to cut from a standard output. Try this procedure.

■ PROCEDURE 1A

```
$ cat >chop
# use special variables to select parts of standard output

first=$1; second=$2                     # capture arguments
time=`date | cut -c$first-$second`      # chop output from date
echo $first $second $time
ctrl-d
$
```

This chop procedure will allow you to select different parts of the output from date. Try

```
$ sh chop 1 3
1 3 Wed
$ sh chop 5 7
5 7 Jan
$ sh chop 1 10
1 10 Wed Jan 22
$ sh chop 12 19
12 19 08:31:32
```

You can refine this procedure by making it possible to enter the command to use in the command substitution (who instead of date, for example).

3.3.3 Refinement: Adding Arguments

To make the chop procedure in Section 3.3.1 more useful (or at least more interesting), we can use $3 in place of date. This is done in Procedure 1b.

■ PROCEDURE 1B

```
$ cat chop
# use special variables to select parts of output to chop

first=$1; second=$2
part=`$3 | cut -c$first-$second`          #chop
```

```
echo $first $second $3 $part
$
```

Now we can enter any command we wish and start chopping. Try

```
$ sh chop 1 20 who
1 20 bbaggins tty02
$ sh chop 15 17 who
15 17 02
```

In the last run of chop, we isolated the terminal number being used by bbaggins. This procedure can be further refined (to almost nothing).

3.3.4 Refinement: Throwing Out the Deadwood

In Procedure 1b in Section 3.3.3 we really do not need to use the variables first, second, *and* part. In fact, the actions in this procedure can be compressed into one line in the following way:

■ PROCEDURE 1C

```
$ cat chop
# use special variables to choose parts of output to chop

echo 'chopped part: ' `$3 | cut -c$2- $2`
$
```

Now try executing this slimmed-down procedure. We leave it until the exercises to experiment further with this procedure. Let's look at some other uses of the set command.

3.4 THE set COMMAND AND STANDARD SHELL VARIABLES

The set command by itself will return all the settings for the standard shell variables:

```
$ set
HOME=/usr/you
IFS=

MAIL=/usr/spool/mail/you
PATH=:/usr/you:/bin:/usr/bin:/usr/you/bin
PS1=$
PS2=>
TERM=vt100
```

The definitions of HOME, MAIL, PATH, and TERM will come from your .profile, if you have one. You can use the echo command to inspect these variables individually. You can also make direct changes to these variables. For example, you can change your PATH in the following way:

```
$ mkdir lib                    # make new directory
$ PATH=PATH:$HOME/lib          # define new path
$ echo $PATH
:/usr/you:/bin:/usr/bin:usr/you/bin:/usr/you/lib
```

Now the shell will look for commands in your lib directory if it does not find them in the other directories specified by the old PATH. This new PATH value will not become permanent unless you install it in your .profile, which is easy to do:

```
$ cat >>.profile               #append to .profile
PATH=$PATH:/$HOME/lib
ctrl-d
$
```

Now use the dot command to execute the new profile to "tell" the shell about the new .profile:

```
$ . .profile                   # execute .profile
```

In changing your .profile, it is possible to destroy this file or accidentally wipe out your PATH so that the shell can no longer find commands you type.

3.4.1 What to Do in Case You Ruin Your .profile

In Section 3.4 an addition to PATH was appended to the .profile. Disaster will strike if you overwrite instead of append to this file in the following way:

```
$ cat >.profile                # mistakenly overwrite file
PATH=$PATH:/$HOME/lib
ctrl-d
$
```

Now you have lost most of your original PATH *and* you have lost your definition of HOME. So you will definitely have a problem giving the shell further commands (a cat or ls, for example). You can remedy this problem by giving a simple redefinition of PATH as follows:

```
$ PATH=:/bin:/usr/bin          # keep it simple
```

Then you can rebuild your .profile with ed or vi or with cat. If all else fails, log off and log on again. This will give PATH its default value. Unfortunately, if you still have your ruined .profile in your home directory, you will have further problems. It is best to fix your .profile before you log off.

Here is good strategy to use to help you in case you lose your .profile:

Damage control measure:
Save a hard copy of your present .profile *and* make a new copy of your profile every time you modify this file.

You will find that your .profile is one of the most important files in your Unix environment. You will probably also find great ways to make it better and more suitable for your own needs. So save a hard copy of this file in case you accidentally wipe out your .profile.

There are other ways you can customize your environment. For example, the PS1 and PS2 variables are shell variables used to define your terminal prompts. There is also an IFS shell variable used to define the characters which delimit the parts of a command line.

3.4.2 The Internal Field Separator (IFS) Characters

The IFS variable displayed by set in Section 3.4 has the values ' ' (space) and newline, which are used by the shell as argument separators. You add a tab to this list of separators by redefining IFS:

```
$ IFS='<space><tab>
<newline>'
$
```

Single quotes are put around the field separator characters to protect them from misinterpretation.

3.4.3 The PS1 (primary) and PS2 (secondary) Prompts

If you enter a line that the shell considers incomplete, the shell will print the PS2 character (a > by default). Here is an example:

```
$ (cd /usr/bin; file * |
>grep executable |
>tee -a $HOME/verbs |
>wc -1 |
>tee -a $HOME/verbs)
     5
$
```

In this example, the shell keeps issuing the secondary prompt (>) until you finish. This set of commands finds all the files in /usr/bin that are executable (these will be labelled "not open for reading" for a non-system administrator). Notice how the commands found go into your $HOME/verbs as well as the count found by wc. You can personalize your environment by changing the prompts used:

```
$ PS1='yes?'                  # change primary prompt
yes?
yes?
yes? PS2='huh?'
yes? (cd /usr/bin; file * |
huh? grep commands)
style:   commands text
uupick:  commands text
xref:    commands text
yes?
```

To make permanent these changes to PS1 and PS2, put them into your .profile. If you run set now, you will see the changes made so far to your shell variables. The * by itself names a very useful shell variable.

3.4.4 The Value of *

An asterisk (*) by itself is used to hold the names of all the files in your current directory. To see this, first get a copy of your current directory:

```
$ ls | 5                # check your directory
act0        act1        act2        act 3       Bergson
bin         c           ........................
$
```

Now try using the * with the echo command as follows:

```
$ echo *                      # see your directory names
act0 act1 act2 act3 Bergson bin c ....
$
```

This is a very useful shell variable. You can do a global print of the files in your directory by using

```
$ cat * | pr            # global file print in pages
```

You can clean a directory selectively by typing

```
$ rm -i *               # global removal scan
act0 ?  n
```

```
act1 ?  n
act2 ?  n
act3 ?  n
temp ?  y
     .
     .
     .
```

You can terminate execution of this command by hitting your DEL (delete) key. Later you will see how the * by itself can be used in shell control structures (discussed in Chapter 4).

To make the variables defined in your .profile or in any command procedure you build available to subsequent shells, you can use the export command.

3.4.5 Exporting Variables to Child Processes

Without the line

```
export HOME PATH PS1 PS2 IFS
```

the values given to these variables for your login shell when it runs your .profile (each time you log in) will not be known to any new shell. Instead, any new shell which runs on behalf of your login shell will use the *default* values of these variables:

SPECIAL VARIABLE	DEFAULT VALUE(S)
HOME	/usr/you
PATH	:/bin:/usr/bin
PS1	$
PS2	>
IFS	<space><newline>

The export command marks variables (not just the special shell variables) for export from the login shell to any subsequent shells. When the export command is used inside a procedure to export procedure variables to other shells, the result is a call-by-value.

3.4.6 Calls-by-value

We can use the export command inside a procedure so that selected variables "known" to the current shell will be known to subsequent shells. In other words, one procedure can call another one *with its values*. Try the following procedure.

■ PROCEDURE 2A

```
$ cat chop                                    # new chop
# use special variable to select parts of output to chop
part=`$3 | cut -c$1-$2`
saveit                                        # activate saveit
echo $part
$
```

Procedure 2a relies on the use of the following saveit procedure:

■ PROCEDURE 3

```
$ cat saveit
echo $part | tee -a results
$
```

Procedure 2a (the new chop) activates saveit without exporting any variables. The shell which runs saveit (Procedure 2a) will not "know" the values of variables used by chop. Here is a sample run:

```
$ chop 1 7 date
Wed Jan
$
```

Saveit did not get the value of part when it was activated by Procedure 2a. Procedure 3 (saveit) just printed a newline. We can change this by using the export command inside Procedure 2a:

■ PROCEDURE 2B

```
$ cat chop
# use special variable to pick parts of output to chop
part=`$3 | cut -c$1-$2`
export part
echo $part
$
```

Now if we run chop, we get the following results:

```
$ chop 1 7 date
Wed Jan                    from saveit
Wed Jan                    from Procedure 2b
$ cat results
Wed Jan                    from call by value
$
```

You can only export forwards (from parent to child shell). An offspring shell can let the login shell know values by saving them in a temp file, which can be inspected by a procedure run by the login shell. Experiments with this idea are left for exercises. Notice that you can also export any of the special shell variables to subsequent shells. To see this, try experimenting with exporting $1, $2, and $3 from chop to saveit.

The set command has another important use: debugging.

3.4.7 Using the set Diagnostic Modes in Debugging

You can use the set command to track what processes do when they are running using the set diagnostic modes. There are two of these modes:

-x print commands and their arguments as they are executed
-v print shell input lines as they are read

You can tell which diagnostic options are supplied to the current shell by typing

```
$ echo $-        # print current diagnostic flags
s
```

An **s** by itself means that the diagnostic modes are turned off. You can turn these diagnostic modes on in the following ways:

```
$ set -v         # print shell input lines
$ echo $-        # print current modes
echo $-            result of -v mode
vs
$
```

Notice that now each line read by the current shell will be echo-printed. You can force the shell to print commands and their arguments with

```
$ set -x         # print commands, arguments
set -x             from set -v
$ echo $-        # check diagnostic modes
echo $-            from set -v
+ echo svx         from set -x
xvs                from echo $-
$
```

To turn either of these diagnostic modes off, type

```
$ set +xv         # turns both modes off
set +xv             from v
+ set +xv           from x
$ echo $-         # check settings
s                   x and v modes are turned off
$
```

It helps to experiment with these commands inside command procedures to see what happens to your settings in subsequent shells forked on behalf of a shell with x and v set. This will be dealt with in exercises.

You can customize your environment further by using the trap command in your .profile.

3.5 CUSTOMIZING YOUR ENVIRONMENT WITH THE trap COMMAND

The trap command is used to catch interrupts, which occur for various reasons. The trap command responds to signals like those in the following table:

Shell Signals

SIGNAL NUMBER	CAUSE OF SIGNAL (AND CONSEQUENT INTERRUPT)
0	exit from shell (current shell stops running)
1	hangup (your phone connection)
2	interrupt (with your DEL key)
3	quit
9	kill (cannot be caught or ignored)
15	generated by kill(1), terminate process

The trap command has the following sequence:

`trap command-sequence ‹signals to trap on›`

You can use the trap command to cause one or more commands to be run when you log out (type control-d, which signals a zero). The C shell in 4.2/4.3BSD Unix runs a .logout file each time you log out. (For an explanation of the C shell .logout file, turn to Section 8.2.4.) You can use the trap command to make the sh shell do the same thing. Here is a sample .logout file:

```
$ cat >.log out                              # build .logout
# have sh run this file when you logout
echo `Total blocks used so far = ' `du -s`
```

```
ctrl-d
$
```

Make your .logout executable:

```
$ chmod +x .logout
```

Now set up the following trap command in your .profile:

Enhanced .profile

```
$ cat >>.profile
trap $HOME/.logout 0
ctrl-d
$
```

Now run your .profile using the dot command to see the results:

```
$ . .profile
```

If you log out now, the trap command in your .profile will catch signal 0 when you type **ctrl-d:**

```
$ ctrl-d
Total blocks used so far = 351

login:
```

You can tell the kernel to ignore interrupts and continue running a command by using a trap. Here is an example:

☐ EXPERIMENT 7

```
$ cat >check
# see who's logged on
sleep 3600; who >>users
ctrl-d
$ trap ' ' 1 9; $HOME/check
```

The empty ' ' is a *null command sequence* which tells the shell to ignore interrupts. Unfortunately, if you run check with this trap, you will lose control of your login shell—you will lose your $ prompt! Theoretically, check will run forever, since you have insulated it from interrupts (except for the DEL key). It may be desirable to have some commands run indefinitely. You can tell the kernel to create background processes for such commands, so that you can retain control of your current shell.

3.6 EXECUTING A COMMAND IN THE BACKGROUND

You can tell the kernel to execute a command while you are using your login shell to do something else. Then the kernel will synchronize two or more processes running concurrently. This is called *background processing*. An ampersand (**&**) is used to specify a background process. Here is an example:

```
$ welcome &                      # run welcome in background
763
$ Hello, world! with PID for current process = 763
$
```

Now try the following experiment which will initiate a background process that searches your /usr/bin for files that are commands texts *and* that appends both the output from grep and from wc to a $HOME/verbs file.

☐ EXPERIMENT 8

```
$ (cd /usr/bin; file * |
> grep commands |
> tee -a $HOME/verbs |
> wc -l >>$HOME/verbs) &
473
$                        # you get $ back while process runs
```

If you type ps, you will see the shell running the background process (with PID = 473). You can continue working with your login shell *while* the background process is running. You can exploit this idea in terms of the trapping for the check command in Section 3.5 as follows:

```
$ cat >>.profile
(trap ' ' 1 9; $HOME/check) $
ctrl-d
$ . .profile              # start background process
```

Now check will run in the background even if you hang up or use the kill command. If you want to make a process oblivious to hangups, you can also use the nohup command as in

```
$ (nohup $HOME/check) &    # ignores signal = 1
569
$
```

Now once every hour during the day the $HOME/users file will have the list of logged on users appended to it regardless of whether or not you are logged on. You can see what processes are running now, if you type

```
$ ps
  PID TTY TIME COMMAND
  532  02  0:06 sh         login shell
  569  02  0:01 sh         background process
  576  02  0:00 sleep      background process
  577  02  0:04 ps         foreground process
```

This is a weaker version of the trap command we just used. It is not immune to signal = 9. We can kill $HOME/check with

```
$ kill -9 569      kills background sh
```

If you run the ps command, you will probably find that the sleep command is still running. Experimenting with trap and nohup will help reveal their secrets. Once you start $HOME/check, your users file will start filling up. So you will either have to kill check or clean your users file to prevent your disk from getting swamped.

The **$!** is another useful shell variable.

$! is the shell variable used to hold the PID of the last process run in the background.

To inspect $! type

```
$ echo $!         # Inspect background PID
569               sample PID
$
```

The shell also maintains an exit status variable.

3.7 THE $? EXIT STATUS VARIABLE

Each command returns an exit status upon completion. An *exit status* is a value returned to the shell which indicates what happened. Here is a selection of these values:

Exit Status Values

EXIT STATUS	MEANING
0	normal exit (command ran successfully)
false	(some non-zero value) for abnormal exit
k	forced exit status value produced by the exit command

To see this, try the following experiment.

☐ EXPERIMENT 9A

```
$ cpp                              # mistaken command
cpp: not found                     error message from sh
$ echo $?                          # print exit status
1                                  status
$ echo 'I love mountain air.'
I love mountain air.
$ echo $?
0                                  success status signal
$
```

You can use the exit command to force your own status signals to be returned to the shell. Try the following variation of Experiment 9a.

☐ EXPERIMENT 9B

```
$ cat >response
echo 'start processing . . . . . . . '
exit 99                            # exit with 99
echo 'lost in space . . . . . . . . '
ctrl-d
$ sh response                      # execute command
start processing . . . . . . . . .
$ echo $?                          # exit status = ?
99
$
```

Notice that we use sh to execute the response procedure. Also notice that the output from

```
echo 'lost in space . . . . . . . . . . . . '
```

does not show up in the output from response. The exit command actually aborts execution of the response procedure. The shell never reaches the third line of this procedure. Can you guess what will happen when the following experiment is run?

☐ EXPERIMENT 9C

```
$ . response      # now what?
```

The exit command (this is exit [2]) is described in Part 2 of the Unix Programmer's Manual.

> The **exit** command terminates a process.

There are still other ways to execute a command.

3.8 BATCH PROCESSING: DELAYED EXECUTION OF A COMMAND

The **at** command makes it possible for you to specify the time (and optional date) when a command is run. It has the following syntax:

```
at time <date> file
```

This command squirrels away a copy of the file specified in the at command line and later (at the specified time) is used as input to sh. In effect, the at command makes batch processing possible.

> A *batch process* accumulates commands to be run at specified times (this is done by at, which sets up a sequence of jobs to be run by the **/usr/lib/atrun** program).

For example, try

```
$ at 5pm <welcome              # execute welcome @ 5pm
job 506998600.a at Fri Jan 24 17:00:00 1986
```

In this example, the input to at is the welcome file. The same thing can be accomplished less awkwardly (but less compactly) in the following way:

```
$ at 5:01pm
who | grep susu
ctrl-d
job 507041400.a at Fri Jan 24 17:01:00 1986
$
```

Notice in both cases that a 24-hour clock is used to store the times that were entered. You can employ 24-hour (military) time when you use at:

```
$ at 18:35
cat * | pr | lp
ctrl-d
job 507042400.a at Fri Jan 24 18:35:00
$
```

If you do not specify a date, the current date will be used to schedule your job. You can implement the **at** command with a different date in the following way:

```
$ at 1am Jan 25
cat * | pr | lp
ctrl-d
job 589001223.a at Sat Jan 25 01:00:00
$
```

This allows you to run such things as a massive print job at a less critical time (at 1 A.M., for example). You can tell which batch jobs have been logged by using the **-1** option:

```
$ at -1
507042400.a    Fri Jan 24 18:35:00    1986
589001223.a    Sat Jan 25 01:00:00    1986
     .
     .
     .
```

You can use the **-r** to remove a batch job:

```
$ at -r 507042400.a
```

This removes the batch job numbered 507042400. If you schedule a batch job too close to the current time, it may not run. This can be explained in terms of what is known as the granularity of the at command. The *granularity of at* refers to how often the **/usr/lib/atrun** command is run.
    You can also specify a +-increment in minutes, days, weeks, months, or years. Here is an example:

```
$ at 7am mon +10 day
mail susu <message
ctrl-d
$
```

This batch job mails susu a letter (in the message file) ten days from next Monday. Delayed execution is also possible.

3.9 PUTTING A COMMAND TO SLEEP: SUSPENDED EXECUTION

The sleep command can be employed to delay execution of a command for a number of seconds. To set up an egg timer, type in the following procedure:

■ PROCEDURE 4A

```
$ cat >egg
sleep $1; echo '<control-g><control-g><control-g>'
ctrl-d
$
```

Now you can delay the execution of the echo command (ringing the egg-timer bell) in the following way:

```
$ sh egg 10
ring ring ring      after 10 seconds
$
```

You will find that there is an upper limit on the number of seconds you can specify to delay execution of a command. In Seventh edition Unix, the upper limit is 65,536 seconds. The same is true for System V Release 2.0. You do not want to run the sleep command in the foreground.

You will put your current shell to "sleep" if you run the sleep command in the foreground. That is, you will not get the $-prompt back until the sleep command has run its course.

So it is a good idea to combine delayed execution with background execution of a command. We can run the egg-timer command procedure in the following way:

```
$ (sh egg 10) &      # run background process
766
$
```

In this way you get the shell prompt back immediately, which means you are free to do something else until your egg timer wakes up (rings). The egg-timer procedure can be refined so that it prints a message specified by a command line argument.

3.9.1 Refinement: Suspended Printing of a Message

The egg-timer command procedure in Section 3.9 can be made more useful and more general by adding a provision for a second argument in the command line for egg:

■ PROCEDURE 4B (REFINEMENT)

```
$ cp egg egg2                        # save old procedure
$ cat >egg
# delay printing of a message
```

```
sleep $1; echo "$2"
ctrl-d
$
```

Now this procedure is almost an automated short-term message service. Try

```
$ (sh egg 300 "coffee time!") &
562
$
```

In five minutes this new timer procedure will print

```
$ coffee time!
```

Notice how the double quotes are used in Procedure 4b to allow for a second argument made up of more than one word. Without the the double quotes, Procedure 4b would print

```
$ coffee
```

Can you see why? Are the double quotes necessary in both the command line *and* around $2 in Procedure 4b? The command line used to run the egg procedure is not the easiest to type. We can refine the egg procedure further to simplify this command line.

3.9.2 Refinement: Embedded Background Processing

We make it easier to run the egg procedure in Section 3.9.1 by embedding the &- command inside the next procedure.

■ PROCEDURE 4C

```
$ cp egg egg3                  # save a copy of old egg
$ cat > egg
# print reminder after a specified time
(sleep $1; echo "$2") &
ctrl-d
$
```

Now we have automated the background processing of the egg procedure. It will always run in the background. Here is a sample run:

```
$ sh egg 300 "coffee time!"
$
```

This is a lot simpler to type. Here is a challenge question about this sample run:

CHALLENGE:
Why is the PID for background processing not printed for the egg procedure when it is executed?

We can simplify this command line further by making Procedure 4c executable:

```
$ chmod +x egg      # make egg executable
```

Now we can execute Procedure 4c in the following way:

```
$ egg 300 "coffee time!"
$
```

When the egg command does wake up, you may not get the $-prompt back after the message is printed. Just type a newline (press your <**enter**> or <**return**> key) to get the $-prompt back.

3.10 SUMMARY

A *process* is an environment in which a program executes. The *environment* for a program in execution consists of an address space (region of memory) and actions by the processor within that address space. The execution of every command leads to the creation of a new process. The new process will either be an execution environment for a named executable binary program or the running of a new shell on behalf of the current shell for a named command procedure. A *command procedure* is a file of commands. A *command* either identifies an executable binary program or a command procedure. Most of the built-in Unix shell commands identify executable binary programs. One of the more intriguing pastimes of a Unix programmer is tracking the processes created when commands are executed.

There are a variety of ways to execute a command. Exploring the various methods used to execute commands has been the chief task of this chapter. A summary of these methods is given in the following table.

Ways to Execute a Command

METHOD	EXAMPLE
1. $ <command>	$ date
2. $ chmod +x <procedure> $ <procedure name>	$ chmod +x welcome # sect. 3.2.2 $ welcome
3. multiple commands	$ cd /usr/bin; grep a*
4. (multiple commands)	$ (cd /usr/bin; grep a*)
5. sh <command>	$ sh welcome
6. . <command>	$. welcome
7. exec <welcome>	$ exec welcome

Ways to Execute a Command (continued)

METHOD	EXAMPLE
8. $<variable>	$ do=welcome; $do
9. `<command>`	$ echo "who's logged on:" `who`
10. <command> **&**	$ welcome &
11. at <time> <date> command	$ at 2:30am Jan 29
	> cat * | pr | lp
	ctrl-d
	job 507041400.a at ...
	$
12. sleep <seconds> command	$ sleep 60; who

The shell maintains a powerful set of special variables which can be separated into the following groups:
1. command-line variables ($#, $*, $0 . . . $9, "$*", "$@")
2. names variable (*)
3. process variables ($$, $!, $?)
4. exit status variable ($-)

These special variables are extremely useful in developing general-purpose command procedures. In addition to these special-purpose variables, the shell also maintains various environment variables. You see these environment variables by typing

```
$ set
```

You can give your shell environment variables new settings by incorporating them into your profile, which is run every time you log in. One of the advantages of Unix is the latitude users have in tailoring their working environment to individual needs and tastes.

3.11 REVIEW OF COMMANDS, SYMBOLS, AND KEYWORDS

The following section reviews the commands, symbols, and keywords introduced in this chapter.

3.11.1 Commands

COMMAND	ACTION
&	background processing command
.	execute command as part of current process
at	delayed execution of a command
cat *	print files in current directory

3.11.1 Commands (continued)

COMMAND	ACTION
export	exports variables to subsequent shells
rm -i *	interactive removal of files
set '<command>'	sets special argument-line variables
set <return>	displays environment variables being used
set -xv	sets diagnostic modes
sleep	suspended execution
trap	detects signals & executes command sequence
wc -w	prints word count in a file

3.11.2 Symbols

SYMBOL	INTERPRETATION
(...;...)	fork new shell to run multiple commands
'...'	command substitution with left, single quotes
$	default, primary sh prompt
$$	PID of current process which is running
$#	number of command-line arguments
$*	shell arguments
$0	command-verb
$1,...,$9	command-line arguments
"$*"	command-line arguments as one word
"$@"	separate command-line arguments
$-	shell diagnostic modes
$!	PID of last background process
$?	exit status
$<variable>	if variable = command, executes command
>	default, secondary sh prompt
' '	null command sequence (see Section 3.5)
" "	null command sequence
"...'...'..."	removes special meaning of single quote
*	holds names of files in current directory
IFS	Internal Field Separator
PS1	primary shell prompt
PS2	secondary shell prompt
sh	name of Unix shell (also a command)

3.11.3 Keywords

KEYWORD(S)	EXPLANATION
background processing	processing command concurrent with shell
batch process	sequence of commands collected in a group to be run at specified times
call-by-value	export variables to subsequent shells
child shell	shell spawned by the kernel on behalf of the shell currently running
command procedure	file of commands

3.11.3 Keywords (continued)

KEYWORD(S)	EXPLANATION
command substitution	output from command (inside ` `) is made part of command line
command-verb	first word in command line (action part command line)
current process	execution environment for program which is currently running
delayed execution	batch processing (with at)
diagnostic modes	set -xv (see Section 3.4.7)
-v	prints commands, arguments as they are executed
-x	prints shell input lines as they are read
exit status	status of process which has completed
exporting variables	give subsequent shells copies of variables defined in current shell
fork	spawn process (done by kernel on behalf of current process)
granularity of at	how often /usr/lib/atrun is executed
internal field separator	characters used to separate fields (see Section 3.4.2)
null command sequence	' ' or " " (used with trap command)
PID	Process IDentity number
process	environment in which a program executes
program	instructions plus data
special shell variables	record-keeping by shell for processes and command lines (see Section 3.3–3.4)

3.12 EXERCISES

1. Add to your .profile so that '$ ' is printed instead of a '$' (no space after $) as the shell prompt.

2. Modify your .profile so that while you are logged on, a new snoopy procedure is executed which
   a. executes every 15 minutes
   b. prints name, location (terminal), time, and date for a person named (you pick person's name), if that person is logged on or logs on while you are processing
   Note: snoopy should run in the background.

3. Set up a .login file while is run by the shell when you log off so that
   a. your .profile "tells" the login shell about .logout
   b. your .logout file kills the snoopy process, which started running when you logged in
   Hint: use cut, grep, and ps to do this.

4. (Refinement) Improve the .logout file in Exercise 3 by using UID (unique id variable) which
   a. is put into your .profile
   b. is assigned $! immediately *after* the snoopy procedure in Exercise 2 is activated by the login shell
   c. is used by grep (instead of the most recent value of $!) to kill the snoopy process.
   Give a sample run.

5. (Alternative) Show how to kill the snoopy process from Exercise 2 before you log out. Give a sample run.
   Hint: use the UID from Exercise 4.
6. (Alternatives) Show how to restart the snoopy process after it has been killed in Exercise 5. Show at least five different ways to do this. Give sample runs.
7. (Spiral effect) Set up ten different command procedures having the structure of acts 0 through 3 in Section 3.1. That is, have act0 activate act1, which activates act2, and so on. Unlike acts 1 and 2 in Section 3.1, your acts 1 through 9 should have a final ps command. Then
   a. give a sample run
   b. mimic Figure 3.1 and trace the births, deaths, and revivals of processes resulting from the execution of act0
8. (Refinement) Make acts 1 through 9 of Exercise 7 run in the background using an embedded &-command in these procedures. Explain what happens when act0 is executed.
9. (Refinement) The nice command can be used to lower the priority of a process (other processes will run before ones which are activated with the nice command). Its syntax is

```
nice [-number (1 to 10)] command [arguments]
```

Here is an example:

```
$ nice -5 snoopy &        # run snoopy in background
```

(Higher numbers like -8 mean lower priority; the default is -10.) Modify acts 1 through 9 of Exercise 8 so that they are run with a lower priority. Give a listing of the new versions of these procedures and use ps to trace what happens when act0 is executed. Give a sample run which is annotated to explain what has happened.

10. (Refinement) Modify your .profile using the nice command to run snoopy (from Exercise 2) in the background at the lowest priority. Give a listing of the new .profile.
11. Put a copy of your .profile in a file called backup. Then destroy your .profile by typing

```
$ cat >.profile
ctrl-d
$
```

Now give the steps you must employ to
a. recover your PATH without retyping your complete .profile (show at least two ways to do this)
b. recover your complete .profile
c. Activate your new .profile without logging off
Note: devise one or more experiments to demonstrate the success of your recovery methods.

12. The following command procedure has an infinite loop, which means it will run indefinitely if it is executed:

```
$ cat >Halley
while :
  do
```

```
        sleep 5          # sleep for 5 seconds
     done
  ctrl-d
  $
```

The Halley command procedure says "while true do sleep 5" (the colon [:] is the shell symbol for true). Do the following with Halley:
a. execute Halley in the background
b. print $!
c. kill Halley
d. run ps to verify success of (c)

13. Use nohup to execute Halley (from Exercise 12) in the background. Then repeat steps b. through d. of Exercise 12.
14. (Refinement) Embed the background (&) command inside the Halley procedure in Exercise 12. (Do this by enclosing the while loop—from **while** to **done**—inside parentheses followed by the & command.) Repeat steps b. through d. of Exercise 12.
15. Use nohup to execute the refined Halley procedure from Exercise 14 and repeat steps b. through d. of Exercise 12.
16. Run Experiments 1a and 1b in Section 3.2.1 and comment on what you find.
17. Remove the parentheses from the command lines in Experiments 1a and 1b in Section 3.2.1 and comment on how execution of the new command lines differs from what you found in Exercise 16.
18. Run Experiment 2 in Section 3.2.1 without the parentheses used in that experiment. Comment on what you find when the new command line is run.
19. Run Experiment 3 in Section 3.2.2 and identify the PIDs which are printed.
20. Explain what happens when you type

```
  $ sh date
```

21. Explain what happens when you type

```
  $ . date
```

22. Run Experiment 4 in Section 3.2.4 and explain what you find.
23. Explain what happens when you type

```
  $ exec date
```

while your login shell is running.
24. Run Experiment 5 in Section 3.2.5 and explain what you find.
25. Explain what happens when you execute the following line:

```
  $ echo 'The date' `date` 'says it's winter.'
```

26. Show how to correct the problem in Exercise 25.
27. Run Experiment 6 in Section 3.2.6 for a list of users on your system. Explain how the experiment works.

28. (Refinement) Modify the team file used in Experiment 6 (in Section 3.2.6) so that the following command line can be used:

    ```
    $ mail `team` <welcome
    ```

29. Write a command procedure named sv (short for "see variables") which does the following things:
    a. prints only $1
    b. uses the shift command to give $1 new values
    c. repeats steps a. and b. five times
    Give sample runs using the following arguments:
    d. tumty tumty tum toes!
    e. Halley's comet was visible in 1986

30. (Refinement) Add to sv from exercise commands to print the remainder of the special command-line variables. Give sample runs using d. and e. from Exercise 29.

31. (Refinement) Embed the background command & in Procedure 1c in Section 3.3.4 and add to this procedure a line which causes the following message to be printed:

    ```
    chopping completed by process with PID = <PID
    printed here>
    ```

    Have this procedure print its own PID in the printed message. Give sample runs with
    a. chop 1 20 who
    b. chop 1 20 ls
    c. chop 1 10 chop
    d. chop 1 10 ps

32. Write a procedure called clean which does the following:
    a. uses $1 to select directory to change to
    b. changes to directory $1
    c. interactively removes files you select with y
    Give a sample run with
    d. ```
       mkdir exp; tee this1 this2 this3 this4 this5
       ctrl-d
       $ tee that1 that2 mariner5 mariner6
       ctrl-d
       $
       ```

    Remove the this and keep the that and mariner files.
    Hint: See Section 3.4.4.

33. Modify Procedure 3 in Section 3.4.6 so that
    a. it creates a variable next
    b. assigns to next characters 3 and 4 of part (from Procedure 2b in the same section)
    c. makes it possible for Procedure 2b to inspect and print a copy of next *after* Procedure 3 (saveit) has finished executing
    Give sample runs.

34. (Refinement) Export from Procedure 2b to Procedure 3 in Section 3.4.6 all of its arguments. Then modify Procedure 3 to print the exported values. Give sample runs.
       ```

35. (Refinement) Install set -xv in both Procedures 2b and 3 from Exercise 34. Give sample runs of Procedure 2b and explain the results (mimic the technique used in Section 3.4.7).
36. Run Experiment 8 in Section 3.6 using the dot command and explain what happens.
37. Convert the command line in Experiment 8 (its parentheses, multiple commands, *and* &) into a procedure called mop (for "more procedures"). Then explain what happens when you
    a. run mop with
    b. run mop with exec
    c. run mop with sh
    d. run mop with **at 7:30pm**
    e. run mop with **sleep 10**
38. Use at to put act0 (from Exercise 2), blastoff (from Section 3.2.5), and mop (from Exercise 37) into the batch stream. Now show
    a. how to list processes which have been batched
    b. how to remove each of these batch processes
39. Write a zap procedure which
    a. displays list of batch processes (use the same ones from Exercise 38)
    b. uses $1 to remove a batch process
    c. prints new list of batch processes
    Give a sample run.
40. (Refinement) Modify zap from Exercise 39 so that it
    a. prompts for a value for UID
    b. reads a value for UID for a batch process
    c. removes the process with the entered UID
41. What is the answer to the challenge question in Section 3.9.2?
42. Besides the methods of executing a command listed in Section 3.10, give a list of various new ways to execute the egg command (Procedure 4c in Section 3.9.2).
    Hint: try combining the old ways to provide new ways to execute egg.

The next exercise refers to the following files:

```
$ cat x
echo 'xxxx . . . x \c'
$cat y
echo 'yyyy . . . y \c'
$cat z
echo 'zzzz . . . z \c'
```

43. What is output (printed on your screen) by the following command lines (assume that x, y, z are executable)?
    a. $ x | y
    b. $ x | y | z
    c. $ x | y | z &
    d. x & y & z
    e. (x;y)
    f. (x;y) & z
    g. (x;y) & (x;z)

3.13 REVIEW QUIZ

Indicate whether the following statements are true or false.

1. You will log yourself off if you execute your .profile with the dot command *while* your login shell is running.
2. Variables "known" to your login shell must be exported to be known to any subsequent shells.
3. If you export the variable x in your login shell, then x will be known to all subsequent shells.
4. Your .profile is run by your login shell every time a new shell is started running on behalf of the login shell.
5. Running the exec command while you are in your login shell will log you off.
6. You can make a process immune to hangups.
7. The /usr/lib/atrun runs files batched by at.
8. "$*" and "$@" both use shell arguments.
9. The * holds the names of all processes that have been run since you logged on.
10. The shell prompt $ cannot be changed.

3.14 FURTHER READING

Bourne, S. R. The Unix System. Reading, MA: Addison-Wesley, 1983. See 2.7.3 on process management.

Foxley, E. Unix for Super-Users. Worthingham, England: Addison-Wesley, 1985. See Chapter 6 on the shell, especially Sections 6.1–6.3.

IEEE Trial-Use Standard Portable Operating System for Computer Environments. New York: IEEE, 1986. See Section 2.3 on uses of the term "process."

Kernighan, B., and B. Pike. The Unix Programming Environment. Englewood Cliffs: Prentice, 1984. See Chapter 3 on the shell, especially Section 3.5 on the use of backward quotes.

Poole, P. C. and N. Poole. Using Unix by Example. Reading, MA: Addison-Wesley, 1986. See Section 5.3.3 on monitoring jobs.

Rochkind, M. J. Advanced Unix Programming. Englewood Cliffs: Prentice, 1985. See Sections 1.3 and 1.4 on processes and signals.

Silvester, P. P. The Unix System Guidebook: An Introductory Guide for Serious Users. New York: Springer-Verlag, 1984. See Chapter 4 on the command shell.

Walton, I. and C. Cotton. The Complete Angler or The Contemplative Man's Recreation. London: Henry G. Bohn, 1856.

4 Command Procedures

. . . As Mozart knew: many of his compositions that make one catch one's breath are misleadingly simple, they seem to be made just out of practically nothing!
—*Edsger W. Dijkstra, 1972.*

The shell is both a programming language and a command language and is often referred to as the command interpreter of the Unix system.
—*S. R. Bourne, 1983.*

4.0 AIMS

- Introduce shell control structures
- Distinguish between various forms of the **if** statement
- Show various forms of the **while** and **until** control structures
- Show how shell programming can be used to automate many tasks using command procedures
- Illustrate the use of the expr command to perform arithmetic operations on integers
- Show how to use the expr command to compare strings
- Review shell metacharacters
- Give an overview of shell pattern matching methods
- Examine various ways to evaluate shell variables
- Introduce recursive procedures
- Explore ways to make procedures robust

4.1 INTRODUCTION TO COMMAND PROCEDURES

The shell is both a command language *and* a programming language. For the most part we have used the shell as a command language in making requests of the Unix kernel. These requests are made with built-in commands like date or with user-defined commands like egg (from Section 3.9). A *command procedure* is a file of commands that can be made executable. Command procedures are also called *shell procedures* or *shell scripts*. In recent publications the favored term is *command procedure*. You can use chmod to make a command procedure executable. Once a command procedure is executable, it can be used just like the built-in commands. This is in fact what we did, for example, to the egg procedure in Section 3.9.2:

```
$ chmod +x egg
$ egg 3600 "dinner time!"
$
```

This illustrates the use of the shell as a command language. We are asking the shell to fish through command lines to find commands which lead to the creation of child processes on behalf of the current shell. Each new process provides an environment in which a program (identified by a command) executes.

The shell can also be used as a programming language. The sh shell has a variety of control structures similar to those found in C or Pascal (if, case, and while, for example). The syntax for these control structures is picky and different from the syntax used in Pascal or C. These control structures can be used to develop powerful command procedures. In addition, the shell provides for the use of string-valued variables as well as a rich set of relational operators which can be used to compare strings.

The shell does not provide for arithmetic. However, there is a built-in expr command, which can be used to handle arithmetic with integers. The expr command is normally used in command substitutions like the following one:

```
$ count=5000                      # initialize count
$ count= expr $count + 1000       # add 1000 to count
```

So, if count begins with a value of 5,000, this statement will assign 5,000 + 1,000 to count. The expr command has a set of integer operators, including a % operator (like the Pascal mod operator) and / (like the Pascal div operator). There is no provision for real-valued operands.

The sh shell supports recursive procedures. A procedure can call itself like the following one:

☐ EXPERIMENT 1 (DANGER AHEAD)

```
$ cat >call
call
ctrl-d
$ chmod +x call
$ call &
18527
$
```

This call procedure will call itself an indefinite number of times (not forever, for reasons we will explain later). If you fail to execute call in the background (with &), you will lose control of your keyboard. Eventually, the shell process running this recursive call command will die—even if you forget to kill it.

In this chapter we will use the shell as a programming language to create new commands. A practical result of this new use of the shell will be the creation of a collection of commands that can be put into your $HOME/bin. These $HOME/bin commands will make it possible to customize your working environment even further.

The beauty of programming the shell is the simplicity and the ease of using the results. Command procedures do not have to be compiled, which saves time. In many cases command procedures can take care of housekeeping tasks more simply than C programs that do the same thing. Shell programming also provides a testing ground for future programs written in C or some other language. Shell programming is powerful because of the incredible number of built-in commands which can be used to fashion new commands.

4.2 CONTROL STRUCTURES

A *control structure* specifies a departure from the normal sequential execution of an instruction. The control structures are supported by the sh shell, as shown in the following table:

Control Structures

TYPE	SYNTAX	EXAMPLE
1. selection		
1.1 if:	if <condition> then <commands> fi	if [$x = 0] then echo $x fi
1.2 if:	if <condition> then <commands> else <commands> fi	if [$x = 5] then echo $x else echo 'ohoh' fi

1.3 if:	if <condition>
	then <commands>
	  elif <condition>
	    then <commands>
	fi
		if [$x = 5000]
		then echo 'ohoh...'
		  elif [$x = 0]
		    then :
		fi

1.4 case	case word in
	  pattern) <commands>;;
	  .
	  .
	  .
	esac
		case $vowel in
		  a) echo 'yes...';;
		  *) echo 'ohoh...'
		esac

Control Structures (continued)

TYPE	SYNTAX	EXAMPLE
2. iteration		

2.1 for	for name in \<list\>
	  do
	    \<commands\>
	  done
		for i in a b c dog cat
		  do
		    echo 'i =' $i
		  done

2.2 while	while \<condition\>
	  do
	    \<commands\>
	  done
		while :
		  do
		    sleep 5
		  done

2.3 until	until \<condition\>
	  do
	    \<commands\>
	  done
		until false
		  do
		    sleep 5
		  done

3. exit	break	while :
		  do
		    sleep 5; exit
		  done

4. next	continue	while :
		  do
		    sleep 5; continue
		  done

In the following sections we look more closely at various ways to set up and use these control structures.

4.2.1 Selection Control with a Simple if Statement

A *statement* specifies an action for a machine to perform. There are three forms of the **if** statement. In its simplest form, an if statement specifies the following actions:

1. if-part: test whether a condition is true or false
2. then-part: perform action following the **then,** provided the if-part tests true. Otherwise, the then-part is ignored and the process continues on the next line of a procedure.

There is more than one way to test the condition specified in the if-part. This can be done by enclosing the condition to be tested inside square brackets as in the following examples:

```
if [ "$user" = susu ]           # test value of $user
then
    mail $user <message         # if $user is susu
```

```
fi
if [ "$#" -eq 0 ]                       # test value of $#
then
    echo 'usage: command [args]'
fi
```

Notice that in both cases an equality is tested. These two if statements have some subtle features. First, notice that the left square bracket [is followed by a space. Similarly, the right square bracket] is preceded by a space. These spaces are a necessary part of the syntax of an if-condition written with square brackets. Older versions of Unix require the use of the test command instead of the more concise square brackets shown in the above examples. Here is a rewrite of the above if-statements using the test command:

```
if (test "$user" = susu)                # test for equality
then
    mail $susu <message                 # then-part action
fi
if (test "$#" -eq 0)                    # test for equality
then
    echo 'usage: command [args]'
fi
```

The test command has many uses which we will explore later in this chapter. Unix System V and Xenix-5 support both ways of writing conditions (either with the test command or with square brackets [ ]) for if-statements. The Seventh edition of Unix requires the use of the test command. You will have to check which method is supported by your system.

Second, notice that the equal sign (=) is used to test equality of strings, whereas a **-eq** is used to test equality of integers. These are examples of *relational operators,* which are used to compare values. There are a variety of relational operators available; the following table lists and illustrates their use:

Relational Operators

NOTE: assume $user = "Goldberry"
         $x = "person"

OPERATOR	CONDITION	MEANING	VALUE
		For Strings	
		test for ...	
-z	[-z "$user"]	strings with 0 length	false
-n	[-n "$user"]	strings with non-0 length	true
=	above example	equality of strings	?
!=	[$x != tom]	inequality of strings	?

Relational Operators (continued)

OPERATOR	CONDITION	MEANING	VALUE
		For integers	
		test for ...	
-eq	above example	equality of integers	?
-ne	[5 -ne 2]	inequality of integers	true
-lt	[5 -lt 4]	less than	false
-gt	[1 -gt 0]	greater than	true
-le	[1 -le 0]	less than or equal	false
-ge	[1 -ge 0]	greater than or equal	true
		For files	
		test for ...	
-d	[-d ../]	directory file	true
-f	[-f egg]	ordinary file	true
-s	[-s .]	file with non-zero length	true

For safety's sake, it is usually a good idea to use double quotes to enclose a variable name which is part of a condition, even if the variable represents an integer. Otherwise, if the parts of a variable are separated by spaces, they will be misinterpreted by the shell. The following experiment illustrates this idea:

☐ EXPERIMENT 2A

```
$ letters=a b
b: not found
$
```

In Experiment 2a we don't even get started because we did not enclose the parts of the argument inside quotes. This is remedied in the next form of this experiment:

☐ EXPERIMENT 2B

```
$ letters="a b"                        # now $letters = "a b"
$ if [ $letters = "a b" ]
> then
>    echo $letters 'equals 2 letters separated by a space.'
> fi
test: unknown operator b
$
```

Since we did not enclose $letters inside quotes in Experiment 2b, the 'b' in "a b" is misinterpreted by the shell as an unknown operator. We can remedy this problem with the quotes used in the next version of this experiment:

☐ EXPERIMENT 2C

```
$ if [ "$letters" = "a b" ]
> then
>     echo $letters 'equals 2 letters separated by a space.'
> fi
a b equals 2 letters separated by a space.
$
```

For the convenience of those who must use the test command to set up if-statements, Experiment 2c can be rewritten as follows:

☐ EXPERIMENT 2D

```
$ if (test "$letters" = "a b")
> then
>     echo $letters 'equals 2 letters separated by a space.'
> fi
a b equals 2 letters separated by a space.
$
```

In addition to the relational operators, the shell also supports the Boolean operators shown in the following table:

Boolean Operators

OPERATOR	SAMPLE	MEANING	VALUE
-a	[5 -gt 0 -a 5 -lt 6]	conjunction (and)	true
-o	[5 -gt 6 -o 5 -lt 2]	disjunction (or)	false
!	[! -d $HOME/x]	negtion (not)	?

A Boolean operator is evaluated in terms of a table like the following one:

Truth Tables

NOTE: <expr> = <expression>

	OR-OPERATOR				AND-OPERATOR		
CONDITION		VALUE	CONDITION		VALUE	CONDITION	VALUE
<expr> -o <expr>			<expr> -a <expr>			! <expr>	
true	true	true	true	true	true	true	false
false	true	true	false	true	true	false	true
true	false	true	true	false	false		
false	false	false	false	false	false		

CONTROL STRUCTURES   **137**

In other words, the only time

<expression> -a <expression>

tests true is when both "anded" expressions are true. By contrast, the only time

<expression> -o <expression>

tests false is when both "or'd" expressions are false. For example, try the following experiment:

☐ EXPERIMENT 3

```
$ if [ `ls | wc -l` -gt 50 -a . -eq "$HOME" ]
> then
>    echo $HOME 'needs cleaning.'
> fi
      .
      .
      .
$
```

Experiment 3 demonstrates some of the remarkable versatility of the shell. This statement tells the shell to do the following things:

1. Use 'ls | wc -l' (command substitution) to embed the count of the files in the current directory into this command line;
2. test if 'ls | wc -l' is greater than 50 *and*
3. test if the current directory is your login directory, then
4. print the 'needs cleaning' message, if the expressions on *both* sides of the **-a** (and) are true and then print the **$** prompt, otherwise
5. ignore the then-part and print a **$.**

You can turn Experiment 3 into the beginning of a useful ckdir procedure in the following way:

■ PROCEDURE 1A

```
$ cat >ckdir
# check size of login directory
if [ `ls | wc -l` -gt "$1" -a . -eq "$HOME" ]
then
    echo $HOME 'needs cleaning.'
fi
```

```
ctrl-d
$
```

Then

```
$ sh ckdir 50
```

will check if your login directory has more than 50 files, for example. Notice that we replaced the constant 50 used in Experiment 3 with the position parameter $1. Procedure 1a is not robust, since it will not execute if you forget to type a test argument. A procedure is *robust* if it is capable of handling bad input. A robust procedure will recover and do something, even if it is activated with a faulty command line (missing arguments or wrong arguments, for example). We can make Procedure 1a more robust by using nested if-statements:

■ PROCEDURE 1B

```
$ cat >ckdir
# check number of files in login directory
if [ "$#" -ne 0 ]
then
    if [ `ls | wc -l` -gt "$1" -a . - eq "$HOME" ]
    then
        echo $HOME 'needs cleaning.'
    fi
fi
ctrl-d
$
```

Now if you type

```
$ sh ckdir
```

the inner if-statement of Procedure 1b will be skipped. This procedure can be improved further by adding a provision for typing an appropriate message, if you forget to enter an argument. This can be done with the if-then-else form of an if-statement.

4.2.2 Double Alternatives with an if/then/else

An **if** statement with an **else** clause directs the machine to choose between two alternatives:

1. Perform the **then** part, provided the **if** condition tests true, otherwise
2. perform the **else** part when an **if** condition tests false.

Try, for example, the following experiment with an **if** statement:

☐ EXPERIMENT 4

```
$ if [ . -eq "$HOME" ]
> then
>     echo 'total files = ' `ls | wc -l`
> else
>     cd
>     echo 'total files = ' `ls | wc -l`
> fi
   .
   .
   .
$
```

This says that if you are not in your home directory, then (in the **else** clause) change back to your home directory and print a message. Notice that the **then** part *and* the **else** clause can have more than one command. (In Experiment 4, the **else** clause has two commands, cd and echo.) The **if** command has the following syntax:

```
if <condition>
then <command(s)>
else <command(s)>
fi
```

This form of the if statement can be used to improve Procedure 1b in the following way:

■ PROCEDURE 1C

```
$ cat >ckdir
# check number of files in your home directory
if [ "$#" -ne 0 ]
then
    if [ `ls | wc -l` -gt "$1" -a . - eq "$HOME" ]
    then
        echo $HOME 'needs cleaning.'
    fi
else
    echo 'usage: ckdir [value]'
fi
ctrl-d
$
```

You can make this procedure more general by dropping the requirement that the current directory must be your login directory. This refinement is left for an exercise.

We can combine what we have seen so far in the following example.

4.2.3 Example: Searching Directories

We can write a command procedure to solve the following problem:

Problem:
Change to a specified directory and search for all files with a specified type. Compute how many files are found. Test if no files of the specified type have been found. If files are found, append the names of these files to a file in the login directory as well as the count of the number of files found. If no files are found, then append a 'not found' message to the file in your login directory.

The first part of this problem was solved in Experiment 8 in Section 3.6. We combine the code in Experiment 8 with the use of an if-statement in the following procedure:

■ PROCEDURE 2

```
$ cat >search
# search directory for files with specified type
cd $1; file * |
grep commands |
tee -a $HOME/temp
count=`wc -l $HOME/temp | cut -c6-7`
if [ "$count" -eq 0 ]
then
    echo $1 'has no commands texts' >>$HOME/verbs
else
    echo $1 'has' $count 'commands texts:' >>$HOME/verbs
    cat $HOME/temp >>$HOME/verbs
fi
rm $HOME/temp
echo 'Search completed.'
ctrl-d
$
```

There are many ways to simplify and enhance Procedure 2:

1. Make Procedure 2 robust by checking for zero arguments (it depends on $1 being the name of a directory—it will fail if $ = 0);
2. eliminate the use of the $HOME/temp file (do everything with $HOME/verbs). If $HOME/temp is eliminated, then
3. devise a means of putting the file count *and* origin (name of directory) at the beginning of a list of files; or
4. introduce the use of $2 positional parameter to specify the file type to search for (instead of limiting this search procedure to commands texts). Searches like the following one will be possible:

```
$ search /usr/bin directory    # find directories
. . . . . . . . . . . . . . . . . . . . . . .
$ search /bin commands
. . . . . . . . . . . . . . . . . . . . . . .
$ # and so on
```

For now these improvements are left for future work.

The shell also provides a special **elif** form of the **if** statement to handle two or more alternatives.

4.2.4 Selecting Multiple Alternatives with an elif

An if-statement with an **elif**-part has the following syntax:

```
if <condition>
then
    <command(s)>
    elif <condition>
    then
        <command(s)>
    else                        # optional else-part
        <command(s)>
    elif <condition>            # optional added elif
    then
        <command(s)>
    else                        # optional else-part
        <command(s)>
        .
        .
        .
fi
```

Here is a sample use of the **elif:**

☐ EXPERIMENT 5A

```
$ month=`date | cut -c5-7`
$ if [ "$month" = Dec -o "$month" = Jan ]
> then
>     echo 'Keep the snow off your roof ... '
>     elif [ "$month" = Feb -o "$month" = Mar ]
>     then
>         echo 'Put a souvenir icicle in the freezer.'
>     elif [ "$month" = Apr ]
>     then
>         echo 'Watch the trees bud ... '
> fi
```

```
keep the snow off your roof ...
$
```

Since you have 12 months to play with, Experiment 5a has lots of other forms.

The sh shell also provides a case statement to handle selection from among multiple alternatives.

4.2.5 Multiple Alternatives with the case Statement

The **case** statement provides a convenient way to simplify **if** statements with more than one **else** or **elif.** Try, for instance, rewriting Experiment 5a:

☐ EXPERIMENT 5B

```
$ month=`date | cut -c5-7`
$ case "$month" in
>     Jan|Dec) echo 'Keep the snow off your roof ... ';;
>     Feb|Mar) echo 'Put a souvenir icicle in your freezer';;
>     Apr) echo 'Watch the trees bud ...';;
> esac
```

Thanks to the **case** statement, Experiment 5b is more concise than Experiment 5a. The vertical line | represents an **or** operator so that

```
Jan|Dec) echo 'Keep ... ';;
```

reads

```
"Jan or Dec then echo 'Keep ... '"
```

The last double semicolon (;;) in Experiment 5b is optional. If you think you will be adding more alternatives to a **case** statement, then it is desirable to leave this last ;; (this will save you some typing *and* a possible syntax error, if you forget to tack on the ;; to the old last line).

There is a problem with Experiment 5b. What happens if the current month is one of the seven not covered by the **case** statement in Experiment 5b? As a rule, this will just mean that nothing happens (the **case** statement caused no action). In Experiment 5b you would get the prompt back. You handle this problem of "unexpected strings" by using an asterisk (*). A * is a wildcard pattern which will match any string. To see this, try putting Experiment 5b into a procedure:

■ PROCEDURE 3A

```
$ cat >reminder
# experiment with the case statement
```

```
# month=`date | cut -c5-7`
month="May" in
case "$month" in
  Dec|Jan) echo 'Keep the snow off your roof ...';;
  Feb|Mar) echo 'Put a souvenir icicle in the freezer,';;
  Apr) echo 'Watch the trees bud ... ';;
  *) echo 'Take a vacation.'
esac
ctrl-d
$
```

Procedure 3a employs a software engineering technique:

Turn an action into a comment by inserting a # at the beginning of a command line. This will save you typing and allow you to experiment with a portion of an old procedure.

In Procedure 3a we masked the following line with a comment:

```
# month=`date | cut -c5-7`
```

Then we added an experimental value of month to Procedure 3a to see what would happen. Since * is a pattern which matches any string, the * will match 'May' and

```
Take a vacation.
```

will be printed. We can simplify Procedure 3a by using a command substitution as follows:

■ PROCEDURE 3B

```
$ cat >reminder
# experiment with the case statement
case `date | cut -c5-7` in
  Dec|Jan) echo 'Keep the snow off the roof ...
  Feb|Mar) echo 'Put a souvenir icicle in the freezer.';;
  Apr) echo 'Watch the trees bud ... ';;
  *) echo 'Take a vacation.'
esac
```

Now the output from the command substitution in Procedure 3b becomes the value used by the **case** statement.

The case statement has many uses. For example, we can use this statement to automate the creation of files.

4.2.6 Example: Automating File Creation

Here is a procedure to automate file creation:

■ PROCEDURE 4A

```
$ cat >ap
# automate the creation of files
case $# in
  1) tee $1;;           # append kb input to $1
  2) tee -a $2 <$1;;    # append $1 to $2
  *) echo 'usage: ap file1 [ file 2 ]'
esac
ctrl-d
$
```

Now type

```
$ chmod +x ap
```

Then to create a new file, try Procedure 5a.

■ PROCEDURE 5A

```
$ ap exe
# procedure to automate making files executable
# procedure to automate making files executable

chmod +x $1
chmod +x $1
ctrl-d
$
```

The ap procedure (Procedure 4a) echo-prints each line you type, which gives you a way to verify that you have entered the correct lines. In the second case in Procedure 4a (when $# = 2), the first file is appended to the second one you name. Here is a sample use of this second case:

```
$ ap exe exe2                    # append exe to exe2
# procedure to automate making files executable

chmod +x $1
$
```

In this case, ap prints a copy of what it has appended to exe2. This happens to be helpful, since the exe procedure can be improved. (We save the old version of exe in exe2 to build a little history of the evolution of a procedure.) Procedure 5a (or exe) works for only one file and is not robust, since it does nothing about zero arguments. Try using ap again to write a new version of exe:

■ PROCEDURE 5B

```
$ ap exe
# Procedure to automate making files executable
# Procedure to automate making files executable

chmod +x $*
chmod +x $*
ctrl-d
$
```

Now type

```
$ sh exe exe
```

to make exe itself executable. (We will have an exercise for making Procedure 5b robust so that it will recover in case you forget to give exe one or more arguments.) From now on, we can use exe to make one or more files executable as in

```
$ exe ap    # make ap executable
```

Both ap and exe are candidates for your own $HOME/bin directory, which we explore further in this chapter.

If you want to turn off the echo produced by tee in Procedure 4a, then use a cat instead of tee. The ap procedure can be revised with ed in the following way:

■ PROCEDURE 4B (FROM ED SESSION)

```
$ ed ap
147
P
* g/tee/s//cat/gp
    1) cat >$1;;
    2) cat -a $2 <$1;;
* /-a $2/
    2) cat -a $2 <$1;;
* s/-a $2/>>$2/p
    2) cat >>$2 <$1;;
* 1,$p
# Automated file creation (idea from Bourne [1983]).
```

```
case $# in
  1) cat >$1;;
  2) cat >>$2 <$1;;
  *) echo 'usage: ap file1 [file2]'
esac
* w
146
* q
$
```

In this use of ed, we have done the following things:

1. Global substitution with g/tee/s//cat/gp (this also causes each edited line to be printed);
2. find line to change with /-a $2/;
3. make substitution with s/-a $2/>>$2/p (this also prints the edited line); and
4. print entire text with 1,$p.

It is possible to automate some of these steps (we show how to do this later in the chapter).[*] In the beginning you will probably find Procedure 4a handy (reassuring) in preparing and adding to procedures. Once you gain confidence in your typing, you will probably prefer not to see every line you type echo- printed by tee. Then you will find Procedure 4b helpful. Notice how Procedure 4b differs from Procedure 4a:

If you type a single argument in a command line which uses Procedure 4b (or ap), what you type will overwrite $1 (this is handy, if you are not adding to or redoing $1 files). By contrast, Procedure 4a always concatenates onto the file specified by $1 whenever a single argument is used.

Other options can be added to Procedure 4b to make it more versatile (handle option 1 of Procedure 4a, for example). This is left for an exercise. In the remainder of this chapter Procedure 4b will be used to create new files. We will do this, for example, by typing

```
$ ap sample
< enter lines of new file >
ctrl-d
$
```

---

[*]For more information about ed, see Appendix B. The idea for Procedure 4b comes from Steve Bourne (1983).

Using a **case** statement, there are a variety of ways to select an action. Here are some examples:

1. command substitution
2. combinations like

   `a[pt] implies ap|at`

3. otherwise case: any pattern with *
4. wildcards like

   `scan* implies scant|scanner| ...`

Try the following experiment to see how these cases work:

☐ EXPERIMENT 6 (ANOTHER PROCEDURE)

```
$ ap e
# experiments with case lists
case $1 in
  `date | cut -c5-7`) echo 'On this date in history ... ';;
  a[pt]) echo $1;;
  -[aeiou]) echo $1;;
  -t|-i|-g|-e|-r) echo $1;;
*) echo $1 'is the otherwise case'
esac
ctrl-d
$
```

Notice that

  `-[aeiou]` is equivalent to `-a|-e|-i|-o|-u`

Also notice that the values in the case list must be distinct (duplicate case list values cause ambiguous selection). The best way to see this is to try various ways of activating Experiment 6. Try, for example,

```
$ exe e                            # make e executable
$ e apt
apt is the otherwise case.
$ e ap
ap
$ e scanner
scanner
$ e -ae
-ae is the otherwise case.
```

CHAPTER 4 / COMMAND PROCEDURES

```
$ e -a
-a
$                          # and so on
```

Until now, we have been preoccupied with selection control structures. The shell also has several powerful iteration control structures.

4.3 ITERATION CONTROL STRUCTURES

The shell provides two forms of iteration control structures:

1. Indexed iteration with a **for** statement, and
2. conditional iteration with either a **while** or an **until** statement.

4.3.1 Indexed Iteration with a for Statement

A **for** statement has the following, somewhat strange syntax:

```
for <index> [ in <list> ]
   do
      <action(s)>
   done
```

A **for** index without a list of values is assigned the first positional parameter (or $1, if it exists), then $2, and so on, until the parameter list has been used up. The following **for** loop illustrates this idea:

```
$ ap loop1
for i
  do
     echo '   argument = ' $i
  done
ctrl-d
$
```

If we make loop1 executable, then experimenting with this form of the **for** statement is possible:

```
$ exe loop1
$ loop1 Day broke, grey.
    argument = Day
    argument = broke,
    argument = grey.
$
```

You can make a **for** statement scan the current directory by using the * as follows:

ITERATION CONTROL STRUCTURES   **149**

```
$ ap loop2
for i in *       # list = current directory
  do
     echo $i
  done
ctrl-d
$
```

We can also explicitly supply a list of values to be assigned to the **for** index. Try, for instance, the following loop:

```
$ ap loop3
for name in amy susu tom sophie abigail mary
  do
     mail $name <message
  done
ctrl-d
$
```

Now if you run loop3, a message will be sent to each person in the supplied list. This is obviously an awkward way to specify a list of values for name. You can also use command substitution to do this. Try the following experiment:

☐ EXPERIMENT 7

Build separate mailing list

```
$ ap ilist
you sadams susur amyp jtolkien jthurber blampson
ctrl-d
$
```

Construct message to mail

```
$ ap message
Why is it that most hackers confuse Halloween and Xmas?
Because 31 (oct) = 25 (dec).
Jon Bentley, "Programming Pearls," CACM, April, 1984.
ctrl-d
$
```

Now use command substitution

```
$ ap mgram
# use command substitution to supply index values
for name in `cat ilist`
   do
      mail $name <message
```

CHAPTER 4 / COMMAND PROCEDURES

```
    done
ctrl-d
$
```

Make mgram executable

```
$ exe mgram
```

Mail your message

```
$ mgram
$
```

You can see how this works without bothering your friends by putting one or more copies of your own name in the ilist file. To see this, try typing

```
$ ap ilist
you you you you you you you you
ctrl-d
```

Now try

```
$ mgram
```

You have just sent eight copies of a message to yourself. Check your mail to verify this.
    Conditional iteration is also possible in sh shell procedures.

4.3.2 Conditional Iteration with while and until

An iteration will continue as long as the **while** condition tests true or you use a **break** to exit from the loop. Try the following experiment:

☐ EXPERIMENT 8

```
$ ap loop5
# experiment with a while loop
answer=y
while [ "$answer" != "n" ]
   do
      echo 'again? \c'; read answer
   done
ctrl-d
$
```

If you execute loop5, the iteration inside the **while** loop will continue until you type something besides **y**. You can force an exit from any loop by using the break command. Here is a session with ed to produce a modified version of loop5:

```
$ ed loop5
113
P
*/echo/
    echo 'again? \c'; read answer
*a
    if [ "$answer" = "N" ]
    then
        break
    fi
.
*1,$p
# experiment with a while loop
answer=y
while [ "$answer" != "n" ]
  do
     echo 'again? \c'; read answer
     if [ "$answer" = "N" ]
     then
         break
     fi
  done
*w
169
*q
$
```

Now if you run loop5, you will exit from the loop if you enter **N** or satisfy the while condition by typing **n**.

There are many ways to set up an infinite **while** loop. Since the : command always returns a value of true, you can use

```
$ while :
>    do
>       # command(s)
>       continue
>    done
```

This loop will run forever unless you include inside this loop either a break command (to exit from the loop) or an exit command (to exit from the running shell). You can also use any condition which always tests true like

```
$ while [ 2 -gt 0 ]
     do
        # command(s)
        continue           # continue iteration
     done
```

The iteration in a **while** loop will not occur at all if the **while** condition tests true

CHAPTER 4 / COMMAND PROCEDURES

initially. If it is desirable to have at least one iteration when a condition might test false the first time, then an **until** loop is a better choice. As long as the **until** condition tests false, iteration inside an **until** loop will continue. Try, for example, the following experiment:

☐ EXPERIMENT 9

```
$ set `ls`
$ until [ $# -eq 0 ]
>    do
>       shift; echo $# '\c'
>    done
116 115 114 113 112 111 110 109 . . .
$
```

An infinite **until** loop can be set up using

```
$ until false
>    do
>       # command(s)
          continue         # continue iteration
>    done
```

In both cases, the minimum number of iterations for either a **while** or **until** loop is zero. Notice that an **until** loop does not behave like a Pascal **repeat** loop, which always has at least one iteration. The **until** condition in a Pascal **repeat** loop is *not* tested until after the first iteration. You can get the same effect as with the Pascal **repeat** loop in several ways with the shell. Here is an example:

Equivalent Loops

PASCAL REPEAT LOOP	SHELL UNTIL LOOP

repeat
  write(count);
  count := count - 1
until (count <= 0)
	case `test $count -le 0` in
	  *) echo $count
	    count=`expr $count - 1`
	esac
	until [$count -le 0]
	  do
	    echo $count
	    count=`expr $count - 1`
	  done

In both cases, at least one value of count will be printed. The line

```
count=`expr $count - 1`
```

ITERATION CONTROL STRUCTURES   **153**

uses the expr command to subtract one from count (the output from this command substitution is assigned to count). A more detailed presentation of the expr command is given in Sections 4.5 and 4.6.

In the next section we begin developing a housecleaning procedure that uses a variety of control structures.

4.3.3 Example: Housecleaning Procedure

The aim of this section is to developing a procedure to take care of the following problem:

PROBLEM:
Write a housecleaning procedure (call it hc) which does the following things:
1. Tests for $\# = 1$ (one argument, which is a directory name)
2. Initializes the position parameters with the names in the entered directory,
3. Gives repeated access to housecleaning choices:
   -c (continue) -d (view directory) -h (help)
   -q (quit)   -r (rm directory)   -v (view)
4. Makes hc robust by catching faulty input.

We can use a **case** statement more than once to take care of checking for an invalid command line and selecting your housecleaning choice. Here is a first attempt at solving this problem.

■ PROCEDURE 6A

```
$ ap hc                                 # create hc procedure
# housecleaning procedure
case $# in
  1) place=$1                           # save directory name
     set `ls $1`                        # init. pos. parameters
     while [ $# -ne 0 ]
     do
        echo 'choice -[cdhqrv]: \c'; read choice; echo
        case "$choice" in
          -c) shift;;
          -d) ls $place;;
          -h) echo 'options: '
              echo '          -c (continue)'
              echo '          -d (directory)'
              echo '          -h (help)'
              echo '          -q (quit)'
              echo '          -r (remove)'
              echo '          -v (view)';;
          -q) break; break;;
          -r) rm $place/$1;;
          -v) cat $place/$1;;
        esac
     done;;
```

```
        *) echo 'usage: hc directory-name'
esac
ctrl-d
$
```

This is a bare-bones solution to the housecleaning problem. Procedure 6a is not robust for many reasons. It will fail right away if the argument you enter is not the name of a directory. You can fix this by typing

■ PROCEDURE 6B

```
$ ed hc
/1)/
   1) place=$1                    # save directory name
a
      if [ -d $place ]
      then
.
/*) echo/
   *) echo 'usage: hc directory-name'
.-
p
   done;;
d
a
   done
  fi;;
.
w
1112
q
$
```

Hc will also fail if the first name in an entered directory is itself the name of a directory. We can correct this problem by shifting the position parameters to the left repeatedly until a regular file is found. Here is an ed session to do this:

■ PROCEDURE 6C

```
$ ed hc
/set/
   set `ls $1`
a
   until [ -f $place/$1 ]
      do
         shift
      done
```

```
     .
     w
     1156
     q
     $
```

Now if $place/$1 is a directory name initially, then the **until** loop in Procedure 6c will shift the position parameters repeatedly to find a regular file. There is still a problem with this start-up feature of hc, which is posed as a challenge problem:

> **CHALLENGE (problem 1):**
> Modify Procedure 6b so that if a directory has *no* regular files, an appropriate message will be printed and control will be returned to the parent shell.

Once we get into the **while** loop, the same problem of finding a regular file occurs when you choose the **-c** option:

The **-c** option only shifts to the left by one, leaving open the possibility that the next directory name is the name of a directory.

Here is a preliminary solution to this problem using a **while** loop:

■ PROCEDURE 6D

```
$ ed hc
/-c)/
     -c) shift;;
s/;;//p
     -c) shift
a
        while [ -d $place/$1 ]
          do
             shift
          done;;
.
w
1175
1,$p
# housecleaning procedure
case $# in
  1)place=$1                          # save directory name
    if [ -d $place ]                  # for robustness
    then
        set `ls $1`                   # init. pos. parameters
```

```
              until [ -f $place/$1 ]      # for robustness
                do
                  shift
                done
              while [ $# -ne 0 ]
                do
                  echo 'choice -[cdhqrv]: \c'; read choice; echo
                  case "$choice" in
                    -c) shift
                        while [ -d $place/$1 ]
                          do
                            shift
                          done;;
                    -d) ls $place/$1;;
                    -h) echo 'options: '
                        echo '          -c (continue)'
                        echo '          -d (directory)'
                        echo '          -h (help)'
                        echo '          -q (quit)'
                        echo '          -r (remove)'
                        echo '          -v (view)';;
                    -q) break; break;;
                    -r) rm $place/$1;;
                    -v) cat $place/$1
                  esac
                done
           fi;;
      *) echo 'usage: hc directory-name'
esac
q
$
```

This inner **while** loop will continue shifting the position parameters as long as a regular file is not found. Notice that there is still a serious problem with the **-c** option:

> **CHALLENGE (problem 2):**
> The inner **while** loop in Procedure 6d may shift too far (when $# becomes zero). Add a "break out" feature to this option, so that you exit from the procedure (with an appropriate message, if shifting makes $# = 0) as a result of not finding another regular file.

Notice that Procedure 6d is not robust for another reason: the inner case statement does not handle invalid choices. You can fix this as follows:

■ PROCEDURE 6E

```
$ ed hc
/-v)/
        -v) cat $place/$1;;
```

```
            a
 *) echo ' options: -[cdhqrv]'
            .
            w
-1210
            q
$
```

This gives the inner **case** statement of hc an "otherwise" condition. This will make hc run more smoothly. Finally, you might want to consider adding echo statements to hc like

```
echo 'current file: ' $place/$1
```

This will tell you which file is available before you make a menu choice, if you print this message at the start of each iteration.

We have been accumulating a backlog of unexplained ideas in talking about the various control structures:

1. uses of the test command
2. arithmetic with the expr command
3. various forms of shell variables

First we look at the test command.

4.4 EVALUATING CONDITIONS WITH THE test COMMAND

The test command is used to evaluate conditions. It has the following form:

test -[rwfdstzn] expression
  -r true if file exists and is readable
  -w true if file exists and is writable
  -f true if file exists and is not a directory
  -d true if file exists and is a directory
  -s true if file exists and has non-zero size
  -t [fildes] true if open file whose file descriptor is *fildes* (1 by default) and is associated with a terminal device
  -z [string] true if length of string is is zero
  -n [string] true if length of string is non-zero

Each of the conditions written in square brackets in the preceding sections can be rewritten with the test command surrounded by parentheses (curved brackets) instead of the square brackets. For example, we search for directory names in your current directory by using

```
$ for i in *
>   do
>     if (test -d $i)
>       then
>         echo 'directory: ' $i
>     fi
>   done
directory: bin
directory: lib
directory: exp
$
```

In this example, the test command must return a value of true (its exit status must be zero!) before

```
echo 'directory: ' $i
```

is executed. If $i tests false as a directory, then the exit status from executing the test command will be 1. You can see this more clearly by printing the exit status returned by the test command for some examples:

```
$ test -d egg; echo $?      # is egg a directory?
1                           # No! (tests false)
$ test -f egg; echo $?      # is egg a reg. file?
0                           # Yes (tests true)
$ test -s yikes; echo $?    # Does yikes exist?
1                           # No
$ test -r date; echo $?     # is date readable?
1                           # No
$ test -w date; echo $?     # is date writable?
1                           # No
$
```

More than one test option can be combined in the same command line:

```
$ test -d $HOME -a -r $HOME    # is it a readable dir?
0                              # Yes!
$
```

It is this hidden feature of the test command, the exit status it produces after each test, that is surprisingly useful. Here is a sample application:

☐ EXPERIMENT 10

```
$ ap ck
# use exit status returned by the test command
test -s $1
case $? in
  0) test -d $1
     case $? in
       0) echo $1 'is a directory';;
       1) echo $1 'is an ordinary file'
     esac;;
  1) echo $1 'does not exist!'
esac
ctrl-d
$
```

Here are some sample uses of the ck command:

```
$ exe ck                          # make ck executable
$ ck yes
yes does not exist!
$ ck bin
bin is a directory
$ ck ck
ck is an ordinary file
$
```

In writing command procedures it is often necessary to perform elementary arithmetic with the expr command.

4.5 ARITHMETIC WITH THE expr COMMAND

The expr command is used to evaluate expressions, including operations on strings (comparisons and character counts). Here is a summary of the arithmetic operations with this command, as shown in the following table:

Arithmetic with expr

OPERATOR	SAMPLE EXPRESSION	VALUE	EXIT STATUS
+	expr 5 + 1	6	0
+	expr 5 + −5	0	1
−	expr 5 − 5	0	1
*	expr 5 '*' 5	25	0
*	expr 5 '*' $HOME	(invalid)	2
/	expr 7 / 2	3	0
%	expr 7 % 2	1	0

Notice that it is necessary the enclose the *(multiplier) operator inside quotes (single, usually) to prevent the shell from misinterpreting *. Also notice how the exit status returned by expr varies in the following ways:

Exit Status Returned by expr

EXIT STATUS	EXPLANATION
0	evaluated expression is neither null nor 0
1	evaluated expression is null or 0
2	expression is invalid

These arithmetic operators can be combined in one expression to be evaluated. Try, for example,

```
$ expr 5 -7 % 2           # 5 - (7 mod 2) (Pascal)
4
$ expr `expr 5 -7` % 2    # (5 - 7) mod 2 (Pascal)
0
```

The second of the above examples illustrates the possibility of "nesting" expr commands (as long as command substitution is used). The expr command is commonly used to change the value of a numeric variable. Try typing

```
$ count=5
$ count=`expr $count '*' 7`; echo $count
35
$
```

Here is a more practical use of this idea:

■ PROCEDURE 7

```
$ ap rove
# track shifted values of positional parameters
count=1
for i in *
  do
    echo $count "th argument = $i
    count=`expr $count + 1`
  done
ctrl-d
$
```

If we execute rove, we get

```
$ exe rove
$ rove
1 th argument = Bergson
2 th argument = bin
3 th argument = act0
4 th argument = act1
      .
      .
      .
$
```

You might want to tune rove so that you can enter the directory to rove around in, *and* fix it so that it prints

```
1 st argument = Bergson
2 nd argument = bin
3 rd argument = act0
4 th argument = act1
```

You can solve the second part of this tune-up problem with a case statement.
The expr command can also be used to compare strings.

4.6 COMPARING STRINGS WITH THE expr COMMAND

The colon (:) is an expr string comparison operator. Here is the syntax for such a comparison:

```
$ expr <string1> : <string2>
```

If the expr command determines that string2 is a substring of string1, then it will return the number of characters in string2. Here are some sample comparisons:

```
$ expr 'tumtytum!' : 'tum'
3
$ expr 'tumtytum!' : 'tatum'
0
$ expr 'tumtytum!' : '!'
1
$
```

It is possible to make the expr command return the number of characters in string1 using a combination of two of the following pattern matching rules:

Pattern Matching Rules

CHARACTER	PATTERN	EXAMPLE
^	match beginning of line	$ expr 'tumty' : '^u' 0
$	match end of line	$ grep 'u'$ /usr/dict/words adieu bateau ....
.	match any single character	$ expr 'tumty' : '..' 2
*	repetition of previous match	$ ls | grep 'scan*' | 5 scanb scane scanf ....
.*	match any pattern	$ expr 'tumty' : '.*' 5
-	any characters in an interval	$ ls [a-z]* | 5 <lists all files with names in lowercase>
[string]	match any characters in **string**	$ expr 'tumty' : [t-u] 1 <matches **tut**>
?	match any single character	$ ls e? ex
\	escape	$ expr 'tum.c' : \. 1

In the above table notice that the combination of a dot (which matches any single character) and an asterisk (repetition of previous match) gives us a way to tell the expr command to compute the length of a string. To see this, try typing

```
$ expr ' tumtytummmmmmmmmmmmmm!' : '.*'
22
$
```

Using the escape character (\), a .*, the grouping symbols ( ) and a sequence of dots, we can use the expr command to select characters in a string. To see this, try the following experiment:

☐ EXPERIMENT 11

```
$ t='tumtytummmmmmmmmmmmmm!'
$ part=`expr $t : ' ..... \(.*\)'`    # skip 1st 5 char's
$ echo $part
tummmmmmmmmmmmmmm!
$
```

The dots . . . . . each specify a character to skip at the beginning of the t-string. The backslash (\) is used to prevent misinterpretation of the parentheses (used as grouping symbols). Recall that parentheses are used to run a sequence of commands inside a subshell. Parentheses are examples of metacharacters. A *metacharacter* is a character like * or (and) which has special meaning for the shell. Here is a list of metacharacters used by the shell:

Shell Metacharacters

METACHARACTER	MEANING	EXAMPLE
^	old name for pipe	(avoid)
|	new name for pipe	$ ls -l | grep '^d' <list dir names>
(<commands>)	run commands in subshell	$ (date; who)
*	current directory names	$ cat *
?	any single character	$ ls ?e
#	begin comment	$ # start comment
'<string>'	take characters literally	$ echo 'date' date
`<commands>`	command substitution	$ echo 'date:' `date` date: Sun Feb ...
"<string>"	take characters literally	$ echo "Jim's house."
;	command terminator	$ date; who
&	background command	$ date &
$<number>	shell position parameters	$ echo $1
$<symbol>	holds special values	$ echo $? $- $# # etc.
$<string>	variable substitution	$ t=5; echo $t
>	redirect output	$ ls >list
<	redirect input	$ mail susu <message
>>	append output	$ ls >>list
<<	here document	$ grep '2' <<! 72 30000 2001 ! 72 2001
<com1>&&<com2>	if com1 tests true, then run com2 (same as **if**)	$ [5 -lt 7]&&date Sun Feb ...
<com1>||<com2>	if com1 tests false, then run com2	$ [5 -gt 7]||who <who will run>

Most of these metacharacters are familiar (the ? and << are new). In pattern matching, the trick is to enclose these metacharacters inside quotes to turn off their special meaning to the shell. The .* in Experiment 12 illustrates this idea. The .* is a wildcard used in

164   CHAPTER 4 / COMMAND PROCEDURES

```
expr $t : ` ..... \(.*\)'
```

to specify all characters in t *to the right of the first five characters* (specified by the five dots .....). We had to use the backslash (\ ) to turn off (escape) the special meaning of the metacharacters ( ). Parentheses can be used in pattern matching with the expr command, provided we escape their special meaning as shell metacharacters. Try some variations of Experiment 12 to see how this works. Better yet, try

> **CHALLENGE (problem 3):**
> Set up a procedure (call it strip) which allows you to enter a string (to assign to t) and to enter the number of leading characters to skip.

You can use a similar technique to strip characters from the end of a substring. For example, try

```
$ echo `expr $t : '\(.*\).........'`
tumtytummmmmm
```

You can strip characters off both ends by using the following technique:

```
$ echo `expr $t : '..... \(.*\)......'`
tummmmmmmmm
$
```

Finally, here is an experiment which uses the : operator to count the characters in a string as follows:

☐ EXPERIMENT 12

```
$ echo 't has ' `expr $t : '.*'` ' characters.'
t has 22 characters.
$
```

Adding this capability to the strip procedure from Challenge problem 3 gives us a fourth Challenge problem:

> **CHALLENGE (problem 4):**
> Modify strip from Challenge problem 3 so that
> 1. strip gives the length of t
> 2. strip gives the length of the substring of t

Many other uses of the expr command are given in expr(1) of Bell (1983).
  Shell programming usually depends on the use of different forms of shell variables. The shell provides several ways to evaluate variables.

4.7 EVALUATION OF SHELL VARIABLES

So far we have liberally used the following forms of shell variables:

Shell Variables

FORM	MEANING	EXAMPLE
variable substitution	$-prefix to specify value	`echo $t`
command substitution	assign output to variable	`t='ls'`
special shell var's	variables used by shell	`set <return>`
position parameters	hold shell arguments	`set 'ls'`
other shell parameters	$?, $-, $#, $!, $*, "$@"	`echo $?`

You can specify alternative values to use by typing

```
$ error='usage: name value'
$ echo ${1-$error}
usage: name value
```

In this example, if $1 has no value, then $error is printed. We can use this idea to modify Procedure 4c in Section 3.9.2 (the egg timer) so that alternate lists can be entered *and* make egg almost fail-safe (give it robustness so that it will run for any set of arguments):

■ PROCEDURE 8 (see section 3.9.2)

```
$ ap egg                                          # start over
# print a reminder later

message="coffee time!"
(sleep ${1-300}; echo ${2-$message}) &
ctrl-d
$
```

Then we can run egg in the following ways:

```
$ exe egg                    # make egg executable
$ egg                        # no arguments
coffee time!                 5 minutes later
$ egg 600                    # 1 argument
coffee time!                 10 minutes later
$ egg 3600 "dinner time!"    # 2 arguments
dinner time!                 60 minutes later
```

Procedure 8 is still not completely fail-safe. We disrupt the running of egg by typing

166 CHAPTER 4 / COMMAND PROCEDURES

```
$ egg "dinner time!"            # $1 must be numeric
$ usage: sleep time
coffee time!
```

The boldfaced part of this sample run of egg shows an error message because the sleep command needs an integer argument representing a number of seconds. Since there is no $2 argument in

```
$ egg "dinner time"    # $2 is missing
```

the default message

```
coffee time!
```

is printed by

```
echo ${2-$message}
```

The message gets printed right away instead of some time later.

> **CHALLENGE (problem 5):**
> Make egg robust for all arguments.
> Hint: use x=`expr 300 \| $1` (if $1 is null, the expr command will assign 300 to check).

An alternative value can be assigned to a variable with no assigned value using the following technique:

```
$ echo ${yes='definitely!'}
definitely                       since yes has no value
```

You can use a ? to get the following results:

```
$ echo ${yes?}
definitely!
$ echo ${nonsense?}
nonsense: parameter null or not set
$ something="It's almost springtime . . . "
$ echo ${nope?$something}
nope: It's almost springtime . . .
$
```

The statement

```
echo ${var1?$var2}
```

is useful in building error messages into procedures with faulty input. For example, we might want to use

EVALUATION OF SHELL VARIABLES **167**

```
$ error='argument is null or not set'
$ echo ${1?$error}
1: argument is null or not set
```

Finally, if a variable has been assigned a value, use an alternative value specified by the + operator as follows:

```
$ echo ${something+$yes}
definitely!
```

Here is a table summarizing the ways to evaluate shell variables:

Ways to Evaluate Shell Variables

METHOD	MEANING	EXAMPLE
$name	evaluate name	$ name='Unix'; echo $name
${name}	evaluate name	$ echo ${name}
${var1-var2}	if var1 not defined, use var2 else use var1	$ echo ${name-whoops} Unix
${var1=value}	assign value to var1, if var1 is not defined else use var1	$ echo ${stop=.}
${var1?value}	if var1 is not defined print value, else use var1	$ echo ${nope?"ohhhhh"} nope: ohhhhh
${var1+value}	use value, *if* var1 is defined, otherwise nothing	$ echo ${x+$name} Unix

As a convenience in supplying standard input to a command, the shell has a here document facility.

4.8 HERE DOCUMENTS

A *here document* specifies standard input to a command. Here documents are surrounded by some delimiter like ! or 'begin' to mark the boundaries of the input to a command. Here is an example:

```
$ grep '305' <<!
(305) 734-2771
(612) 746-2555
(306) 991-0001
!
(305) 734-2771
```

CHAPTER 4 / COMMAND PROCEDURES

Here documents are remarkably useful. For example, we can automate some of the messier features of ed by supplying the lines normally typed into ed. Here is a procedure called gsub (for "global substitutions") which illustrates this idea:

■ PROCEDURE 9

```
$ ap gsub                           # create gsub file
ed $3 <<!                           # begin here document
g/$1/s//$2/gp                       # global substitution
w
!echo 'edited text:'
g/^/p                               # global print
!echo 'global substitution completed'
q
!                                   # end of here document
ctrl-d
$
```

Now you can use gsub to make global substitutions inside a text. The lines in the here document are the same ones you would type if you were to run ed to make a global substitution and verify what you have done. This command has the following syntax:

```
usage: gsub old-string new-string file
```

To see this, try the following experiment:

☐ EXPERIMENT 13

```
$ ap text                                    # create text
Tom went walking on up the Withywindle to tell
Goldberry about UNIX and Tunix but instead stopped off
to look for gold and he ... lost track of time.
ctrl-d
```

Sample run of gsub

```
$ gsub "UNIX and Tunix" "Unix and Tunis" text
150
to tell Goldberry about Unix and Tunis about
150
edited text:

Tom went walking on up the Withywindle
to tell Goldberry about Unix and Tunis but instead
stopped off to look for gold and he ... lost track of
time.
$
```

Notice that gsub is not robust. This procedure will fail if incorrect arguments and the wrong number of arguments are used to activate gsub.

> **CHALLENGE (problem 6):**
> Make gsub robust.

Recursive command procedures (ones that call themselves) are also possible.

4.9 RECURSIVE PROCEDURES

A *recursive procedure* calls itself. Unless you specify otherwise, each time a command procedure calls itself, a new subshell (child process of the current shell) starts running to execute the recursive procedure. This cannot go on indefinitely because there is a limit to the number of offspring a shell can have. To see this, try

```
$ ap call
call
ctrl-d
$ sh call &
767
$
```

While the call procedure is running, type

```
$ ps
```

You will probably be surprised at the ps table which is *eventually* printed (you will probably have to wait a while before it is printed). If variables are passed to a subshell, each parent will maintain a copy of the old value of the passed variable. Then, if a recursion is finite (and stops before an overflow condition occurs), the old values of the passed variables will be restored in reverse order. Each time a parent shell is revived, the next old value will be restored. Here is a procedure to demonstrate this idea:

■ PROCEDURE 10

```
$ ap mirror                                        # recursive procedure
# experiment with recursion

if [ $1 -ne 0 ]
then
  echo 'count =' $1
  mirror `expr $1 - 1`                             # recursive call
```

```
fi
echo ' old value of $1 = ' $1         # restored values
ctrl-d
$
```

Here is a sample run of mirror:

```
$ exe mirror                          # make mirror executable
$ mirror 3
count = 3
count = 2
count = 1
  old value of $1 = 0
  old value of $1 = 1
  old value of $1 = 2
  old value of $1 = 3
$
```

There is a way to force mirror to run with the shell it starts with. This will make it possible for mirror to run much longer because the excess baggage created by endless subshells is no longer present.

> **CHALLENGE (problem 7):**
> Modify mirror (Procedure 10) so that it runs recursively without creating a succession of subshells. Do the same thing with call.

To bring together many of the ideas discussed so far in this chapter, we will develop a recursive procedure to solve the following problem:

> **PROBLEM:**
> List all files in all subdirectories of a given subdirectory.

Here is the beginning of a procedure to solve this problem:

■ PROCEDURE 11

```
$ ap sd                               # scan directories
# recursively search for directories to list

cd $1; echo $HOME/$1; ls -l
for name in *
  do
    if (test -d $name)
    then
        sd $ name                     # recursive call
```

RECURSIVE PROCEDURES 171

```
        fi
     done
ctrl-d
$
```

The sd procedure does the following things:

1. Changes to directory named by $1 (notice that this is the source of a possible error);
2. prints $HOME/$name directory name;
3. lists directory; and
4. scans the $name directory for the name of the *next* directory and calls itself with

```
sd $name
```

if a directory name is found.

If a directory has 20 subdirectories, then 20 shells will start running to track down and list each of these subdirectories. Notice that each received shell picks up where it left off and continues scanning the directory it was in. Here is a sample run of sd:

```
$ exe sd                            # make sd executable
sd lib
/usr/you/lib
total 4
-rw-r--r--    1    you    unix      67 Jan  9 10:10 Texas
drwxr-xr-x    4    you    unix      80 Dec 22 11:24 pkgs
-rw-r--r--    1    you    unix     419 Dec 28 11:11 index
drwxr-xr-x    2    you    unix     128 Jan  2 17:53 tools
/usr/you/pkgs
total 0
/usr/you/tools
total 4
-rw-r--r--    1    you    unix    2296 Jan 20 17:03 commands
-rw-r--r--    2    you    unix    1545 Dec 29 19:32 xref
```

You have probably noticed that sd is not robust. This is a good place to use a case statement like

```
case $# in
  0) echo 'usage: sd directory-name';;
  *) .......
esac
```

There are many variations of the sd procedure, depending on what results are to be produced. We could just as easily

1. List a file name, and
2. prompt to see if some operation is to be done on the file (cat or rm, for example).

The sd procedure also provides a means of generalizing the hc ("housecleaning") procedure in Section 4.3.3.

4.10 SUMMARY

The sh shell can be programmed. There are a variety of control structures which make it possible to modify the normal sequential execution of command lines in a procedure. A *control structure* specifies a departure from normal sequential operation of commands. Control structures can be classified in the following ways:

Control Structures

CONTROL STRUCTURE	TYPE OF CONTROL	ACTION SPECIFIED BY STRUCTURE
if	selection	select action based on the evaluation of some condition
case	selection	select action (from among multiple alternatives) by matching a value with a case constant
for	iteration	indexed repetition of an action
while	iteration	conditional repetition of action
until	iteration	conditional repetition of action

Shell programming can be used to automate many tasks typically performed during an average Unix session. For example, some of the more cumbersome **ed** command lines can be simplified using a here document inside a command procedure. A *here document* specifies standard input for a command. The gsub procedure simplifies the problem of making global substitutions with ed.

Command procedures should be made robust. A *robust procedure* is a procedure that is immune to failure which occured as a result of bad input. There is no provision in gsub for catching an incorrect number of arguments. We can make gsub robust by using the **case** control structure, for example, to check for improper commands lines used to run gsub. It is generally true that the shell control structures provide means of making procedures robust.

Recursive procedures are also possible. A *recursive procedure* is one that calls itself. Unless you use the . or exec command to make a recursive call, a new subshell will be created each time a recursive call is made. The production of subshells by recursive calls is a significant limiting factor in the number of such calls that can be made. Recursion offers yet another way to program the shell.

4.11 REVIEW OF COMMANDS, SYMBOLS AND KEYWORDS

This section reviews the commands, symbols, and keywords introduced in this chapter.

4.11.1 Commands

COMMAND	ACTION
break	exit from a loop
case	selection control
continue	continue iteration
expr	perform arithmetic
for	indexed iteration
if	test condition to select an action
test	test condition
while	conditional iteration of an action
until	conditional iteration of an action

4.11.2 Symbols

SYMBOL	USAGE
-a	and operator
-o	or operator used in **if** conditions
!	not operator
[ ]	test condition inside square brackets
:	command which always returns value true
: (expr)	expr string comparison operator
* (case)	matches any string
. (expr)	matches any character
? (case)	matches any character
.* (expr)	matches any pattern
-[xy] (case)	same as -x	-y
	(case)	or operator
)	end of case list (example: -[xy])...
\	escape
;;	separate alternatives in **case** structure
$var	variable substitution
${ }	evaluate variables inside { }
<<	starts here document (input to a command line from lines of document)
x&&y	same as "if x then y"
x||y	same as "if not x then y"
$	match end of line
^ (expr)	match beginning of line
- (expr)	interval of characters (example: [a-z])

4.11.3 Keywords

KEYWORD(S)	EXPLANATION
control structure	specifies departure from normal sequential execution of command lines
else clause	specifies an alternative action when an **if** condition tests false
exit status	value returned by a command (0 = true, 1 = false, for example) Example: `$ grep idea /usr/dict/words` has an exit status of 1, if nothing is output by grep, that is, idea is not found, (see Section 4.5)
here document	specifies standard input to a command (see Section 4.8)
metacharacter	character with special meaning for shell
recursive procedure	procedure which calls itself
relational operator	operator used to compare values
robustness	resistant to failure
robust procedure	resistant to failure as a result of bad input (see Section 4.13)

4.12 EXERCISES

1. Make Procedure 4C (called egg) in Section 3.9.2 robust (resistant to failure as a result of faulty command lines used to execute egg). Give sample runs to show various cases.
2. What is the limiting factor on the number of recursive calls made by the call procedure in Experiment 1 in Section 4.1?
3. Modify the call procedure in Experiment 1 in Section 4.1 so the limiting factor discussed in Exercise 2 is eliminated. In other words, modify call so that it runs longer than the call procedure in Experiment 1. Do the following things:
   a. Put a counter in the call procedure in Experiment 1 which counts the number of recursive calls made.
   b. Put a counter in the modified call procedure for *this* exercise which counts the number of recursive calls made. Give ample runs of both versions of call.
4. Why is it important to run call in the background in Experiment 1 in Section 4.1?
5. Write a command procedure which uses command line arguments to illustrate how each of the control structures in the table in Section 4.2 functions. Give sample runs.
6. Explain the difference between
   a. break and exit
   b. break and continue

7. Write a command procedure (call it myif) which illustrates the use of each of the relational operators used in **if** condition (see Table 4.2.1 for a list of these operators). There is a restriction: do this with a single **if** condition using a combination of Boolean operators. Use positional parameters in your **if** condition so that various arguments can be used to test your massive condition. Give sample runs.

8. Explain the difference between
   a. != and -ne
   b. = and -eq

9. Write a command procedure called cmp (for "compare") which can be used to illustrate the use of the -a and -o operators (see Section 4.2.1) for various arguments. Give some sample runs.

10. Modify the myif procedure in Exercise 7 so that you print the exit status returned by **if** each time it is run. Give a sample run.

11. Modify ckdir (Procedure 1b, Section 4.2.2) so that any directory can be checked. Give a sample run.

12. Make ckdir in Exercise 11 robust by checking if an entered argument is the name of a directory. Print an error message (display correct usage) if a faulty argument is used. Give a sample run.

13. Make the four improvements to the search procedure suggested at the end of Section 4.2.3. Give sample runs to demonstrate how the new search procedure works.

14. Improve the case statement in the reminder procedure (Section 4.2.5, Procedure 3b) so that it handles all months (all forms of months: all upper case (JAN), all lower case (jan), all usual abbreviations (for example, jn for june or jly for july), and complete spellings (for example, september). Give a sample run.
    Hint: use [ ] to specify possible values.

15. Make exe (Procedure 5b in Section 4.2.6) robust. Give a sample run.

16. Add to Procedure 4b (the ap procedure in Section 4.2.6) the following provisions:
    a. a option so that typed lines are appended to $2 without echo- printing each entered line
    b. -e option so that typed lines are appended to $2 and are echo-printed
    c. -c option to specify that $1 is to be appended to $2
    d. robustness feature: when arguments are used, make sure they do not represent directory names
       Give a sample run.

17. Make mgram (Experiment 7 in Section 4.3.1) robust by printing an error message if ilist is empty and exiting from the procedure. Give a sample run.

18. Make mgram in Exercise 17 more robust by printing an error message if the message file is empty. Give a sample run.

19. Write the snoopy procedure (Exercise 2 in Chapter 3) using either an **until** or **while** control structure which repeatedly checks if a specified person is logged on. Print a message if that person is logged on. Fix up snoopy so that you can use an argument to specify the person to look for.

20. Make snoopy from Exercise 19 robust by guaranteeing that a search is made only if an entered name is the name of a person listed in /usr. Give a sample run.

21. Modify snoopy in Exercise 20 so that the exit status from grep is printed each time grep is run.

22. Make snoopy from Exercise 21 run with a default person's name, if snoopy is run without any argument. Install the new snoopy in your .profile and give a sample run.

23. Explain what happens if a continue command is used instead of the break command in modified version of loop 5 in Section 4.3.2.
24. Give an answer to Challenge problem 1 in Section 4.3.3.
25. Give an answer to Challenge problem 2 in Section 4.3.3.
26. Improve the hc procedure in Section 4.3.3 by printing the name of each file which is inspected or visited.
27. Give a sample run of a built-in command which forces that command to have an exit status of
    a. 0
    b. 1
    c. 2
28. Write a command procedure called sum which computes the sum from 1^2 to $\$i^2$. Give some sample runs.
29. Use the suggestions at the end of Section 4.5 to fine tune the rove procedure.
30. Write a procedure called extract which allows the following options:
    a. -c to count characters in an entered string
    b. -b to print first k characters of an entered string
    c. -m to print k middle characters of an entered string
    d. -e to print k end characters of an entered string
    Give a sample run.
31. Make extract from Exercise 30 robust by
    a. making sure an entered k-value does not exceed the length of an entered string
    b. printing a usage message if an unexpected option is entered
    c. printing a usage message if the wrong number of arguments are entered
       Give sample runs to illustrate each case.
32. Answer Challenge problem 3 in Section 4.6.
33. Answer Challenge problem 4 in Section 4.6.
34. Answer challenge problem 5 in Section 4.7.
35. Answer Challenge problem 6 in Section 4.7.
36. What is the maximum value of count that can be used with the recursive mirror procedure in Section 4.9 on your system?
37. Modify the mirror procedure from Section 4.9 so that a subshell is not created each time a recursive call is made. Explain why a sample run of this modified mirror differs from the run in Section 4.9. (This is Challenge problem 7 in Section 4.9.)
38. Add to the sd ("search directory") procedure in Section 4.9 the changes suggested at the end of that section. Give a sample run.
39. (Refinement) Add the sd procedure (Section 4.9) to the hc procedure (Section 4.3.3) so that *after* housecleaning is finished in an entered directory, housecleaning can be continued (if desired) in each subdirectory of a given directory.

4.13 REVIEW QUIZ

Indicate whether the following statements are true or false.
1. **if** can be the name of a file in one of your directories.
2. The exit status returned by grep will be 1 if a grep-search for a pattern results in failure.

3. The **until** iteration always iterates an action at least once.
4. A **while** loop always has zero or more iterations.
5. A **for** loop always has a fixed number of iterations.
6. Every **until** loop can be rewritten as a **while** loop.
7. Shell procedures can be recursive.
8. The sh shell has no provision for arithmetic.
9. The colon (:) is the expr command integer comparison operator.
10. The period (.) matches any single character when used with the expr command.

4.14 FURTHER READING

Bourne, S. R. The Unix System. Reading, MA: Addison-Wesley, 1983. See Chapter 4 on the sh shell.

Dijkstra, E. W. "Notes on Structured Programming" in O.-J. Dahl, E. W. Dijkstra, C. A. R. Hoare. Structured Programming. Orlando, Florida: Academic Press, 1972. See Section 7 of Part 1 on control structures.

Pike, R. and B. W. Kernighan. Program Design in the Unix Environment. AT&T Bell Laboratories Technical Journal, vol. 63, no. 8, part 2 (October 1984), pp. 1595–605. See Section II for a discussion of the cat command.

5 Procedure Design

You should not have to pay for those features you do not need.
—*Mullender and Tanenbaum, 1985.*

The guiding principle for making the choice [whether to add a new option or write a new program] should be that each program does one thing.
—*Pike and Kernighan, 1984.*

5.0 AIMS

- Suggest techniques helpful in designing new procedures
- Illustrate how preconditions and postconditions can be used to spot weaknesses in procedures
- Use various forms of scaffolding in developing procedures
- Illustrate the use of stepwise refinements in developing command procedures
- Show new uses of recursive procedures
- Develop various scanners
- Suggest ways to do massive file deletions
- Develop extensions of the Hewett and Gosling method of bundling software into distribution files
- Begin using several new commands
- Suggest various tools to put into your $HOME/bin directory

5.1 INTRODUCTION TO PROCEDURE DESIGN

There are essentially two kinds of user-defined command procedures:

1. Procedures containing sequences of commands without control structures like

```
$ cat where
# show current directory
echo ' working directory: ' `pwd`
    $
```

2. Procedures with control structures that change the normal sequential execution of commands like

```
$ cat snoopy
# see who's logged on
until who | grep $1
  do
    sleep 600                    # sleep 10 minutes
  done
$
```

Both kinds of user-defined procedures are common. The first kind of procedure is put together usually to save typing, neaten up, and explain the output from one or more commands. The two commands **pwd** and **where** do essentially the same thing:

```
$ pwd
/usr/you
$ sh where
working directory: /usr/you
```

The value of **where** might just be that its output is "friendlier," and "where" is easier to remember than the more cryptic "pwd." The second kind of user-defined procedures gives us another way to customize our use of the shell. The use of shell control structures allows us to specialize our use of the built-in commands. Both types of user-defined commands can be used to tailor a working environment to individual needs and tastes.

The idea is to use the old tools to create new tools. A *tool* is a useful procedure. This is really a design principle taken from Bergson, which is used by McIlroy, Pinson, and Tague (1978) to introduce the 7th edition of Unix:

Bergson design principle:
Use old tools to develop new tools.

Usually tools can be used either by themselves or in connection with other tools. We can use the built-in commands like who and grep to build needed new commands like snoopy. General purpose tools are best. Instead of typing

```
$ (until who | grep susu
>     do
>            sleep 600
>            done) &
5678
$
```

we can save time by putting these lines into a new command procedure (call it snoopy) and typing

```
$ sh snoopy susu &
6201
$
```

Notice that snoopy not only saves time, it also uses the $1 positional parameter to provide a general solution to a problem. To watch for when nwirth logs in instead of "susu," we can just as easily type

```
$ snoopy nwirth &
7506
$
```

  This chapter is chiefly about the development of useful command procedures to put in $HOME/bin (your bin directory) for everyday use. Since this becomes a matter of personal taste, the procedures developed in this chapter are problem-oriented, merely intended as suggestion of various ways to solve common problems. In a Unix environment the following problems often repeatedly crop up:

A Selection of Typical Problems

PROBLEM	SOLUTION
lots of scrap files	bin/del to delete unwanted files
unwanted processes	bin/zap to kill unwanted processes
finding subdirectories	bin/sd to list subdirectories
finding dated files	bin/dirt to list dated files
bundling software	bin/bundle to bundle software
mailing files	bin/send to send files
searching through a file	bin/search to search for an item
making files executable	bin/exe to make a file executable
printing in columns	bin/5 to print in 5 columns
	bin/6 to print in 6 columns, etc.

This chapter suggests various procedures to put into your $HOME/bin directory to solve these typical problems. It also suggests some techniques for designing procedures that are both useful *and* robust (resistant to failure as a result of bad input).

5.2 PROCEDURE DESIGN TECHNIQUES

C. R. Vick (1984) suggests that the fundamental objective of *software engineering* is to provide sound engineering principles, practice, and tools that can be used to support each of the phases of the software life cycle. In the development of software, a *life cycle* can be identified with the following stages:

Software Life Cycle

STAGE	EXAMPLE
1. specify problem requirements	detect who's logged on
2. design solution	run who and grep repeatedly
3. code/debug	create snoopy command
4. test/validate	run snoopy with various names
5. maintain/	use snoopy command
modify/	try all different time intervals for sleep command used by snoopy (repeat steps 1 through 4 again)
revalidate	more work with snoopy

In this section we explore the following procedure design techniques:

Sample Procedure Design Techniques

TECHNIQUE	EXPLANATION
1. scaffolding	displaying intermediate procedure values; turning old command lines into comments
2. preconditions	input specifications (sufficient condition for a program to start running: enough arguments? correct arguments? and so on)
3. postconditions	output specifications (assuming a procedure terminates, these specify the results of a procedure)
4. assertions	claims about procedure actions
5. test data	determining data to use to test correctness of a procedure
6. robustness	resistance to failure as a result of bad input
7. stepwise refinements	decomposition of a task into subtasks (of a procedure into subprocedures)

In the following sections we explore these design techniques in more detail.

5.2.1 Scaffolding

In developing procedures, especially ones that won't behave (produce unexpected, wrong, *or* no results), it is helpful to use scaffolding. The term *scaffolding* refers to extra program components added to assist in program development. Typical scaffolding includes such components as

1. stubs: empty software components
2. simulated portions of a future program
3. test data generators and other helper programs used to support the development and testing of a program

For example, the empty statement inside the following case command serves as scaffolding for future actions triggered by $#$ being either 1 or 2:

```
case $# in
   0) echo 'usage: command arguments(s)'; ;
   1|2)    ; ;                          # scaffolding
   *) echo '.......'
esac
```

Stubs can be used to represent future program components. You can turn an old action-line in a procedure into scaffolding by inserting a comment at the beginning of a line. Here is an example:

```
case $# in
   0) echo 'usage: command arguments(s)'; ;
   1|2)    ; ;                          # scaffolding
# *) echo '.......'                     scaffolding
esac
```

Now the last case in this instance of the **case** command is employed as scaffolding. Making this line a comment removes it from the action-part of the command. This is a helpful technique to use with fairly complex procedures that will not work. The idea is to turn suspected problem command lines into comments to isolate the source of a problem. In effect,

---

Scaffolding switch:
Inserting a # at the start of a command line allows us to turn a command line "off," and removing a leading #-sign allows us to turn an old command line "on."

PROCEDURE DESIGN TECHNIQUES

5.2.2 Identifying Preconditions and Postconditions

An assertion about required input for a procedure is a *precondition* for the execution of the procedure. For example, a username is necessary input in

```
$ cat snoopy
# precondition: $1 must be a user name

until who | grep $1
  do
    sleep 600                                    # sleep 10 minutes
  done
```

Specifying a precondition tells us what data are needed to run a procedure. Preconditions also point to potential trouble spots in executing a command. In this example, it is clear that snoopy is not robust for two reasons:

1. no check is made if one argument has been used to activate snoopy
2. if there is one argument, no check is made to see if $1 is a username in /usr

Similarly, a *postcondition* is an assertion about the result which is expected from a program. With snoopy, for instance, we can make the following assertions:

```
$ cat snoopy
# precondition: $1 must be a username
# postcondition: $1-line output by who will be printed
                 if $ logs on while snoopy is running
      .
      .
      .
$
```

In effect, preconditions and postconditions give us ways to test the correctness of a program. These assertions give us a way to track down "ghosts" that make running procedures go wrong, thus giving us a way to verify procedure correctness. It is also helpful to get used to making assertions about program actions which will always occur during the execution of a loop.

5.2.3 Invariant Assertions

An *invariant assertion* is a claim which holds true before and after each iteration of a loop. We can make the following assertion about the **until** loop in snoopy:

```
$ sleep 600 will run as long as grep has no output
```

The **until** loop in snoopy depends on the test of the following condition:

```
who | grep $1
```

The exit status from grep will be 1 (false), if grep does not match a line from the output from who with the $1-pattern. This sample assertion is invariant—always true when the snoopy **until** loop is running. Assertions have a hidden benefit: they suggest test data which might be used to validate a program.

5.2.4 Test Data

Test data also give us a way to check procedure correctness. The trick is to look for test data that push a running procedure, that make a running procedure falter. This is easy to see with snoopy, if we execute this procedure as follows:

```
$ snoopy &
1627
$ usage: grep [ -bchlnsvy ] ...
```

The system will print this usage error message, since the activation of snoopy without an argument makes grep fail (grep uses $1 as the pattern to search for in the output from who). Test data give us a way to determine the robustness of a procedure.

5.2.5 Robustness

A procedure is *robust* if it is resistant to failure as a result of bad input. We know snoopy is not robust. Both the sample precondition in Section 5.2.2 and the test in Section 5.2.4 tell us this. We can begin making it robust in the following way:

■ PROCEDURE 1A

```
$ cat snoopy
# precondition: $1 is a username
# postcondition: line with $1 (from who) is printed,
#                if $1 logs on while snoopy is running

case $# in
   1) until who | grep $1
         do
            sleep 600                    # sleep 10 minutes
         done; ;
   *) echo 'usage: snoopy user-name'
esac
```

Now no matter how many arguments we type, snoopy will run, and detect either 0 arguments or excessive arguments. However, Procedure 1a will fail if an entered name is not in /usr. We can fix this as follows:

■ PROCEDURE 1B (ED SESSION)

```
$ ed snoopy
304
/case/
case $# in
a
    1) ls | grep $1                   # see any mistake?
        if [ $? -eq 0 ]
        then
            until who | grep $1
              do
                sleep 600           # sleep 10 minutes
        else echo 'usage: $1 must be a user name in /usr'
        fi;;
.
.=
14
p
        fi;;
15,18d
1,$p
# precondition: $1 is a user name
# postcondition: line with $1 (from who) is printed,
#                if $ logs on while snoopy is running
case $# in
    1) ls | grep $1                   # see any mistake?
        if [ $? -eq 0 ]
        then
            until who | grep $1
              do
                sleep 600                      # sleep 10 minutes
              done
        else echo 'usage: $1 must be a user name in /user'
        fi;;
    *) echo 'usage: snoopy user-name'
esac
w
416
q
$
```

Now try experimenting with snoopy (run in the background). It should check if the name you enter is in /usr before the **until** loop is run. To see this, try the following experiment:

☐ EXPERIMENT 1

```
$ snoopy &
1797
$ usage: snoopy user-name
$ snoopy susu &
1799
$ usage: $1 must be a user name in /usr
$ snoopy you &
1804
$ usage: $1 must be a user name in /usr
```

Notice that the third sample run produces an unexpected result, since **you** is in /usr. In fact there is a mistake in Procedure 1b —/usr was omitted in

```
1) ls | grep $1
```

We should have

```
1) ls /usr | grep $1
```

A few test data led us to discover this omission, which is easily corrected with another ed session:

```
$ ed snoopy
416
/1)/
    1) ls | grep $1          # see any mistake?
s/ls/ls \/usr/p
    1) ls /usr | grep $      # see any mistake?
w
421
q
$
```

(Notice how the blackslash is used in

```
s/ls/ls \/usr/p
```

to escape the usual meaning of the slash (/): a / is used by ed as a delimiter.) Typically the development of one procedure leads to others which need to be written. This often occurs as a result of stepwise refinement of a plan of action.

5.2.6 Stepwise Refinements

The idea of using stepwise refinements as a way of developing programs comes from Niklaus Wirth (1971). The idea is to decompose a program into subprograms gradually, to decompose a task into subtasks. To see this, we need to start with a problem:

PROBLEM:
Write a message to a user when that person logs on.

Here is the beginning of a solution to this problem:

■ PROCEDURE 2A

```
$ cat >tgram
# send a message to a user who logs on
# precondition: $1 must a user name in /usr

# check if $1 is logged on           (scaffolding)
if [ $? -eq 0 ]
then write $1 <message
fi
$
```

If you have a non-empty message file, Procedure 2a can be tested in the following way:

☐ EXPERIMENT 2

```
$ cat message
[Scaffolding] includes dummy software components or
stubs
(Vick, Ramamoorthy, 1984).
$
$ tgram you &
1894
$ you
   you         tty02       Feb 15 19:33
               Message from you ...

[Scaffolding] includes dummy software components or
stubs
(Vick, Ramamoorthy, 1984).
(end of message)
$
```

Procedure 2a can be refined by replacing the scaffolding with a command to serve as our system sleuth. Sounds like a job for snoopy! So try using snoopy in Procedure 2b:

■ PROCEDURE 2B (ED SESSION)

```
$ ed tgram
181
/check/
# check if $1 is logged on          (scaffolding)
d
i
snoopy $1
.
w
139
1,$p
# send a message to a user who logs on
# precondition: $1 must be a user name in /usr

snoopy $1
if [ $? -eq 0 ]
then write $1
then write $1 <message
fi
q
$
```

Now snoopy will be activated by tgram and will run until you log off or the $1 user logs on. At that point, the **if** command in tgram tests whether the exit status from snoopy is 0. A message is written to the $1 user, if $? is zero (this means grep found $1 in the output from who). Notice that the **if** statement is not really necessary (snoopy always returns zero, since it continues running until $1 logs on). Also notice that tgram is not robust (the precondition tells us this!).

In the following sections we use these design techniques to develop procedures for solving the list of problems given in Section 5.1.

5.3 DELETING FILES

A simple

```
$ rm SomeFile
```

can be used to delete SomeFile. It is common to have many files to delete at the end of a Unix session. So it would be handy to solve the following problem:

PROBLEM
Automate deleting files, starting with the most recent files, display each filename and make it possible to pick the files to delete.

We can solve this problem as follows:

1. input: directory listed in time-order
2. display each filename
3. input: choice (**y** to rm, **n** to ignore, **q** to break)
4. check chosen file to avoid attempting to delete a subdirectory
5. repeat steps 2 through 4

We can use the command substitution 'ls -t' to set the position parameters for a del command. Then we can use "$@" in a **for** loop to pick the filenames to display. Here is a first attempt to solve this problem:

■ PROCEDURE 3A

```
$ cat >del
#
# automate file deletion
# 'precondition: file names

for i in "$@"
   do
      echo '    ' $i '? \c'
      read choice
      case $choice in
         y*|Y*) # ckfile  (scaffolding--hidden procedure
                #           to check if $i is a directory)
                # if $i is not a directory, then
                    rm $i;;
         n*|N*) ;;           # do nothing
         q*|Q*) break
      esac
   done
echo
ctrl-d
$
```

This del procedure depends on the use of command lines like the following ones:

```
$ del SomeFile                                # for one file
    SomeFile ? q
$ del copy1 copy2 copy3 bin
    copy1 ? n
    copy2 ? y
    copy3 ? y
    bin ? y                                   mistake!
rm: bin directory
$
```

CHAPTER 5 / PROCEDURE DESIGN

An attempt to delete $HOME/bin caused an error message and del was interrupted (we get the shell prompt $ back). This says del is not robust. The precondition for del tells us del is not robust in another way: $i must be a filename (del does not check for that). We can use the hidden ckfile to handle both of these problems. If we use command substitution with del, we can supply del with a complete list of filenames as follows:

```
$ del `ls -t`
    del ? n
    copy1 ? y              copy1 is deleted
    copy2 ? q              break
$
```

This is awkward, making del difficult to use. An alternative way to accomplish the same thing is to embed 'ls -t' inside del. So the **for** loop in del would have the following form:

```
for name in `ls -t`
    do .......
```

Now we can activate del simply by typing

```
$ del
```

which is easier to do. We still need to take care of the problem of making sure $name is not a directory name (we can develop the hidden ckfile procedure to take care of this). The ckfile procedure should have the following features:

1. input: $1
2. check file type of $1 (use set 'file $1')
3. use exit to return an exit status corresponding to a file type

Recall how the **file** command works. The output from **file** has the following syntax:

```
            file-name: file-type
```

So, for example, we can type

```
$ file snoopy
snoopy: commands text
$
```

In the ckfile procedure we will use, the fact that the second field in the output from **file** specifies the file types. You can see this by typing

```
$ set `file snoopy`
$ echo $2
commands
$
```

Finally, recall that the **exit** command has the following syntax:

```
$ exit <number>
```

We use this fact to give $? a value meaningful to us (and to del, for example). These features are implemented in the following procedure:

■ PROCEDURE 4

```
$ cat >ckfile
# check for empty directory
# precondition: $1 must be a file name
# postconditions:
# exit status = 0 signals a non-empty subdirectory
# exit status = 1 signals an empty subdirectory
# exit status = 2 signals a non-subdirectory file
# exit status = 3 signals some other kind of file
old=$1                          # protect $1 from set command
set `file $1`                   # check file type = $2
case $2 in
   ascii|commands|English) exit 2; ;
   directory) set `ls -1 $old`              # is $2 empty?
           case $2 in
               0) exit 1;;                   # $2 is empty
               *) exit 0                     # $2 is non-empty
             esac; ;
   *) exit 3
esac
```

The sole purpose in the life of this ckfile procedure is to give $? a meaningful value. Notice that ckfile uses the fact that

```
ls -1 <directory-name>
```

prints a list which begins with

```
total <number> .................................
```

So

```
set `ls -1 $old`
```

assigns the number of files in the $old directory to $2. Procedure 4 (ckfile) can be run by itself to see how it works. Try the following experiment:

☐ EXPERIMENT 3

```
$ chmod +x ckfile                   # make ckfile executable
$ ckfile snoopy; echo ?
2
$ ckfile bin; echo $?
0
$ ckfile /bin/grep; echo $?
3
$
```

Using stepwise refinement, we can replace the scaffolding in Procedure 3a with ckfile:

■ PROCEDURE 3B (AFTER ED SESSION)

```
$ cat del
# delete selected files
# precondition: none
# postcondition: changed directory

for name in `ls -t`
   do
      echo $name '? \c'                # display file name
      read choice
      case $choice in
         y*|*) ckfile $name            # check file type
                  case $? in
                     2) rm $name;;
                     *) echo 'rm not permissible'
                  esac;;
         n*|N*) ;;                     # do nothing
         q*|Q*) break                  # exit from loop
      esac
   done
echo
```

These changes make del more robust. Ckfile actually does more than is needed by del. For example, del does not need to know if $name identifies an empty directory. This feature of ckfile will be useful later when we develop a procedure to bundle software to mail. You can see how Procedure 3b (the new del) works by trying the following experiment:

☐ **EXPERIMENT 4**

```
$ del
        del    ? n
        ckfile ? n
        bin  ? y                    wrong choice!
rm not permissible
        tgram? q
$
```

Notice that del is easier to use now. We no longer have to type

```
$ ls `ls -t`
```

Notice also how del catches our attempt to delete $HOME/bin (previously this choice would have caused del to be interrupted and to stop running). Now del catches the wrong choice (a **y** to delete $HOME/bin), prints an error message, and continues running—it is more robust. Procedure 3b can be refined further. We can make del useful by adding the following features:

1. make

```
$ del                   # no arguments
```

   the default case (the current directory is scanned by del—this is Procedure 3b)
2. permit, for example,

```
$ del ./bin             # select directory to scan
```

   so that we can select the directory to weed out unwanted files

Notice that if we add this second feature to del, we also must cope with a new robustness problem: an argument list for del must be

1. Empty or
2. contain a directory name (this must be checked!).

It will be necessary to run a careful check of the argument list for del each time to ensure robustness. These added capabilities for del are left for future work.

The solution to the problem of zapping (killing) unwanted processes is similar to the one used in del.

5.4 ZAPPING UNWANTED PROCESSES

If the PID (process id number) is known for a process, then we can remove a process by typing

```
$ kill <PID>
```

The ps command can be used to determine the PIDs for running processes. It would be handy to have a zap command in $HOME/bin to automate killing unwanted processes. Here is a preliminary solution to this problem (outline of a plan):

■ PROCEDURE 5A

```
$ cat >zap
#
# zap processes using PID's found by some means
# precondition: none
# postcondition: some processes may have been zapped

echo 'menu:'
echo '----> y) to zap process;'
echo '----> n) to continue listing PIDs;'
echo '----> q) to quit.'
echo; echo; echo 'current processes: '; echo; ps -f
#
# scaffolding:
#              pick PIDs to zap
#
sleep 10                                  # bookkeeping time
echo 'remaining processes:'
ps -f
```

This zap procedure depends on a hidden pick procedure to take care of

1. getting each PID
2. soliciting choice
3. acting on choice

We can develop a pick procedure in stages, starting with picking a PID to display. This can be done using a here document in the following way:

■ PROCEDURE 6A

```
$ cat >pick
#
# pick out PIDs
#
grep -v 'PID' >temp <<!
uid=`ps -f`
!
```

```
#
# scaffolding:
#              selecting PIDs in temp to display
ctrl-d
$
```

The **-v** grep option says "print all input lines not matching the pattern." Notice that the output from ps -f contains PID in the heading:

```
$ ps -f
    UID  PID  PPID  C    STIME      TTY   TIME  COMMAND
    you  182     1  0  10:32:57      02   0:07  -sh
    you  344   182 37  12:16:14      02   0:04  ps -f
```

The current version of pick (Procedure 6a) uses

```
grep -v 'PID' >temp <<!....
```

to ignore the heading produced by ps -f and put the remaining lines from ps -f (contained in UID in the here document) into a temp file. Now we need to replace the scaffolding in pick with apparatus to "cut" out the PIDs to display. This can be done with the following **for** loop:

```
for process in `cut -c10-13 temp`
    do ....
```

This **for** loop uses the fact that the PID occupies columns 10 through 13 in each line printed by ps -f. This gives us a new version of pick:

■ PROCEDURE 6B (AFTER AN ED SESSION)

```
$ cat pick
#
# zap unwanted processes
# precondition: none
# postcondition: possibly fewer running processes

ps -f                              # display current processes
grep -v 'PID' >temp <<!
uid=`ps -f`
!
for process in `cut -c10-13 temp`
   do
      echo '     ' $ process '? \c'    # display PID
      read choice; echo
```

```
      case $choice in
        y*|Y*) kill $process;;
        n*|N*)  ;;                    # do nothing
        q*|Q*) break;;
        *) echo 'usage: y|n|q'
      esac
   done
rm temp
$
```

This pick procedure is busy. It lists the PIDs one at a time, giving us a chance to select an action. Now we use pick to remove the scaffolding in zap (Procedure 5a) as shown in the following procedure:

■ PROCEDURE 5B (AFTER ED SESSION)

```
$ cat zap
#
# zap processes using pid's found by pick
# precondition: none
# postcondition: some processes may have been zapped

echo 'menu:'
echo '----> y) to zap process;'
echo '----> n) to continue listing PIDs;'
echo '----> q) to quit.'
echo; echo; echo 'current processes:'; echo; ps -f
pick                          # instead of scaffolding
sleep 10                      # bookkeeping time
echo 'remaining processes:'
ps -f
$
```

The command

```
sleep 10
```

gives Unix time to update its process list before we attempt to run ps -f again. To see how this new version of zap works, try the following experiment:

□ EXPERIMENT 5

```
$ snoopy susu &               # start process
7967                          # start process
$ snoopy nwirth &
8001
```

ZAPPING UNWANTED PROCESSES **197**

```
$ zap                                    # run zap
   menu:
   ----> y) to zap process;
   ----> n) to continue listing PIDs;
   ----> q) to quit.

   current processes:

UID   PID    PPID   C    STIME    TTY   TIME   COMMAND
you    34       1   0  10:32:57   02    0:00   -sh
you  7967      34   0  14:06:10   02    0:00   [ sh snoopy ]
you  7979    7967   0  14:06:14   02    0:00   sleep 600
you  8001      34   0  14:06:19   02    0:00   [ sh snoopy ]
you  8009    8001   0  14:06:23   02    0:00   sleep 600
          .
          .
          .
      34 ? n
    7967 ? y
    7979 ? q
<new process table will be printed after 10 second
wait>
$
```

Refinements of zap are possible.

5.5 REFINEMENT: ADDING OPTIONS TO zap

The new zap procedure introduced in Section 5.4 can be improved by letting users select the ps option used by pick:

---

ps options (a selection):
- **-e:** print information about all processes
- **-d:** print information about all processes except process group leaders
- **-f:** generate full listing
- **-l:** generate long listing

This would mean zap would activate pick with an argument (form of ps output list to use). This would be the list displayed by pick *before* the "picking" starts. The pick procedure can be improved by displaying the process name (instead of PID) and using the corresponding PID (saved somewhere) to kill an unwanted process. This would make zap easier to use. Otherwise we have to keep cross-referencing the PID (printed by pick) with the process table printed by ps. These improvements are left for exercises.

There are many procedures that can be developed to manage directories.

5.6 SCANNING DIRECTORIES

When directories become massive, then it is helpful to have commands like the following ones:

Directory Scanners

COMMAND	ACTION
dirt	list all files for a given date
ds	list all subdirectory names of a directory
dira	list all subdirectories of a given directory
dirs	list all files since a given date
dirz	list all empty files

In the following sections we develop the dirt, ds, and dira commands shown in the above table, starting with ds. The remaining two scanners are left for exercises.

5.6.1 Scanning a Directory for Subdirectories

We can scan a directory for its subdirectories by piping the output from ls -l to grep in the following way:

■ PROCEDURE 7A

```
$ cat >ds
# list subdirectories of a directory
# precondition: none

ls -l | grep '^d'
ctrl-d
```

Then

```
$ sh ds
```

will display all subdirectory names in the current directory. This ds command can be made more versatile by making a listing of the current directory as a default condition and allowing for the possibility of entering the name of a directory to scan. This is done as follows:

■ PROCEDURE 7B (AFTER AN ED SESSION)

```
$ cat ds
# list subdirectories of a directory
```

```
# precondition: either empty argument list or the name
#               of a directory to scan

case $# in
  0) ls -l | grep '^d';;
  1) ls -l $1 | grep '^d';;
  *) echo 'usage: ds [directory-name]'
esac
$
```

The new ds command is not robust. It will fail if it is activated with an argument which is not the name of a directory. You can remedy this problem by using the ckfile procedure (this is Procedure 4 in Section 5.3) in

```
1) ckfile $1
```

in the **case** command in Procedure 7b. The technique used in ds can be used to solve the problem of listing dated directory entries.

5.6.2 Scanning Directories for Dated Entries

To isolate and print a list of directory entries with a given date, we can use the following technique:

■ PROCEDURE 8A

```
$ cat >dirt
# list files created (or changed) on a given date
# precondition: $1 must be month and day

ls -l | grep "$1"
ctrl-d
$
```

This version of dirt will work if we use the following technique:

```
$ dirt "Feb 16"
-rwxr-xr-x  1  you  unix    640 Feb 16 10:56 ckfile
-rwxr-xr--  1  you  unix    291 Feb 16 11:14 del
       .
       .
       .
```

In this sample run, dirt displays all the files dated Feb 16. This works fine as long we remember to type a command line in this special way (the month and date inside double quotes). Why not let dirt do this work for us? Let dirt group the month and day together for us. This can be done using the following procedure:

■ PROCEDURE 8B (AFTER AN ED SESSION)

```
$ cat dirt
# list all files created (or changed) after a given date
# preconditions: $1 must give month
#                $2 must give day

ls -l | grep "$1 $2"
$
```

Now we can run dirt using

```
$ dirt Feb 16
```

There is still a hidden problem with dirt. The ls -l command lists days like Feb 9 (with two spaces) differently than it lists days like Feb 16 (with one space). To see this, type

```
$ ls -l
-rwxr--r--   2   you   unix     64 Feb  1 09:17 trial
-rw-r--r--   1   you   unix   6146 Jan 29 11:36 unixref

                              source of problem
```

We can take care of this problem by having dirt inspect the size of $2 each time. That is, try the procedure that follows:

■ PROCEDURE 8C (AFTER AN ED SESSION)

```
$ cat dirt
# list all files created or changed after a given date
# preconditions: $1 must give month
#                $2 must give day

case $2 in
  [1-9] ls -l | grep "$1  $2";;    # with 2 spaces!
  *)    ls -l | grep "$1 $2"       # with 1 space
esac
$
```

There are many reasons why dirt is not robust:

1. no check is made on the correctness of $1 and $2
2. no check is made on the number of arguments (two are necessary)
3. no check is made on the size of $2, if the entered day is greater than 9 (what if 31 is entered for a month like February?)

Making dirt robust is left for future work. Next, we develop a dira command to scan all subdirectories of a given directory.

5.6.3 Scanning All Subdirectories of a Directory

The problem of listing all subdirectories of a given directory was partially solved with Procedure 11 (the original sd command) in Section 4.9. We are in a position now to make the earlier sd command more robust by using the new ckfile command from Section 5.3. Here is a new version of the sd command:

■ PROCEDURE 9 (AFTER AN ED SESSION)

```
$ cat sd
# list subdirectories of a given directory
# precondition: $1 is a directory name
# postcondition: listing of $1 & its subdirectories

echo $1; ls -lt $1
for name in $1/*
   do
      ckfile $name            # check for non-empty dir
      case $? in
        0) set `ls -l $name`  # reset positional param's
           sd $name;;         # recursive call
        *)                    # do nothing
      esac
   done
$
```

Unlike in the old version of sd (in Section 4.9), we now use the ckfile command to guarantee that (1) $name is a directory name (checked by the old sd) *and* (2) if $name is a directory name, then this directory must be non-empty.

The precondition given in the new sd procedure points to a problem: sd will fail, if either no argument is given or a wrong argument is given. If we type

```
$ sd ./susu
```

and "susu" is not a subdirectory name, sd will fail. The sd command will also fail if we type

```
$ sd                          # no argument!
```

The recursive method used in the sd procedure can also be used to develop extensions of the Hewett and Gosling method of bundling software.

5.7 HEWETT AND GOSLING METHOD OF BUNDLING SOFTWARE

Kernighan and Pike (1984) give credit to Alan Hewett and James Gosling for inventing the following method of grouping files together into a single file:

■ PROCEDURE 10A

```
$ cat >bundle
# Hewett and Gosling method: using recursion, bundle
# designated files into a single distribution file.
# precondition: arguments are file names
# postcondition: here documents attached to cat >$name

for name
   do
       echo "cat >$name <<!"
       cat $name
       echo "!"
   done
ctrl-d
$
```

When bundle is run, the expression

```
cat >$name <<!
```

is written to a destination file (notice that this is the beginning of a here document). Then, the text for a here document is built when

```
cat $name
```

is executed, which writes the contents of the $name file to the designated file. Finally, echo "!" writes the exclamation point (!) to the designated file (this closes the here document which has been built inside the designated file). To use this version of bundle, these steps must be followed:

1. Run bundle with

```
$ bundle [file [file] ] >[destination file]
```

This collects copies of the designated files into a single destination file. Then

2. execute the destination file to "unbundle" the texts of the original files into separate files by repeatedly using

```
cat >$name <<!
<text from old file>
!
```

If pkg is the name of a file containing the output from bundle, then you can unbundle pkg by typing

```
$ sh pkg
```

To see how bundle works, try the following experiment:

☐ EXPERIMENT 6

```
1  $ bun tgram dirt >lib/pkg     # bundle files in lib
2  $ cd lib
3  $ cat pkg                     # show bundled files
4  cat >gram <<!
5  # send a message to a user who logs on
6
7  snoopy $1
8  write $1 <message
9  !
10 cat >dirt <<!
11 # list files created (or changed) on a given date
12
13 case $2 in
14    [1-9]) ls -l | grep "$1     $2";;
15    *) ls -l | grep "$1 $2"
16 esac
17 !                                              $ unbundle pkg
18 $ sh pkg
19 $
```

When you type

```
$ sh pkg
```

the here documents in pkg will be fed to corresponding files created by redirecting the output from cat (the shell runs cat repeatedly when you sh the pkg file). In Experiment 6, lines 4 and 10 show the places where cat is used to send the lines of a here document to a named file (first tgram, then dirt).

Can you see why bundle is not robust? No check is made to see if the entered arguments are names of regular files. The bundle command does not check if $#$ is zero (nothing happens in this case). Finally, since no check is made if a regular file is empty, time may be wasted writing empty here documents for empty regular files. A modified version of ckfile (from Section 5.3, Procedure 4) could be used to take care of this third problem.

CHALLENGE (problem 1):
Make bundle robust.

This version of bundle is limited to collecting together files designated in a command line like

```
$ bundle snoopy tgram >pkg
```

which puts snoopy and tgram into here documents inside the pkg file. Using the recursive techniques used earlier in the sd ("search directory") procedure in Section 5.6.3, we can put together a recursive version of bundle.

5.7.1 Bundling Software Recursively

The aim of this section is to develop a solution to the following problem:

PROBLEM:
Collect all files in a given directory and all of its subdirectories into a single distribution package, which can be unbundled using the Hewett and Gosling method.

Even slight changes in the sd procedure in Section 5.6.3 will give us a new version of bundle which will solve this problem in an elegant way. Here is a procedure to do this:

■ PROCEDURE 10B (AFTER AN ED SESSION WITH 10A)

```
$ cat bundle
# Extension of the Hewett and Gosling method of bundling
# software using recursion
# precondition: none (redirection to pkg is advised)
# postcondition: collection of here documents output
#                to designated file (screen, by default)

beginning=$pwd                     # to get back to .
cd $1
for name in *
   do
      ckfile $name                 # robustness feature
      case $? in
         0) bundle $name;;         # non-empty directory
         1) ;;                     # do nothing
         2) echo "cat >$name <<!"  # bundle $name
            cat $name
            echo "!";;
         *)                        # do nothing
      esac
   done
cd $beginning                      # to original directory
$
```

You now have the capability of bundling together all files in a designated directory *and* all of its subdirectories. Notice that once inside the **for** loop of this new version of bundle, the following things occur:

1. ckfile checks the $name file type
2. depending on the exit status of ckfile, the next action is chosen (with the **case** command):

2.1 bundle calls itself, if ckfile finds a non-empty directory of the given directory (exit status = 0)
2.2 do nothing, if ckfile finds an empty directory
2.3 add here document for $name, if ckfile finds that $name is a regular file

Notice that ckfile does not check if $name is non-empty, if $name is regular file (this is a future refinement of ckfile). To run this new version of bundle, try the following technique:

```
$ bundle lib | tee lib/pkg
```

In this way, what goes into lib/pkg will also be printed on your screen. In some ways, bundle is almost too powerful. If you type

```
$ bundle $HOME | tee $HOME/pkg
```

then *all* of your files in $HOME and all of your subdirectories will be bundled in $HOME/pkg. Unless you intend to send someone every file you own or you want a quick way to archive all of your files, you will probably want to use bundle more conservatively. You might want to try the following steps:

1. set up a maildrop subdirectory
2. use maildrop to store files to be bundled later
3. run bundle on maildrop

Once you have bundled files in some pkg file, you send these to a friend using

```
$ mail friend <pkg
```

To see how this new version of bundle works, try the following experiment:

☐ EXPERIMENT 7

```
$ pwd                           # show current directory
/usr/you
$ mkdir maildrop
$ cat >maildrop/joyce
echo 'riverrun, from swerve of shore to bend of bay...'
ctrl-d
$ cp tgram maildrop
$ mkdir maildrop/pearls
$ cat >maildrop/pearls/amadeus
echo 'tralala...tralala...tweedledee...tweedledum...'
ctrl-d
```

Now use bundle to package software

```
$ bundle maildrop | tee maildrop/pkg
cat >joyce <<!
echo 'riverrun, from swerve of shore to bend of bay...'
!
cat>amadeus <<!
echo 'tralala...tralala...tweedledee...tweedledum...'
!
cat >tgram <<!
# send a message to a user who logs on

snoopy $1
write $1 <message
!
$ pwd                       # check final directory
/usr/you
```

Notice how the amadeus file in maildrop/pearls gets bundled before bundling continues in the original maildrop directory with

```
cat >amadeus <<!
echo 'tralala...tralala...tweedledee...tweedledum...'
!
```

(It is the boldface part **cat >amadeus** which comes into play when the pkg file is unbundled [executed].) Even though bundle has moved back and forth through the target directory and its subdirectories, we still end up in the original /usr/you directory. To unbundle pkg, type

```
$ sh pkg         # this should not be done in maildrop
```

If you sh pkg inside the maildrop directory, you will overwrite the original maildrop files with copies of the originals (a waste of time!) and copies of the files from each of the subdirectories of maildrop (amadeus in maildrop/pearls, for example). It would be better to see how this unbundling works by executing pkg in your $HOME directory, for example.

This new version of bundle has a major weakness: it does not restore files in pkg to their original subdirectories. So, for instance, if you mail pkg to a friend, an

```
$ sh pkg
```

will not create a pearls subdirectory for the amadeus file.

5.72 Unbundling into Subdirectories

With a slight modification to the bundle procedure (Procedure 10b), we can build into the bundled software a provision for "unbundling" files into their original subdirectories. Here is a procedure to do this:

■ PROCEDURE 10C (AFTER AN ED SESSION)

```
$ cat bundle
# Extension of Hewett and Gosling bundling method
# precondition: $1 must be a directory name
# postcondition: bundled files

beginning=$pwd; cd $beginning; cd $1
for item in *
  do
     name=$1/$item
     echo "echo $name 1>&2"           # to see unbundling
     ckfile $item
     case $? in
        0) echo "mkdir" $name          # key new step!
           bundle $name;;              # recursive call
        1) ;;                          # do nothing
        2) echo "cat >$name <<!"       # bundle
           cat $item                   # cat $item
           echo "!";;
        *)                             # do nothing
     esac
 done
cd $beginning
$
```

It is necessary to unbundle a pkg file built by this new version of bundle in your $HOME directory. Otherwise, the references to directories in pkg (the bundled file) will get jumbled. It is best to experiment with bundle to see how it works, which is really quite astounding. Try Experiment 8:

□ EXPERIMENT 8

```
$ bundle maildrop | tee $HOME/pkg
echo maildrop/joyce 1>&2
cat >maildrop/joyce <<!
echo 'riverrun, from swerve of shore to bend of bay...'
!
echo maildrop/pearls 1>&2
mkdir maildrop/pearls
```

```
echo maildrop/pearls/amadeus 1>&2
cat >maildrop/pearls/amadeus <<!
echo 'tralala...tralala..tweedledee...tweedledum...'
!
echo maildrop/tgram 1>&2
cat >maildrop/tgram <<!
# send a message to a user who logs on

snoopy $1
write $1 <message
!
$
```

The boldfaced part of Experiment 8 indicates a mkdir command line which has been put into the pkg file. This time when we execute (with sh) the pkg file, the command

```
mkdir maildrop/pearls
```

will be run to set up the pearls subdirectory. This is followed by the line

```
cat >maildrop/pearls/amadeus <<!
```

which copies the here document to the amadeus file in the pearls subdirectory.

This new version of bundle is not robust (it will be necessary to check for the following things):

1. possibility of zero arguments
2. attempt to run bundle with a non-directory name
3. attempt to bundle an empty $name file

In addition, it would be helpful to add scaffolding to bundle to show what happens when bundle is run (use pwd, for example, to print the working directory name after cd is run each time).

CHALLENGE (problem 2):
Add scaffolding to bundle to show what happens when this procedure is executed.

To experiment with this new version of bundle in your own account, try setting up dummy directories like $HOME/maildrop and $HOME/mail/pearls. Then, put some sample (dummy) files into these new directories. Type

```
$ bundle maildrop | tee $HOME pkg
```

Before you try unbundling pkg in your own account, remove the maildrop and maildrop/pearls directories. Then unbundle pkg by typing

```
$ sh pkg
```

which will recreate the original maildrop and maildrop/pearls directories.

5.8 OTHER SCANNERS

There are many useful scanners you may want to consider putting into your $HOME/bin directory. Here are some sample scanners:

Some General-purpose Scanners

SCANNER	ACTION(S) BY SCANNER
cksp	check spelling in a text
gred	single case version of grep
mole	months left (from entered month to end of year)
0	phone directory assistance (find entry or entries)
scanf	scan directory for files with current date
xref	cross-reference commands with procedures
uxref	cross-reference Unix commands with definitions

To put together a spelling checker, we will need to use some new commands.

5.8.1 A Spelling Checker

Most Unix systems have a /usr/dict/words file, which we will use to solve the following problem:

> **PROBLEM:**
> Scan a given text and print out all words not found in /usr/dict/words.

We can solve this problem by doing the following things:

1. Eliminate all punctuation marks and put words in text in a column; to do this, try

   ```
   tr -cs "[A-Z][a-z]" "[\012*]" <text
   ```

2. Since all words in /usr/dict/words are not in lower case (the online dictionary includes proper names like Aaron and acronyms like AAA) and assuming we are only interested in checking the spelling of words other than proper names and acronyms, we can employ **tr** to replace upper case

letters (words that begin a sentence, for example) in a target text with corresponding lower case letters; this can be done as follows:

```
tr "[A-Z]" "[a-z]" <text
```

3. Use **sort** to put the words in your text in order.
4. Use **uniq** to eliminate duplicate words.
5. Use the **comm** command to select words not common to two files; this can be done by using

```
comm -23 input /usr/dict/words
```

Before we try putting these steps together, we will experiment a bit with some of these commands to see how they work in various contexts. Try the following experiment:

☐ EXPERIMENT 9

```
$ cat >message
He asked, 'Why??????????????'
$
```

Now set up a procedure which uses tr

■ PROCEDURE 11A

```
$ cat >slim1
# Eliminate duplicate entries

tr -s "[A-Z][a-z]" <$1
ctrl-d
$ #now use slim on the message file
$ #
$ sh slim1 message
He asked, 'Why?'
$
```

In Experiment 9 the duplicate ?'s do not appear in the output from tr. The original message file remains the same. Next, we want to put the words of a text into a single column. The following procedure does this:

■ PROCEDURE 11B

```
$ cat <slim2
# Put words in a text into a single column

tr -cs "[A-Z][a-z]" "[\012*]" <$1
ctrl-d
$
```

The 012 in slim2 is the ASCII code (in octal) for a linefeed (this produces a newline). The non-alphabetic characters are coverted into newlines. Here is a sample use of slim2:

```
$ sh slim2 message
He
asked
whyyyyyyyyyyyyyyyy
$
```

We can combine the technique used in slim2 with a second use of the tr command to start building a cksp ("check spelling") procedure in the following way:

```
$ sh slim2 message | tr "[A-Z]" "[a-z]"
he
asked
whyyyyyyyyyyyyyyyy
$
```

Now all capital letters (the "H" in "he," for example) will be eliminated from the output using this technique. Using this technique, the cksp procedure will have the following form:

■ PROCEDURE 12A

```
$ cat >cksp
# check spelling
# precondition: $1 is file to be scanned for misspelled words
# postcondition: suspect words (not found in /usr/dict/words)

tr -cs "[A-Z][a-z]" "[\012*]" >$1 |
tr "[A-Z]" "[a-z]" |
sort
# scaffolding:
#             eliminate duplicate words
#             compare words in $1 with those in dictionary
```

```
#          print suspect words
#
ctrl-d
$
```

If we run cksp on the message in Experiment 9, we get

```
$ sh cksp message
asked
he
whyyyyyyyyyyyyyyyyy
$
```

To finish cksp (Procedure 12a), we can use the uniq command to eliminate duplicate words. To see this, we will use cksp together with the uniq and head commands on a more elaborate message shown in the next experiment:

☐ EXPERIMENT 10

```
$ cat >message
One of the primary functions of an operating system is
providing a file storage capacity (Lampson, 1981).
ctrl-d
```

Use uniq on output from cksp

```
sh cksp message | uniq -c | head -8
1 a
1 an
1 capacity
1 file
1 function
1 is
1 lampson
2 of
```

The **head** command prints the leading lines from an input file (it will print the first ten lines, if no line count is given). For example,

```
$ head /usr/dict/words
```

will print the first ten words of your spelling dictionary. If we pipe the words coming from cksp to uniq, then to sort, then to head, we can produce a list of the most commonly used words in a text. Here is a procedure to do this:

■ PROCEDURE 13

```
$ cat >freq
# word-frequency scanner
# precondition: $1 names a message file

cksp $1 |
sort |
uniq -c |
sort -r
ctrl-d
$
```

Then freq can be used as follows:

```
$ chmod +x cksp freq                    # make files executable
$ freq message | head -5
   2 of
   1 the
   1 system
   1 storage
   1 storage
   1 providing
$
```

The -r option for sort reverses the ordered list based on the values of the first field of each line (frequency counts are sorted in reverse order by the freq command). The freq comand (Procedure 13) uses what is known as an *idiom,* which has the following form:

Idiom

FORM	EXAMPLE
sort <option(s)> <file |	sort <sample |
uniq <option(s)> |	uniq -c |
sort <option(s)>	sort -r

Idioms are commonly used in shell programming. We can use these ideas to produce a new version of cksp:

■ PROCEDURE 12B (AFTER AN ED SESSION WITH 12A)

```
$ cat cksp
# check spelling
# precondition: $1 names a message file
```

```
# postcondition: suspect words

tr -cs "[A-Z][a-z]" "[\012*]" <$1 |
tr "[A-Z]" "[a-z]" |
sort |
uniq >temp
# scaffolding:   pick out suspect words
#                print results
$
```

So, for example, this new version of cksp produces results like the following one:

☐ EXPERIMENT 11

```
$ cat <message
To the tintinnabulation that so musically wells
    From the bells, bells, bells, bells,
       Bell, bells, bells-- (Poe, 1845).
ctrl-d
```

Now use cksp on this message file

```
$ cksp message | 3
bells             from              musically
poe               so                that
the               tintinnabulation  to
wells
$
```

This experiment relies on the use of the following print procedure:

■ PROCEDURE 14

```
$ cat >3
# Use procedure name to determine how many columns to use

pr -$0 -t -l1 $*
ctrl-d
$
```

which uses $0 (the procedure name, which is 3) to specify the number of columns to print without a header (the -t option) with a page length of 1 (the -l1 option).

Finally, we need to use the **comm** command to scan the spelling dictionary and isolate words in a message not found in the dictionary. The **comm** command has the following syntax:

OTHER SCANNERS   **215**

comm [- [123]] file1 file2
    (has 3 column output:
        column 1: lines only in file1
        column 2: lines only in file2
        column 3: lines common to both files)
   - in place of file1 means standard input
   -12 prints only lines common to both files
   -23 prints only lines in first file but *not* in second file (or file2)

Obviously, comm is a very powerful command. Before we try incorporating comm into cksp (Procedure 12b), it will help to try some experimenting with this command:

☐ EXPERIMENT 12

```
$ cat >f1
Once upon a time and a very good time it was...(Joyce,
1916)
ctrl-d
$ cat >f2
...there was a moocow coming down along the
road...(Joyce).
ctrl-d
```

                     Now use comm on f1 and f2

```
$ cksp f1 >first; cksp f2 >second; comm first second
                                a
                along
and
                coming
                down
good
it
                                                joyce
                moocow
once
                road
                the
                there
time
upon
very
                                                was
```

216   CHAPTER 5 / PROCEDURE DESIGN

The words "a," "Joyce," and "was" appear in both sample files in Experiment 12. We can single out the words appearing in the first file, but not in the second file, by using

```
$ comm -23 first second | 5
and       good       it        once      time
upon      very
```

which is the list of words in the first column shown in Experiment 12. It is this second form of the comm command which we need to replace the final bit of scaffolding in cksp (or Procedure 12b):

■ PROCEDURE 12C (AFTER AN ED SESSION 12B)

```
$ cat cksp
# check spelling
# precondition: $1 names a message file
# postcondition: suspect words

tr -cs "[A-Z][a-z]" "[\012*]" <$1 |
tr "[A-Z]" "[a-z]" |
sort |
uniq >temp
comm -23 temp /usr/dict/words |
6
rm temp
$
```

This version of cksp produces an extra temp file, which is used by the comm command. However, also notice that we can use the dash (-) with the comm command to specify that comm uses its standard input instead of filel (or temp in Procedure 12c). If we use this feature of comm, we can simplify cksp as follows:

■ PROCEDURE 12D (AFTER AN ED SESSION)

```
$ cat cksp
# check spelling
# precondition: $1 names a message file
# postcondition: suspect words are printed in 6 columns

tr -cs "[A-Z][a-z]" "[\012*]" <$1 |
tr "[A-Z]" "[a-z]" |
sort |
uniq |
comm -23 - /usr/dict/words |
6
$
```

You can expect this version of cksp to produce a result like the following one on the quote from Lampson in Experiment 10:

```
$ cksp message
a            functions     lampson      operating     providing
```

Finally, notice that cksp still is not complete because it is not robust (the precondition tells us this). A check should be made of $1 to make sure it names a regular file. There is a second potential problem with cksp: the printed words may not fit in six columns (the words from Poe's "Bells," for example, must be printed in no more than three columns by pr). Also notice that /usr/dict/words may not be a good measure of the spelling correctness of your letters, messages, and so on. It would be good to build a personalized version of the /usr/dict/words file, putting into this file the specialized words you use.

5.8.2 Gred, a Single-result Greplike Command

If we use ed and a here document, we can produce the following greplike command:

■ PROCEDURE 15

```
$ cat >gred
# search for a single line containing a pattern
# precondition: $1 is a search pattern
#               $2 names a file to be searched

ed $2 <<!
/$/
1
.=
q
!
ctrl-d
$
```

If gred finds a line matching the pattern ($1), it will print that line *and* the line number of the printed line. Here is a sample use of gred:

☐ EXPERIMENT 13

```
$ head -50 /usr/dict/words >temp; gred 'ate$' temp
305
```

```
abate
25
$
```

In other words, "abate" is the 25th word in our version of /usr/dict/words *and* it is the first word which ends with the "ate" (the $ at the end of "ate$" tells ed to match the pattern with the end of a line). Try using patterns like '^ abe', for example, to see what turns up in your version of the spelling dictionary. We used head to strip off part of this dictionary, since the whole dictionary is too big for ed (roughly 25,000 lines). Try experimenting with head to test the upper limits of your version of ed.

5.8.3 Using cal to Print a Partial Calendar

The cal command has the following syntax:

---

cal [month] year
Note: cal prints a calendar for a given year (for a single month, if the month is specified, which must be a number between 1 and 12). Cal has no options. The year can be between 1 and 9999.

For example, try typing

```
$ cal 9 1752
   September 1752
S   M Tu  W Th  F   S
         1  2 14 15 16
17 18 19 20 21 22 23
24 25 26 27 28 29 30
```

It is also possible to type

```
$ cal September 1752
```

which produces the same result. The cal command will print out a calendar for an entire year, if you type, for example,

```
$ cal 1752
```

which is an interesting calendar year because of the month of September. It would be handy if we had a command to print out the remaining months from a given month to the end of a given year. The following procedure stub suggests how to do this:

■ PROCEDURE 16

```
$ cat >mole
# print months left in year
# preconditions: $1 identifies a month
#                $2 identifies a year

case $1 in
   jan*|Jan*) mo=1;;
   feb*|Feb*) mo=2;;
   mar*|Mar*) mo=3;;
   apr*|Apr*) mo=4;;
   may*|May)  mo=5;;
   jun*|Jun*) mo=6;;
   jul*|Jul*) mo=7;;
   aug*|Aug*) mo=8;;
   sep*|Sep*) mo=9;;
   oct*|Oct*) mo=10;;
   nov*|Nov*) mo=11;;
   dec*|Dec*) mo=12
esac
# scaffolding: use $mo to control how many months
#              are printed
ctrl-d
$
```

Before we worry about the obvious robustness problems with this version of the mole command, we need to devise some means of advancing an entered value of the mo variable repeatedly until it is greater than twelve. Sounds like a job for the expr command! We can use the following technique to do this:

```
until [ $mo -gt 12 ]
  do
     cal $mo $2
     mo=`expr $mo + 1`
  done
```

We leave it for an exercise to replace the scaffolding in mole with this **until** loop and to make mole robust. If this is done, you should find that you can get results like the following one:

```
$ mole Nov 2001
    November 2001
S   M Tu  W Th  F  S
               1  2  3
4   5  6  7  8  9 10
11 12 13 14 15 16 17
18 19 20 21 22 23 24
25 26 27 28 29 30
```

```
    December 2001
S   M  Tu  W  Th  F   S
                      1
2   3  4   5  6   7   8
9  10  11 12 13  14  15
16 17  18 19 20  21  22
23 24  25 26 27  28  29
30 31
```

Later, you will see that many variations of mole are possible using the awk programming techniques given in Chapter 7.

5.8.4 A Phone Directory Scanner

A command named 0 (after "dial 0 for operator") is another useful tool to add to your $HOME/bin directory. This is really a specialized use of the grep command in terms of a particular phone directory file set up somewhere convenient in your directory system (try $HOME/lib/phonebk, for example). Here is a sample phonebk file:

```
$ cat >$HOME/lib/phonebk
Peterson, J.L. 2310 El Camino Blvd., S.C., CA (408) 986-2000
Baggins, B. down under hill, unlisted
Dijkstra, E.W. Santa Clara, CA (408) 986-7133
Langman, S. Englewood Cliffs, NJ (201) 551-4413
Yes, O. Mankato, MN (507) 345-2221
Holt, R.C. Newton, MA (617) 964-4353
```

The trick now is to put together a procedure designed to search through just this phonebk file as follows:

■ PROCEDURE 17

```
$ cat >0
# phone directory service
# precondition: $1 specifies a pattern
grep $1 $HOME/lib/phonebk
```

Now you can use 0 in all sorts of ways to ferret out information from your on-line phonebk file. For example, you can list all entries with a 408 area code by typing

```
$ sh 0 408
Peterson, J.L. 2310 El Camino Blvd., S.C., CA (408) 986-2000
Dijkstra, E.W. Santa Clara, CA (408) 986-7133
```

It is left for future work to improve 0, to make it robust. We can also use grep to pick out the files in a directory with the current date.

5.8.5 Another Directory Scanner

We can use

```
$ set `date`; echo $2 ' ' $3
Feb     23
```

to initialize the positional parameters. Notice that $2 will be assigned the current month; $3, the current day. Then we can use the following technique to list files with the current date in your current directory:

■ PROCEDURE 18

```
$ cat >tidy
# use tidy ("today's directory") to list today's files

set `date`
ls -lt . | grep "$2 $3"
ctrl-d
$
```

Now try typing

```
$ sh tidy
-rwxr-xr-x  1 you    unix       373 Feb 23 13:44 mole
-rw-r--r--  1 you    unix       385 Feb 23 12:56 temp
-rw-r--r--  1 you    unix        78 Feb 23 12:44 message
```

For reasons mentioned earlier (in Section 5.6.2), tidy is not robust. Notice that tidy will not work if the current date has a day between one and nine (there will be two spaces between the month and day in the directory listing produced by ls -lt). In addition, you might consider generalizing tidy so that by default (without an argument) tidy prints today's files for your current directory. Otherwise, if you enter a directory name, tidy would scan that directory for files with the current date. Finally, if you make tidy recursive (like sd, in Procedure 9 in Section 5.6.3), you can get a complete list of files with the current date.

5.9 OTHER FILES FOR YOUR $HOME/bin DIRECTORY

The ap and exec commands from Chapter 4 should probably be added to your $HOME/bin directory. We have refrained from using these commands until now in this chapter to avoid any ambiguity and to make clear what was being done. I have found the ap and exec commands to be the most commonly used ones in my bin directory.

You may also want to set up some specialized commands to handle various printing problems. A pl ("print line") command should prove useful:

■ PROCEDURE 19

```
$ cat >pl
# print line of dots

for dot in 1 2 3 4 5 6 7
   do
      echo '..........\c'
   done
echo
ctrl-d
$
```

The pl command is fast enough to be useful. For example, type

```
$ echo; pl ; echo '      Tunis behaves like Unix'; pl
```

```
.......................................................
                Tunis behaves like Unix
.......................................................
```

The pl command would be useful in setting up table headings. Variations of the pl command are possible. It could be refined so that the default is a line of 70 dots. Otherwise, a numeric argument could be used to specify a multiple of five dots (the desired echo command could be selected with a case statement). The idea is to avoid doing any arithmetic inside the pl command procedure, which would make pl unacceptably slow.

It would also be helpful to have a center command like the following one:

■ PROCEDURE 20

```
$ cat >center
# center cursor or printhead

                                                    \c'
echo '
ctrl-d
$
```

Then, for instance, you can type

```
$ echo; pl; center; echo 'Tunis and Unix'; pl
```

```
.......................................................
                 Tunis and Unix
.......................................................
```

The simplicity of the center command suggests leaving it as is. You might want to create an indent command to handle various multiples of seven spaces to indent before printing. This is left for an exercise.

We have been piling up quite a few new commands. It helps to set up a special personal commands file together with a special-purpose xref command to cross-reference new commands with standard Unix commands.

5.10 CROSS-REFERENCING NEW COMMANDS

Here is a sample cross-reference file of new commands in your $HOME/lib directory:

```
$ cat >$HOME/lib/cref
snoopy case ls grep if until echo sleep
tgram if write <
del for $@ echo read case ckfile break
pick for cut grep ps echo read case break kill rm
ckfile set case exit `ls -l`
zap echo ps pick sleep
ds case $# ls grep echo
dirt case grep ls
ctrl-d
$
```

Next it would be helpful to keep this file sorted. We can do this with

```
$ sort $HOME/lib/cref
ckfile set case exit `ls -l`
del for $@ echo read case ckfile break
     .
     .
     .
```

Then we can put together a special-purpose scanner for this file using the following procedure:

■ PROCEDURE 21

```
$ cat >xref
# print lines of cref matching a specified pattern
# precondition: $1 is a pattern

sort $HOME/lib/cref | grep $1
ctrl-d
$
```

Then xref can be used to list all lines that match an entered pattern. Try typing

```
$ echo; pl; center; echo "xref'd commands"; pl; xref
ckfile
............................................................
xref'd commands
............................................................
del for $@ echo read case ckfile break
ckfile set case exit `ls -l`
```

In developing new command procedures, you may find (as I have) that having easy access to paradigms is helpful. In this context, a *paradigm* is an example which shows how you have used commands in earlier procedures. It is easy to forget all the twists and turns taken earlier when designing new procedures. It does not take much time to add lines to your $HOME/cref file after a working session. Later, quick reference to files having commands you have used before can serve as a source of new ideas. Finally, a file like $HOME/cref offers a good workshop for practice use of the sort command. We will return to this idea later in the text.

5.11 SUMMARY

Software engineering is concerned with processes used to develop software. In this chapter, we have suggested how the following software engineering methods can be used to develop new command procedures:

1. Scaffolding: various extra products (suggestive comments, stubs, test-data generators, for example) used to further the development of a procedure.
2. Preconditions: assertions about necessary input.
3. Postconditions: assertions about necessary output.
4. Other assertions: claims about program segments.
5. Test data: data used to test procedure performance.
6. Stepwise refinements: fleshing out a procedure step-by-step (with added commands in the case of shell procedures).

A procedure does not have to be long or complex to be useful. A simple procedure like snoopy has the simplicity of a Mozart composition and yet is remarkably powerful. Sometimes a new command procedure just involves saving typing. The xref procedure in Section 5.10 or the 0 phonebook procedure illustrates this idea. The xref command saves our typing, for example,

```
$ sort $HOME/lib/cref | grep 'ckfile'
```

We can now do the same thing with

```
$ xref ckfile
```

Often, designing a new procedure means narrowing the use of a familiar command. A scanner like dirt in Section 5.6.2 offers an illustration of this idea. With dirt, we have narrowed and specialized the use of the ls command to allow us to inspect a part of a directory (all files with a given date). A simple command like dirt can prove surprisingly useful when it is easier to remember the day we worked but not the files we built for that day.

Ultimately, it is your $HOME/bin directory which you should be using to keep commonly used commands. This gives you another way to tailor your working environment.

5.12 REVIEW OF COMMANDS, SYMBOLS, AND KEYWORDS

This section reviews the commands, symbols, and keywords introduced in this chapter.

5.12.1 Commands

COMMAND	ACTION
cal	prints all or part of calendar
comm	compare files
comm -23 × y	prints lines in x which are not in y
comm -23 - y	prints lines in standard input which are not in y
echo "cat >$name <<!"	output is a command line (used by the Hewett and Gosling bundling method)
grep -v expr file	finds and prints all lines in file which do *not* match the expr-pattern
head file	prints first ten lines of file
head -8 file	prints first eight lines of a file
ps -f	long form of process table
set 'date'	initialize positional parameters with date
set 'ls -lt'	initialize positional parameters with output from ls -lt
sort file	sorts file based on the leading field of each line of a file
sort -r file	sorts file in reverse order
tr -s "[a-z]" file	squeezes file, eliminating duplicate lowercase letters of file
uniq file	eliminates duplicate lines of file
uniq -c	eliminates duplicate lines of file and appends a count of the number of occurrences of each line
write	used to communicate a message on-line

5.12.2 Symbols

SYMBOL	USAGE
.=	ed command to print line number of current line
i	ed insert command
$?	exit status
\ /	escape usual meaning of / (see Section 5.2.5 for an example with ed)

5.12.3 Keywords

KEYWORD(S)	EXPLANATION
assertions	claims about actions performed by a procedure
bundling	putting files into a distribution file
distribution file	collection of files which is unable to be bundled
idiom	uniq bracketed by sort command
invariant assertion	claim about procedure relation which does not vary (typically part of a loop)
postcondition	result of running a command
precondition	assertion about input to a procedure
robustness	resistance to failure as a result of bad input
scaffolding	extra products used to develop software
scanner	procedure used to search through a file for lines that match a pattern
software life cycle	typical stages in software development: 1. specify problem/requirements 2. design solution 3. code/debug 4. test/validate 5. maintenance/modify/revalidate
stepwise refinement	isolate key segments (reducible to procedures) in developing software
stub	empty software component
test data	input data used to test correctness of a procedure
unbundling	using sh on a distribution file

5.13 EXERCISES

1. Modify snoopy (Procedure 1b in Section 5.2.5) so that it automatically runs in the background. Using your own name, give a sample run.
2. Add to the list of postconditions for snoopy from Exercise 1.
3. Fix snoopy from Exercise 2 so that
   a. by default, sleep 60 will be used if $# equals 1. Otherwise,
   b. sleep $2 second, provided $# is 2. Give a sample run.
4. Make snoopy from Exercise 3 robust by assuring that when $# is 2, $2 is in the interval from min to max (use min = 5 and max = 600 to test this new version of snoopy). Give a sample run with bad data like "ten seconds" for $2.
5. Give the complete ed session used to make the changes in Exercises 1 to 4. Use 1,$p to list the modified snoopy file after each major change is made.
6. Modify tgram (Procedure 2b in Section 2.5.6) so that it automatically runs in the background. Give a listing and a sample run.
7. Add to ckfile (Procedure 4 in Section 5.3) a provision for checking if a regular file is non-empty (return an exit status of 2, if it is non-empty; 4, if it is an empty regular file). Imitate Experiment 3 in testing this new version of ckfile. Give sample runs.
8. Modify del (Procedure 3b in Section 5.2.6) so that it takes into account the new ckfile command from Exercise 7. A file should be removed if ckfile returns an exit status of either 2 or 4. Give a sample run.

9. Modify del from Exercise 8 so that ckfile is used to print only the names of regular files for possible removal. In other words, a filename should not be displayed if it is not the name of a regular file. Give a sample run.
   Note: this will mean ckfile will have to be moved from where it is in Procedure 3b to a new position.
10. Carry out the refinement of zap (Procedure 5b in Section 5.4) described in Section 5.5. Give sample runs.
11. Write a dirs directory scanner procedure to list all files since a given date. The dirs command should have the following syntax:

    usage: dirs [date] [directory-name]

    If you type

    ```
    $ dirs
    ```

    the current date and current directory should be used by dirs. (The current date and directory name are optional arguments.) If only the date is used as in

    ```
    $ dirs Feb 5
    ```

    then by default the current directory should be scanned. It should also be possible to select both the date and directory to scan using dirs. Give a sample run.
    Hint: use the IFS shell variable to do this:
12. Give preconditions and postconditions for dirs in Exercise 11. Add comments to dirs to indicate these conditions.
13. Make dirs from Exercise 11 robust. Give a sample run.
14. Write a dirz directory scanner procedure to list all empty files in a given directory. The dirz command should have the following syntax:

    usage: dirz [directory name]

    If we type

    ```
    $ dirz
    ```

    then by default the current directory should be scanned for empty files (including directories). It should be possible to specify the directory to scan as in

    ```
    $ dirz bin
    ```

    The dirz command should have output taken from ls -lt. Give sample runs for both cases.
15. Make ds (Procedure 7b in Section 5.6.1) robust. Give a sample run.
16. Make dirt (Procedure 8c in Section 5.6.2) robust in terms of the list of problems given at the end of Section 5.6.2. Give sample runs.
17. Make sd (Procedure 9 in Section 5.6.3) robust. Give some sample runs.
18. Solve Challenge problem 1 in Section 5.7. Give sample runs.

19. Modify bundle (Procedure 10b in Section 5.7.1) so that only non-empty regular files are bundled.
20. Solve Challenge problem 2 in Section 5.7.2. Give sample runs.
21. Write a uxref cross-reference procedure which cross-references Unix commands with definitions in terms of entered search patterns. The uxref procedure has the following syntax:

    usage: uxref pattern
    Construct a ucref file with entries like the following one:

COMMAND	EXPLANATION
du	summarize disk usage
echo	echo arguments
ed	text editor
file	determine file type
find	find files

    The xref command should allow the user to type a list of all ucref lines that match an entered pattern. Give some sample runs.

22. Write a slim procedure that replaces all multiple spaces with single spaces, and which has the following syntax:

    usage: slim file

    Give a sample run on a sample message file with the following entry:

    ```
    $ cat >message
    Anticipatory documentation and scaffolding tend to have
    two major economic         implications for        the
    software life cycle:
       1. They reduce overall costs...
       2. They tend   to  front-load the software manpower
          distribution.
    --B.W. Boehm, 1984.
    ctrl-d
    ```

23. Add to slim from Exercise 22 the capability of specifying the number of spaces to reduce to a single space (double spaces to single spaces, all triple spaces to a single space, and so on). Give a sample run using the message file from Exercise 22.
24. Write a rev (for "reverse") command procedure that reverses each line of input. The rev command has the following syntax:

    usage: rev file

    Here is a sample use of rev:

```
$ cat >list
fold
song
someone
tintinnabulation
along
gold
riverrun
ctrl-d
$ rev <list
dlof
gnos
enoemos
noitalubannitnit
gnola
dlog
nurrevir
$
```

25. (Kernighan-Mashey Rhyming Dictionary Problem)
    Write a rhyme command that takes a list of words as input and produces a rdict ("rhyming dictionary") file. Give a sample run using the list file from Exercise 24.
    Hint: sort the output from the rev command from Exercise 24.

26. Write a tally command procedure that takes a list of words and produces an ordered list in terms of the count of the number of times each word appears in the original list. The ordered list should be printed in ascending order. The tally command has the following syntax:

    usage: tally file

    Experiment with tally using the following file:

    ```
    $ cat >script
    The pounding of the cylinders increased: ta pocketa
    pocketa pocketa pocketa pocketa. The Commodore stared
    at the ice forming on the pilot window. He walked over
    and twisted a complicated set of dials. "Switch on No.
    8 auxiliary!" he shouted.  "Switch on No. 8 auxiliary!"
    repeated Lieutenant Berg.  (James Thurber, 1939)
    ctrl-d
    $
    ```

    Hint: use sort -n in an idiom.

27. Modify tally in Exercise 26 so that it has the following syntax:

    usage: tally -[ad] file

    Fix tally so that it is possible to select either a sorted list of words with tallies in either ascending (the -a option) or descending (the -d option) order. If we type

```
$ tally file
```

the default should be the -a option. Give a sample run using the script file from Exercise 26.

28. Make cksp (Procedure 12d in Section 5.8.1) robust. See the list of suggestions for doing this at the end of Section 5.8.1. Give sample runs.
29. Using gred (Procedure 15 in Section 5.8.2), experiment with your version of ed to see how much of /usr/dict/words can be handled by gred at one time using the technique shown in Experiment 13.
30. (A bit of history) Explain the output from

```
$ cal 9 1752
```

31. (Refinement) Complete mole (Procedure 16 in Section 5.8.3) so that it has the following syntax:

    usage: mole [month] [year]

    In other words, mole should print as follows.

    a. the remaining months of the year are printed, if we type

    ```
    $ mole
    ```

    b. the calendar for the months from an entered month to the end of the current year if we type a command line like

    ```
    $ mole Feb
    ```

    c. the calendar for the months from an entered month to the end of an entered year if we type a command line like

    ```
    $ mole Oct 2001
    ```

    Give sample runs.

32. (Robustness) Make mole from Exercise 31 robust by allowing months to be typed as numbers (1-12) as well as forms like jan or Jan or january or January. Give a sample run.
33. (Robustness) Make 0 (Procedure 17 in Section 5.8.4) robust. Give a sample run.
34. (Robustness) Make tidy (Procedure 18 in Section 5.8.5) robust.
35. (Refinement) Modify tidy from Exercise 34 so that it has the following syntax:

    usage: tidy [directory name]

    In other words, tidy should

    a. by default, give the files with the current date in your current directory if you type

    ```
    $ tidy
    ```

b. give the files with the current date in a designated directory, if you type

```
$ tidy <directory-name>
```

Give some sample runs.

36. (Refinement) Use recursion in tidy from Exercise 35 so that tidy prints all files with the current date in all of your directories if you type

```
$ tidy -a
```

In other words, give tidy the following syntax:

usage: tidy − [a] [directory-name]

37. Write an indent command procedure which indents in multiples of seven and has the following syntax:

usage: indent [1 <= number <= 7]

The indent command should
a. by default, indent seven spaces if we type

```
$ indent
```

b. a multiple of seven spaces if we type a line like

```
$ indent 2
```

Combine the use of indent with sample echo commands to show how indent works.

38. (Refinement) Using the pl command (and possibly center) from Section 5.9 and indent from Exercise 37, modify xref (Procedure 21 from Section 5.10) so that it prints a table of the form:

Cross-referenced Commands

| COMMAND | RELATED COMMANDS |

Use the cref file in Section 5.10 to demonstrate the use of xref.

39. (Refinement) Modify xref from Exercise 38 so that it has the following syntax:

usage: xref -[clm] [pattern] [file]

-c lists distinct command and number of times each command appears in cref as in
  2 ckfile
  3 case
  3 for
  3 until
  7 echo

232 CHAPTER 5 / PROCEDURE DESIGN

-l appends to list of command lines found the least frequently used command and number of times command appears in file as in

```
2 ckfile
```

-m appends to list of command lines found the most frequently used command and number of times command appears in file as in

```
7 echo
```

Notice that if no filename is used, then $HOME/lib/cref is used by default. The new xref command should allow for

a. typing

```
$ xref -c      # to list commands and frequencies
```

b. typing

```
$ xref -l      # lists least frequently used command
```

c. typing

```
$ xref -m      # lists most frequently used command
```

d. typing

```
$ xref -cl     # list plus command with lowest freq.
```

e. typing

```
$ xref -cm     # list plus command with most freq.
```

f. typing

```
$ xref -clm    # combined output
```

g. typing

```
$ xref pattern file
```

h. typing any of the above options with pattern and file as in

```
$ xref -lm pattern file
```

Give sample runs of the new xref using the cref file from Section 5.10.

40. Give pre- and postconditions for xref in Exercise 39.
41. Make xref in Exercise 39 robust.

5.14 REVIEW QUIZ

Indicate whether the following statements are true or false.

1. A postcondition is an assertion concerning procedure input.
2. A procedure with preconditions is always robust.
3. The following yes procedure is an example of a stub:

```
$ cat yes
# yes does nothing
$
```

4. Scaffolding can be added to any user-defined command procedure.
5. Your PATH need not include $HOME/bin to make it possible to run commands in $HOME/bin from your $HOME directory or any of its subdirectories.

Questions 6 through 8 refer to the following procedure:

```
$ cat >do
# print entered name centered between two lines

pl                              # print line of dots
center                          # center cursor
echo $1                         # print name
pl                              # print line of dots
```

6. The do command is robust.
7. If you type

```
$ do Bilboe Baggins
```

then

```
..........................................................
                      Bilboe Baggins
..........................................................
```

will be printed.

8. We would be using stepwise refinement, if we added a provision for **do** to print the current date as part of the heading it prints.
9. The cal command prints a full calendar if you type

```
$ cal
```

10. A scanner is a procedure which typically scans the lines of a file for lines which match a specified pattern.

5.15 FURTHER READING

Boehm, B. W. Software Life Cycle Factors in Vick, C. R., and C. V. Ramamoorthy. Handbook of Software Engineering. New York: Van Nostrand, 1984. See p. 501 on scaffolding.

Joyce, J. Portrait of an Artist as a Young Man. New York: Viking Press, 1916.

Kernighan, B. W., and J. R. Mashey. The Unix Programming Environment in IEEE Selected Reprints in Software. Los Angeles, CA: IEEE Computer Society, 1982. See p. 259 for the rhyming dictionary problem.

Kernighan, B. W., and R. Pike. The Unix Programming Environment. Englewood Cliffs: Prentice, 1984. Section 3.9, pp. 97–99 gives the Hewett and Gosling bundling algorithm. Section 3.5 introduces James Duff's pick program.

Lampson, B. W. Ethernet, Pup and Violet found in Lampson, B. W., M. Paul, and H. J. Siegert. Distributed Systems: Architecture and Implementation. New York: Springer-Verlag, 1981.

Mullender, S. and A. Tanenbaum. A Distributed File Service Based on Optimistic Concurrency Control. ACM Operating Systems Review, vol. 19, no. 5 (December, 1985), pp. 51–63.

Pike, R., and B. W. Kernighan. Program Design in the Unix Environment. AT&T Bell Laboratories Technical Journal, vol. 63, no. 8, part 2 (October, 1984), 1595–605. See Section II for discussion of the **cat** command.

Poe, E. A., "The Bells" in The Works of Edgar Allan Poe. New York: Plymouth, 1929.

Vick, C. R. Introduction: A Software Engineering Environment in Vick, C. R., and C. V. Ramamoorthy. Handbook of Software Engineering. New York: Van Nostrand, 1984. See Section 4 for an overview of software engineering.

6 Filters and Stream Editing

[The stream editor] is convenient because it will handle arbitrarily long inputs, because it is fast, and because it is so similar to ed.
—*Kernighan and Pike, 1984.*

6.0 AIMS

- Introduce filters
- Explore various ways to use members of the grep family
- Introduce stream editing
- Catalog and illustrate various stream editor functions
- Show various ways to construct regular expressions
- Illustrate the use of extended regular expressions by **egrep**
- Show various **sed** equivalents of command lines which use **grep** and **egrep**
- Suggest a solution to the Kernighan-Mashey rhyming dictionary problem
- Suggest how the stream editor can be used to play Lewis Carroll's game of doublets
- Suggest other applications of the stream editor

6.1 INTRODUCTION TO FILTERS AND STREAM EDITING

A *filter* is a procedure which copies its standard input with processing to its standard output. In so doing, a filter reads each line from its input stream, performs zero or more operations on each input line, possibly transforms some of its input lines, and then writes them to its standard output. The tr, uniq, and sort members of the grep family and sed (for "stream editor") commands are examples of filters. The familiar

```
$ grep pattern file
```

illustrates the use of grep to filter its input file and write to its output lines matching a pattern. For example, we can filter the /usr/dict/words file using the following technique:

```
$ grep '^appl' /usr/dict/words | 5
applaud      applause     apple         applejack    appliance
applicable   applicant    application   applied      applique
apply
```

The grep command is an example of a pattern matching filter. In fact, grep gets its name from its pattern matching capability; "grep" stands for "global regular expression print." The grep family of pattern matching filters also includes the **egrep** and **fgrep** commands (the grep command is the oldest of these three filters).

The **egrep** command is more powerful than grep; it accepts a broader range of regular expressions which can either be part of a command line or be taken from a file. For example, **egrep** has an **or** (|) operator, which makes it possible to inspect a given input line in terms of more than one pattern. We can use this idea to write a more powerful version of snoopy as follows:

■ PROCEDURE 1A

```
$ cat snoopy                        # after an ed session
# see who's logged on

case $    in
  2) until who | egrep "$1|$2"      # choice of names
        do
             sleep 600              # sleep 10 minutes
        done;;
  *) echo 'usage: snoopy name1 name2'
esac
$
```

Now you can type

```
$ snoopy susu nwirth &
8679
$
```

to scan the output from who to see whether either of two people is logged on. The

fgrep command works with patterns that are fixed strings that can be taken from a file. For example, we can set up the following name file:

```
$ cat >persons
nadams
mrochkind
pbernstein
tgibbons
jgseiler
ctrl-d
$
```

Now we can modify snoopy so that it uses the names in this persons file to scan the output list from who as follows:

■ PROCEDURE 1B

```
$ cat snoopy                              # after an ed session
                                          # see who's logged on
case $                                    # in
    0) until who | fgrep -f persons       # use names in file
           do
               sleep 600                  # sleep 10 minutes
           done;;
    *) echo 'usage: snoopy'
esac
$
```

This version of snoopy is more powerful than the original one given in Chapter 5. It is also simpler to use and more versatile than the older version (including the version of snoopy which uses egrep). We merely need to edit the persons file to change one or more of the names in our "snoop" list.

The grep command was invented before sed and has enjoyed a long and fruitful life. The sed command is also a filter and is an outgrowth of the Unix editor (ed). The sed stream editor has restricted capabilities (compared with ed) but it can handle an unlimited number of input lines *and* it is fast. Typically, sed takes its input from a pipe or file, processing each line in terms of a sequence of sed commands, and copies the processed lines to its output (usually a screen). It filters the input lines taken from a pipe or file. Since ed can only handle files with limited size, this makes sed an attractive alternative in filtering large files. The stream editor is non-interactive. It also produces no change in an input file that it filters.

Since sed works with the same set of regular expressions used by ed, those who know ed find sed easier to use. For example, we can use the sed **s** (for "substitute") command to make substitutions in input lines having a matching pattern. We can use the **p** (for "print") command to print transformed input lines. Finally, we can use the **-n** sed option to restrict sed output to those input lines that have been changed. To see this, try the following show command:

■ PROCEDURE 2

```
$ cat >show
# show selected files

ls | sed -n 's/^'$1'/cat '$1'/p' | sh
ctrl-d
$
```

The expression ˆ'**$1**' identifies

1. the beginning of a name given by
2. the $1 positional argument value (this is surrounded by single quotes to prevent misinterpretation of the $ by sed)

The command

```
sed -n 's/^'$1'/cat '$1'/p'
```

says to

1. only print the transformed lines (the **-n** option)
2. substitute the beginning of an input line which matches the $1 pattern with

    ```
    cat '$1'
    ```

3. print the tranformed line (thanks to the **p** command)

The show command will allow us to inspect the contents of files with a given prefix. For instance, we can type

```
$ chmod +x show         # make show executable
$ show whoops           # see files with whoops-prefix
                        # check for correct number of arguments

case $# in
   0) ;;                # do nothing
   /) echo 'usage: whoops'
esac
   .
   .
   .
$
```

The pattern in this example is ˆ **whoops** (filenames that begin with 'whoops' like "whoops" and "whoops2"). Again, if we type

```
$ show g
```

then sed is used to select all filenames (output from ls) that have a g-prefix like "gred" and "gsub." The pattern in this case is ^ **g** (filenames which begin with 'g').

In this chapter we will bring together the various features of the grep family. In most cases, sed can be used to write the equivalent of a grep or egrep command. Some features of grep make it easier to use. The grep family also has options not available to sed. Finally, we will explore the various features of sed which make it a powerful programming tool and a remarkable useful filter.

6.2 THE GREP FAMILY

The grep command has the following syntax:

---

grep -[bchlnsvwy] RE [file...]
 RE: regular expression
 -b each line is preceding by the block number in which it is found
 -c count of matching lines is printed
 -h omit file name headers with output lines (7th edition Unix and Xenix-5, only)
 -l only names of files with matching lines are printed
 -n output lines are preceded by relative line numbers
 -s suppress error messages
 -v all but matching lines are printed
 -w search for expression as a word (4.3 BSD Unix, only)
 -y lowercase letters of pattern will match uppercase letters

---

A *regular expression* specifies a set of strings which matches a specified pattern. In effect, regular expressions specify patterns that identify various sequences of characters.

6.2.1 How to Construct Regular Expressions

A *metacharacter* is a character that has a special meaning for a command like sh or grep. Metacharacters recognized by the shell were presented in Section 4.7 (the *, |, and ; are examples). In this section we show how metacharacters can be used to construct regular expressions recognized by members of the grep family, ed and sed. Regular expressions are put together with zero or more of the following metacharacters:

Metacharacters

CHAR	EXPLANATION	REGULAR EXPRESSION
.	matches any character	C.: Cs, CS, C ,Co, CO
*	matches zero or more occurrences of preceding character	bo*k: book, boook
.*	matches zero or more occurrences of any character	s.*ng: song, something
-	any character in an interval	(see next line)
[]	matches any of enclosed characters	[a-z]: any small letter
$	end of line	t$: lines ending with t
^	1. start of line 2. null line 3. exception indicator 4. other cases: 　^[a-z] selects lines beginning with lowercase letter 　^[^a-z] selects lines beginning with uppercase letter 　^[A-Z] selects lines beginning with uppercase letter	^t: lines beginning with t ^$: empty line [^a-z] any capital letter
\	escape character	\. specifies a dot
\(RE\)\1	tagged expression (cannot be used by egrep or fgrep): 1. repeated character 2. repeated string	\(.\)\1: aa, bb, etc. \(.*\)\1: yesyes, nono

You will probably find it helpful to experiment to enter command lines which test the use of each of the metacharacters with the **grep** command. For example, you might try

```
$ grep '^[a-z]' /usr/dict/words
```

to extract all words in the online dictionary that begin with a lowercase letter.

It is possible to have a regular expression which contains no metacharacters. A single character like **t** is a regular expression that matches only itself. Regular expressions can be concatenated ("glued together"). Since a single character is a regular expression, a string like 'mm' (matches lines containing words like *summer* and *tummy*) is also a regular expression. Here are some other examples of concatenated regular expressions:

Concatenated Regular Expressions

RE	MEANING	RE	MEANING	CONCATENATED REs	MEANING
J	just J	[un]	u or n	J[un]	J, Ju, or Jun (for example, June but not junebug)
[0-9]	digit	[0-9]	digit	[0-9][0-9]	any 2 digits
^A	starting	.*e$	ends in e	^A.*e$	begins with A and ends with e

Suppose, for example, we have a file like the following one:

```
$ cat >this
This is Ju...
This is June.
This is Jn weather.
Junebugs come in May.
Yes, justly spoken.
...in the jugular...
Just pass the jello.
Julian and julienne differ.
The word julienne  refers to vegetables cut into thin
strips.
July is named after Julius Ceasar.
Try jiujitsu as well as Tae Kwon Do.
Juggernauts are idols.
```

Then if we use the first of the concatenated regular expressions in the above table, we get

```
$ grep 'J[un]' this
This is Ju...
This is June.
This is Jn weather.
Junebugs come in May.
Just pass the jello.
Julian and julienne differ.
July is named after Julius Caesar.
Juggernauts are idols.
$
```

Most of the lines in *this* file have a sequence of characters that conform to the pattern identified by J[un]. The pattern J[un] selects lines containing J, Ju, or Jun. So the line

```
Julian and julienne differ.
```

is selected because 'Julian' contains 'Ju,' whereas

```
The word julienne refers to vegetables cut into thin
strips.
```

would not be selected by 'J[un]' because 'julienne' starts with a lowercase 'j'. To select only the lines containing lowercase instances of j, ju, and jun, type

```
$ grep 'j[un]' this
Yes, justly spoken.
...in the jugular...
Julian and julienne differ.
The word julienne refers to vegetables cut into thin strips.
$
```

The third of the above examples in the table of concatenated REs has some subtle features that can be made clear by "grepping" on the lines of a sample file. To see this, try entering the following file:

```
$ cat sample
everything
something
song
Sonia sometimes sings softly.
Amos always answers amiably.
Andy is here
June
tututu
to
too
too soooooooooooooon!
$
```

To see how concatenated regular expressions work, try the following experiment:

☐ EXPERIMENT 1

```
$ grep '^A' sample              # lines beginning with A
Amos always answers amiably.
Andy is here
$ grep '.*e' sample             # lines with e
everything
something
Sonia sometimes sings softly.
Amos always answers amiably.
```

```
Andy is here
June
$ grep '.*e$' sample            # lines ending in e
June
Andy is here
$ grep '.*y\.$' sample          # lines ending in y.
Sonia sometimes sings softly.
Amos always answers amiably.
```

Now put first and last RE together

```
$ grep '^A.*y\.$' sample        # A ......... y.
Amos always answers amiably.
```

The asterisk * is called a *closure operator*. When it is appended to a single character like

```
[a-z]*
```

which matches any string with lowercase letters, such a regular expression matches zero or more occurrences of a lowercase letter. It is the longest possible string that is matched by a regular expression of the form

<character> *

Without using your machine, try determining the answers to the following Challenge problem:

> **CHALLENGE (problem 1):**
> What is printed by the following lines?
> 1. grep .* *
> 2. grep -n scan* *
> 3. grep -l robust* *
> 4. grep -l grep*

Tagged regular expressions like

```
\(Su\)\1
```

correspond to any repeated string like

```
'Su' in 'SuSu'
```

and cannot be used with egrep or fgrep. Try the following experiment with your on-line dictionary:

☐ EXPERIMENT 2

```
$ grep '[aeiou]\([aeiou]\)\1$' /usr/dict/words | 5
Hawaii      iii     marquee     Pompeii     viii
```

The tagged regular expression in Experiment 2 matches all words ending with three or more vowels (*plateau,* which is not in our dictionary, is another example). Except for tagged regular expressions, any of the above regular expressions can be used with grep. To test your insight into tagged regular expressions, try solving the following Challenge problem:

> **CHALLENGE (problem 2):**
> What is printed by grep in the following lines?
>
> ```
> $ pattern='\([aeiou][aeiou]\)\1'
> $ grep $pattern$ /usr/dict/words
> $ pattern='\([aeiou]\)\1'
> $ grep $pattern$ /usr/dict/words
> $ grep $pattern'.'$ /usr/dict/words
> ```

Finally, the '^' (up-arrow) can be used to specify any character *not* contained in a pattern. Here are some examples:

```
[^a-z]    specifies any non-lowercase letter
[^a-zA-Z] specifies characters which are not letters
[^ok]     any character which is not 'o' or 'k'
^[^Tt]    start of a line not beginning with 'T' or 't'
```

In addition, extended regular expressions can be used with egrep.

6.2.2 Extended Regular Expressions for egrep

The 'e' in egrep stands for "extended" and egrep is used for extended pattern matching. The egrep command has the following syntax:

---

egrep [option(s)] RE [file]
   RE   regular expression
   option(s) same as grep plus
   -f RE is taken from a file (**fgrep** also)

A file consisting of regular expressions (one per line) can be used by egrep to search a file for lines having a matching pattern. Try the following experiment to see this:

☐ EXPERIMENT 3

```
$ cat >match                    # build pattern file
^$
e$
y
ctrl-d
$
```

Now use match with egrep

```
$ egrep -f match sample
everything                              matches y
Sonia sometimes sings softly.           begins with S
June                                    ends in e
Andy is here                            ends in e
Amos always answers amiably.            matches y
```

Notice how egrep works in Experiment 3: egrep prints a line in the sample file if a match is found between any pattern in the match file and the current input line. The egrep command also permits the following additional regular expressions:

1. <single character regular expression> + that matches one or more occurrences of the character as in

    o+ which matches 'o' in 'to' or 'oo' in 'too'

    Try typing

    ```
    $ egrep o+ sample
    ```

2. <single character regular expression>? that matches zero or one occurrence of the single character as in

    o? which matches ' ' or 'o' in 'to'

3. the | (vertical line) can be used to specify alternative regular expressions as in

    ```
    $ egrep 'song|sing|tututu' sample
    song
    Sonia sometimes sings softly.
    tututut!
    ```

Note: A newline can be used instead of the | to separate alternative patterns as in

```
$ egrep <sample 'song
>             sing
>             tututu'
$
```

The file called *this* created in Section 6.2.1 provides a good example of how egrep at times can be superior to grep. We can use | ('or' operator) with egrep to select lines containing words beginning with J, Ju, Jun or j, ju, jun by typing

```
$ egrep 'J[un]|j[un]' this
This is Ju...
This is June.
This is June weather.
Yes, justly spoken.
      .
      .
      .
```

Notice if we want to select from the file called *this*, all lines containing words that begin with J or j, we can use

```
$ egrep 'J|j' this
```

In addition to alternative regular expressions, egrep has the following feature: parentheses ( ) can be used to form extended regular expressions. Here are some examples:

```
$ egrep 'sings (tututu|softly)' sample
Sonia sometimes sings softly.
```

The pattern

```
'sings (tututu|softly)'
```

specifies either 'sings tututut' or 'sings softly' (notice the importance of the space). If we eliminate the space in the above pattern, we specify an entirely different pattern as in

```
$ egrep 'so(o+|mething)' sample      # notice no space
something
too sooooooooooooon!
```

You can also use

```
$ egrep '(ing)+' /usr/dict/words
```

to find words like *ringing, ping*, or *thing*.

THE GREP FAMILY   **247**

The members of the grep family are not programmable whereas it is possible to program the stream editor, which is also used in pattern matching.

6.3 STREAM EDITING

The stream editor is another example of a filter. Like the members of the grep family, sed writes its input to its output. In the process, sed can be used to perform operations on its input lines. The sed command has the following syntax:

---

sed [-n] [-e script] [-f file] [file(s)]

   -n output only processed lines

   -e (optional) says what follows is a sed script containing editing commands

    -f causes script to be taken from file [files] optional input file

---

To demonstrate the features of sed, we will use the following lines from William Blake:

```
$ cat >blake
To see a world in a Grain of Sand,
And a Heaven in a wild Flower,
Hold Infinity in the palm of your hand,
And Eternity in an hour.
A Robin Redbreast in a Cage
Puts all Heaven in a Rage.
--W. Blake, Auguries of Innocence, 1789.
```

A sed script containing editing commands has the following syntax:

    [address [, address]] function [arguments]

An *address* is used by the stream editor to select lines for editing. There are several kinds of addresses: a decimal number or $ (for last input line) or regular expression (also called *context address*). That is, a sed address can be one of the following:

1. A decimal number that counts the lines of input as in

```
$ sed '2q' blake
To see the World in a Grain of Sand,
And a Heaven in a wild Flower,
```

In this example, the **q** is the sed quit function. This sed command says "copy first 2 lines of blake to output and quit." A sed address can also be

2. a **$**, which addresses the last line of input as in

```
$ sed -n '$p' blake
--W. Blake, Auguries of Innocence, 1789.
```

In this sample sed command, the **-n** says "do not copy non-addressed lines to the standard output." The **$p** addresses the last input line of blake (the **$** specifies this) and then the sed print function **p** tells sed to print the addressed line. Finally, a sed address can be

3. a regular expression, which is also called a *context address* (an input line is viewed as the context for a regular expression) as in

```
$ sed -n '/[Hh]old/p' blake
Hold Infinity in the palm of your hand.
```

This sample sed command line identifies any line containing either 'Hold' or 'hold' and the sed **p** function tells sed to print lines containing the pattern.

A sed command line can have 0, 1, or 2 addresses which is interpreted by sed as follows: (1) zero addresses tells sed to apply instructions to every input line as in

```
$ sed <blake 'w poem'
```

which uses the sed **w** ("write") function to write all lines of the blake file to the poem file *as well as* to the standard output. This sample sed command line has no addresses; (2) one address tells sed to apply command line instructions to all lines that match the given address as in

```
$ sed -n <blake 's/a/A/p'         # substitute A for a
To see A world in a Grain of Sand,
And A Heaven in a Wild Flower,
      .
      .
      .
```

where **a** is the context address used to identify lines of the blake file. The sed **s** ("substitute") function tells sed to substitute an 'A' for just the *first* occurrence of an 'a' in lines containing this letter. So, for example, sed outputs

```
To see A world in a Grain of Sand,
```

without changing the remaining three a's in this line from Blake; and (3) two addresses (separated by a comma) tells sed to apply the sed command line to the first line matching the first address *and* all subsequent lines until a line is found that matches the second address. Then the same steps are repeated until the end of the input file is reached. Here is an example:

```
$ sed -n <blake '/see/,/palm/p'          # 2 addresses
To see a world in a Grain of Sand,
And a Heaven in a wild Flower,
Hold Infinity in the palm of your hand.
```

Notice that the first printed line has a matching 'see' and the printing continues until a line containing 'palm' is found. The second printed line matches neither pattern but is printed because it is between lines containing the first and second addresses.

There are a variety of sed functions used in specifying how to process an input line.

6.3.1 Stream Editor Functions

A *function* instructs sed how to process input lines. All functions are named by a single character.

In the fourth of the above examples, notice that the second line that is inserted has a misspelling:

> Is the Artists Jealousy.

It should read

> Is the Artist's Jealousy.

This forms the basis for the following Challenge problem:

> **CHALLENGE (problem 3):**
> Devise a means of using the stream editor insertion function \i to insert the following line into the sample lines of Blake's poem:
>
> > Is the Artist's Jealousy.

In the last example in the above table, the r ("read") function reads the lines of the temp file after the line with the matched address. The w ("write") command is used in connection with the s ("substitute") function. Whenever a substitution is made, the w function writes the changed input line to a designated file. Here is another, somewhat simplified example which uses the w function:

☐ EXPERIMENT 4A

```
$ cal mar 1986 | sed -n 's/M/Mon/w /dev/tty'
     Monarch 1986
  S Mon Tu W Th F S
```

sed Functions

FUNCTION	MEANING	EXAMPLE
d	delete lines	$ sed '/^[AHP]/d' blake To see a world in a grain of Sand, --W. Blake, Auguries of Innocence, 1789.
n	next line	$ sed <blake 'n d' To see a world in a grain of Sand, Hold Infinity in the palm of your hand, A Robin Redbreast in a Cage --W. Blake, Auguries of Innocence, 1789.
a\	append lines (insert after)	$ sed <blake '/^[TAH-]/d' | > sed 'a\\ > A dove-house .... ' Puts all Heaven in a Rage. A dove-house ....
i\	insert lines (insert before)	$ sed <blake '/^[TAHP]/d' | > sed '/Blake/i\\ The poison of the Honey Bee Is the Artists Jealousy.' The poison of the Honey Bee Is the Artists Jealousy. --W. Blake, Auguries of Innocence, 1789.
c\	change lines	$ sed <blake '2q' | > sed '/^A/c\\ > And a Heaven in a ....' To see a world in a Grain of Sand, And a Heaven in a ....
p	print line	$ sed -n '/Blake/p' --W. Blake, Auguries of Innocence, 1789.
s	substitute	$ sed -n <blake 's/W\./Wm\./p' --Wm. Blake, Auguries of Innocence, 1789.
g	substitute globally	$ sed -n <blake '/^T/p' | > sed 's/a/A/g' To see A world in A GrAin of SAnd,

w	write to file	$ sed -n <blake '/^T/p' |
		> sed 's/a/A/g
		> w temp
		> '
		To see A world in a GrAin of SAnd,
		$ cat temp
		To see A world in A GrAin of SAnd,

r	read from file	$ sed '/world/r temp' blake To see a world in a Grain of Sand, To see A world in A GrAin of SAnd, :

STREAM EDITING   **251**

Multiple functions can be used in the same sed command line as in the revised version of Experiment 4a:

☐ EXPERIMENT 4B

```
$ cal Mar 1986 | sed -n 's/M/Mon/w /dev/tty
>                        s/2 /*/w /dev/tty
>                        s/ 2/**/w /dev/tty
>
       Monarch 1986
   S Mon Tu W Th F S
   *  3  4  5  6  7  8
   9 10 11 1* 13 14 15
  16 17 18 19**0 21 22
  23**4 25 26 27 28 29
```

The output from the w function in Experiment 4b goes to your terminal, since /dev/tty is the device file for your terminal. The sed command also has a **&** operator that tells sed to replace **&** with a matched pattern. Here is another version of Experiment 4 which shows this:

☐ EXPERIMENT 4C

```
$ cal Mar 1986 |
> sed '1q' |
> sed 's/M/\.&on\./p'
    .Mon.arch 1986
```

Notice how the **M** (the pattern) replaces **&** in the printed line.

The **g** function is a time-saver. To see this, we will show how to make multiple substitutions in the same input line in two different ways. A sample of the first way to do this is shown in the next experiment:

☐ EXPERIMENT 5A

```
$ date |
> sed 's/:/#/' |
> sed 's/:/#/'
Fri Feb 28 11#52#44 CST 1986
```

If there had been three colons in the input line in Experiment 5a, only two of them would have been changed to a #-sign. We can do the same thing more simply using the **g** ("global") function as in the following experiment:

☐ EXPERIMENT 5B

```
$ date |
> sed 's/:/#/g'
Sat Mar  8 12#43#05 CST 1986
```

Experiment 5b can be rewritten another way using the stream editor flow-of-control functions which are summarized in the following table:

Flow-of-control Functions

FEATURE	MEANING	EXAMPLE
!	don't do	$ sed -n <blake '/^[AHP-]/!p' To see a world in a Grain of Sand,

{	grouping	$ sed -n <blake '/\.$/ {
		> w temp
		> }
		> '
		$ cat temp
		And Eternity in an hour.
		Puts all Heaven in a Rage.

q	quit
	(after current
	line is written
	to output)
		$ sed -n <blake '/\.$/ {
		> w temp
		> q
		> }
		> '
		$ cat temp
		And Eternity in an hour.

:<label>	branch address	<see next line for example>
b<label>	branch to label	$ sed <blake ':again > s/^T/t/p > bagain > ' to see a world in a Grain of Sand, [An infinite loop results from this command line. Can you see why? Press your DEL (delete) key to exit from the loop.]
b	branch to end	$ sed -n <blake '/^[AHP]/ { > p > b > } > w temp > ' And a Heaven in a wild Flower, Hold Infinity in the palm of your hand, And Eternity in an hour. A Robin Redbreast in a Cage Puts all Heaven in a Rage

STREAM EDITING 253

Flow-of-control Functions (continued)

FEATURE	MEANING	EXAMPLE

t<label>	test &	$ cat temp
		To see a world in a Grain of Sand,
		--W. Blake, Auguries of Innocence, 1789
		$ sed -n <blake '/^[TH]/ {
		> :yes
		> s/a/A/p
		> tyes
		> q
		> }
		> '
		To see A world in a Grain of Sand,
		To see A world in A Grain of Sand,
		To see A world in A GrAin of Sand,
		To see A world in A GrAin of SAnd,

In the last of the examples in the above table, notice how the **q** function works. As long as the **t** ("test") function in **tyes** detects that a substitution has been made by the stream editor, the processor branches back to scan the same input line again for another possible substitution of 'A' in place of 'a.' Once this test performed by **tyes** fails (produces a value of false), the stream editor continues processing on the next line (the one containing the **q** function). The **q** ('quit') tells the stream editor to terminate the editing of input lines. No further lines are processed by sed.

Returning now to Experiment 5b in a whimsical way, we write its equivalent using the **t** ("test") function as follows:

☐ EXPERIMENT 5C

```
$ date |sed    ':again
>              s/:/\./
>              tagain
>              '
Sat Mar 8 14.55.12 CST 1986
```

There are also multiple-line forms of the n, d, and p functions that are useful.

6.3.2 Multiple Input-line Functions

The multiple-line forms of the n, d, and p functions are given in the following table:

Multiple-line Functions

FUNCTION	EXPLANATION
N	*appends next* input line to the current line in the pattern space (this contrasts with the **n** function, which *replaces* the current input line with the next input line).
D	*deletes* up to and including the first newline in the current pattern space (if the pattern space has no imbedded newlines, the **D** function works the same as the **d** function).
P	*prints* first part of the pattern space (this works the same as the **p** function, if the pattern has no imbedded newlines).

To see how the **N** function works, try the following experiment:

☐ EXPERIMENT 6A

```
$ sed <blake 'n
>            D'
To see a world in a Grain of Sand,
Hold Infinity in the palm of your hand,
A Robin Redbreast in a Cage
--W. Blake, Auguries of Innocence, 1789
```

Now use N instead of n

```
$ sed <blake 'N
>            D'
$
```

Since the next line is appended to the current input line by **N** in Experiment 6a, all of the input lines are deleted by **D**. To see how **d** differs from **D**, we can vary Experiment 6a as follows:

☐ EXPERIMENT 6B

```
$ sed <blake 'N
>              /^A/ {
>                    d
>                    }
>              '
To see a world in a Grain of Sand,
And a Heaven in a wild Flower,
Hold Infinity in the palm of your hand,
And Eternity in an hour.
```

STREAM EDITING 255

In Experiment 6b, pairs of input lines are appended together separated by newlines. So, for example, the **N** function appends the first two lines together:

```
To see a world in a Grain of Sand, \nAnd a Heaven
in a wild Flower,
```

Now the uppercase A in 'And' is no longer at the beginning of a line. This explains why the first two pairs of lines fail to match the pattern '/^ A/'. However, notice that the third pair of lines begins with an uppercase A, so the **d** function comes into play. The **d** function deletes everything in the pattern space whether there is an imbedded newline or not. This contrasts sharply with what happens when the **D** function is used in the following variation of Experiment 6b:

☐ EXPERIMENT 6C

```
$ sed <blake 'N
>               /^A/ {
>                    D
>                    }
>               '
To see a world in a Grain of Sand,
And a Heaven in a wild Flower,
Hold Infinity in the palm of your hand,
And Eternity in an hour.
Puts all Heaven in a Rage.
--W. Blake, Auguries of Innocence, 1789
```

Now the line

```
Puts all Heaven in a Rage
```

gets printed because the **D** function deletes that part of the pattern space *up to* the first newline (there is one imbedded newline in the pattern space between 'Cage' and 'Puts'). To test your insight into how the **d** and **D** function, try answering the following Challenge problem:

> **CHALLENGE (problem 4):**
> Why is the following line printed by Experiment 6c?
>
> ```
> --W. Blake, Auguries of Innocence, 1789
> ```

Finally, to see how the **P** function works, we can modify Experiment 6c as follows:

☐ EXPERIMENT 6D

```
$ sed -n <blake 'N
>                 /^A/ {
>                      P
>                      }
>                 '
A Robin Redbreast in a Cage
```

Notice how the **P** function used in Experiment 6d prints only the part of the pattern space (up to the first newline):

```
A Robin Redbreast in a Cage/nPuts all Heaven
in a Rage.
```

You can see this more clearly if you use **p** instead of **P** in Experiment 6d. We leave this for an exercise. Finally, the stream editor has a powerful set of "hold and get" functions.

6.3.3 Hold and Get Functions

The stream editor has a set of hold and get functions useful for setting aside input for later use. These functions are used to save and retrieve input. They are listed with examples in the following table:

Hold and Get Functions

FN	MEANING	EXAMPLE
h	hold pattern space (overwrite hold area contents)	(see illustration for g function)

g	get contents of hold area (destroys previous pattern space)	$ sed <blake '/^[TH]/h
		$ g
		
		To see a world in a Grain of Sand,
		And a Heaven in a wild Flower,
		Hold Infinity in the palm of your hand
		And Eternity in an hour.
		A Robin Readbreast in a Cage
		Puts all Heaven in a Rage.
		Hold Infinity in the palm of your hand

H	hold pattern space (appends to contents of hold area)	(see illustration for G function)

STREAM EDITING   **257**

Hold and Get Functions (continued)

FN	MEANING	EXAMPLE
G	get contents of hold area (appends to previous pattern space)	$ sed <blake '/^[TH]/H $ G To see a world in a Grain of Sand, And a Heaven in a wild Flower, Hold Infinity in the palm of your hand And Eternity in an hour. A Robin Redbreast in a Cage Puts all Heaven in a Rage. --W. Blake, Auguries of Innocence, 1789 To see a world in a Grain of Sand, Hold Infinity in the palm of your hand
x	exchange	$ sed -n <blake '/^[TH]/p' | sed 'h n x' To see a world in a Grain of Sand, To see a world in a Grain of Sand,

Obviously, these five get and hold functions are tricky to use. At times, it may be convenient to overwrite the contents of the hold area, for which the **h** function is ideal. Otherwise, you will want to use the **H** function. Here is a problem that can be solved using the hold and get functions:

Problem:
Repeatedly strip the end-letter from a word, saving the various forms of the shortened word. Do this for a list of words and print out all forms of each word.

For example, if *nighttime* is in a list of words, then it should be possible to print

```
nighttime
nighttim
nightti
nightt
night
nigh
nig
ni
n
```

The steps needed to do this can be written in pseudocode (program description) in the following way:

258 CHAPTER 6 / FILTERS AND STREAM EDITING

```
(* precondition: file of words (call it whims);
   postcondition: transformed list of words        *)
begin
   repeat
      get word from whims file;
      append word to hold area;
      repeat
         substitute null for end character;
         append transformed word to hold area
      until no further substitutions are possible
   until all words in whims have been filtered
end
```

The trick now is to interpret the steps of this algorithm using the sed get and hold functions. Here is a procedure to do this:

■ PROCEDURE 3

```
$ cat >strip
# repeatedly strip end-letters from words in a list
# precondition: list of words in a file called whims

sed <whims 'H
            :again
               s/.$//g
               H
            tagain
            $ G
          '
ctrl-d
$
```

It is possible to use the stream editor to write the equivalent of most commonly used grep family command lines.

6.4 sed EQUIVALENTS OF grep FAMILY COMMANDS

In this section we suggest various ways to write the equivalent of some grep command lines. For instance, the sed command also has a special = function used to print the line number of an output line. Here is an example:

```
$ sed -n <blake '/And/ { =
>                        p
>                        }
>                      '
```

```
2
And a Heaven in a wild Flower.
4
And Eternity in an hour.
```

Notice that this use of sed produces almost the same result as the **-n** grep option in

```
$ grep -n <blake And
2:And a Heaven in a wild Flower,
4:And Eternity in an hour.
```

By contrast, the output from the equivalent sed command appears on separate lines. We can use sed to filter the output from grep **-n** as follows:

```
$ grep -n <blake And |
>sed 's/^../line & /p'
line 2: And a Heaven in a wild Flower,
line 4: And Eternity in an hour.
```

Notice how the **&** sed operator allows us to insert into the replacement expression the pattern found:

1. s/ ../line & /p first substitutes a **2:** in place of **&** which gives the replacement 'line 2: ' (notice the spaces!)
2. s/ ../line & /p next substitutes a **4:** in place of **&** giving the new replacement expression 'line 3: '

This leads to the following Challenge problem:

> **CHALLENGE (problem 5):**
> Use only sed to produce the same results given by
>
> ```
> grep -n <file pattern
> ```

The sed command can be used to write the equivalent of most commonly used grep command lines. For example, we can write the equivalent of the | egrep operator in the following procedure:

■ PROCEDURE 4A

```
$ cat >snoopy
# see who's logged on

who | egrep -n ''$'|'$2''
ctrl-d
$
```

We can execute snoopy and guarantee at least one output line using the following technique:

```
$ sh snoopy nobody you
8:you      tty42           Mar  8 09:48
```

This says you are the eight person in the list printed by who. We can use sed to write the equivalent of Procedure 4a as follows:

■ PROCEDURE 4B

```
$ cat >snoopy
# see who's logged on

who | sed -n '/'$1'/ { =
                       p
                      }
                /'$2'/ { =
                       p
                      }
                '
ctrl-d
```

Now if we execute snoopy (Procedure 4b), you can expect a result similar to the following one:

```
$ sh snoopy nobody you
8
you        tty42           Mar  8 09:48
```

You might want to try an extension of the idea in Procedure 4b expressed in the following Challenge problem:

> **CHALLENGE (problem 6):**
> Assuming the persons file has a list of usernames, use sed to write the equivalent of the following command line:
>
> ```
> $ who | egrep -f persons
> ```

The stream editor has a variety of uses. We show some of these uses in the next few sections, starting with the rhyming dictionary problem.

6.5 THE KERNIGHAN-MASHEY RHYMING DICTIONARY PROBLEM

Kernighan and Mashey (1982) suggest the following method of constructing a rhyming dictionary:

1. develop a rev ("reverse") command to reverse the letters in a sequence of words
2. use rev as follows to build a rhyming dictionary:

```
$ rev <list | sort | rev >rhymes
```

For example, if list contains the words *gold, dust, water, mold,* and *first,* the rev and sort commands can be used to transform (filter) these words as follows:

```
                dlog           dlog           gold
                tsud           dlom           mold
rev <list -->   retaw | sort --> retaw | rev --> water
                dlom           tsrif          first
                tsrif          tsud           dust
```

We can use the stream editor to write a rev procedure. To make it easier to see how this is done, we will write the following sequence of procedures:

```
strip <list --> gold | scalp --> d | bunch --> dlog | bee -->dlog
                gol              l              dlog
                go               o
                g                g
```

Not shown in this sentence of commands is a hidden zapln command, which will be used to eliminate unwanted newlines. The strip command comes from Procedure 3 (Section 6.3.3). The scalp command will strip ("scalp") the end-letter off each input line as follows:

■ PROCEDURE 5

```
$ cat >scalp
# scalp last letter off the end of each input line

sed ':again
    /^../ s/^.//g
    tagain
    '
ctrl-d
$
```

As long as there are two or more characters on an input line, the scalp command will peel off (replace with a null) the first letter of each letter pair. So if list has only the words *gold* and *yes* in it, here is the result of using the strip and scalp commands on this list file:

```
$ scalp <list | strip
d
l
o
g

s
e
y
```

We can use the stream editor to filter the output from strip and collect the single letters on successive lines onto a single output line. Here is a bunch procedure to do this:

■ PROCEDURE 6

```
$ cat >bunch
# collect single letters on separate lines into one line
sed ':over
     /^./ N
     /\n$/ {
            p
            b
           }
     s/\n//
     tover
    '
ctrl-d
$
```

The bunch procedure used the **N** function to append successive lines (this has the effect of putting single letters together). The imbedded newlines (produced by **N**) are eliminated by

```
s/\n//
```

The bunch command prints the collected letters each time a newline is detected. Here is a sample run with strip, scalp, and bunch:

```
$ strip <list | scalp | bunch
dlog
dlog

sey
sey
```

The idea now is to eliminate the extra newlines produced in the output from bunch. We will do this with the following zapnl procedure:

■ PROCEDURE 7

```
$ cat >zapnl
# zap newlines

sed '/^$/d'
ctrl-d
$
```

If we combine the use of strip, scalp, bunch, and zapnl on the list file, we get

```
$ strip <list | scalp | bunch | zapnl
dlog
dlog
sey
sey
```

Finally, we need a procedure to eliminate duplicates in the output from zapnl. We call this the bee procedure:

■ PROCEDURE 8

```
$ cat >bee
# eliminate duplicate words

sed -n 'p
        n
        '
ctrl-d
$
```

This is handy use of the **n** function, which allows us to print alternate lines only, starting with the second line. Putting the strip, scalp, bunch, zapnl, and bee procedures together, we get the following result:

```
$ strip <list | scalp | bunch | zapnl | bee

dlog

sey
```

These separate commands (new filters) give us the ingredients for a rev command:

■ PROCEDURE 9

```
$ cat >rev
# reverse the letters in a list of words

strip <list | scalp | bunch | zapnl | bee
ctrl-d
$
```

The rev procedure can be simplified; we leave this for an exercise.
    The stream editor can be used to set up word games like the one in the next section.

6.6 LEWIS CARROLL'S GAME OF DOUBLETS

Lewis Carroll (1879) devised a game called doublets which has the following rules:

1. start with any pair of words, each with the same number of letters like *gold* and *dust*
2. link the two words together by interposing other words that differ from each other by only one letter, such as

>   gold
>   mold
>   told
>   toll
>   doll
>   dull
>   duel
>   duet
>   dust

More than one solution to a doublet is possible. For example, we can have

>   gold
>   gild
>   gilt (a young sow)
>   gist
>   gust
>   dust

The idea is to construct a doublet with the fewest number of links. We can use the stream editor to find possible links for a doublet using the following procedure:

■ PROCEDURE 10

```
$ cat >links
# find word links for Lewis Carroll's game of doublets

sed -n </usr/dict/words '/^'$1''$2''$3'$/p'
ctrl-d
$
```

This links procedure can be run in the following ways:

1. find words with fixed end-letters and varying in-between words as in

   ```
   $ sh links s .. s
   sans
   suds
   ```

   This produces a list of four-letter words that begin and end in 's.' Then we can
2. find words with a varying end-letter as in

   ```
   $ sh links d us .
   dusk
   dust
   ```

   or
3. find words with a varying first letter as in

   ```
   $ sh links . us t | 6
   bust    dust    gust    just    lust    must
   oust    rust
   ```

For links to be useful in a game of doublets, the process will have to be made more flexible. It should be combined with a decision-making procedure that can be used to select letters until (if ever) the second word in a doublet is found.

We can also use the stream editor to customize our use of the **cal** command.

6.7 FILTERING THE OUTPUT FROM cal

The stream editor can be used to solve the following problems:

1. print the remaining weeks in the current month
2. print the remaining days in the current month

6.7.1 Printing the Remaining Weeks in the Month

The stream editor can be used to filter the output from the **cal** command so that only the remaining weeks in the current month are printed. Here is a first try at writing a wleft procedure to do this:

■ PROCEDURE 11A

```
$ cat >wleft
# print remaining weeks in the current month
# precondition: output from cal
# postconditions: 1) heading from cal output
#                 2) selected weeks from cal output

set `date`
day=$3; mo=$2; yr=$6
cal $mo $yr | tee temp | sed '2q'
#
# scaffolding: select remaining weeks from temp
#
rm temp
ctrl-d
$
```

This first version of the wleft command merely prints the heading from the current month as in

```
$ sh wleft
    March 1986
S M Tu W Th F S
```

We can use a while loop to replace the scaffolding in Procedure 11a so that the following actions are repeated:

1. use the stream editor on temp to select a line in the temp file having the current $day value
2. advance the value of day to the next week and repeat step 1 while $day is less than or equal to 31

Here is a new version of wleft with the scaffolding removed:

■ PROCEDURE 11B (AFTER AN ED SESSION)

```
$ cat wleft
# print remaining weeks in the current month
```

```
set `day`
day=$3; mo=$2; yr=6
cal $mo $yr | tee temp | sed '2q'
while [ $day -le 31 ]
  do
     case $day in
        [1-9]) sed -n <temp '/ '$day'/p'; ;
        *) sed -n <temp '/ '$day'/p'
     esac
      day=`expr $day + 7`
      done
rm temp
$
```

This version works sometimes. For example, if day = 9 for March 1986, we get

```
$ sh wleft
     March 1986
 S   M  Tu   W  Th   F   S
 9  10  11  12  13  14  15
16  17  18  19  20  21  22
23  24  25  26  27  28  29
30  31
```

However, wleft does not work for values of day greater than 24. For instance, if day equals 25, then the last week of the month will not be printed. Also notice that if day = 12 for the month of March 1986, for example, then

```
March 1986
```

will be printed twice. This happens since ' 19' is part of the heading output by cal. This leads to the following Challenge problem:

> **CHALLENGE (problem 7):**
> Make wleft robust.

In other words, find a way to make wleft work for all possible days. The second of the above wleft robustness problems is solved in the next section. It turns out that we can use the stream editor to isolate the remaining days of the current month.

6.72 Filtering Out the Remaining Days of the Month

The problem of printing remaining days in the current month can be separated into two subproblems:

1. printing the heading for the current month
2. isolating the remaining days in the current month

The first problem can be solved using the same method given in Procedure 11b. However, this method has a drawback because it relies on the use of the tee command to create a temp file. This is both inefficient and slow. It would be better to rely entirely on the stream editor to solve both problems. Here is the beginning of a procedure to do this:

■ PROCEDURE 12A

```
$ cat >dleft
# print remaining days in current month
# precondition: output from cal must be filtered
# postconditions: 1) isolate heading output by cal;
#                 2) isolate remaining days output by cal.

set `date`
day=$3; mo=$2; yr=$6
cal $mo $yr | sed -n '/[JFMASOND]/ {
                                    p
                                    b
                                    }
                      '
#
# scaffolding: filter remaining lines output by cal
#
ctrl-d
$
```

This version of dleft will produce the same result as the first version of wleft (Procedure 11a) more quickly. It will also eliminate the possibility that the first line output by **cal** will be printed more than once (this can happen with Procedure 11a). Now we need to use sed to filter the remaining lines in the pipe in dleft. We can do this in two steps:

1. use spaces to mask the days in the current week prior to the current day
2. print the weeks following the current week

A second edition of dleft that solves the problem of isolating the remaining days is on the next page.

■ PROCEDURE 12B (AFTER AN ED SESSION)

```
$ cat dleft
# print remaining days in the current month

set `date`
day=$3; mo=$2; yr=$6
cal $mo $yr | sed -n '/[JFMASOND] {
                                        p
                                        b
                                        }
                        /'$day'/ {
                                :mask
                                /^ *'$day'/ {
                                                p
                                                blast
                                                }
                                        s/[0-9]/ /
                                        tmask
                                :last
                                n
                                s/^./&/p
                                tlast
                                q
                                }
                        '
$
```

In this second version of dleft, the mask loop takes care of masking unwanted days with spaces. Notice no masking occurs before the current week. Notice also that /'$day'/ identifies the line from **cal** containing the current day. Once this line is found by the stream editor, then

```
/^ *'$day'/
```

is used in a subtle way. This pattern specifies a modified output line from **cal** which has the following form:

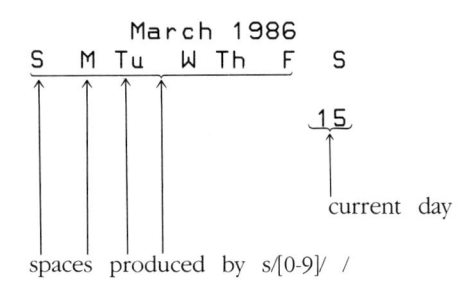

```
        March 1986
S   M   Tu  W   Th  F   S
↑   ↑   ↑   ↑   ↑
                    15
                    ↑
                    current day
|   |   |   |   |
spaces produced by s/[0-9]/ /
```

270 CHAPTER 6 / FILTERS AND STREAM EDITING

Until all the characters prior to the current day are masked by spaces, the **t** ("test") function in **tmask** continues sending the stream editor back to this line containing the current day to insert spaces into this line. Once all the columns up to the current day are filled with spaces, *then* the pattern /^ *'$day'/ (all spaces up to '$day') selects the current line for processing by

```
{
  p
  blast
}
```

The **b** ("branch") function in **blast** sends the stream editor to the section of this procedure labeled by **last.** Then the last loop takes care of printing the remaining weeks after the current week. The dleft command is incredibly fast. It demonstrates the admirable efficiency of the stream editor. The dleft command is also a good one to add to your .profile. You might want to try extending the dleft command so that it prints the remaining days in the current year instead of just the current month.

If you are using Ultrix-11, the dleft command procedure will have to be modified:

Caveat:
Ultrix-11 is a Unix look-alike from DEC (Digital Equipment Corporation) for its 16-bit PDP-11 machines. The Ultrix-11 cal command requires the numeric form of a month as in

```
          cal 3 1986
```

instead of

```
          cal Mar 1986
```

To make it possible to run dleft with Ultrix, a case statement like the following one should be added to dleft:

```
case $mo in
   Jan) mo=1; ;
   Feb) mo=2; ;
      .
      .
      .
esac
```

6.8 SUMMARY

A *filter* copies its input (with possible processing) to its output. For example,

```
$ sed -n 'p' blake
```

merely copies its standard input to its standard output, thanks to the **p** ("print") command. Members of the grep family and the stream editor are examples of filters.

The grep ("global regular expression print") was developed before the stream editor. Almost all forms of grep can be written using the stream editor. Because of its senior status in the Unix commands repertoire *and* because grep is often easier to use then sed, grep continues to be widely used in Unix programming. Both members of the grep family and the stream editor depend on the use of regular expressions.

A *regular expression* specifies a pattern used to identify a set of strings. For example, a single character like 't' is a regular expression that identifies all strings containing this letter. Regular expressions are typically constructed using what are known as metacharacters. A *metacharacter* is a character that has special meaning for the shell or for a filter like the stream editor. The metacharacter '.', for instance, represents any single character. Then the regular expression

```
't..n'
```

identifies words like *teen* or *then*.

The stream editor is extremely powerful because of its versatility and speed. Unlike members of the grep family, the stream editor is programmable. It has its own extensive set of control functions, which makes it possible to select and iterate actions performed by the stream editor. Unfortunately, procedures written with the stream editor tend to be cryptic, making them difficult to read. It takes considerable patience *and* practice to learn to use sed.

6.9 REVIEW OF COMMANDS, SYMBOLS, AND KEYWORDS

This section reviews the commands, symbols, and keywords introduced in this chapter.

6.9.1 Commands

COMMAND	ACTION
cal	prints calendar
egrep	extended global regular expression print
fgrep	fixed strings used to filter input
grep	global regular expression print
sed	stream editor

6.9.2 Symbols

SYMBOL	USAGE
RE	regular expression
^RE	identifies RE at beginning of line
[^RE]	identifies all strings not containing the RE inside the square brackets
^[^RE]	identifies all strings at the beginning of a line which do not match the RE inside the square brackets
*	closure operator
't*n'	identifies words like *teen* or *between*
'[th]*'	identifies words like *too* or *through*
[ ]	matches exactly *one* of the enclosed characters
[th]	matches 't' or 'h'
/dev/tty	identifies your terminal
( )	grouping symbols used to construct extended regular expressions for **egrep**
|	alternation operator used to construct an extended regular expression for **egrep**

6.9.3 Keywords

KEYWORD(S)	EXPLANATION
closure operator	*
concatenate REs	connect regular expressions
context address	regular expression
doublet	name of word game devised by Lewis Carroll
extended RE	available to **egrep**
'yes|no'	identifies 'yes or no'
'ok (yes|no)'	identifies 'ok yes' or 'ok no'
filter	copies its input to its output
function	stream editor command
whole-line:	d ("delete")
	n ("next line")
	a ("append line[s]")
	i/ ("insert line[s]")
	c/ ("change line[s]")
substitute:	s ("substitute")
	g ("global sustitution")
	p ("print line")
	w ("write to file")
input-output:	p ("print addressed lines")
	w ("write addressed lines to file, which is overwritten")
	r ("reads addressed lines and appends them after matched lines")
multiple line:	N ("next line")
	D ("delete first part of pattern space")
	P ("prints first part of pattern space") see Section 6.3.2

6.9.3 Keywords (continued)

KEYWORD(S)	EXPLANATION

hold and get:	h ("hold pattern space in hold area")
	   Note: this overwrites old hold area
	 g ("gets contents of hold area")
	   Note: this overwrites old pattern space
	 H ("append pattern space in hold area")
	 G ("appends contents of hold area to pattern space")
	 x ("interchange contents of pattern space and hold area")

flow of control:	b ("branch to end of list of editing commands") b<label> ("branch to labeled line in list of editing commands") t<label> ("test if substitution has been made by the stream editor") q ("quit stream editing") see Section 6.3.1

6.10 EXERCISES

1. Write a filter (call it nl for "number lines") which processes its input by numbering the lines it prints. Give a sample run using the blake file given in Section 6.3.
2. Give a list of filters available on your Unix system.
3. List things grep can do that sed cannot do.
4. Which of the three members of the grep family can be used in place of the other two grep commands? If you think this is not possible, then give instances that make each member of the grep family indispensable.
5. Write a command line using grep exlusively that can be used instead of
   a. egrep 'T|H' blake
   b. egrep 'a (wild|Cage)' blake

The next seven exercises refer to the following text file:

```
$ cat >sample
The initial prototype network software was done for
the PDP-11/70 computers running unix system III.
Since native mode unix system implementations are
similar, porting the network software and drivers to
the VAZ-11/780 computer was straightforward, but
making the implementation consumed months of effort
because of hardware interface problems.
--T.E. Fritz, J.E. Hefner, T.M. Raleigh, 1984.
```

6. Use sed to write a pick command that prints the last word of each line of the sample file. The new pick command will have the following syntax:

   pick filename

7. (Refinement) Modify the pick command in Exercise 6 so that it has the following syntax:

   pick -[w#] filename

with the **-w#** option that makes it possible to specify which word (according to its **#**-position) in each input line will be selected by pick. Give a sample run using
   a. pick -w2 sample # the second word of each line of sample
   b. pick -w3 sample # the third word of each line of sample

8. (Refinement) Modify the pick command in Exercise 7 so that it has the syntax

   pick -[w#] [eRE] filename

with the new **-e** option that makes it possible to select lines with matching substrings from lines of a file. This -e option will be independent of the -w option. Give a sample run with
   a. pick -e 'unix' sample # lines containing unix
   b. pick -e 'i..n' sample # lines with matching pattern

9. Use sed to write a gsub ("global substitution") command with the syntax

   gsub old-string new-string filename

so that gsub replaces each occurrence of the old-string by the new-string. Give a sample run with
   a. gsub unix Unix sample # replace 'unix' by 'Unix'
   b. gsub 'native mode' 'native-mode' sample
   Note: gsub should print only the modified lines.

10. (Refinement) Modify gsub in Exercise 9 so that it has the syntax

   gsub -[a] old-string new-string filename

with the **-a** option that allows the user to choose to have all lines of an input file printed by gsub. The new gsub command procedure should begin with a statement of pre- and post- conditions for this procedure. Give a sample run using
   a. gsub -a 'unix' 'UNIX' sample
   b. gsub -a '#' ' # ' gsub

11. Modify snoopy (Procedure 1a in Section 6.1) so that it has the syntax

   snoopy -[t] [seconds]

with the **-t** ("time") option that allows a user to specify the granularity of snoopy (how many seconds snoopy is put to sleep between checks for names in the output from who).

12. Write a Bgrep ("Berkeley grep") command with the following syntax:

   Bgrep -[bchlnsvwy] RE files

with a **-w** ("word") option present in 4.2/4.3 BSD Unix that permits the user to search for an expression as a word. This means the word *some* will not match *something* or *someone*. Give a sample run with
   a. Bgrep -w 'straight' sample
   b. Bgrep -w 'net' sample
   c. file you create that demonstrates this feature
   d. Bgrep -w 'J[un]' this # use **this** from Section 6.2.1
Note: Bgrep should have all of the other features of grep listed in Section 6.2, except possibly the **-h** option.

13. Using the blake file from Section 6.3, devise separate experiments to illustrate each of the options for grep.
14. Give a solution for each of the parts of Challenge problem 1 in Section 6.2.1.
15. Give a solution for each of the parts of Challenge problem 2 in Section 6.2.1.
16. Rewrite the following experiments using egrep:
    a. Experiment 1, Section 6.2.1
    b. Experiment 2, Section 6.2.1
17. Rewrite Experiment 3 (in Section 6.2.2) using sed. Give a sample run.

The next seven exercises refer to the following text file:

```
$ cat >thurber
There were others. Gertie Straub: big, genial, and
ruddy, a collector of pints of rye (we learned after
she was gone), who came in after two o'clock one
night from a dancing party at Buckeye Lake and
awakened us by bumping into and knocking over
furniture. "Who's down there?" called mother from
upstairs. "It's me, dearie," said Gertie, "Gertie
Straub," "What are you doing?" demanded mother.
"Dusting," said Gertie.
ctrl-d
```

18. (Refinement) Use sed to modify pick from Exercise 8 so that it has the following syntax:

    pick -[-w#] [eRE] [1#] filename

    with a new **-1** ("line") option that allows the user to select the number of lines of a file to be printed starting with the top line. Give a sample run with
    a. pick -1 3 thurber
    b. pick -1 4 thurber | pick -2
19. Use the thurber file to illustrate each of the sed functions given in the table at the beginning of Section 6.3.1.
20. Give an answer to Challenge problem 3 in Section 6.3.1.
21. Use the thurber file to illustrate the sed flow of each control function given in Section 6.3.1.
22. Use the thurber file to illustrate each of the sed multiple line functions in the table given at the beginning of Section 6.3.2.
23. Give an answer to Challenge problem 4 in Section 6.3.2. Give another example to prove your point. Use the thurber file in your illustration.
24. Use the thurber file to illustrate each of the hold and get functions given in the table at the beginning of Section 6.3.3.
25. Give an answer to Challenge problem 5 in Section 6.4.
26. Give an answer to Challenge problem 6 in Section 6.4.
27. Use sed to write a succ ("successor") command that will have the syntax

    succ character

so that for a given character, this command will find the next character (if there is one) in the ASCII scale.
Note: you should find a copy of the ascii character set in

`/usr/pub/ascii`

Give a sample run with
a. succ z

28. (Refinement) Modify the succ command from Exercise 27 so that it has the syntax

                succ - n   character

so that
a. it has a new **-n** option that can be used to specify how many successors of an entered character to find. For example,

`succ -5 Z`

will find the next five characters after 'Z' on the ascii scale.
It will print the entire printable ascii character set (from ' ' to '~') if succ is run without an argument.
Give sample runs with
a. succ -6 Z
b. succ -10 ' '
c. succ

29. (Robustness) Make the succ command in Exercise 28 robust. If the successor of an entered character does not exist, then have a wrap-around feature so that the successor is taken from the beginning of the ascii scale. For example, we would be able to obtain the following result:

```
$ succ -5 '~'
del nul ^A ^B ^C
```

Give sample runs with
a. succ -6 '~'
b. succ -10 '~'

30. Write a pred ("predecessor") command with the syntax

                pred character

so that pred finds the character immediately preceding the entered character on the ascii scale. Give sample runs with
a. pred a
b. pred A

31. (Refinement) Modify the pred command from Exercise 30 so that it has the syntax

                pred -[n] character

with a new **-n** ("next") option that permits us to select how many predecessor characters are printed. Give sample runs with
a. pred -5 A
b. pred -10 a

32. (Robustness) Make the pred command in Exercise 31 robust so that it has the following wrap-around feature: if the predecessor for a character does not exist, then it will be taken from the end of the ascii scale. This will make it possible to run pred as follows:

```
$ pred -10 '^A'
nul del ~ } | { z y x w
```

Give sample runs with
a. pred -10 'nul'
b. pred -45 '#'

33. Write an encrypt command with the syntax

    encrypt file

so that each character (except spaces) is replaced by its successor in the ascii scale. Give a sample run with
a. encrypt thurber
b. encrypt blake   # take blake from Section 6.3

34. (Refinement) Modify the encrypt command from Exercise 33 so that it has the following syntax:

    encrypt [-n] [-p] file

with the following options: **-n,** to specify the offset to use in selecting either a successor or predecessor character (for example,

```
encrypt -5 blake
```

would replace each character of blake by its fifth successor on the ascii scale), and **-p,** use predecessor to encrypt text. Notice that by default the successor of each character will be used, if the **-p** option is not used. It will be possible to type

```
encrypt -5 -p blake
```

to replace each character of the blake file with its fifth predecessor in the ascii scale. Give sample runs with the file called blake (from Exercise 18) with
a. encrypt -10 blake
b. encrypt -5 -p blake

35. (Refinement) Modify the encrypt command from Exercise 34 so that it has the syntax

    encrypt -[dnp] files

with the **-d** ("decrypt") option that allows the user to specify an encrypted file that the encrypt command will decrypt (give back the original plaintext). The encrypt command will produce the original plaintext if we use the **-d** option as well as exactly the same options that were used to encrypt the original text. Then encrypt will reverse the encryption steps used. For example,

```
$ cat sample
love
$ encrypt sample
mnwf
$ encrypt -d sample
love
```

and

```
$ encrypt -2p sample
jmtc
$ encrypt -2dp sample
love
```

It should now be possible to encrypt more than one file at once as in

```
$ encrypt blake thurber sample
```

Give sample runs with
a. encrypt -3p blake
   ncrypt -3dp blake
b. encrypt -p blake
   encrypt -dp blake
c. encrypt -5 blake
   encrypt -5d blake

36. (Robustness) Make encrypt from Exercise 35 robust to detect attempts to decrypt a directory.
37. Show ways to simplify the procedures used by the rev command in Section 6.5.
38. Give an answer to Challenge problem 7 in Section 6.7.1. Give sample runs.
39. Use sed to write a dtoday ("directory today") command with the syntax

    dtoday [directory-names]

   so that
   a. dtoday (by itself) lists the files in the current directory with the current date
   b. dtoday . (same as [a])
   c. dtoday bin (lists bin files with current date)
   d. dtoday bin lib (lists bin and lib files with current date)
   Give a sample run with
   a. dtoday
   b. dtoday bin
   c. dtoday.
40. (Robustness) Make dtoday from Exercise 39 robust to prevent possible non-directory names from being used as arguments to run this command. Give a sample run.

41. Use sed to write a btoday ("before today") command which can be used to list files without today's date. This command should have the syntax

    btoday [directory-names]

    so that
    a. btoday (by itself) list files in the current directory without today's date
    b. btoday . (same as [a])
    c. btoday bin (lists bin files without today's date
    Give sample runs with
    a. btoday
    b. btoday .
    c. btoday bin

42. (Refinement) Modify the btoday command from Exercise 41 so that it has the syntax

    btoday -[i] [date [date] [dir-names]

    with the **-i** ("interval") option that makes it possible to select a date interval for files to be listed by btoday. Then we can have
    a. btoday
    b. btoday [directory] (try btoday bin)
    c. btoday 'Feb 5' (files with Feb 5 date in .)
    d. btoday 'Feb 5' bin
    e. btoday -i 'Feb 5' 'Feb 7' (files between Feb 5 & 7 in .)
    f. btoday -i 'Feb 3' 'Mar 9' bin (files in bin dated between Feb 3 and Mar 9)
    Use a, b, and c to give sample runs.

43. (Robustness) Make btoday from Exercise 42 robust. Give a sample run using a mistaken non-directory name to run btoday.

44. (Refinement) Modify the dleft (Procedure 12b in Section 6.7.2) so that it has the syntax

    dleft -[a]

    with the new **-a** ("all") option that allows the user to list the remaining days in the current year.

45. (Refinement) Modify the dleft command from Exercise 44 so that it has the syntax

    dleft -[a] [month] [year]

    making it possible to
    a. list the remaining days from the current day until the end of the specified month as in

    ```
    $ dleft -a April      # days left until end of April
    ```

    (Note: if the current month comes *after* the specified month, the dleft should list all days from January until the end of the specified month—January to April, for example.)
    b. list the remaining days from today until end of year specified as in

    ```
    $ dleft -a Dec 2010
    ```

    Give a sample run using a and b.

46. (Robustness) Make the dleft command from Exercise 45 robust. Give sample runs with the following bad input:
    a. dleft -a thurber   # thurber is not a month!
    b. dleft -a April 10000 # year is too big for cal

6.11 REVIEW QUIZ

Indicate whether the following statements are true or false.
1. The sort command is a filter.
2. If the stream editor executes the **b** command, the editor branches to the beginning of the list of editing commands being used.
3. The stream editor **t** command tells the shell to run the time command.
4. It is not possible to used extended regular expressions with the **grep** command.
5. Tagged regular expressions cannot be used by **egrep**.
6. The alternation operator | can be used to construct regular expressions acceptable to **grep**.
7. The stream editor has no alternation operator.
8. \(.*\)\1 is an example of a tagged regular expression.
9. The stream editor can take its input from a pipe.
10. The following command line is unacceptable:

```
grep -l grep *
```

6.12 FURTHER READING

Blake, W. Auguries of Innocence in Poets of the English Language, eds.: W. H. Auden and N. H. Pearson. New York: Viking, 1950.

Carroll, L. Doublets game in T. Augarde. The Oxford Guide to Word Games. New York: Oxford University Press, 1984. See Chapter 21.

Fritz, T. E., J. E. Hefner, and T. M. Raleigh. A Network of Computers Running the Unix System. AT&T Bell Laboratories Technical Journal, vol. 63, no. 8, part 2 (October 1984), 1877–896.

Kernighan, B. W. and J. R. Mashey. The Unix Programming Environment. Selected Reprints in Software. Los Angeles: IEEE, 1982. See p. 259 for rhyming dictionary problem.

Kernighan, B. W. and P. Pike. The Unix Programming Environment. Englewood Cliffs, N. J.: Prentice, 1984. See pp. 108–14 on the stream editor.

McMahon, L. E. SED—A Non-interactive Text Editor. Unix Programmer's Manual, volume 2, New York: Holt, Rinehart and Winston, 1983. See pp. 440–50.

Thurber, J. Thurber Carnival. New York: Dell, 1945. See A Sequence of Servants.

7 awk Programming Methods

[awk] syntax is remarkably terse, even by the Trappist standards of UNIX. . . . —David Budgen, 1984.

7.0 AIMS

- Identify the structure of awk programs
- Illustrate various patterns acceptable to awk
- Call attention to special features of awk variables, arithmetic, and functions
- Show how output from an awk program can be formatted
- Identify and illustrate awk control structures
- Present ordinary as well as associative arrays
- Introduce Bentley anagram classes
- Develop and illustrate the use of a random number generator
- Show various ways that awk can interact with the shell
- Compare awk and C

7.1 INTRODUCTION TO FEATURES OF awk

The awk language is named after its inventors, Alfred Aho, Peter Weinberger, and Brian Kernighan. Its design borrows features from many sources, especially from sed, from SNOBOL4, a string-processing language developed at Bell Labs during the 1960s, and from the C language. It is not necessary to know C to program in awk but familiarity with C helps. Many features of awk syntax resemble but are subtly different from C syntax. Unlike C, the data type of a variable is determined *by awk* from the context in which a variable is used. In addition, awk syntax, especially in formatting output and its control structures, is simpler than C syntax. Because awk programs do not need to be compiled, awk offers an ideal tool for developing programs that can later be rewritten more efficiently in C or some other language.

The awk language offers a powerful text processing facility with the following features:

1. awk partitions each input line (called a record) into fields that can be processed individually. This makes it possible to extract desired parts of an input line for processing.
2. awk recognizes a variety of patterns, including the full range of regular expressions recognized by sed, Boolean conditions (like those available in C), pattern ranges, special BEGIN and END patterns which trigger actions *before* any input is processed and *after* all input lines have been processed, and combinations of patterns.
3. Arrays, including associative arrays like box["a"], box["b"], . . . , box["z"] (for a box array where each array element is associated with a letter) in awk, make it possible to restructure input data.
4. Multiple output streams from an awk program are possible (the same input can be processed and pieces of the output from an awk program can be funneled to more than one output file *or* program).
5. Thanks to a variety of control structures imported from C, various kinds of iteration and conditional selection of awk program actions are possible.
6. A variety of variables, including built-in, shell command line variables, and user-defined variables can be used in awk programs.
7. awk provides various means to communicate with the shell, including concatenation (with > and >>) of awk output to shell files and piping of awk output to shell programs.

Because of its versatility, awk has a variety of uses: report generation (printing expanded tables that include totals and various statistics derived from an input stream), data transformation (simple text transformations such as formatting a text so that each line includes a line number), and data validation (making sure the fields of each input line are correct, for example). This chapter introduces the various features of awk. In addition, it suggests some of the ways awk can be used.

7.2 STRUCTURE OF awk PROGRAMS

awk programs have the following basic forms:

1. With one or more specified patterns and an implied action. (Note: the implied action is output lines that have a matching pattern.)

```
awk '
        pattern      # single pattern
    ' filename
```

EXAMPLE
Print lines of /usr/dict/words that begin with a lowercase letter:

```
awk '
     /^[a-z]/
   ' /usr/dict/words
```

or

```
awk '
     pattern       # multiple patterns
     pattern
           .
           .
           .
     pattern
   ' filename
```

2. awk also has a basic template with a specified action to perform on an input line that matches a pattern:

```
awk '
     pattern { action }    # single action
   ' filename
```

EXAMPLE:
Exit from running program when a line ending with a lowercase 'e' is found:

```
awk '
     /[e]$/ { exit }
   ' /usr/dict/words
```

or

```
awk '
     pattern { action       # multiple actions
               action
                  .
                  .
                  .
               action }
   ' filename
```

3. Without a pattern and with one or more specified actions to perform on *each* input line:

```
awk '
       { action }
     '
```

or

```
awk '
       { action }
            .
            .
            .
       { action }
     '
```

Examples of this form of awk programs are given in Section 7.3.
4. With reference to a file containing the body of an awk program (pattern-{action} pairs). (Note: for record-keeping purposes, it is helpful to use a .awk extension on files containing awk pattern {action} pairs, but this is not necessary.)

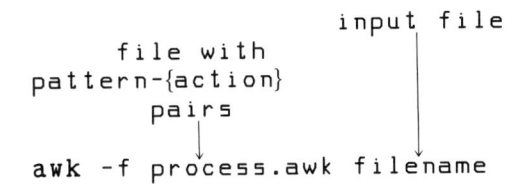

```
                        input file
      file with            |
 pattern-{action}          |
       pairs               |
         |                 |
         ↓                 ↓
awk -f process.awk filename
```

EXAMPLE:
(Note: the double vertical line || is the awk symbol for the "or" operator.) Output lines containing Unix "or" C "or" . . . using

```
$ cat process.awk /Unix/ || /C/ || /kernel/ || /shell/
$ awk -f process.awk /usr/dict/words
```

Every awk program has an implied loop of the following form:

> **while** not end of input **do begin**
> process current input line;
> get next input line
> **end**

In other words, after an awk program processes an input line, it automatically fetches the next input line (if there is one) to be processed. Ordinarily, an awk program will continue processing input lines until it reaches the end of an input file. Every awk program must specify a pattern and/or an action to perform. When an

STRUCTURE OF awk PROGRAMS   **285**

awk program has no specified actions, there is always a default action: *output input lines matching specified patterns*. Lines output by an awk program will be printed on your terminal screen if you do not specify an output file besides the standard output. It is important to notice that awk program texts have free form (you are free to choose how much to indent pattern-{action} pairs, for example). As a matter of good programming style, it is advisable to align pattern-{action} pairs that appear on separate lines of the same program.

An awk program partitions *each* input line into fields that can processed separately.

7.3 RECORDS AND FIELDS

Each input line is called a *record*. The current input line is assigned to $0. The parts of an input line separated by blanks and/or tabs are called *fields*. The first field is assigned to $1, the second to $2, and so on. The built-in awk variable $NF holds the value of the *last* field of the current input line. Also notice that the sequence $1, $2, ..., $NF contains private awk variables that should not be confused with shell variables. Here is an illustration of this idea of awk input line fields:

```
$cat samplelines
The quick brown fox jumped over the lazy dog's back.
$ awk '
>       { print $0 }
>       { print $1, $5, $NF }
>     ' samplelines
    [ output printed on screen by this program: ]
The quick brown fox jumped over the lazy dog's back.
The jumped back.
```

This awk program also illustrates two uses of the built-in **print** command, which makes it possible to print all or parts of a record. Each input line has many other built-in variables associated with it. The variable NR holds the number of the current input record. Its final value will then be the total number of input lines that have been processed. The value of the built-in awk variable NF (not to be confused with $NF) equals the number of fields of the current input line. The value of the *length* variable equals the number of characters in the current input line. Here are some sample uses of awk variables NF, NR, and length:

1. Numbering lines of printed text:

```
$ cat Asimov
    "Who--is Robbie?"
    "He's a robot, sir." She stretched to tip-toes.
Isaac Asimov, I, Robot, 1950.
$
$ awk ' { NR, " ", $0 } ' Asimov
1      "Who--is Robbie?"
```

```
    2    "He's a robot, sir." She stretched to tip-toes.
    3    Isaac Asimov, I, Robot, 1950.
$
```

2. Experimenting with $NF, NF, length, and NR:

```
$ awk ' { print NR, $NF, NF, length } ' Asimov
1 Robbie?" 2 18
2 tip-toes. 8 48
3 1950. 5 29
$
```

Length is a built-in awk function. Without an argument, length will return the number of characters in an input line. This function can also be used to obtain the length of a specified field as in

☐ EXPERIMENT 1

```
awk '
       /'ae'$/ { print NR, $1, length ($1)
     ' /usr/dict/words >temp
```

This awk program will print the lengths of all words in the on-line dictionary which end in 'ae' as well as the line number where each word occurs. Here is some sample output produced by this experiment:

```
$ head temp
94 abscissae 9
582 algae 5
715 alumnae 7
795 amoebae 7
998 antennae 8
2818 brae 4
8606 formulae 8
12396 lacunae 7
12498 larvae 6
12269 Mae 3
$
```

The awk program in Experiment 1 found 254 words ending in 'ae' in /usr/dict/words on our system.

QUIZ:
What words in /usr/dict/words would the following awk program output?

```
awk '
      /[ae]$/ { print NR, $1, length ($1) }
    ' /usr/dict/words
```

There are a variety of patterns that can be used in awk programs.

7.4 PATTERNS

Regular expressions can be used as patterns in awk programs. The methods of handling regular expressions with sed carry over in awk programming. That is, a regular expression used as a pattern in an awk program is enclosed by /. Here are some examples:

Sample Uses of Regular Expressions

awk pattern-{ action } PAIR	RESULT
/Unix/ { print $NF }	print last field of lines that contain 'Unix'
/^Unix/ { print $0 }	prints lines that begin with 'Unix'
/[Unix]$/ { print $1 }	print first field of lines that end in 'U' or 'n' or 'i' or 'x'
/Unix/ && /C/	print lines containing 'Unix' and 'C'

So far we have focused on how awk processes input lines one at a time. It is possible to specify one or more actions that are performed by an awk program *before* input lines are processed (this is done with a BEGIN pattern). It is also possible to specify one or more actions that an awk program performs *after* the last input line has been processed (an END pattern tells awk to do this "tail-end" processing).

7.4.1 BEGIN and END Patterns

To specify one or more actions for an awk program to perform before it begins processing input lines, use a BEGIN pattern in the following way:

```
awk '
      BEGIN { action
                  .
                  .
                  .
              action }
      pattern { action }
  '
```

For example, to print a heading for a report concerning selected input lines, try the following experiment:

☐ EXPERIMENT 2A

Note: assume input file called report contains lines with the following information:

PC-model   date-sold   RAM   monitor-type   fixed disk   cost

```
awk '
     BEGIN { print "model", "  date sold", "   cost"
             print "--------------------------------" }
     /XT/  { print $1, " ", $2, " ", $6 }
     /AT/  { print $1, " ", $2, " ", $6 }
     /RC/  { print $1, " ", $2, " ", $6 }
   ' report
```

Suppose, for example, that the report file has the following lines:

```
$ cat report
Jn 7.27.85 128K color none 1200
PC 7.23.85 256K mono  none 2200
PC 5.20.85 64K  mono  none 1800
AT 9.11.86 1M   color 30M  4500
PC 9.12.86 128K color none 2400
RC 1.15.87 1M   mono  30M  8200
```

Then the program in Experiment 2a would produce the following output:

MODEL	DATE SOLD	COST
AT	9.11.86	4500
RC	1.15.87	8200

In this sample report file, notice that each input line represents a computer that has been sold. For this reason, the final value of NR will represent the total number of units sold. We could add this information to the report printed by Experiment 2a using the END pattern in the following way:

☐ EXPERIMENT 2B

Note: append the following lines to the awk program in Experiment 2a.

```
awk '
         .
         .
         .
     END  { print "--------------------------------"
            print "total units sold = ", NR }
   ' report
```

A variety of conditional (or Boolean) expressions can be used as awk patterns.

7.4.2 Conditionals

Here is a table showing awk relational operators and sample awk patterns:

awk Conditionals

OPERATOR	MEANING	SAMPLE PATTERN	MEANING
Boolean Operators			
`||`	or	`/^b/ || /b$/`	lines that begin or end with 'b'
`&&`	and	`/^b/ && /t$/`	lines that begin with 'b' and end with 't'
`!`	not	`!/^b/`	lines not beginning with 'b'
Comparison of Strings			
`~`	matches	`$6 ~ /Jul/`	6th field matches Jul
`!~`	does not match	`$6 !~ /Jul/`	6th field not Jul
Comparison of Numbers			
`>`	greater than	`$1 > 5`	1st field > 5
`==`	equals	`$3 == " "`	3rd field is empty
`<`	less than	`$2 < 2001`	2nd field < 2001
`!=`	not equal	`$2 != 2001`	2nd field not 2001
`>=`	greater than or equal	`$6 >= 55`	6th field >= 55
`<=`	less than or equal	`$6 <= 55`	6th field <= 55

Notice that the ~ (tilde) operator is used to check for matching strings, whereas the == operator checks for equality between numbers. Here is a sample awk program that uses both of these operators to select directory entries:

☐ EXPERIMENT 3

Note: post-conditions: (1) print Jul files with 50 bytes; (2) print bytes, filenames for files at least 100 bytes; (3) print number of files in directory.

```
ls -l . | awk '
             $6 ~ /Jul/ && $5 == 50 { print $0 }
             $5 >= 100              { print $5, $NF }
                 END                { print NR, " files" }
             '
```

Notice that the awk program in Experiment 3 takes its input lines from a pipe. Pattern ranges are also possible.

7.4.3 Pattern Ranges

A pattern range has the following format:

$$\text{pattern, pattern } \{ \text{ action } \}$$

This format says to process all lines having a pattern in the specified range. For example, to list all directory files in a specified byte range, we can use the following experiment:

☐ EXPERIMENT 4

Note: post. print all directory files, starting with the first occurrence of a file using 50 bytes and the next occurrence of a file with 100 bytes.

```
$ cat scan
ls -l . | sort +4 |
         awk '
               $5 == 50, $5 == 100 { print NR, $0 }
         '
```

If we wanted to select all directory lines, starting with filenames beginning with the letter 'e' until the first occurrence of a filename beginning with the letter 'k,' for example, we can use the following script:

☐ VARIATION ON EXPERIMENT 4

Note: post. print all directory lines, starting with filenames beginning with 'e' and ending with the *first* occurrence of a filename beginning with the letter 'k.'

```
$ cat scan2
ls -l . | sort +8 |
         awk '
               $NF ~ /^e/,$NF ~ /^k/ { print NR, $0 }
         '
```

Notice that so far we have not attempted to use shell variables inside an awk program. It is possible to do this by enclosing shell variable names inside quotes.

7.4.4 Using Shell Arguments Inside awk Programs

To distinguish between awk field variables and shell variables inside an awk program, the shell variables are enclosed inside quotes as in Experiment 5.

☐ EXPERIMENT 5

Note: pre. '$1' = shell argument identifying month post. print directory lines for a given month.

```
$ cat seemonth
ls -lt . | awk '
              $6 ~ /'$1'/ { print NR, $0 }
'
```

For example, we see all files for the month of July by typing

```
$ seemonth Jul
8  -rwxr-xr-x   1   you group    79 Jul 20 11:57 seemonth
   .
   .
   .
12 -rwxr-xr-x   1   you group   104 Jul 20 11:57 filter
```

Using this method of quoting shell arguments, we can write the awk equivalent of the following command line (select directory listings for a given day) with grep:

```
ls -lt . | grep '<month> <day>'
```

Here is a sample use of this command line:

```
ls -lt . | grep 'Jul 18'    # selects July 18 directory files
```

We can do the same thing with awk using

```
$ cat seeday
ls -lt . | awk '
              $6 ~ /'$1'/ && $7 ~ /'$2'/
'
```

This seeday procedure would be activated using

```
$ seeday Jul 18
```

This procedure can be simplified, if we allow for filenames of the form Jul18:

```
$ cat seeday
ls -lt . | awk '
              /'$1'/ && /'$2'/
'
```

The seeday procedure leads to the following challenge problem:

CHALLENGE (problem 1):
Using awk, write a seedays procedure with the following features:

usage: seedays 1st-month day final-month day
pre. '$1', '$3' = 1st, final months
　　　'$2', '$4' = 1st, final days
post. directory files starting with $1 $2
　　　and ending with $3 $4

The awk language supports a full range of arithmetic operations as well as an assignment operation for both numbers and strings.

7.5 VARIABLES, ARITHMETIC, AND ASSIGNMENTS

Unlike shell variables, all user-defined *and* most built-in awk variables require no $-prefix when their values are used in an awk program. The built-in NR and NF variables are examples. A list of built-in awk variables is given in the following table:

Built-in awk Variables

VARIABLE	MEANING
$0	current input line
$i	ith field of current input line, i >= 1
'$i'	ith shell argument, i >=1
'$<name>'	value of shell variable $<name>
$NF	last field of current input line
FILENAME	name of current input file
FS	field separator character (by default this is either a blank or tab, which can be changed)
NF	number of fields in current record
NR	number of current records (equals total number of records upon completion of processing input file)
OFMT	output format for numbers (by default %g is used where a numeric argument is printed in style d (integer) or style f (float) or style e (exponential format); see printf(3S), Unix [1983])
OFS	output field separator (by default, a blank)
ORS	output record separator (by default, a newline)
RS	input record separator (by default, a newline)

The data type of a variable is determined by awk from the context. To assign a value to a variable, awk has a variety of assignment operators. The simplest of these is the '=' operator which has the following syntax:

variable-identifier = <numeric or string-value>

(The assignment operator '=' reads "is replaced by" *and* should not be confused with the '==' equality operator.) Here are some sample assignment statements in an awk program:

```
$ echo 'yes tumtytum!' |
> awk '
>     { first = length ($1); second = length($2)
>       sum = first + second
>       print $1, first, $2, second, "total = ", sum }
> '
```

In awk, variables are preinitialized. You can verify this by trying the following experiment:

☐ EXPERIMENT 6

```
$ echo 'awk is a deterministic finite automation.' |
> awk '
>     BEGIN { sum1 = 0 }
>         { print "sum1 = ", sum1, "sum2 = ", sum2
>           sum1 = sum1 + length($1)
>           sum2 = sum1 + length($2)
>           print $1, sum1, $1, "+", $2, "=", sum2 }
> '
```

The BEGIN line in Experiment 6 is unnecessary, since both sum1 and sum2 have been initialized to zero by awk. The first print statement verifies this. In fact, you should find that only sum1 gets printed, since sum2 is undefined *until* it is assigned a value. A string variable can be set up in an awk program with an assignment statement as in

```
BEGIN { sample = "a string is an example of an RE" }
      { print sample, "has length", length(sample) }
```

Notice that the sample awk program in Experiment 6 also does some simple arithmetic (it computes the sum of the two lengths, first and second). Arithmetic in awk programming is very much like arithmetic in C. Here is a table of awk operators that are organized by precedence (in decreasing order):

Operator Precedence Table

OPERATORS	ACTION	PRECEDENCE
++ --	increment, decrement	(highest)
* / %	multiply, divide, remainder	
+ -	add, subtract	
> >= < <= == ~ !~	comparisons	
!	negation	
&&	and	
||	or	
= += -= *= /= %=	assignment	(lowest)

The ++, --, and assignment operators are imports from the C language (they work the same way as in C). Here are some paradigms to demonstrate how these operators are used:

Sample Uses of awk Operators

STATEMENT	EQUIVALENT STATEMENT	ACTION
i++	i = i + 1	adds 1 to i
j--	j = j - 1	subtracts 1 from i
sum += i	sum = sum + i	adds i to sum
half *= .5	half = half * .5	multiplies half by .5
sum /= total	sum = sum / total	computes ratio (as a real)
sum %= total	sum = sum % total	computes remainder (as an integer)

In addition to unformatted output provided by the built-in print command, awk also provides a printf command for formatted output.

7.6 FORMATTED OUTPUT WITH printf

The syntax for the built-in printf command is similar to the syntax for printf in C:

> printf "conversion character-list," output-list

Here are some sample uses of printf:

```
printf "\t%s\n", "POSIX (Portable Operating System Unix)"
printf "%s    %d\n", "total lines = ", NR
printf "%s %6.2f", "average = ", sum/NR
```

In general, except for the parentheses used by printf(3) in C, the same formatting specifications used in C can be used by printf in awk. Here is a table of these specifications:

awk printf Format Specifications

SPECIFICATION	MEANING
\n	newline
\t	tab
%d	signed integer
%nd	signed integer right justified n columns
%c	single character
%nc	single character right justified n columns
%e	scientific notation (example: 1.66667e+00 = e-format for 5/3)
%f	floating point (real) format (example: 1.66667 = f-format for 5/3)
%<col>.<dec>f	floating point right justified col columns with dec places to the right of the decimal point
%c	single character
%nc	single character right justified n columns
%s	null terminated string
%ns	string right justified n columns
%o	unsigned octal integer
%x	unsigned hex integer

Notice that it is possible to right justify each formatted value by inserting a constant between the % and the conversion character being used. Here are examples of this:

```
printf "%20d %10d", 21, 34         # col's 20 and 30 used
printf "%30.2f %30e", 5/3, 5/3     # col's 30 and 60 used
printf "%20s %30d", "yes", 3       # col's 20 and 50 used
```

As a more practical application of awk formatting, we can set up a procedure to format the output from the time command in the manner of the C shell in the following way:

Sample processing time:

```
sh format              csh format


$ time who             % time who
<list of users>        <list of users>

real 1.0               0.1u 0.3s 0:01 17%
user 0.1
sys  0.3
```

The real time reported by the time command represents the total elapsed time (not CPU time) needed to execute a command. The sum of the remaining two times represents the CPU time needed to execute a command. In this sample run of the time command, it took 1 second to list the current users of the system, 0.1 seconds of time executing a command, 0.3 seconds in the Unix system. The C shell reports these times in a more concise format and also displays the percentage of CPU to real time used by a command. We can use awk to convert the sh shell output from the time command to a format fairly close to the C shell (or csh) format in the following way:

■ PROCEDURE 1A

Notice how the shell argument $1 is used in this program.

```
   $ cat stopwatch
1  time $* 2>y                        # isolate standard error
2  cat $1 'processing time (sh form):' `cat y`
3  awk '
4         /^'r'/ { r = $2 }           # capture real time
5         /^'u'/ { u = $2 }           # capture user time
6         /^'s'/ { s = $2 }           # capture system time
7  END    { p = (((u + s) / r) * 100)
8           printf "%s %s", "'$1'", "processing time (csh form):"
9           printf "%6.2fu %6.2fs %6.2fr %6.2f%\n",u,s,r,p }
10        ' y
11 rm y
```

Notice that the time command writes its output both to its standard output (by default) *and* to its standard error. What we do in the stopwatch procedure is redirect the output to the standard error file or to a temporary file called y. The y file will hold the output from the time command. The next trick is to capture the numeric values in y which then can be used to compute the percentage of CPU to real time used. The output from stopwatch is not exactly the same as the output from time produced by the C shell. Here is a sample run of stopwatch:

```
$ sh stopwatch who
<output from who>
who processing time (sh form): real 1.2 user 0.0 sys 0.3
who processing time (csh form): 0.00u 0.30s 1.2r 25.00%
```

The output from stopwatch differs slightly from the C shell form of the output from the time command. The real time 1.2 seconds would be written 00:01 by the C shell time command. To see this, switch over to the C shell by typing

```
$ csh
% time who
<output from who>
0.1u 0.4s 0:02 20%
%
```

(Notice that the processing time for who varies.) To return to the Bourne (sh) shell (get back the $ prompt), type control-d:

```
% <control d>
$
```

We say more about the C shell in the next chapter. We can mimic the output from the C shell time command more closely by using an awk control structure.

7.7 CONTROL STRUCTURES

The awk language provides a variety of control structures that are summarized in the following table:

awk Control Structures

CONTROL	SYNTAX	EXAMPLE
if	**if** (condition) statement	**if** ($1 = = $'$1') print $1
else	**if** (condition) statement **else** statement	**if** ($1 = = $'$1') printf "$NF = = %s", $NF **else** print NR, NF, $0
for	**for** (expr1; cond.; expr2) statement	**for** (i = 1; i < = 89; i + +) sum + = $1

awk Control Structures (continued)

CONTROL	SYNTAX	EXAMPLE
	for (i in array) statement	**for** (i in table) print i, table [i] (needed in exercise 8)
while	**while** (condition) statement	**while** (1 > 0) print "forever . . ."

break	break	**while** (1 > 0) {
		sum + +
		if (sum > 5)
		   break
		print "sum = %d", sum
		}

exit	exit	**while** (1 >0) **if** ($1 = = '$1') exit **else** sum + +

next	next	**if** (sum = = 3)
		next
		else {
		print NR, $0
		sum + +
		}

The break statement causes an iteration to terminate, whereas an exit statement causes processing of input lines to halt. If an awk program has an END statement and an exit statement is executed, the END statement will be executed next. To see this, try the following experiment:

☐ EXPERIMENT 7

Note: sample uses of break and exit.

```
$ cat breaker
cal $1 | awk '
            /Ma|Ap|Ju/ { i = 1
                    while (i != 6) {
                       if (i == 3)
                         break
                       else
                         print NR, $i, i++
```

```
                    if (NR > 10)
                        exit
                    }
                }
        END { print "final: ", NR, NF, $NF }
'
```

Here is a sample run of breaker:

```
$ sh breaker 1987
6 Jan 1
6 Feb 2
14 Apr 1
final:  14 3 Jun
```

You should find that breaker prints the same thing regardless of the year you enter. Notice that the break statement serves to cause awk to exit from the while loop early. Also notice how the END statement in breaker gets executed after the exit statement terminates the processing of the input from the pipe. To vary what breaker does, try the following Challenge problem:

> **CHALLENGE (problem 2):**
> Modify breaker in Experiment 7 so that (a) the week of the 20th is printed for Jan, Feb, Apr and (b) the initial pattern takes the months sought from shell arguments as in
>
> ```
> $ sh breaker 1987 Ja Fe Ap
> ```

Here is a second version of stopwatch (Procedure 1a, Section 7.6) which uses the awk **if** statement to obtain output that is closer to the output from time in the C shell:

■ PROCEDURE 1B

Note: changes to original stopwatch occur in lines 4, 5, 6, and 13.

```
1  $cat stopwatch
2  time $* 2>y
3  awk '
4       /^'r'/ { r = $2; sec = r % 60
5                if (r > 60) {
6                   min = r/60; min %= 1 }
7              }
8       /^'y'/ { u = $2 }
9       /^'s'/ { s = $2 }
10      END { p = (((u + 2) / r) * 100)
11            printf "%s %s", "'$1'",
                        "processing time (csh form:)"
12            printf "%6.2fu %6.2fs", u, s
```

300   CHAPTER 7 / awk PROGRAMMING METHODS

```
13              printf "  %d:%d %6.2%\n", min, sec, p }
14         ' y
15 rm y
```

This new version of stopwatch has an output that is closer to an acceptable format for real time in minutes and seconds. In lines 5 and 6, we use an **if** statement to determine if the timed command has taken more than 60 seconds. The changes in lines 4 through 6 (which compute values for min and sec) are reflected in the new format for the real time in line 13. Here is a sample run of the new stopwatch:

```
$ stopwatch wc /usr/dict/words
   23739   23739   194186   /usr/dict/words
wc processing time (sh form): real 8.7 user 6.0 sys 1.8
wc processing time (csh form): 6.00u 1.80s 0:8 89.66%
```

There is still a problem with the format of the csh form of real time. In this sample run, stopwatch should have printed 00:08 instead of 0:8 to represent the fact that it took wc 8 seconds to obtain the line, word, and character counts for the online dictionary. To make this possible, a second **if** statement could be used to check if the value of sec is less than 10 (in that case, sec could be formatted with a leading zero). Yet another **if** statement could be used to check whether the value of min is less than 9. Improving stopwatch further becomes the basis for the following Challenge problem:

>   **CHALLENGE (problem 3):**
>   Use awk control structures so that stopwatch (Procedure 1b) replicates the reported output from the time command.

In addition to these control structures, awk provides a variety of built-in functions.

7.8 BUILT-IN FUNCTIONS

A summary of built-in awk functions is given in the following table:

Built-in awk Functions

Legend: 'expr' stands for 'expression'; 'str' = 'string'; e = 2.71828 (approximately); exp(1) = e; x is in radians, not degrees (1 radian = 57.2958 degrees); pi = 3.1415927 (approximately)

FUNCTION	ACTION	EXAMPLE	
cos (x)	computes cosine of x in radians	cos(pi/4)	# = 0.7071
sin (x)	computes sine of x in radians	sin(pi/6)	# = 0.5

Built-in awk Functions (continued)

FUNCTION	ACTION	EXAMPLE	
exp(expr)	compute e^{expr}	exp(3)	# = 20.0855
log(expr)	computes $\log_e$ expr	log(exp(1))	# = 1
		log (10)	# = 2.30259
sqrt(expr)	square root of expr	sqrt(2)	# = 1.414
int(expr)	computes trunc(expr)	int(2.71828)	# = 2
length(str)	no. of char's in str	length ("yes")	# = 3
getline( )	gets next input line = 1 if not EOF	getline ( )	# = 0 if EOF
index (s1,s2)	position of s1 in s2	index("tumtytum!", "ty")	# = 4
sprintf(x,f,o)	assigns output a to string x with format f	see sprintf(3S), Unix, [83]	
split(s,x,c)	splits s string into x[1], ...,x[n] on character c *and* returns n (= 0, if c is not in s)	split("tumtytum!",box,"t")	
substr(s,p,n)	returns substring of s with n characters starting at position p	substr("hello", 4,2)	# = lo

awk supports the use of arrays, which we present in detail in Section 7.9. The split and sprintf functions build arrays. Each of these functions returns the size of the array it has built. To see this, try the following experiment with the split function:

☐ EXPERIMENT 8

```
$ cat capture
# separate out a string into substrings
awk '
    { n = split("'$1'", box, "'$2'")
      for (i = 1; i <= n; i++)
         printf "\t%d\t%s\n", i, box [i] }
'
$ cat dummyfile
yes
$
$ sh capture tumtytumtytumtoes! t <dummyfile
```

302   CHAPTER 7 / awk PROGRAMMING METHODS

```
    1
    2       um
    3       y
    4       um
    5       y
    6       um
    7       oes!
```

Notice how split operates on a target string. It splits a target string into substrings, starting with the first character *after* the character specified by the third split argument and ending with the next occurrence of the specified character. In the sample run of capture (in Experiment 8), notice box[1] is empty. The split function scans a target string from left to right. The first substring obtained by split represents all the characters (from left to right) up to the first occurrence of the specified character. In addition, the split function outputs the number of substrings which it has found in an input string (this numeric value is assigned to n in the capture procedure in Experiment 8). To see this more clearly, try the following sample run of capture:

```
$ sh capture tumtytumtytumtoes! u <dummyfile
    1       t
    2       mtyt
    3       mtyt
    4       mtoes!
$
```

where the split function splits the target string as follows:

```
scan left:

box[1] = t (only character before 'u')
 ↑box[2] = mtyt
  ↑  box[3] = mtyt
      ↑  box[4] = mtoes!
          ↑
 tu     |
    mytyu   |
        mtytu  |
             mtoes!
```

The substr function works differently. It extracts from a target string a single substring, which begins position p and contains n characters. The arguments of the substr function can be explained as follows:

```
        extract substring from target string
                start extraction at position p
                        substring has length n
             ↓         ↓              ↓
substr(target, position-p, length-n)
```

To see how substr works, try the following experiment:

☐ EXPERIMENT 9

```
$ cat partition
# input words are split into characters separated by spaces
awk '
     { for (i = 1; i <= length($1); i++)
         printf "%s %c", substr($1, i, 1), " "
       printf "\n" }
   ' $1
$ cat list
pans
pots
opt
snap
stop
begin
being
$ sh partition list
p a n s
p o t s
o p t
s n a p
s t o p
b e g i n
b e i n g
$
```

Later we will show how to use the partition procedure in Experiment 9 to find what are known as anagram classes. First, we need to see how to employ arrays in awk programs.

7.9 ARRAYS

An *array* is a collection of items. Each item in an array is identified by its position in the collection. For example, in the box array set up by the split function in Experiment 8 the items are strings extracted from a target string. The values of i in the sample run in Experiment 8 represent the number of substrings stored in the box array by split. Note that from split ("tumtytumtytumtoes!", box, "u"), we get

position i	box[i]
1	t
2	mtyt
3	mtyt
4	mtoes!

To set up arrays in awk programs, we need to do the following things:

1. specify an array name
2. devise a means of assigning values to an array index
3. devise a means of filling an array with selected items

For example, suppose we need to fill an array with filenames in a directory in time order. We can do this using the values of NR to assign filenames to positions in a name array. To see this, try

☐ EXPERIMENT 10

```
$ cat collect
awk '
       { name[NR] = $NF }
   END { printf "\t%s\t%s\n", "index", "filename"
         for (i = 2; i<= NR; i += 2)
            printf "\t%d\t%s\n", i, name[i] }
   '
$
```

The collect procedure in Experiment 10 will fill the name array with the values of $NF from the input lines. If we pipe the output from ls -lt to collect, this procedure will fill the name array with the filenames in your directory in time order. Then collect arbitrarily selects the filenames in even-numbered positions in the name array to print in a table. Here is a sample run of collect:

```
$ chmod +x collect
$ ls -lt | collect
      index          file name
       2             collect
       4             partition
       6             breaker
       8             hello.exe
      10             hello.c
       .              .
       .              .
       .              .
```

The beauty of awk is its simplicity. We can use an array in an awk program to create a variation of the shell head command in the following way:

☐ EXPERIMENT 11

```
$ cat fromtop
# select lines to process
```

```
awk '
    BEGIN { min = '$1'; max = '$2' }
          { line[NR] = $0 }
    END   { for (i = min; i <= max; i++)
                printf "%d\t%s\n", i, line[i] }
'
$
```

The fromtop procedure allows us to select lines from an input file for processing. For example, we print lines 3 through 5 of an input file in the following way:

```
$ chmod +x fromtop
$ fromtop 3 5 <list
3       opt
4       snap
5       stop
```

and lines 3 through 5 of your current directory by typing

```
$ ls -lt | fromtop 3 5
3       -rwxr-xr-x 1 you unix   180 Aug 1 08:21 collect
4       -rw-r--r-- 1 you unix    68 Aug 1 07:39 list
5       -rwxr-xr-x 1 you unix   124 Aug 1 07:50 partition
```

Associative arrays are also supported by awk.

7.9.1 Associative Arrays

In awk it is possible to use a field of an input line as the index of an array and associate name-value pairs. The result is what is known as an associative array. For example, the following mototal procedure associates with each month in a directory the total storage used during that month:

■ PROCEDURE 2

```
$ cat mototal

# determine total storage used for each month

ls -lt . |
awk '
  $6 != prev { sum++; prev = $6; name[sum] = $6 }
             { total[$6] += $5 }
  END { printf "\t%s\t%s\n", "month", "storage used"
        for (i = 1; i <= sum; i++)
          printf "\t%s\t%d\n",name[i],total[name[i]] }
'
```

CHAPTER 7 / awk PROGRAMMING METHODS

The mototal procedure does the following things:

1. Increments sum if the month field ($6) of the ls -lt output differs from the previous value of **prev** (notice that initially prev has a null value, so prev will not equal $6—this means the first line from the pipe will cause sum to be incremented, giving sum a value of 1).
2. name[sum] will hold the month-name (each time a new value is assigned to prev, the new month-name or $6 is assigned to name[sum]).
3. total is an associative array. So, for example, if the first four lines output by ls -lt are for the month of July, here is what happens to the total array:

```
output from ls -lt          assignments to total

-rwxr-xr-x ...  288 Jul ...   total["Jul"] += 288
-rwxr-xr-x ...  168 Jul ...   total["Jul"] += 168
-rw-r--r-- ...    4 Jul ...   total["Jul"] += 4
-rwxr-xr-x ...   68 Jul ...   total["Jul"] += 68
```

In other words, total associates with "Jul" the sum 288 + 168 + 4 + 68 or 528 bytes of storage.

4. Notice how the values in the name array are used to select values in the total array when the awk reaches the END pattern in mototal.

Here is a sample run of mototal:

```
$ sh mototal
        month       storage used
        Aug         1492
        Jul         47177
        Jun         471
        Mar         1901
        Feb         2734
        Jan         433
        Dec         2377
```

The mototal procedure is good enough to put in your bin. It will provide you with a miniature history of your Unix usage for the current year. In Section 7.9.2 we give a further illustration of associative arrays along with a sample use of the awk -f option.

7.9.2 Example: Scanning /usr/dict/words

It is typical for an on-line dictionary to have a mixture of words that begin with upper- and lowercase letters. To count the number of upper- and lowercase a's and b's, for example, try the following experiment:

☐ EXPERIMENT 12

```
$ cat assoc.awk
/^'a'/ { box["a"] += 1 }
/^'A'/ { box["A"] += 1 }
/^'b'/ { box["b"] += 1 }
/^'B'/ { box["B"] += 1 }
END { printf "\t%s\t%s\t%s\t%s\n","ltr","count","ltr","count"
   printf "\t%c\t%d\t%d\n","a",box["a"],"A",box["A"]
   printf "\t%c\t%d\t%c\n","b",box["b"],"B",box["B "] }
```

Now try typing

```
$ awk -f assoc.awk /usr/dict/words
```

On our system, the assoc.awk produced the following output after scanning /usr/dict/words:

letter	count	letter	count
a	1309	A	348
b	1202	B	398

There is an alternative way to compute the tallies in the associative box array. Since we always increment by 1, we can employ the more concise + + operator in assoc.awk in the following way:

```
/^'a'/ { box["a"]++ }
```

Arrays make it possible to manipulate input data in a variety of ways. For example, we can use arrays to construct what Jon Bentley (1986) calls anagram classes.

7.9.3 Example: Bentley Anagram Classes

An *anagram class* consists of all words that can be obtained by interchanging the letters of a given word. Here are some examples of anagram classes that were found in /usr/dic/words on our system:

>   ascent secant stance
>   avocet octave vocate
>   caret carte cater crate trace
>   danger gander garden

Here is a technique that can be used to obtain these anagram classes:

Algorithm for Obtaining Anagram Classes

[Note: the steps in the following algorithm refer to partition and to three hidden procedures:

partition: from Experiment 9
select: performs a selection sort on letters
combine: combines corresponding words into word pairs
squash: forms anagram classes]

I. Sort letters of each word in the original list (save sorted letters in a temp file)

parse		p a r s e		aeprs	
mode		m o d e		demo	
time		t i m e		eimt	
spare		s p a r e		aeprs	
emit	partition →	e m i t	select →	eimt	temp →
dome		d o m e		demo	
ada		a d a		aad	
spear		s p e a r		aeprs	

II. Concatenate the original list with the temp file, combine corresponding pairs, sort the list of pairs and combine corresponding pairs into anagram classes.

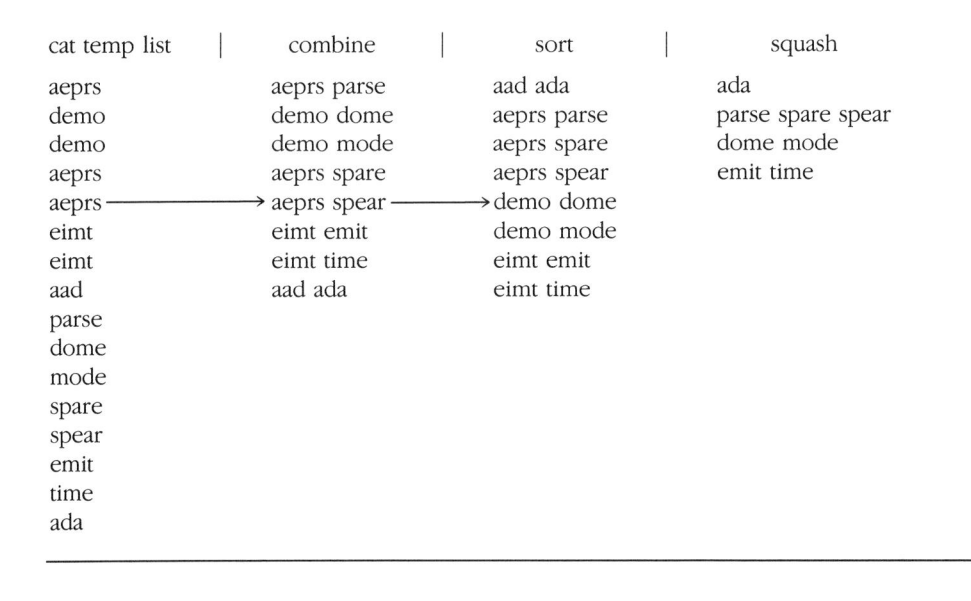

cat temp list	|	combine	|	sort	|	squash
aeprs		aeprs parse		aad ada		ada
demo		demo dome		aeprs parse		parse spare spear
demo		demo mode		aeprs spare		dome mode
aeprs		aeprs spare		aeprs spear		emit time
aeprs ──→		aeprs spear ──→		demo dome		
eimt		eimt emit		demo mode		
eimt		eimt time		eimt emit		
aad		aad ada		eimt time		
parse						
dome						
mode						
spare						
spear						
emit						
time						
ada						

In other words, the algorithm to obtain anagram classes can be implemented using the following enigma procedure:

ARRAYS 309

■ PROCEDURE 3

(Implementation of anagram class algorithm)

```
$ cat enigma
partition $1 | select > temp
cat $1 temp | combine | sort | squash
```

The select operation performs a selection sort, which uses the following algorithm (written in Pascal):

```
1   begin
2     for i := 1 to listsize do begin
3       pos := i;                           (*an i, not 1*)
4       for k := pos + 1 to listsize do (*scan*)
5         if list[k] < list[pos] then pos := k;
6       swap(list[i], list[pos])
7     end
8   end
```

In other words, in each scan of the list (lines 4 and 5), the smallest list item is found (in location pos) and is swapped with the current beginning list entry until all sublists of the list have been scanned. This is an easy sort to implement in awk, which is done in the following select procedure:

■ PROCEDURE 4

```
$cat select
#selection sort letters of a word

awk '
    { for (i = 1; i <= NF; i++) list[i] = $i}
    # selection sort:
    { for (i = 1; i <= NF; i++) {
       pos = i
       for (k = pos + 1; k <= NF; k++)
         if (list[k] < list[pos]) pos = k
       t = list[i]; list[i] = list[pos];
       list[pos] = t
       }
    }
    { for (i = 1; i <= NF; i++)
        if (i < NF)
           printf "%s", list[i]
        else
           printf "%s\n", list[i] }
```

Using the partition procedure from Section 7.8 and select, we can carry out part I of the anagram class algorithm. To see this, try typing

```
$ partition list | select
aeprs
demo
eimt
aeprs
eimt
demo
aad
aeprs
```

This will produce the list of sorted letters that go into the temp file used by enigma. To complete the implementation of the anagram class algorithm, we need the combine and squash procedures. After we concatenate the original list and temp files, the following combine procedure forms pairs of corresponding words:

■ PROCEDURE 5

```
$ cat combine
# combine output from select with original list

awk '
            { comb[NR] = $0 }
    END     { h = int(NR/2) + 1
              for (i = 1; h <= NR; i++) {
                 print comb[i], comb[h]
                 h++
              }
            }
    '
```

Apart from the rest of enigma (Procedure 3), you can experiment with combine in the following way:

```
$ partition list | select >temp
$ cat temp list | combine
aeprs parse
demo mode
eimt time
aeprs spare
eimt emit
demo dome
aad ada
aeprs spear
```

To complete the implementation of enigma (Procedure 3), we need a squash procedure to take the output from sort to gather together all words that belong to a single anagram class. The following squash procedure is essentially the same as the squash procedure suggested by Jon Bentley (1986):

■ BENTLEY'S SQUASH PROCEDURE

```
$ cat squash
# see Bentley, Programming Pearls, Prentice-Hall, 1986, p. 20

awk '
       $1 != prev { prev = $1; if (NR > 1) printf "\n" }
                  { printf "$s ", $2 }
       END        { print "\n" }
   '
```

If you use the enigma procedure to obtain anagram classes from your on-line dictionary, it is best to run enigma in the background and redirect the output from enigma to some temporary file (call it classes, for example). Notice the following warning message in using enigma on your on-line dictionary:

> Warning: be sure the input file for enigma contains only words that begin with lowercase letters. Also, enigma will be extremely slow in scanning a large file.

To guarantee that the input file contains only lowercase letters, try using the following procedure:

```
$ cat lowercase
# filter out all lines not beginning with a lowercase letter

grep '^[a-z]' $1
```

For example, we can use the lowercase procedure to set up a targetfile as follows:

```
$ sh lowercase >targetfile
```

Then make each of the procedures enigma uses executable *and* make enigma executable; then type

```
$ enigma targetfile >classes &
```

You may be surprised at how many anagram classes enigma puts into the classes file. On our system, enigma found 817 anagram classes with three or more words.

We can bring together a variety of built-in functions to produce random numbers.

7.9.4 Random Numbers and Frequency Tables

A sequence of numbers is *random* if each number of the sequence is equally likely to occur. Here is a procedure that can be used to produce fairly random numbers:

■ **PROCEDURE 6**

(random number generator)

```
$ cat rnd
date | awk '
       BEGIN { low = '$1'; high = '$2' }
             { seed = substr($4, 7, 2)
               seed = seed*3.14159
               seed = sqrt(seed)
               seed -= int(seed)
               rnd = low + seed*(high - low + 1)
               print int(rnd) }
      '
```

The rnd procedure uses the seconds output by date as a seed in computing a random number in the specified range. To see this, try typing

```
$ rnd 2 99
88
```

For example, suppose date gives

```
$ date
Mon Aug 4 08:59:11 PDT 1986
```

Then rnd uses substr($4, 7, 2) to select eleven seconds as the value of seed. Then seed makes the following computations:

```
seed = 11
seed = 11 + 3.14159 = 34.55749
seed = sqrt(seed) = 5.87856
seed = seed - int(seed) = 0.87856
rnd = low + seed * (high - low + 1)
    = 2 + 0.87856 * (99 - 2 + 1)
    = 2 + 86
    = 88
```

which is in the specified random number range 2 to 99. The rnd procedure has a variety of uses. For example, we can use it to simulate the roll of a die as shown in the following dice experiment:

■ EXPERIMENT 13

(simulating rolls of a die)

```
$ cat dice
# simulate rolls of a die
# pre. $1 equals number of rolls of die
# post. random numbers in the range from 1 to 6

count=1
while (test $count -le $1)
  do
    echo `rnd 1 6`          # calls rnd with range 1,6
    count=`expr $count + 1`
  done
echo
```

Here is a sample run of dice:

```
$ dice 5
3
6
4
5
1
```

A good random number generator will produce values that are uniformly distributed. For example, if we type

```
$ dice 600
```

the rnd procedure should produce roughly 100 1's, 100 2's, and so on. We can use an array in an awk program to print the distribution of values produced by rnd:

☐ EXPERIMENT 14

(building frequency tables)

```
     $ cat freq
     # check frequencies of values produced by rnd
1    awk '
2            /1/ { tally[1]++ }
```

314 CHAPTER 7 / awk PROGRAMMING METHODS

```
3              /2/ { tally[2]++ }
4              /3/ { tally[3]++ }
5              /4/ { tally[4]++ }
6              /5/ { tally[5]++ }
7              /6/ { tally[6]++ }
8              END { print
9                    print "die     ", "No.    ", "frequency"
10                   print
11                   for (i = 1; i <= 6; i++) {
12                      printf "%2d %8d %7s", i, tally[i], " "
13                      j = 1
14                      while (j <= int(tally[i]/5)) {
15                         printf "%1s", "*"
16                         j++
17                      }
18                   print
19                   }
20                 }
21            '
```

Notice that the awk print statement can be used without arguments. (This is the case in lines 8 and 10 of Experiment 14.) By itself, the print statement will perform differently when not employed relative to either a BEGIN or END pattern (without arguments, print will output a copy of the current input line). When print appears without arguments relative to a BEGIN or END pattern (as in Experiment 14), print causes a newline to be output.

Now try piping the output from dice (Experiment 13) into freq. Here is a sample run of freq:

Warning: slow processing ahead. Process in the background.

```
$ dice 600 | freq &

die       No.     frequency

1         143     ***************************
2         102     *******************
3         114     **********************
4          90     ******************
5          97     *******************
6          54     *********
```

There are a variety of ways in which awk programs can interact with the shell.

ARRAYS   **315**

7.10 INTERACTING WITH THE SHELL

It is possible for an awk program to interact with the shell in the following ways:
1. quoted shell variables *and* arguments used as arguments in awk programs
2. redirection of awk output using > and >> to files specified by quoted filenames
3. piping awk output to files specified using quoted filenames

We have already made repeated use of quoted shell arguments in shell programs (seemonth in Experiment 5, Section 7.4.4, for example). It is also possible to use the same quoting system to reference shell variables inside awk programs. To see this, try the following experiment:

☐ EXPERIMENT 15

```
$ cat idea
# referencing shell variables in an awk program

past=1936
future=2010
awk '
      BEGIN { difference = '$future' - '$past' }
            { print '$past', '$future', difference }
   '
```

The idea procedure in Experiment 15 performs arithmetic on the shell variables past and future. This procedure produces the results that follow. Note that for the sake of demonstration *only,* the following dummyfile is used to run idea:

```
$ cat dummyfile
yes
$ sh idea <dummyfile
1936     2010     74
```

The output from an awk program can be redirected using either > or >>. For example, to save a list of the files listed for a specified month in your current directory, try

■ PROCEDURE 7A

```
$ cat savemonth
# make list of files for a specified month

ls -lt . | awk '
                  /'$1'/ { print $0 >>"month"; sum++ }
                  END { print sum, "entries saved." }
                '
```

To see how savemonth works, try typing

```
$ sh savemonth Jun
```

Then savemonth will append to the month file (specified by "month") all lines of your current directory from June. Since it may be awkward (no pun intended!) to remember to type, try modifying savemonth so that it checks only the first three characters of the month you type (use the built-in substr() function to do this). We can make savemonth more useful by creating a file named after the shell argument used. For example, if we type

```
$ sh savemonth Aug
```

it would be helpful to have savemonth create a file named month.Aug. Here is a new version of savemonth that does this:

PROCEDURE 7B

```
$ cat savemonth
# save entries for specified month in month.'$1'

ls -lt . |
awk '
        /'$1'/ { print $0 >>"month.'$1'"; sum++ }
        END { print sum, "entries saved in month.'$1'" }
    '
```

Now savemonth produces the following result:

```
$ sh savemonth Jul
28 entries saved in month.Jul
```

To pipe the output from an awk program to a shell procedure (either a built-in shell procedure like wc or sort or a user-defined procedure like mototal), it is necessary to enclose a referenced shell procedure inside quotes. For example, to sort the values in the tally array in the freq procedure from Experiment 14, try adding the following line to freq:

PIPING OUTPUT FROM AN awk PROGRAM

(Note: add the following lines between lines 19 and 20 of the freq procedure in Section 7.9.4, Experiment 14.)

```
for (i = 1; i <= 6; i++)
  print tally[i] | "sort"
```

In this sample use of a pipe inside an awk program, the values of the tally array are fed to the built-in sort procedure. Thanks to the various ways that it is possible to communicate the output from an awk program to the shell, we can have multiple output streams from the same awk program. For example, the modified version of freq now has two output streams, one to your terminal screen and a second piped to sort. This feature of awk would make it possible, for instance, for an awk program to generate more than one report saved in multiple files.

Although awk syntax resembles C syntax, it differs from C in a variety of ways.

7.11 COMPARISON OF awk AND C

The awk and C languages differ in the following ways:

Differences between awk and C

ITEM	awk	C
variables	without type declaration	required declaration of the data type of *each* variable
printf	printf "format", args	printf("format", args);
separator	either ; or newline	; must be used to separate statements
patterns	in pattern-action pairs used in scanning input	1. regular expressions not used 2. comparisons are part of a conditional used by an **if** or **while** or **switch** statement, for example
execute	no compiling	executable module must be produced by C (compiling is always necessary)
speed	slow	usually an order of magnitude faster

You might want to try the following simple experiment to see how much faster C can be compared with awk:

☐ EXPERIMENT WITH C

The following are three different programs that do the same thing.

In C

```
$ cat response
# include <stdio.h>
```

```
main ()
  {
   printf("\t\t%s\n", "Hello, world!");
  }
```

<h3 style="text-align:center">in awk</h3>

```
$ cat response.awk
{ printf "\t\t%s\n", "Hello, world!" }
```

<h3 style="text-align:center">in sh</h3>

```
$ cat response.sh
echo '\t\tHello, world!'
```

To compile the response.c file, use

```
$ cc -o response.exe response.c
```

This will cause you C compiler to produce an executable module called response.exe, which you can run by typing

```
$ response.exe
          Hello, world!
```

To see how fast response.exe is compared with the corresponding program written in awk or in sh, try typing the following. Note that here is the content of the dummyfile used in this experiment:

```
$ cat dummyfile
yes

$ time response.exe
               Hello, world!
real      0.4
user      0.0
sys       0.2

$ time sh response.sh
               Hello, world!
real      1.0
user      0.0
sys       0.5

$ time awk -f response.awk dummyfile
               Hello, world!
real      2.1
user      0.0
sys       0.5
```

In other words, response.exe is more than twice as fast as either its response.sh or response.awk counterparts. Even so, it is easier (and usually faster) to use awk to develop a program, since there is no need to compile experimental awk programs. By contrast, every time a change is made in a C program, that program must be recompiled before the new version can be run. **awk** is an ideal tool for developing programs. Once an awk program performs correctly, it is easy to rewrite an awk program in C because of the similarity between awk and C syntax. If awk is used in developing programs, then it is desirable to work with small modules like those in enigma (Procedure 3, Section 7.9.3). Then, working awk modules can easily be rewritten in C (or with some other compiler) to speed up the development of other modules being used in a pipeline. That is, it is possible to use C and awk programs together in the *same* pipeline. To see this, try the following experiment:

☐ EXPERIMENT 16

```
$ cat together
# pipe the output from a C program to awk
response.exe | awk '
                     { print NR, "... ", $NF, NF }
                   '
```

Now try typing

```
$ sh together
1 ...   world! 2
```

You will find, for example, that enigma is extremely slow if you employ it to find the anagram classes in a large file like /usr/dict/words. The enigma procedure does perform satisfactorily on small test files, however. So, once you have enigma working, it would be better to replace individual modules with corresponding C programs. For instance, we can replace partition, select, and combine by a single, very concise, extremely efficient C program.

7.12 awk LEADS TO C

The awk language provides a versatile software development tool. C and awk syntax closely resemble each other, which makes it easy to implement an awk program in C. Since awk programs do not have to be compiled, awk provides an ideal laboratory for developing small program modules. The speedier, more efficient C counterpart of a working awk module offers a production-level alternative once we are satisfied with the performance of an awk module. There is a paradox in this. Although it is easier and faster to test programming ideas in awk, there is a severe drawback to awk: slow processing. The slowness of awk programs shows up in processing large files with awk. The enigma procedure illustrates this slowness. As long as enigma is limited to processing small files, its performance is satisfactory. To see this, try the following experiment:

☐ EXPERIMENT 17 (processing speed of awk)

```
$ cat words
parse
mode
dome
spare
spear
emit
time
ada
$ time enigma words
ada
parse spare spear
dome mode
emit time
real         34.6
user          5.9
sys           6.1
```

The 34 seconds it takes enigma to process the words file is tolerable. However, try typing

```
$ time enigma /usr/dict/words &
```

It takes enigma several hours to process the on-line dictionary. The awk modules that enigma uses can be rewritten in C to make enigma faster. For example, suppose we replace the partition, select, cat, and combine procedures used by enigma with a single C program (call it gather.c). (A listing for gather.c is given in Appendix D.) Then, after compiling gather.c to obtain gather.exe, we find the anagram classes in the on-line dictionary by using the following procedure:

```
$ cat findgrams
# finds anagram classes

gather.exe <$1 | sort | squash >classes
```

First, try out findgrams with the words file from Experiment 17 by typing

```
$ time sh findgrams words

real         8.4
user         0.4
sys          1.7
```

This contrasts with the 34 seconds it took enigma in Experiment 17 to do the same thing. The speed of findgrams is even more dramatic when it processes the on-line dictionary. To see this, try

```
$ time sh findgrams /usr/dict/words &
328
$
real          8:51:4
user          7:40.2
sys             40.2
$ wc classes
   22779   23739   240704   classes
```

In other words, while the enigma process requires hours, it takes findgrams (with the help of gather.c) just eight minutes to create a file with 22,779 lines (most of these are single word classes). The classes file also contains many proper names (words beginning with capital letters). To cut the classes down to a more reasonable size (isolate all lines that begin with a lowercase letter), try typing

```
$ grep '^[a-z]' classes >finalcopy
```

Multiple output streams from an awk program are possible. For example, we can use the following procedure to fetch the anagram classes containing two or more words contained in finalcopy:

```
$ cat supercatch
# awk program with multiple output streams

awk '
        NF == 2 { sum2++; print $0 >>"2 class" }
        NF == 3 { sum3++; print $0 >>"3 class" }
        NF == 4 { sum4++; print $0 >>"4 class" }
        NF == 5 { sum5++; print $0 >>"5 class" }
        NF == 6 { sum6++; print $0 >>"6 class" }
         END { print sum2, sum3, sum4, sum5, sum6 }
   '
```

Now we can use supercatch to separate out the anagram classes in the finalcopy file in the following way:

```
$ sh supercatch {finalcopy
727 77 15 1
```

In other words, the speedier findgrams procedure has found 727 anagram classes with two words; 77 with three words; 15 with four words; one with five words. Notice that the supercatch procedure produces separate files containing these anagram classes. To do this, try typing

```
$ cat 5class
caret carte cater crate trace
```

A subtle feature of awk is its treatment of each input line as a record that is split into fields. The fields of a record are recognized by awk in terms of its built-in field separator variable, FS. By default, FS character matches either a tab or blank. So, for instance, awk partitions this line as shown in the following sample awk record:

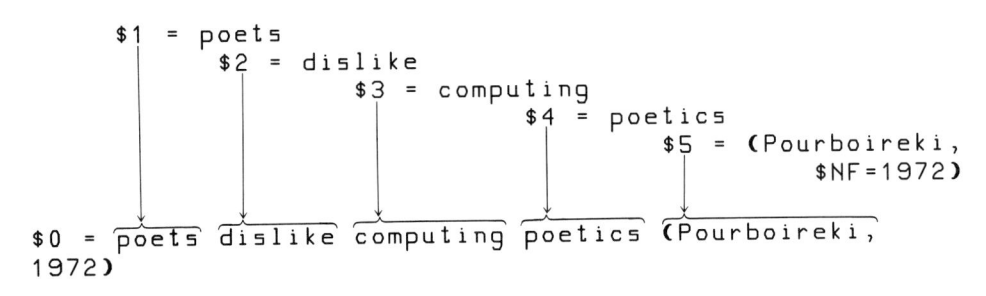

```
        $1 = poets
            $2 = dislike
                $3 = computing
                    $4 = poetics
                        $5 = (Pourboireki,
                            $NF=1972)

$0 = poets dislike computing poetics (Pourboireki,
1972)
```

That is, $0 holds the current record. In addition, awk assigns to NF the number of fields in $0 (NF equals 6 in the above sample record).

7.13 SUMMARY

One of the beauties of awk is its simplicity. Without much fuss, it does not take long to put together fairly powerful awk programs. The trick is to get used to the variety of ways that pattern-action pairs can be set up in awk programs. Part of the reason awk programs tend to be short is the implied loop in every awk program. That is, on its own, an awk program gets the next input line once it has finished processing the current record. In addition, awk syntax is simpler than C. Typically, the C equivalent of an awk program will be longer, since awk determines the data type of a variable by context. By contrast, in C it is always necessary to specify the data type of each variable. C is terse, awk is terser.

7.14 REVIEW OF SYMBOLS AND KEYWORDS

This section reviews the symbols and keywords introduced in this chapter.

7.14.1 Symbols

SYMBOL	USAGE
' awk text '	right single quotes delimit an awk text
/ pattern /	right slashes / / delimit an awk pattern

7.14.1 Symbols (continued)

SYMBOL	USAGE
{ <statement(s)> }	{ } delimit awk statements which specify actions for awk to perform
;	; used as awk statement separator
newline	separator for awk statements
NR	record number
NF	number of fields in a record
$NF	holds last field of current record
$0	holds current record
$i, i >= 1	$i holds ith field of current record
'$i', i >= 1	'$i' specifies ith shell argument
'$<identifier>'	'$<identifier>' specifies a shell argument to be used by awk
"n"	newline
"t"	tab
%format><character>	specifies conversion character and format for argument to be printed by printf
,	separate extreme values in a pattern range
,	argument separator for print, printf
||	or
&&	and
!	not
=	assignment operator
+= -= *= /= %=	other assignment operators
==	equals (x == a reads "x equals a")
!=	not equal
> >= < >=	relational operators
~	matches (x ~ /Unix/ reads "x matches "Unix")
!~	does not match (/VMS/ !~ /Unix/ reads "VMS does not match Unix")
++	unary increment operator (sum++ is the same as sum += 1 or sum = sum + 1)
--	unary decrement operator (diff-- is the same as diff -= 1 or diff = diff - 1)

7.14.2 Keywords

KEYWORD(S)	EXPLANATION
anagram	transposition of letters of a word or phrase to form a new word (example: parse -- aerps)

7.14.2 Keywords (continued)

KEYWORD(S)	EXPLANATION
anagram class	collection of words derived from a given word
array	collection of items
associative array	associates name-value pairs
awk	token that begins each awk program
AWK	acronym (usually written in lowercase in deference to Unix) representing the names of the inventors of awk, Aho, Weinberger, and Kernighan
BEGIN	pattern used to specify action(s) to be performed by awk *before* processing of an input file begins
break	terminate an iteration (see Experiment 7, Section 7.7)
cc	command used to compile a C program
csh	command used to switch to a C shell
END	pattern used to specify action(s) to be performed by awk *after* processing the lines of an input file
exit	terminates processing by awk of input file (does not terminate an awk program if there is an END pattern; see Experiment 7)
field	name of component of a record
pattern	used by awk to select actions to perform relative to a segment of an input line that matches a pattern.
patterns recognized by awk:	
1. RE	regular expression (same as those recognized by ed or sed)
2. BEGIN	identifies preprocessing to be done by awk
3. END	identifies postprocessing to be done by awk
4. conditionals	Boolean expression that evaluates to true or false
5. ranges	specifies initial and final values found in input file lines as well as corresponding actions to be performed relative to lines in the range
POSIX	Portable Operating System (from UN)IX, name of IEEE Standard 1003 which specifies an operating system based on Unix. Available from: IEEE, Inc., 445 Hoes Lane, Piscataway, NJ 08854.
record	current input line
selection sort	repeatedly selects minimum values in sublists of a list until list values are in ascending order (see Procedure 4, Section 7.9.3). Also see J.P. Linderman (1984) for discussion of sort command. See Horowitz and Sahni (1984) on selection sorting.

7.15 EXERCISES

1. Write a many procedure with the following specification:

   ```
   many [ list of filenames ]
   action: counts the number of lines in each file
   specified in the many command line and appends a
   comment to each input file of the following form:

        # total: <integer> lines
   ```

   Give a sample run of many with
   a. dummyfiles one, two, three containing lists of words of varying lengths in many one two three
   b. many many

2. Write a linecount procedure that computes the average number of lines of files in your current directory. Give a sample run.

3. Write a bytecount procedure that computes the average number of bytes of files in your current directory. Give a sample run.

4. Give a sample awk program that illustrates each of the four forms of awk programs specified in Section 7.2.

5. Implement Experiments 2a and 2b in Section 7.4.1 and give a sample run.

6. Implement a variation of Experiment 3, Section 7.4.2 (call your procedure sysuse) with the following specification:

   ```
   sysuse [ -fd ] [ month ] [ day ]
     options: -f  all files
              -d  directories
     action: production of the following table:

        file name   date      storage
        _____

                    total:
                    average:

   pre. 1. -f specifies that a storage usage table be
              produced for all months
              example: sysuse -f
         2. -d specifies directory storage table be
              produced
              example: sysuse -d
         3. [ month ] specifies month for storage table
              examples: sysuse Jun
                        sysuse -d Jun
         4. [ day ] specifies day for storage table
              example: sysuse -d Jun 30
   ```

   Note: shell arguments should be evaluated by awk *and* pattern ranges should be used to handle multiple months and days. Give a sample run for each of the above cases (vary the months and days, if your directory contains other months and days).

7. Implement a generalization of the scan procedure in Experiment 4, Section 7.4.3, with the following specification:

```
usage: scan [ -ns ] [ letter range ] [ byte range ]
  options: -n  specifies that a string range will be given
           -s  specifies that a byte range will be given
  examples: scan -n 'd' 'e'  (files with names
beginning with d or e)
            scan -s 50 100   (files in the byte range
from 50 to 100)
  post. segment of current directory in specified
range
```

Give a sample run.

8. (Wheel of Fortune): write a procedure called wheel with the following specification:

```
usage: wheel [ -acv ] filename
  options: -a  frequency of all consonants and all vowels
               used in words in target file
           -c  frequency of all consonants used in target
               file
           -v  frequency of all vowels used in target file
  post. wheel prints a ten column table with following form:

       ltr fr   ltr fr   ltr fr  ...  ltr fr
```

Give a sample run with
a. wheel -a /usr/dict/words (or /usr/dict/web)
b. wheel -c /usr/dict/words (or /usr/dict/web)
c. wheel -v /usr/dict/words (or /usr/dict/web)

9. (Refinement): refine the wheel procedure from Exercise 8 in the following way:

```
usage: wheel [ -acv ] [ number ] filename
  examples: wheel -a 4 /usr/dict/words (prints 4 consonants
              and vowels with highest frequency)
            wheel -c 5 /usr/dict/words (prints 5 consonants
              with highest frequency)
            wheel -v 1 /usr/dict/words (prints vowel with
              highest frequency)
```

Give a sample run of wheel for each of the above examples.

10. Implement Experiment 5, Section 7.4.4, and give a sample run.
11. Give a list of differences between sed and awk.
12. Solve Challenge problem 1, Section 7.4.4. Give sample runs.
13. The binary log of a number (written lg n) can be computed using ln n/ ln 2 (in awk, log n/ log 2). Write a log2 procedure in awk with the following specification:

EXERCISES **327**

```
usage: log2 [ -i ] [ incr ] [ low, high ]
action: computes binary logs of numbers between the low
        and and high values
option: -i specifies increment
post: log2 prints a multicolumn table with the
      following form:

         lg n      value       lg n       value

examples: log2 10 100   (prints binary logs of all numbers
                        between 10 and 100).
          log2 -i 10 10 10000 (prints binary logs all
                              numbers between 10 and 1000
                              incremented by 10 as in

         lg n      value       lg n       value

         lg 10     3.32        lg 20      ?
           .         .           .          .
           .         .           .          .
           .         .           .          .
```

Give sample runs for the above examples.

14. (Refinement): log2 from Exercise 13 computes the log of a number base 2. The log of a number base x can be computed using log n/log x. Refine log2 to satisfy

```
usage: log2 [ -bi ] [ base ][ incr ] [ low, high]
 option: -b specifies base to use (default is 2)
 examples: log2 -b 10 5 100 (computes log base 10 for
                             numbers in 5,100 interval)
           log2 -bi 10 2 5 100 (computes log base 10 for
                                numbers in 5,100 interval
                                incremented by 2)
```

Give a sample run for the above examples.

15. Solve Challenge problem 2, Section 7.7. Give some sample runs.
16. Solve Challenge problem 3, Section 7.7. Give some sample runs with
    a. stopwatch wc /usr/dict/words
    b. stopwatch stopwatch who
    c. stopwatch ls
17. (Refinement): refine stopwatch from Exercise 16 so that it satisfies the following specifications:

```
usage: stopwatch [ -bc ] [ command ]
 options: -b print both forms of processing time
          -c print only C shell form of processing time
```

Give some sample runs with
   a. stopwatch -b wc /usr/dict/words
   b. stopwatch -c wc /usr/dict/words
18. Implement Experiment 8 and give some sample runs.
19. Write the C language equivalent of partition in Experiment 9, Section 7.8. Give some sample runs with
   a. list file given in Experiment 9
   b. last twenty entries of your online dictionary
20. (Refinement): refine mototal (Procedure 2, Section 7.9.1) so that it satisfies

```
usage: mototal [ -dm ] [ month(s) ] [ day(s) ]
  option: -d specifies range of days to find storage used
          -m specifies range of months to find storage used
    examples: mototal (storage for all months)
              mototal Jun Sep (storage for specified months)
              mototal -m Jun Aug (storage for months in range)
              mototal -d Jun 10 15 (storage used during
                        specified days)
```

Give a sample run for above examples.

21. Implement select (Procedure 4, Section 7.9.3) and give some sample runs with
   a. partition <head -20 /usr/dict/words | select
   b. partition <tail -20 /usr/dict/words | select
22. Implement combine (Procedure 5, Section 7.9.3) and give some sample runs with
   a. output from 21a
   b. output from 21b
23. Implement enigma (Procedure 3, Section 7.9.3) and give some sample runs.
24. Implement dice (Experiment 13, Section 7.9.4) and give some sample runs.
25. Implement freq (Experiment 14, Section 7.9.4) and give some sample runs.
26. (Refinement): refine freq from Exercise 25 so that it satisfies

```
usage: freq [ -c ] [ number ]
  option: -c   specifies frequency count each star represents
              in table printed by freq
    examples: freq -c 10 (each star represents 10 occurrences)
              freq -c 3  (each star represents 3 occurrences)
```

Give sample runs with the above examples.

27. Write a shuffle procedure in awk that simulates shuffling a poker deck (52 cards, 13 cards in each suit) that satisfies

```
usage: shuffle
  post. list of 52 distinct random numbers.
```

Give some sample runs.
Hint: the following Pascal procedure given to me by David Ranum (private communication) shuffles a poker deck:

```
type
  DeckType = array[0..51] of integer;
procedure shuffle(var deck: DeckType);
var ind1, ind2, num, temp: integer;
begin
  for ind1 := 0 to 51 do begin
    num := trunc(rndm * 100);
    ind2 := (ind1 + num) mod 52;
    temp := deck[ind1]; deck[ind1] := deck[ind2];
    deck[ind2] := temp
    end
end;  (*shuffle*)
```

Give some sample runs of shuffle.

28. Write a craps procedure in awk that satisfies

```
usage: craps [ -p ]
  option: -p prints picture dice faces turned up.
  post. prints dice face totals turned up after a roll.
  rules: 1. if total is 7 or 11 on first roll, you win
         2. if total is 2, 3, or 12, you lose
         3. on any other total, keep rolling until either
            one of the totals in case 2 turns up or you
            roll the same total again (you win)
```

Give some sample runs of craps.

29. Write a krnd (for "Knuth random") procedure in awk which implements the following algorithm (written in Pascal) to generate random numbers:

```
function krnd(var seed: real): real;
begin
  seed := (637 * seed) mod 9423;
  krnd := seed/9423
end;  (*krnd*)
```

(The krnd algorithm is derived from Knuth [1973].)

30. Implement krnd from Exercise 29 in the dice procedure from Experiment 13, Section 9.4.4. Give some sample runs.

31. Test randomness of krnd with the freq procedure, Experiment 14, Section 9.4.4. Give some sample runs.

32. Write a sidebyside procedure that satisfies

```
usage: sidebyside [ low, high ]
  action: prints frequencies of numbers in low, high interval
          produced by rnd (Procedure 6, Section 9.4.4) and
          by krnd (Exercise 30) in a table of the form:

                    rnd                      krnd
          n         frequency      n         frequency
```

Give some sample runs with
a. sidebyside 1 6
b. sidebyside 1 52

33. Write a cipher procedure in awk that satisfies

```
usage: cipher key filename
post: prints message in encrypted form where each character
      in your message is replaced by a distinct random
      number (for each line in message file), which is
      derived relative to current input line using

      seed = key * (position of character in line)
```

[Note: spaces must be encrypted also.]

Give a sample run with indicated messages in a message file:
a. cipher 0.5 'tumtytumtoes!' (in message)
b. cipher 0.271828 'Sell short.' (in message)
c. cipher 2.6 'Meet me Spade's corner at 6 p.m.' (in message)

34. Write a decipher procedure in awk which satisfies

```
usage: decipher key filename
post.prints decryption of contents of file using key
```

Give sample runs with encrypted messages from Exercise 33.

35. Doublets is a game taken from the works of Lewis Carroll and is played in the following way: given a pair of words, each with the same number of letters, start with the first word in the doublet and replace one letter at a time to obtain another dictionary word until the last replacement produces the second word in the doublet. Here are some examples:

doublet	solution	doublet	solution
cat, dog	cat	black, white	black
	cot		slack
	dot		stack
	dog		stalk
			stale
			shale
			whale
			while
			white

Write a doublet procedure in awk that accepts a doublet and uses your on-line dictionary to attempt to find the intermediate words leading to a solution to your doublet. That is, doublet should satisfy

```
usage: doublet word word
post: prints failure message if solution to doublet not
      found
```

EXERCISES 331

Give some sample runs with
a. cat, dog
b. dust, gold
c. old, spy
d. red, spy
e. ada, awk
f. iron, cord

36. (Refinement): refine doublet from Exercise 35 so that it allows you to add words to your on-line dictionary to solve your doublet.

37. (Refinement): refine doublet so that it computes your doublet score according to the following rule formulated by Lewis Carroll:

scoring rule: square length + 1 of word used in doublet and subtract 2 for every link (intermediate word used to solve doublet).
example: dust-gust-gist-gilt-gild-gold gets a score of 16 minus 8 = 8.

Give some sample runs.

7.16 REVIEW QUIZ

Indicate whether the following statements are true or false.
1. There are regular expressions acceptable to sed which are not acceptable to awk.
2. An awk program which checks input lines for patterns has an implied case statement.
3. Every awk program has an implied loop.
4. An awk program can be empty (just awk ' ').
5. By default, an awk program that consists merely of patterns will output only those lines not matching a pattern.
6. If yes is the name of an awk variable, then $yes is the value of that variable.
7. NF equals the last field of the current input line in an awk program in execution.
8. NR will be zero in an awk program that processes an empty input file.
9. Procedures written in sed are usually faster than corresponding procedures written in awk.
10. An awk program can process lines taken from a pipe.

7.17 FURTHER READING

Aho, A. V., B. W. Kernighan, and P. J. Weinberger. Awk—A Pattern Scanning and Processing Language. Software—Practice and Experience, vol. 9 (25 December 1978), pp. 267–79.

AT&T Unix Programmer's Manual, volume 1. NY: Holt, Rinehart and Winston, 1983. See pp. 284–85 on printf(3S).

Bailes, P. A. DDA—A Date Definition Facility for UNIX Using AWK. Software—Practice and Experience. Vol. 15, no. 10 (October 1985), pp. 1011–20.

Bentley, J. Programming Pearls. Reading, MA: Addison-Wesley, 1986. See pp. 19–21 on awk and anagrams.

Budgen, D. Making Use of the Unix Operating System. Englewood Cliffs, NJ: Prentice, 1984. See pp. 164–69 on awk.

Carroll, L. in T. Augarde. The Oxford Guide to Word Games. NY: Oxford, 1984. See Chapter 21 on games of Lewis Carroll.

Horowitz, E. and S. Sahni. Fundamentals of Data Structures in Pascal. Rockville, MD: Computer Science Press, 1984. See p. 11 on selection sorting.

Kernighan, B. W. and R. Pike. The Unix Programming Environment. Englewood Cliffs, NJ: Prentice, 1984. See pp. 114–31 on awk.

IEEE. IEEE Trial-Use Standard Portable Operating System for Computer Environments. NY: IEEE, 1986. See Appendix B on relationship of POSIX to C.

Lindeman, J. P. Theory and Practice in the Construction of a Working Sort Routine. AT&T Bell Laboratories Technical Journal. Vol. 63, no. 8, part 2 (October 1984), pp. 1827–844.

Pourboireki, N. Artificial Intelligence and Intelligent Artifice in R. M. Baer. The Digital Villain. Reading, MA: Addison-Wesley, 1972. See Chapter 10 on Echo IV program by Nicholas Pourboireki.

Van Wyk, C. J. AWK as Glue for Programs. Software—Practice and Experience. Vol. 16, no. 4 (April 1986), pp. 369–88.

8 The Joy C Shell

Unix was designed by programmers for programmers.
—Quarterman, Silberschatz, and Peterson, 1985.

8.0 AIMS

- Give an overview of the C shell
- Show how the .login, .cshrc, and .logout files can be used to customize your Unix environment
- Introduce events and event numbers relative to the C shell history mechanism
- Show various applications of C shell aliases
- Introduce C shell programming techniques
- Show how to design various C shell procedures
- Suggest ways to make C shell procedures robust
- Illustrate how procedures written for the Bourne shell can be adapted to the C shell
- Call attention to the benefits of noclobbering
- Present optional filename expansions or globbing

8.1 INTRODUCTION TO THE C SHELL

Recall that a *shell* is a command language interpreter. In a Unix environment, a variety of shells are usually available. So far we have been using the Bourne shell or sh. The sh shell is named after Steve Bourne (1978), who developed it for 7th edition Unix. The C shell was written by Bill Joy (1980) at Berkeley for 6th edition Unix and is a standard feature of the Berkeley Software Distribution of Unix. (In this chapter, we will refer to Berkeley Unix as BSD.) The system name for the C shell is csh. If you are logged in now, you can execute the C shell by typing

```
$ csh       # begin using the C shell

%
```

The **%** is the default prompt for the C shell. Everything you do after this is history. While you are logged in, the C shell maintains a history of previous command lines you have entered. To see this, type

```
history

    1 history

%
```

An old command line is called an *event*. The history command displays both an old command line *and* its event number. An *event number* is a positive integer that specifies when an event occurred; the most recent event has the highest event number. You can use the **set** command to specify how many old events are kept by the history mechanism. For example, to save up to 12 old events, type

```
% set history = 12       # save up to 12 old commands
%
```

The value of $history indicates the size of the history list being maintained. To check the value of $history, type

```
% echo $history
12
%
```

You can customize the C shell prompt so that its event number is displayed along with the %-prompt by typing

```
% set prompt = '\!% '      # notice the space!
5%
```

So far we have typed four command lines. The current blank command line is the fifth event indicated by the 5% prompt. Now check your history by typing

```
5% history                              # display your history
    1 history
    2 set history = 12
    3 echo $history
    4 set prompt = '\!% '
    5 history
6%
```

INTRODUCTION TO THE C SHELL **335**

Notice that the comments (strings that begin with a #) are not preserved by the history mechanism. Just the executable portion of command lines becomes history.

The history mechanism was invented by Warren Teitelman. In Section 8.3 we show several ways of recalling and executing old command-line events.

Bill Joy invented the aliasing mechanism for the C shell. The **alias** command makes it possible to rename command lines using one or more characters. For instance, we can make **h** the alias for **history** by typing

```
6% alias h history
7%
```

Now to see your history, you merely need to type

```
%7 h
     1  history
        .
        .
        .
%8
```

The word 'alias' is not the easiest one to type, especially for amateur typists. To remedy this, you can make **al** the alias for **alias** itself by entering

```
%8 alias al alias      # an alias for alias!
```

This is usually the first alias defined at the beginning of a C shell session. This simplifies aliasing other commands. To see this, try

```
%8 al dir 'ls -a . | pr -5 -t'
```

to define **dir** as an alias for the command line (inside the single quotes) to list all the files in your current directory in five columns. Instead of entering the original command line, you can now enter

```
%9 dir
.              ..             bin       .cshrc    .lastlog
.login         .logout
%10
```

Bill Joy (1986) points to the history and aliasing mechanisms as being at the heart of the C shell. In addition to these time-saving tools, the syntax for C shell command lines makes it easier for C programmers to use. Its syntax is close to the C language. The C shell also has a powerful set of control structures with syntax which closely resembles C.

In addition to the commands available to both the Bourne and C shell, there are a variety of useful built-in C shell commands. Among the latter are a set of job control commands invented by Jim Kulp. These job control commands include a **jobs** command to display processes relative to command lines as well as **fg** and **bg** commands to handle foreground and background processing.

The C shell is available as either the default or as an alternative shell on many Unix systems besides Berkeley Unix itself (Xenix-3, Xenix-5, Ultrix-11, and Ultrix-32, for example). This chapter introduces the basic features of the C shell. It also shows what changes are needed to make procedures written earlier with the Bourne shell compatible with the C shell. We start by looking at ways you can access either the Bourne or the C shell and how you can begin customizing your working environment while you are in the C shell.

8.2 GETTING STARTED WITH THE C SHELL

After you log in, you can determine what your default login shell is by using **grep** to search through the /etc/passwd file for login information relative to your login name. In showing how this is done, we will assume your default login shell is the Bourne shell (with the $-prompt). Try

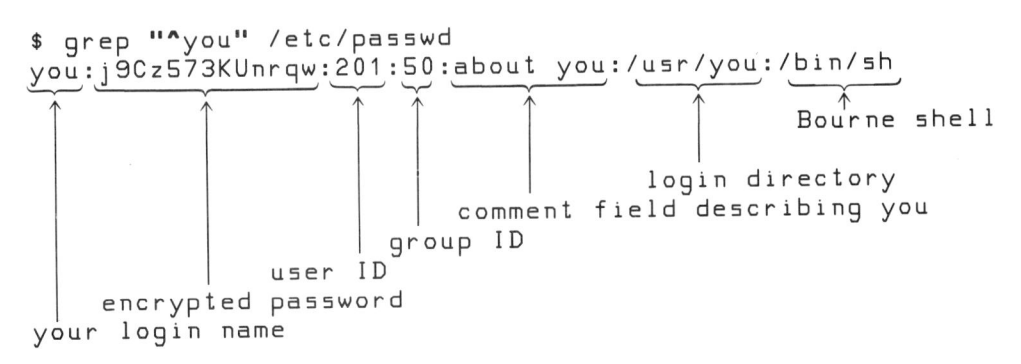

```
$ grep "^you" /etc/passwd
you:j9Cz573KUnrqw:201:50:about you:/usr/you:/bin/sh
```

```
your login name
  encrypted password
              user ID
                group ID
                  comment field describing you
                           login directory
                                    Bourne shell
```

The last field in the above sample entry from /etc/passwd is /bin/sh, which indicates your login shell is the Bourne shell. If your login shell were the C shell, this last entry would be /bin/csh. Your system administrator can change your login shell to /bin/csh by editing the /etc/passwd file. You can move back and forth between the Bourne and C shells by using **csh** and **sh** or the BSD Unix **chsh** ("change shell") command. The **csh** and **sh** commands are preferred because they are simpler to use and can be used in BSD and non-BSD Unix environments.

After you login, you can execute the C shell by typing

```
$ csh                    # execute C shell
%
```

If you are in the C shell and want to change to the Bourne shell, type

```
% sh                     # execute Bourne shell
$
```

If you have logged in under the C shell, executed **sh,** and want to return to the C shell, you can do so either by pressing ctrl-d or entering **exit.** Once you are in the C shell, use either the **printenv** (in BSD Unix) or **env** (in System V Unix or Xenix-5) command to display the settings for your environment variables. Try

```
% env                        # display environment settings
```

Here is sample output from env:

```
HOME=/usr/you
PATH=:/usr/you/bin:/bin:/usr/bin
TERM=vt100
SHELL=/bin/sh
MAIL=/usr/spool/mail/you
```

You can employ the **setenv** command to modify these environment variables. For example, the above sample of SHELL says /bin/sh is the default shell. You can change this for this session only be entering

```
% setenv SHELL /bin/csh              # modify SHELL
% echo $SHELL
/bin/csh
```

To use **vi** you need to make sure TERM has the correct setting. For example, if your terminal is an ansi Standard CRT like the IBM PC AT, then type

```
        % set TERM ansi     # declare terminal type
```

The value of $TERM must match one of the names associated with the /etc/termcap file on your system.

Recall that each time you log in under the Bourne shell, your .profile file will automatically be executed if you have this file in your login directory. It is .profile that makes it possible to customize your environment and automatically initialize environment variables like HOME, PATH, TERM, and MAIL. Similarly, if /bin/csh is your login shell, this program will automatically execute .login and .cshrc files, provided that these files are installed in your login directory.

8.2.1 Customizing Your Environment with .login and .cshrc

Your .profile is a hidden file that is not listed when you type

```
% ls -l ~ | more             # does not list .profile
```

In the C shell, ~ is the same as $home. To see this, type
```
% echo ~          # identifies $home
/usr/you
```

To list the hidden files in your directory, type

```
$ ls -a ~ | more              # display hidden files
```

If you have the .login and .cshrc files in your login directory *and* you log in under /bin/csh, the C shell will automatically execute these files each time you log in. Again, if /bin/csh is your default shell and you have a .logout file in your home directory, the C shell will automatically execute this file each time you log out *while* you are in the C shell. Here is how these files are used:

SPECIAL FILE	USES
.login	1. executed by /bin/csh when you log in under /bin/csh (this *only* happens when the C shell is your default shell)
	2. initialize environment variables using the **set** and **setenv** commands
	3. execute one or more favorite files you have in your ~/bin directory like a modified version of the **dleft** "days left") procedure from Section 6.7.2 which we give in Section 8.5.2
	4. execute one or more Unix commands like **who**
.cshrc	1. executed by /bin/csh when you log in under /bin/csh
	2. **set** special C shell variables
	3. aliases for various favorite command lines
.logout	1. executed by /bin/cshrc when you log out, if /bin/csh is your default shell
	2. do housekeeping chores like saving the output from **date** in a .lastlog file and displaying your disk usage output by **du -s**

If you do not have these files in your login directory, then you might want to start with the following simplified version of .login:

```
% cat > .login                          # sample .login file
#
# .login, version 1.0
#
setenv SHELL /bin/csh
setenv USER you                         # USER identifies login name
setenv MAIL /usr/spool/mail/you
setenv TERM vt100                       # identifies terminal as vt100
set path = (. $home/bin /bin /usr/bin)
set ignoreeof                           # ignore ctrl-d
set noclobber                           # prevent overwriting old files
echo Welcome to the C shell, $USER
echo -n Date and time: `date`
echo " "
ctrl-d
%
```

In the C shell, HOME is preset by default to your login directory. Some versions of Unix automatically use the password file /etc/passwd to initialize the USER (or a LOGNAME) environment variable. Just in case this is not so on your system, we have included a **setenv** command line for USER in the sample .login file. Also notice that the value of TERM in the sample .login file may be appropriate for you. You need to set TERM relative to one of the device names in your /etc/termcap file. (This is a text file which is a data base for terminal types on your system.) Besides the vt100 and ansi terminals, your /etc/termcap file will probably have device names like free100 (Liberty Freedom 100), ti931 (for Texas Instrument 931 VDT), sk8620 (for Seiko 8620), lisa (for Apple Lisa), and so on. To see what your system allows, type

```
% cat /etc/termcap
```

For a list of the type of terminals *currently* being used on your system, type

```
% cat /etc/ttytype
vt100      console
vt52       tty00
vt52       tty01           Sample /etc/ttytype
vt100      tty03
ti931      tty11
ti931      tty12
sk8620     tty13
macterm    tty14
diablnet   diablo
applenet   apple
```

Most Unix environments also have a **tset** ("terminal setup") command, which you will probably want to learn to use in your .login file. This command makes it possible to login on more than one type of device (a default device like a vt100 and some other device you specify). If your default device is an ansi keyboard and your alternative device is a vt100, then you can use the following setup in your .login file:

```
set term = ('tset -m ansi:ansi -m :\?vt100 -r -S -Q')
setenv TERM $term[1]            default terminal
setenv TERMCAP $term[1]         terminal data base
```

---

tset options used:

-m Says map to specified terminal listed in in your /etc/ttytype file.
   Mappings to both ansi and vt100 terminals are given here.
-r Says to display terminal type on diagnostic output.
-S Outputs strings to be put in environment variables.
-Q Suppresses displaying "Erase set to" and "kill set to" messages.

Once you have created your .login file, you can execute it using the **source** command by typing

```
% source .login              # execute your .login file
Welcome to the C shell, jim
Date and time: Tue Jan 20 11:49:44 CDT 1987
%
```

Now if you use either **printenv** or **env**, you can check the results of executing .login. Try

```
% env
HOME=/usr/you
MAIL=/usr/spool/mail/you
PATH=:/usr/you/bin:/bin:/usr/bin
SHELL=/bin/csh
TERM=vt100
USER=jim
```

Notice that the simple .login file has the following additional features:

1. **set noclobber** This prevents accidental overwriting to an existing file—unless you specify otherwise, no overwriting existing files will be permitted.
2. **set ignoreeof** This makes it necessary to use **logout** instead of **ctrl-d** to log off. If the ignoreeof variable is not set, then you must type **ctrl-d** twice to log off.

If you have a .cshrc file in your home directory, this file will also be executed automatically each time you log into the C shell. The .cshrc file is used primarily to initialize variables like history and time and to define your favorite aliases. To see the effects of having a .cshrc file, use an editor (or redirect **cat** as shown below) to create the following sample .cshrc file:

```
% cat > .cshrc
#
# .cshrc, version 1
#

# set up C shell variables

set history = 12            # maintain up to 12 old events
set savehist = 12           # (BSD only) to save history
set prompt = '\% '          # prompt with current event no.
set time = 10               # enables command timing

# build aliases

alias al alias              # make al alias for alias
al lo logout                # simplify entering logout
al h history                # simplify entering history
al cx 'chmod +x'            # to make a file executable
al xcsh 'source -/.cshrc'   # to execute .cshrc
al xlog 'source -/.login'   # to execture .login
al whereis \
'find / -name \!* -print'   # locate a Unix file
al dc \
'ls -a \!* | pr -5 -t'      # print all files in 5 cols.
al dsub \
'ls -l \!* | grep "^d"'     # list subdirectories
ctrl-d
%
```

Now execute this file by typing

```
% source .cshrc
23%
```

Notice the C shell prompt now includes the number of the current event (this is a result of the **set prompt** command line in the .cshrc file you just executed). Once you have executed this version of the .cshrc file (many other versions are possible!), you can now type

```
23% xcsh
24%
```

to execute your .cshrc file. Until you are satisfied with your .cshrc file, you will probably find **xcsh** handy and one of the most commonly used aliases. The history and prompt variables in the sample .cshrc file were explained earlier in Section 8.1. Two additional mystery variables (savehist and time) also are set in the .cshrc file. Here is how they are used:

1. **savehist** (BSD only)   When savehist is set in a BSD Unix environment, this tells the C shell how many history commands to save when you log off and make available again as part of your history when you log in again. When you execute

   ```
   % set savehist = 10
   ```

   the C shell saves the last ten commands you have entered (just before you log out) in a .history file in your login directory. The beauty of this feature of BSD Unix is the restoration of the last ten events in your previous history *without* their being executed again. The restored events taken from .history when you log on are made part of your history for the current login session. By default, savehist is unset.

2. **time** (all versions of the C shell)   When the time variable is set, this enables a command timing feature of the C shell. In executing

   ```
   % set time = 10       # for more than 10 seconds
   ```

   you have told the C shell to display resource utilization statistics for commands requiring more than ten seconds.

Warning: there are instances where you do not want to have the C shell timing execution of commands (when the timing for one slow command goes into a pipe to another command, for example). In Section 8.6.3, we give an example where it is advantageous to **unset time.**

To "turn off" a variable which has been set, use the **unset** command. To see this, try the following experiment:

☐ EXPERIMENT 1

(setting and unsetting the time variable)

```
% set time = 3             # for more than 3 secs.
% whereis vi               # locate vi
/bin/vi
```
....

GETTING STARTED WITH THE C SHELL

```
                0.8u 27.3s 0:46 60%
                % unset time                    # disable timing
                % whereis ed                    # locate ed
                /bin/ed
                ..........................
                %
```

This says **whereis vi** took 0.8 seconds of user time, 27.3 seconds of system time, and 46 seconds of real time with a ratio of (user + system time) to real time or

$$(0.8 + 27.3)/46 = 0.61087$$

or about 60% (the estimate computed by my C shell). By unsetting the time variable in Experiment 1, we turn off the timing function of the C shell. No timing statistics are displayed for **whereis ed.**

In the sample version of .cshrc given in this section, we have also used some special C shell escape characters (single quotes, the backslash \ ) and we employ what is known as an alias argument \!* (to pass any number of arguments to an alias).

8.2.2 C Shell Escape Characters

The sample .cshrc file in Section 8.2.1 has many features that may be new to you. First notice how we set up the alias for the **whereis** command using the backslash \ to escape special shell characters:

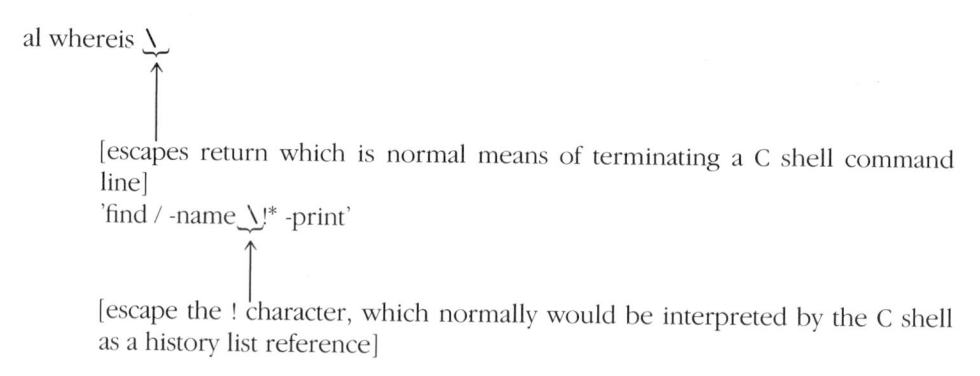

al whereis \

[escapes return which is normal means of terminating a C shell command line]

'find / -name \!* -print'

[escape the ! character, which normally would be interpreted by the C shell as a history list reference]

The backslash is one of the most commonly used escape characters in C shell programming. The \ is an example of a metacharacter. A *metacharacter* is a character that has some controlling role relative to other characters used in a programming language. The ! (exclamation) is itself a metacharacter that is normally interpreted by the C shell as part of a history substitution. For example, to reenter the previous command, type

```
                24% !!
                xcsh
                25%
```

There are many other uses of the ! relative to your history. (These are given in Section 8.3 and in Appendix A.) For now, notice that we have used the \ in the .cshrc file to escape the usual meaning of the !.

Many of the aliases in the sample .cshrc file in Section 8.2.1 also use single quotes in a special way. In the C shell, single quotes are used to prevent variable expansions and command substitutions. To see what effect single quotes have, try the following experiment:

☐ EXPERIMENT 2A

(display $home as a literal string and its value)

```
% echo '$home equals ' $home
$home equals /usr/you
```

Because we enclosed $home inside single quotes in Experiment 2a, the C shell treats '$home' as a literal string (plain characters) instead of treating $home as a variable to be expanded in the output from **echo.** To tell the C shell to expand $home, you must use double quotes *or* no quotes at all. In the C shell, double quotes permit the variable expansion *and* command substitution. To see this, try

☐ EXPERIMENT 2B

(permit variable expansion and command substitution)

```
% echo "$home has `echo $home | wc -c` characters."
/usr/mozart has 11 characters.
```

By using double quotes in Experiment 2b, we have told the C shell to expand the $home variable (use its value). The double quotes in the **echo** command line in this experiment also cause the substitution of the output from **wc -c**. Notice that we get the same effect without using double quotes, as shown in the following variation of Experiment 2b:

☐ EXPERIMENT 2C

(permit variable expansion and command substitution)

```
% echo $home has `echo $home | wc -c` characters.
/usr/mozart has 12 characters.
```

In the sample .cshrc file in Section 8.2.1, we have introduced a **whereis** alias.

GETTING STARTED WITH THE C SHELL **345**

8.2.3 A Note on whereis

On some Unix systems that support the C shell, **whereis** is a standard command (it is in BSD Unix but not in System V or Xenix-5). For those systems not having the built-in **whereis** command, we have included **whereis** as an alias for its primitive equivalent of the much more powerful version of **whereis** available in BSD Unix. This is a good example of an alias that frees us from typing a somewhat complex command line using **find,** which we experimented with in Section 2.5, using the Bourne shell. For example, to locate the **csh** file, type

```
% whereis csh                    # locate csh file
find: cannot open /usr/spool/uucp
/bin/csh
%
```

By typing **whereis csh,** we have entered an alias for

```
find / -name csh -print
```

During the search started by entering **whereis csh,** an attempt is made to access /usr/spool/uucp, which is a restricted file and unreadable. This attempt to access /usr/spool/uucp is displayed along with the location of **csh** in /bin/csh. Finally, notice that the **whereis** alias in .cshrc in Section 8.2.1 introduces the use of an alias argument using \!* which we explain in Section 8.4.2.

8.2.4 Customizing logoff with .logout

Without fanfare you can log off when the C shell is your login shell by typing

```
% logout                         # leave system
login:
```

You can customize logging off by introducing a .logout file in your home directory. Each time you logout, the C shell checks if you have a .logout file in your home directory. If you do, it will execute commands in your .logout file. To see how this works, try setting up the following sample .logout file:

```
% cat > .logout
#
# .logout, version 1.0
#
echo -n "Total blocks used so far:   `du -s`"; echo " "
echo -n "Leaving system at:   `date`"
ctrl-d
%
```

Recall that **lo** is the alias for **logout** defined in the .cshrc file in Section 8.2.1. So you can now leave the system by typing

```
% lo
Total blocks used so far: 238
Leaving system at Wed Jan 21 09:17:47 CST 1987
login:
```

You might want to consider customizing your logout procedure further by using the following technique given by Gail and Paul Anderson (1986).

Anderson method of leaving the C shell:
Each time you log off, use your .login file to execute

date | tee $home/.lastlog

to do two things:

1. Display the output from **date** when you log off.
2. Redirect the output from **date** to a .lastlog file, which you can then use in your .login file to display the date and time of your session with the C shell.

Using this idea, here is a second, enhanced version of .logout:

```
% cat .logout                   # after editing version 1
#
# .logout, version 1.1
#
echo -n "Total blocks used so far: `du -s`"; echo " "
echo -n "Leaving system at `date |tee $home/.lastlog`"
```

Now try logging out and log on again to see the effect of this new version of .logout. Notice it is now possible to modify your .login file to display the contents of the .lastlog file.

8.2.5 Enhanced Version of the .cshrc File

Once you have logged out using version 1.1 of the .logout file in Section 8.2.4, you have a means of customizing your login procedure. To do this, you merely need to type

```
% cat >> .login
echo -n Last time on system: `cat .lastlog`; echo " "
ctrl-d
%
```

For completeness, we show the entire new version of the .cshrc file:

☐ EXPERIMENT 3

(new version of .cshrc)

```
% cat .login                              # after editing
#
# .login, version 1.1
#

setenv SHELL /bin/csh                     # establish SHELL as csh
setenv USER you                           # USER identifies login name
setenv MAIL /usr/spool/mail/you
setenv TERM vt100                         # your terminal may be diff.
set path = (. $home/bin /bin /usr/bin)
set ignoreeof                             # ignore ctrl-d
set noclobber                             # avoid overwriting old files

echo Welcome to the C shell, $USER

echo -n Date and time: `date`; echo " "

echo -n Last time on system:  `cat $home/.lastlog`; echo " "
```

Now test this new version of .cshrc by typing

```
% xlog                                    # use alias from .cshrc
Terminal type is vt100

Welcome to the C shell, jim
Date and time: Wed Jan 21 09:41:29 CST 1987
Last time on system: Wed Jan 21 09:32:36 CST 1987
```

The exclamation mark ! is a vital metacharacter relative to the history mechanism in the C shell. We show how this can be used to tap your history in various ways in Section 8.3.

8.3 RETRIEVING EVENTS IN YOUR HISTORY

A selection of the various uses of the ! relative to the history mechanism are summarized in the following table:

Selection of History Commands

Legend: E = event number, which is a positive integer
 n is a positive integer
 str specifies a string
 $ specifies 'last'
 (*) example given as part of interpretation

COMMAND	EXAMPLE	INTERPRETATION
!!	% !!	reissue previous command
!E	% !5	retrieve, display and execute fifth event
!str	% !v	execute most recent event beginning with v
!$	(*)	!$ specifies the last word of the last command as in

```
% grep "^mozart" /etc/passwd
mozart::231:50:.....................
% cat !$
cat /etc/passwd
root:BbDR7W7WZcISbXE:0:0:Super User:....
```

!?str?	(*)	invokes most recent event containing **str** as in

```
% !?mo?
grep "^mozart" /etc/passwd
mozart::231:50:.....................
%
```

!E:p	% !35:p	displays specified event without executing the retrieved event.

A complete list of C shell history commands is given in Appendix A. The elements of the Selection of History Commands table have been chosen because they are commonly used.

Until now we have pretended that you have been using the default C shell prompt (without the current event number). This simplifies the presentation of many of the C shell command lines. You should notice that by using

```
% set prompt = '\!% '
```

you give yourself a means of seeing how far you have progressed in your current history. The display of the current event number also makes it easier to use many of the history commands. For example, if you have

```
33% xlog
34% xcsh
35%
```

as your current event number and you want to reexecute the second-to-the-last command, you can type

```
35%  !33
xlog
%
```

Strings are sometimes easier to deal with than numbers. Suppose you now have the following history:

```
36%  h
     30   vi .login
     31   cat .login
     32   ls -a . | pr -5 -t
     33   xlog
     34   xcsh
     35   xlog
     36   h
37%
```

You can reexecute the 30th event by typing

```
37%  !v
vi .login
```

which you may find quicker than entering the correct event number. Notice also that the use of !v often eliminates the need to display your history. If you want to display but not execute the 30th event, you can type

```
37%  !30:p
vi .login
38%
```

The event you have displayed also becomes part of your history. In sum, these history commands simplify the reuse of old command lines.

The C shell alias mechanism offers another means of simplifying commonly used command lines.

8.4 ALIASES

The **alias** command has the following syntax:

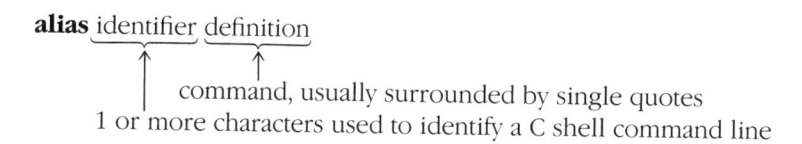

> **alias** identifier definition
>   ↑   ↑
> | command, usually surrounded by single quotes
>   1 or more characters used to identify a C shell command line

Commonly used aliases go into your .cshrc file. You can create temporary aliases otherwise. Try, for example,

```
% al xout 'source ~/.logout'
%
```

if you know you will be making periodic changes to your .logout file during the current session. Now you can execute your .logout file without logging off. To see this, type

```
% xout                           # try out your .logout
Total blocks used so far: 238    .
Leaving system at Wed Jan 21 11:26:57 CST 1987%
```

Notice that after executing **xout** the % prompt appears at the end of the last line displayed. You really do not need to worry about this when you execute your **lo** alias. However, if this bothers you, type

```
% cat >> .logout
echo " "
ctrl-d
%
```

Now

```
% xout
```

will perform more satisfactorily. You can remove aliases with the **unalias** command. For example, to remove the **whereis** alias temporarily, you can type

```
% unalias whereis                      # remove alias
```

You may find that you have aliases in your .cshrc file that you are not using very often but still want to keep. You can have it both ways by turning unwanted aliases in your .cshrc file into comments as in

```
# al whereis \
# 'find / -name \!* -print'
```

In effect, the #-signs turn the whereis alias "off." To restore this alias, just remove the #-signs. Aliases can also be nested.

8.4.1 Nested Aliases

One alias can reference another alias. For example, to save your last five commands, try

```
% al last5 'h | tail -5 | tee .last5'
%
```

Notice that we have embedded the alias **h** in the definition of the **last5** alias. To see how this works, try the following experiment:

☐ EXPERIMENT 4

(Note: define the **last5** alias before you run this experiment.)

```
% last 5                          # see and save last 5 events
    50    al xout 'source ~/.logout'
    51    xout
    52    cat >> .logout
    53    al last 'h | tail -5 | tee .last5'
    54    last5
%
```

Now check the contents of .last5 by typing

```
% cat .last5
```

If your Unix system does not have the **savehist** feature, you may find it helpful to add the last5 alias to your .cshrc file with

```
% cat >> .cshrc
al last5 'h | tail -5 | tee .last5'
ctrl-d
%
```

Then you can tie together your working sessions by adding the last5 command line to your .logout file using

```
% cat >> .logout
last5
ctrl-d
%
```

You have probably noticed from what we said earlier in Section 8.2.4 that you can drop the double quotes used in version 1 of .logout. After using an editor to make this change, we have the following new, enhanced version of the .logout file:

```
#
# .logout, version 1.2
#

echo -n Total blocks used so far: `du -s`; echo " "
echo -n Leaving system at `date | tee $home/.lastlog`; echo " "
last5
```

Then display your former history each time you log on with

```
% cat >> .login
echo Last 5 events:; cat .last5
ctrl-d
%
```

Now use the aliases from Sections 8.2.1 and 8.4.1 to test the new versions of these files:

☐ EXPERIMENT 5

(Note: make the changes (given in this section) to your .cshrc, .logout, and .login files *before* you run this experiment.)

```
% xcsh                              # tell C shell changes
% xout                              # test last5 alias
Total blocks used so far: 248
Leaving system at Wed Jan 21 12:01:45 CST 1987
% xlog                              # see last 5 events
Welcome to the C shell, jim
Date and time: Wed Jan 21 12:03:19 CST 1987
Last time on system: Wed Jan 21 12:01:45 CST 1987
Last 5 events:
     57   cat >> .logout
     58   cat >> .login
     59   xcsh
     60   xout
     61   xlog
%
```

The C shell aliasing mechanism makes it possible to embed arguments in alias definitions.

8.4.2 Alias Arguments

In the sample .cshrc file given in Section 8.2.1 there are several examples of alias definitions with arguments. The alias for dc ("directory in columns") has such a definition:

```
al dc 'ls -a \!* | pr - 5 -t'
         ↑
         alias argument
```

ALIASES 353

The alias argument \!* used in this alias definition has the following interpretation:

1. \ in \!* escapes the usual meaning of the ! (the \ prevents the C shell from interpreting the ! as a history list reference).
2. !* in \!* (in an alias definition) tells the C shell to *substitute* everything but the word 0 in the command line which uses the alias.

The C shell numbers command-line words starting with 0. The alias argument \!* tells the C shell to substitute every word except the word 0 in the command line which begins with an alias. By using \!*, you can pass multiple arguments to an alias. You can use \!^ as an alias argument to tell the C shell to substitute only word 1 of the current command line into the command line named by an alias. To see how the \!* alias argument can be used to substitute words 1 through n of a command line, try experimenting with the **dc** alias in the following way:

```
% dc $home $home/bin        # pass multiple arguments
/usr/you
.           ..         .cshrc      .login
/usr/bin
dleft       snoopy
%
```

Notice that the C shell has passed both $home (word 1) *and* $home/bin (word 2) to the **dc** command line, which is expanded in the following way:

```
ls -a /usr/you /usr/you/bin | pr -5 -t
```

Your $home and $home/bin directories will probably have many more files than we have shown in the above sample execution of the **dc** alias. In this case, you might want to employ the C shell **more** command as in

```
% dc $home $home/bin | more
```

We can invent another alias to experiment with the word 1 \!^ alias argument. Try

```
% al pickone '(echo \!^ | tee temp | wc -w); cat temp; rm temp'
% pickone C++ was invented by Bjarne Stroustrop.
            1
C++
%
```

Just C++ (word 1) is passed to **pickone.** Now try

```
% al pickall '(echo \!* | tee temp | wc -w); cat temp; rm temp'
% pickall C++ suggests incrementing C by 1.
             6
C++ suggests incrementing C by 1.
%
```

You can further customize your working environment while you are in the C shell by specializing the logoff procedure.

Once you become familiar with the potential of the history and alias mechanisms, you may be tempted to overdo a good thing.

8.4.3 A Word of Caution about Your History and Aliases

You should regard your .cshrc file as a home for frequently used aliases. Too many aliases can slow down your processing and chew up memory.

Rule of thumb: limit yourself to ten active aliases in your .cshrc file. Use -signs to put to "sleep" infrequently used .cshrc file aliases.

You will also want to be conservative about the number of events you maintain in your history. You can also chew up memory by making your history too long. As a rule it is best to limit yourself to a value of $history equal to ten or twelve.

All the time you have spent developing Bourne shell procedures has not been wasted. In many cases, the adaptation of procedures given in earlier chapters requires only slight modifications to make them executable in the C shell. In Section 8.5 we introduce the main features of the syntax for C shell procedures and illustrate how Bourne shell procedures can be adapted to a C shell environment.

8.5 C SHELL PROCEDURES

C shell procedures have the following format:

```
# initial comments (pre and post conditions)
# usage: command-verb [options] [argument-list]

command-lines
```

In the C shell, a command line argument which is continued on the next line requires the backslash \ escape character. To see this, try the following procedure which uses **sed** to list all files in your current directory that are empty:

■ PROCEDURE 1

(list all empty files in your current directory)

```
% cat > dirz
# list empty files in current directory
# usage: dirz
```

```
ls -a | sed -n '/^-/p' | \
        sed -n '/'"  0 '"/p'
ctrl-d
%
```

Notice that we used \ to continue the piped output from **sed** to **sed** on the second line of **dirz.** To see how this procedure works, try the following experiment:

☐ EXPERIMENT 6

(scanning directory for empty files)

Note: first create Procedure 1 before you run this experiment. Also, notice that we use **cx,** which is an alias for chmod +x in the .cshrc file in Section 8.2.1.

```
% cat > nothing
ctrl-d
% cat > vacant
ctrl-d
% cx dirz                              # make dirz executable
% dirz
-rw-r--r--      1 you    yourgroup  0  Jan 18 21:48 nothing
-rw-r--r--      1 you    yourgroup  0  Jan 18 21:59 vacant
```

You can use the same trick with the \ with an echo'd text which continues on more than one line as in

```
% echo 'A C shell procedure can be empty, \
which means it will do nothing if it is executed.'
A C shell procedure can be empty,
which means it will do nothing if it is executed.
```

(An empty shell procedure is called a *stub.*) Before we go further, there is an invaluable dbug alias (suggested by Gail and Paul Anderson [1986]) in the .cshrc file in Section 8.2.1:

```
al dbug 'csh -fvx'                      # use to find bugs
```

This dbug command will cause each procedure line being parsed and executed by /bin/csh to be displayed. If there is anything wrong with a line in a procedure, the execution started by dbug will stop at the problem spot and print an error message. To see how this works, try the following experiment:

☐ EXPERIMENT 7

(debugging a procedure that has errors)

■ PROCEDURE 2

```
% cat > no
# number the lines in a specified file
# requires $1 to be a file name
# usage: no filename

awk '( print NR, $0 }' $1
ctrl-d
%
```

Now, make no executable and dbug no by typing

```
% cx no
% dbug no no

awk '{ print NR, $0 }' $1
awk ( print NR, $0 } no
awk: syntax error near line 1
awk: bailing out near line 1
```

Now, edit no, replace the (by { and type

```
% no no
1    # Number lines in a specified file
2    # requires $1 to be a file name
3    # usage: no filename
4
5    awk '{ print NR, $0 }' $1
```

In the **no** procedure, we use $1 for the value of the first argument, which is the same technique we used to specify the first argument in a Bourne shell command line. The C shell also mimics C in referencing command line arguments using various forms of **argv** (called the C Shell *argument vector*).

8.5.1 Referencing Command-line Arguments with argv

A summary of the ways command-line arguments can be referenced in the C shell is given in the following table:

Legend: n is a positive integer

ARGUMENT VECTOR	INTERPRETATION
$#argv	number of command line arguments
$*	all command line arguments
$argv[*]	equals $* (all arguments)
$argv	equals $* (all arguments)
$0	word 0 in command line (file name)
$argv[n]	nth argument (1 <= n <= $*)
$argv[1-n]	arguments 1 through n (1 < n <= $*)
$argv[$*]	last argument
$argv[$#argv]	same as $argv[$*]

A good way to become comfortable with C shell argument vectors is to invent a procedure that uses the various forms of **argv** shown in the table just presented. The easiest way to do this is to employ the simplest form of the C shell **if** statement to prevent attempts to display non-existent arguments. The **if** statement has the following syntax:

>**if** (Boolean expression) **then**
>   command(s)
>**endif**

For instance, we can use the following **if** statement to print a message, provided $#argv is not zero:

>**if** ($#argv != 0) **then**
>   echo All arguments: $argv
>   echo All arguments: $*
>**endif**

The Boolean expression in this **if** statement uses the "not equal" operator != and returns a value of true if an argument line has one or more arguments. For now, this is all we need to know to put together a procedure to experiment with command-line arguments. A more detailed discussion of various forms of the **if** statement is given in Section 8.5.5. Now try the next experiment:

☐ EXPERIMENT 8

(experiments with C shell arguments)
Notice how single quotes are used in the following procedure to escape the usual meaning of the quoted characters.

PROCEDURE 3

```
% cat > allargs
# illustrate the use of C shell arguments
# usage: allargs [zero or more arguments]

echo '$#argv = ' $#argv
if ($#argv != 0) then
   echo '$argv[*] is ' $argv[*]
   echo '$* is ' $*
   echo '$argv is ' $argv
   echo " "                            # print a blank line
   set n = $#argv                      # capture no. of arguments
   echo '$argv[1-$n] (select) : ' $argv[1- $n]
   echo '$0 (name of program) is ' $0
   echo '$argv[1], $1 (first arg.) is ' $argv[1] $1
   echo '$argv[$#argv] (last arg.) is ' $argv[$#argv]
endif
ctrl-d
%
```

Now make allargs executable and try different argument lists:

```
% cx allargs
% allargs                              # with no arguments
$argv = 0
% allargs Mozarts middle name is Amadeus.
$#argv = 5
$argv[*]: Mozarts middle name is Amadeus.
$* is Mozarts middle name is Amadeus.
$argv is Mozarts middle name is Amadeus.

$argv[1-$n] (select) : Mozart's middle name is Amadeus.
$0 (name of program) is allargs
$argv[1], $1 (first arg.) is Mozarts Mozarts
$argv[$#argv] (last argument) is Amadeus.
```

Notice that we used Mozart instead of Mozart's as the first argument. The C shell misinterprets Mozart's when we enter

```
% allargs Mozart's first name is Wolfgang.
Unmatched '.
%
```

If you want the C shell to treat the ' (apostrophe) as just another charater rather than one of it metacharacters, then you must use double quotes as in

```
% allargs "Mozart's" first name is Wolfgang.
```

Now you should find that $argv[1] is taken by allargs as Mozart's.

Unlike the Bourne shell, values are assigned to C shell variables using the **set** command.

8.5.2 Setting Values of C Shell Variables

In the C shell the **set** command is used to assign strings to variables. It has the following syntax:

$$\textbf{set}\ variable\text{-}name\ =\ string$$

For example, to assign the output from **date** to a variable d, type

```
% set d = `date`
```

This contrasts sharply with the way set is used in the Bourne shell using

```
% set `date`
```

which sets the Bourne shell arguments. Here is a comparison of how the two shells use set:

Use of set by Bourne and C Shells

C SHELL	BOURNE SHELL
`% set d = `date``	`$ set `date``
`% echo $d`	`$ echo $*`
`Thu Jan 22 14:06:31 CST 1987`	`Thu Jan 22 14:10:20 CST 1987`
`% echo $d[1]`	`$ echo $1`
`Thu`	`Thu`
`% echo $d[2-3]`	`$ echo $2 $3`
`Jan 22`	`Jan 22`
`% echo $#d`	`$ echo $#`
`6`	`6`
`% set mo = $d[2]`	`$ mo = $2`
`% echo $mo`	`$ echo $mo`
`Jan`	`Jan`

Notice that once a C shell variable has been set, it can be treated either as a single value ($d, for example) or as an array of values ($d[1] through $d[$#d]). With the date variable d, we have $d[1] equal to Thu in the above table. The variable $#d is the number of arguments (the array size identified by the variable d). So $d[$#d] equals the last argument in the d-array or 1987 in the above table as shown as follows. Note that spaces in an assigned string mark the separation between array components in the output from 'date' assigned to d:

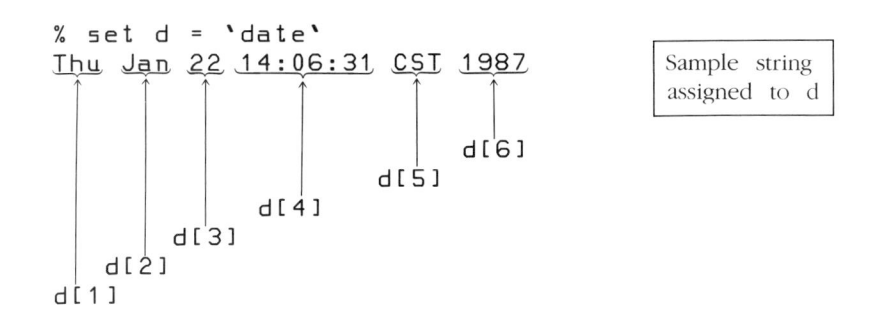

```
% set d = `date`
Thu Jan 22 14:06:31 CST 1987
 ↑   ↑   ↑    ↑       ↑    ↑
 |   |   |    |       |    d[6]
 |   |   |    |       d[5]
 |   |   |    d[4]
 |   |   d[3]
 |   d[2]
 d[1]
```

Sample string assigned to d

The Bourne shell requires the = (equal sign) to assign a value to a variable as in

```
$ count=`ls -a | wc -w`      # count files
$ echo $count
92
$
```

We need to use set in the C shell to assign a value to count as in

```
% set count = `lc -a | wc -w`
% echo $count
92
%
```

You can use set by itself to display variables you already have set by typing

```
% set
argv      ()
d         (Thu Jan 22 14:06:31 CST 1987)
history   10
home      /usr/you
ignoreeof
mail      /usr/spool/mail/you
path      (. /usr/you/bin /bin /usr/bin)
prompt    !%
savehist          5
shell     /bin/csh
status    0
```

The @-symbol is a "synonym" for **set.** If you type

```
% @
```

this will also display the values of all C shell variables. You might want to try some other experiments with C shell variables before going further. For example, we have enough information now to revise the **dleft** ("days left") procedure in Section

6.7.2. In this and the remaining times where we modify Bourne shell procedures to make them executable in the C shell, it is helpful to the use the following "failsafe" method. Note that we illustrate the steps of this method using the **dleft** procedure from Section 6.7.2 (it is typically used by system administrators to modify critically important files like /etc/password):

```
% cp dleft dleft+          # "xerox" copy of dleft
% vi dleft+                # edit dleft+, not dleft
.....................
% mv dleft dleft-          # put old dleft in freezer
% mv dleft+ dleft          # use new version of dleft
```

The idea is to save an old file and make all changes to a copy of the original file. If you consistently use the same technique, you will find it easier later to return to what you had previously. The following procedure is the C shell version of **dleft:**

■ PROCEDURE 4

(Note: this is the C shell form of Procedure 12b from Section 6.7.2. This new procedure uses **set** to assign values to d, day, mo, yr \ to continue **sed** program on more than one line.)

```
% cat dleft+               # file after editing session
# print remaining days in current month
# usage: dleft+

set d = `date`
set day = $d[3]; set mo = $d[2]; set yr = $d[6]
cal $mo $yr | sed -n ' /[JFMASOND] { \
p \
b \
} \
/'$day'/ { \
 :mask \
/^ *'$day'/ { p \
blast \
} \
s/[0-9]/ / \
tmask \
 :last \
n \
S/^./&/p \
tlast \
q \
}'
ctrl-d
%
```

Now make dleft+ executable and try it out with

```
% cx dleft+
% dleft+
     January 1987
   S   M  Tu   W  Th   F   S
                  22  23  24
  25  26  27  28  29  30  31
%
```

What we said about **sed** in Chapter 6 still applies in the C shell, with one important exception. You will probably find that it is often necessary to use the \ to implement multiline programs.

The C shell has a substantial collection of operators that have been carried over from the C language to form expressions *and* to make comparisons.

8.5.3 C Shell Operators

The various C shell operators are brought together in the following precedence table:

C Shell Operator Precedence

Legend for Table types: A = arithmetic assignment operator
                         Ac = compact arithmetic assignment operator
                         B = bitwise operator
                         G = grouping symbols
                         L = logical operator
                         C = comparison operator

OPERATOR	INTERPRETATION	TYPE	PURPOSE
( ) **highest**	value construction	G	change order
+ + − −	add 1, subtract 1	Ac	assignment
~	1's complement	B	reverse bits
!	not	L	negate value
* / %	times, div, mod	A	arithmetic
+ −	sum, difference	A	arithmetic
<< >>	shift left, right	B	manipulate bits
<= >= > <	le, ge, g, l	C	comparison
== != =	equal, not equal	C	comparison
&	and	B	bitwise and
^	xor	B	bitwise xor
|	or	B	bitwise or
&& (BSD only)	prop. operator	L	logical and
|| (BSD only)	prop. operator	L	logical or
= += −= *= /=	assignment	A (Ac)	assignment

C SHELL PROCEDURES

In the C shell we employ the @-symbol to initialize a C shell variable with a numeric value.

8.5.4 Variables with Numeric Values

A C shell numeric assignment statement has the following syntax:

@ variable-name arithmetic-expression

syntax: arithmetic-operator integer

necessary space between @ and variable-name

Arithmetic assignment statements can be expressed either compactly with the c language operators (+ = , -= , *= , /= , + + , and --) or explicitly using the usual arithmetic operators common to both the Bourne and C shells (-, + , *, and /). Here is a cross-reference table showing both forms of arithmetic assignments:

Cross-reference Table of Assignments

(Note: give the result-variable an initial value using % @ result = 10)

ASSIGNMENT (SHORT FORM)	RESULT VALUE	ASSIGNMENT (LONG FORM)	RESULT VALUE
@ result+ +	11	@ result = $result + 1	11
@ result - -	9	@ result = $result - 1	9
@ result + = 20	20	@ result = $result + 20	20
@ result - = 20	-10	@ result = $result - 20	-10
@ result /= 4	2	@ result = $result / 4	2
(none)		@ result = $result % 3	1
@ result *= 11	110	@ result = $result * 11	110

This should be familiar to you, since the same techniques are used by **awk** in arithmetic assignment statements. In addition to arithmetic assignment statements, the C shell also carries over from C the same bitwise, logical, and comparison operators. The bitwise operators may appear strange at first.

8.5.5 Bitwise Operations

To understand the bitwise operators, keep in mind that the machine works with bit-strings in doing its arithmetic (and everything else!). So, for example, when we enter a 7 on a 32-bit machine like a VAX-11, the machine uses

7 as 0000 000 0000 0000 0000 0000 0000 0111 (base 2)

This is the secret behind the C shell (and C as well C++) bitwise operations. Take, for instance, the shift operators << (shift left) and >> (shift right). We can tell the machine to shift the bits of a number to the left by one (in other words multiply by two) by typing

```
% @ result = 7                # give result initial value
% @ result = ($result << 1); echo $result
14
```

Always enclose a bitwise operation inside parentheses.

Here is what happened behind the scenes with the value of 7:

(0111 << 1) shifts 1's to left by 1
    1110 = 1000 + 0110 (base 2) = 8 + 6 (base 10)

Notice how shifting the bits in 7 (or 0111) to the left by one has the same effect as multiplying 7 by 2. It takes less processing time to shift bits than it does to perform a multiply operation. Can you guess the value of result (initially equal to 7) if we enter

```
% @ result = ($result >> 1)    # shift bits right 1
```

You guessed right if you said $result is now 3. Here is why:

(0111 >> 1) shifts 1's to right by 1
    0011 (base 2) = 3 (base 10)

The unit bit perishes ("drops off the edge of the world") if it is shifted right. Notice that shifting the bits of a binary number to the right by one produces the same result we would get if we divided the original number by two.

To experiment with the remaining bitwise operators, try various values with the following procedure:

☐ EXPERIMENT 9

(testing use of the bitwise and logical operators)

```
% cat > operators
# illustrate use of bitwise and logical operators
# usage: operators integer integer
```

C SHELL PROCEDURES **365**

```
@ x = $argv[1]; @ x = $argv[2]
@ z = ($x << 1); echo shift bits of $x left by 1 = $z
@ z = ($x >> 1); echo shift bits of $x right by 1 = $z
echo " "                                 # insert blank line
@ z = ($x ^ $y); echo $x xor $y gives $z
@ z = ($x | $y); echo $x or $y gives $z
@ z = ($x & $y): echo $x and $y gives $z
echo " "; echo "logical operations:"; echo " "
@ z = ~ $x; echo "1's complement of " $x is $z
@ z = ! $x; echo logical negation of $x is $z
@ z = ($x > $y || $y < 100); echo or truth value is $z
@ z = ($x > $y && $y < 100); echo and truth value is $z
ctrl-d
%
```

You will find when you run the operators procedure that $z is 1 if the result of the || (or) operation returns a value of true, otherwise z will be 0. For example,

```
% operators 50 49
```

makes

```
(50 > 49 || 50 < 100) true, so $z is assigned a 1
```

while

```
% operators 500 600
```

makes

```
(500 > 600 || 500 < 100) false, so $z is assigned a 0
```

Similarly, $z will be 1 if the result of the && (and) operation is true, 0, otherwise. Can you guess the value of $z after the && operation in the operators procedure for each of the above pairs of integers?

The ~ complement operator causes the values of bits in a number to be reversed (to 1, if a bit is initially 0; to 0, if originally 1). The & (and), | (or) and ^ (xor or exclusive or) are binary bitwise operators (each one requires two operands) that assign a value to a variable based on the following rules:

Rules for and, or, and xor

OPERATION	NAME	VALUES OF BITS IN ASSIGNED VALUE
&	and	A bit in the result is set *only* when bits in the same position of the operands are also 1, otherwise the assigned bit is 0.

Rules for and, or, and xor (continued)

OPERATION	NAME	VALUES OF BITS IN ASSIGNED VALUE
|	or	A bit in the result is set when either bit (*or* both bits) in the same position in the operands is 1, otherwise the assigned bit is 0.
^	xor	A bit in the result is set when either bit (but not both bits) in the same place is 1, otherwise the assigned bit is 0.

The C shell has a rich variety of control structures that we explore in the next section.

8.5.6 C Shell Control Structures

C shell control structures have concise, easy-to-use syntax and embody the processing power of similar structures found in C. These control structures are brought together in the following table:

C Shell Control Structures

STRUCTURE	EXAMPLE

1. Selection control
if (expr) command
if (expr) then
   command(s)
endif
	`if ($#argv == 0) exit`
	`if ($result == 5 || $result <= 10) then`
	  `echo '$result is ' $result`
	`exit 0`
	`endif`

if (expr) then
   command(s)
else
   command(s)
endif
	`if ($ans == yes) then`
	  `echo $ans is definite`
	`else`
	  `if ($ans == maybe) then`
	    `echo $ans is indefinite`
	  `endif`
	`endif`

switch (str)
   case pattern1:
     command(s)
     breaksw
     ....
	`switch ($argv[1])`
	  `case -a:`
	    `echo $argv[1] starts alphabet`
	    `breaksw`
	  `case -3:`

C Shell Control Structures (continued)

STRUCTURE	EXAMPLE

case nth-pattern
  command(s)
  breaksw
default:
  command(s)
  breaksw
endsw
	`exit 1`
	`breaksw`
	`default:`
	  `echo 'usage: ............'`
	`breaksw`
	`endsw`

2. Iteration control
foreach item (list)
  command(s)
end
	`foreach name ( 'ls' )`
	  `echo $name; head -1 $name`
	`end`

while (expr)
  command(s)
end
	`while ($count > 0)`
	  `echo '............'`
	  `@ count --` `# subtract 1`
	`end`

3. Other forms of control
shift
	`while ($#argv)`
	  `echo $argv[1]; shift`
	`end`

shift variable	`set d = `date``
	`while ($#d)`
	  `echo $d[1]; shift d`
	`end`

goto label break continue onintr label	`goto doorway` [exit from innermost loop] [skip remaining statements inside innermost loop and resume iteration] [branches to label on interrupt (hitting delete key)]

Control structures are usually used in combination with each other. For example, we can use the **foreach** and **if** statements together to solve the following problem:

> **LISTING PROBLEM:**
> List all non-directory files in a chosen directory (use each filename in a heading before each listing).

This problem can be solved using the following technique:

Pseudocode Solution

ACTIONS	C SHELL HINTS (COMMANDS TO USE)
begin	
change to desired directory;	`cd`
for each file in target directory	`foreach`
if file is not a directory then	`if`
display file name	`echo`
display file	`cat`
endif	
endfor	
end	

The idea is to loop through the names in a chosen directory. We bypass a directory name which is itself the name of a directory. This is a good application for the **if** statement. These ideas are implemented in the following procedure:

■ PROCEDURE 5

```
% cat > tylog
# list non-directory files in target directory
# requires $argv[1] be target directory name
# usage: tylog pathname

cd $argv[1]
foreach file (`ls -a $argv[1]`)
   if (! -d $file) then
      echo filename $argv[1]/$file
      echo " "
      cat $file
      echo " "
   endif
   end
ctrl-d
%
```

You may find tylog useful later when you want a copy of each of the files in one of your directories. To use tylog to list the files in your $home/bin directory, for example, type

```
% cx tylog
% tylog $home/bin
```

It would be helpful to invent a procedure to check for files which are nonexistent, or existent but empty.

8.5.7 Example: Checking for Empty or Nonexistent Files

The **test** command introduced in Section 4.4 offers a means of checking for empty or nonexistent files. We can create a procedure (call it isitempty) which combines the use of **test** with the **if** statement and **exit.** In the C shell **exit** has three forms:

Forms of exit

Legend: expr = expression

FORM	ACTION	EXAMPLE	
% **exit** (command)	return to login shell	5% csh 1% exit 2% 6%	# new shell # return # back again
exit	terminates execution of a procedure and assigns to status variable the status of last executed command (0, if successful; 1, if not successful)	% cat sample # use of exit by itself if ($# argv == 0) exit %	
exit expr	terminates execution of a procedure and assigns to status var value of expr(ession)	% cat anotherone # use of exit expr if ($# argv == 0) exit 99 %	

Inside a procedure, **exit** is used either by itself or together with an expression (expr) which is assigned to the **status** variable when the execution of a procedure is terminated by **exit.** Here is an application of these ideas:

■ PROCEDURE 6

```
% cat > isitempty
# test if a file is empty
# requires $argv[1] to be non-empty file for exit 0
#usage: isitempty filename

if ($#argv == 0) then
  echo 'usage: isitempty filename'; exit 1
  endif
test -r $argv [1]
```

```
if ($status > 0) then
  echo $argv[1] does not exist.; exit 1
else
  set size = `ls -l $argv[1]`
  if ($size[5] == 0) then
    echo $argv[1] exists but is empty.; exit 1
  else
    exit 0
  endif
endif
ctrl-d
%
```

The isitempty procedure can be used either by itself or as part of another procedure to add a measure of robustness. First try isitemtpy by itself to see how it works. To see this, try the following experiment.

☐ EXPERIMENT 10

(As a warning, first create the isitempty Procedure 6 before you run this experiment.)

```
% cx isitempty
% isitempty
usage: isitempty filename
% echo $status              # check exit status
1
% isitempty isitempty       # checks itself!
% echo $status              # check status
0
%
```

Now create an empty dummy file for last test of isitempty:

```
% cat > emptyfile
ctrl-d
% ls -l emptyfile
-rw-r--r--   1  you   yourgroup   0  Jan 23 11:30 emptyfile
% isitempty emptyfile
emptyfile exists but is empty.
%
```

Now we can use isitempty to make future C shell procedures robust. The **no** procedure in Section 8.5 offers a simple application of this idea as shown in Procedure 7:

■ PROCEDURE 7

(robust version of no procedure)

```
% cat no                                    # after editing old file
# number lines of a file
#
# no, version 1.1
#
# usage: no filename

if ($#argv == 0) exit 1
isitempty $argv[1]; if ($status >0) exit 1
awk '{ print NR, $0 }' $argv[1]
```

Notice that a variation of the isitempty procedure will be needed to make the tylog procedure from Section 8.5.6 robust. Whenever we execute tylog, we want to avoid attempts to list files in empty or nonexistent directories. There is one glitch you will need to deal with in the isitempty procedure before it meets the needs of tylog, however. To see the source of this problem, try typing

```
% mkdir emptydir
% ls -al emptydir
total 4
drwxr-xr-x    2 you yourgroup        32 Jan 23 11:51 .
drwxr-xr-x    6 you yourgroup       800 Jan 23 11:51 ..
%
```

In other words, the new emptydir directory will *not* be empty! It will have information about the . (current directory) and .. (parent directory) as soon as it is created. So you will need to create an enhanced version of isitempty to check whether an existing file is a directory or non-directory file.

> **CHALLENGE (problem 1):**
> Enhance isitempty to check both directory and non-directory files.

The procedures we wrote earlier for the Bourne shell using sh control structures must be modified before they can be executed in the C shell.

8.6 NEW CLOTHES FOR OLD PROCEDURES

The **ap** procedure (written for the Bourne shell) in Section 4.2.6 makes a good application of the C shell switch statement. Since it is short, only minor changes are needed to create a C shell version of **ap** (call it **ap+**).

8.6.1 Automating File Creation

The **ap** procedure from Section 4.2.6 solves the following two problems:

1. automate creation of a new file
2. automate concatenating the contents of one file onto a second file

The original **ap** procedure used the Bourne shell **case** statement to solve this problem. In the C shell we can employ the **switch** statement to do the same thing. Here are the Bourne and C shell versions of this procedure side by side:

Bourne and C Shell Versions of ap Procedure

C SHELL	BOURNE SHELL
```% cat ap+```	```$ cat ap```
```# Automate file creation```	```# Automate file creation```
```switch ($#argv)```	```case $# in```
```case 1:```	``` 1) cat >$1;;```
``` cat > $argv[1]```	``` 2) cat >>$2 <$1;;```
``` breaksw```	``` 0) echo 'usage: ap fl [fl]'```
```case 2:```	```esac```
``` cat $argv[1] >> $argv[2]```	
``` breaksw```	
```default:```	
``` echo 'usage: ap fl [fl]'```	
``` breaksw```	
```endsw```	

The default clause in the switch statement works the same as the otherwise clause available in some versions of Pascal. The switch statement defaults for *any* values not included in the case lists. This makes the C switch more robust than its case statement counterpart in the Bourne shell.

Notice that there are all sorts of things we can do to improve the ap+ procedure. For example, we can use isitempty from Section 8.5.6 to make ap+ robust—prevent ap+ from attempting to concatenate with an empty file. The ap+ procedure is also a good place to use.

```
unset noclobber
```

so case 2 will always work. That is, we sometimes may want to override noclobber and use concatenation to create a new file. If you type

```
% set noclobber
% who >> thoseofus                    # nonexistent file
thoseofus: No such file or directory
% unset noclobber
% who >> thoseofus                    # creates a new file
%
```

By unsetting noclobber, we make it possible for redirection with >> to create a new file, if the specified file does not exist. We leave it to you to make these changes in the ap+ procedure.

> **CHALLENGE (problem 2):**
> Make ap+ robust.

Since we are creating so many new files, another useful application of the switch statement is a new version of the **del** procedure from Section 5.3.

8.6.2 Automating the Deletion of Old Files

The **del** procedure solves the following housecleaning problem:

1. display directory times in time-order (most recent first)
2. respond to choices:
   y to remove a file
   n to do nothing
   q to terminate execution of **del** (with break)
3. avoid attempting to delete a directory

This is an instance where we need to take input from your terminal. In the Bourne shell this is accomplished by executing the **read** command. There are two ways to do this in the C shell, depending on what version of the C shell you have available:

Ways to Get Input from a Terminal in the C Shell

INPUT COMMAND	EXAMPLE
$<	% echo 'input: '
	% set choice = $<
gets	% set choice = `gets`

If your system does not have a **gets** command available, it is easily created with a C program given in either Kernighan and Ritchie (1978) or Anderson (1986). You will find a copy of a C program to implement gets in Appendix C. We present here the Bourne and C shell versions of the new **del** procedure (we call it **del+**) without attempting to make this new procedure robust (step 3 in the above list) side by side:

Bourne and C Shell Versions of del

C SHELL	BOURNE SHELL
| ```
% cat del+
# pick files to delete
#
# del, version 1.0
#
echo 'options:'
echo 'y to remove file'
echo 'n to save file'
echo 'q to quit.'
echo " "
foreach i (`ls -t`)
  echo -n $i '?'
  set choice = `gets`
  switch ($choice)
    case [yY]:
      rm $i
      breaksw
    case [nN]
      breaksw
    case [qQ]:
      break
      breaksw
    default:
      echo 'Enter y,n or q.'
      breaksw
  endsw
end
echo " "
``` | ```
$ cat del
# pick files to delete
#
# del, version 1.0
#
echo 'options:'
echo 'y to remove file'
echo 'n to save file'
echo 'q to quit.'
echo
for i in `ls -t`
  do
    echo $i '?\c'
    read choice
    case $choice in
      y*|Y*) rm $1;;
      n*|N*) ;;
      q*|Q*) break
    esac
done
``` |

It remains to make del+ robust (you should build into this procedure a check to prevent an attempt to delete a directory).

CHALLENGE (problem 3):
Make del+ robust.

As a final example of the use of C shell control structures, we show a new version of the enigma procedure from Section 7.9.3.

8.6.3 Anagram Classes Revisited

The original version of the enigma procedure written for the Bourne shell in Section 7.9.3 will not change much in the C shell. However, each of the procedures which enigma itself executes needs to be revised to make them executable in the C shell. Here are the Bourne and C shell versions of this procedure:

Bourne and C Shell Versions of enigma

C SHELL VERSION

```
% cat enigma+
# find anagram classes
# enigma+, version 1.0 (C shell)
# usage: enigma+ word-list

partition $argv[1] | select > temp
cat temp $argv[1] | combine | sort | squash > results
rm temp; rm results
```

BOURNE SHELL VERSION

```
$ cat enigma
# find anagram classes
# enigma, version 1.0 (Bourne shell), section 7.9.3
# usage: enigma word-list

partition $1 | select > temp
cat temp $1 | combine | sort | squash
rm temp
```

The individual procedures used by these two versions of enigma *are* different. First, before we go further, make sure you have not **set time** in your .cshrc file. This will cause the enigma procedure to do terrible things (processing times from the slower procedures in enigma will go into the pipe along with the words being processed). Next, we need to escape continuation on more than one line in the **awk** programs used to implement the partition, combine, select, and squash procedures. To save space, only the C shell versions of these procedures (taken from Section 7.9.3) will be given next. Note that each of the following procedures taken from Section 7.9.3 has been edited to make it compatible with the C shell.

■ PROCEDURE 8

```
% cat partition
# split input words into characters separated by spaces
# partition, version 1.0 (for C shell)
# usage: partition listofwords
```

```
awk ' \
        { for (i = 1; i <= length($1); i++) \
            print "%s %s, substr(%1, i, 1), " " \
          print "\n" } \
        ' $argv[1]
%
```

■ PROCEDURE 9

```
% cat select
# selection sort letters of a word
# selection, version 1.0 (for C shell)
# usage: select <list or cat list | select
awk ' \
        { for (i = 1; i <= NF; i++) a[i] = $i } \
        { for (i = 1; i <= NF; i++) { \
            j = i \
            for (k = j + 1; k <= NF; k++) \
              if (a[k] < a[j]) j = k \
            t = a[i] \
            a[i] = a[j] \
            a[j] = t \
            } \
        } \
        { for (i = 1; i <= NF; i++) \
            if (i < NF) \
              print "%s", a[i] \
            else
              printf "%s\n", a[i] \
        } \
        '
%
```

■ PROCEDURE 10

```
% cat combine
# combine output from select with original list
# combine, version 1.0 (C shell)
# usage: cat temp list | combine

awk ' {comb[NR] = $0} \
        END { h = int(NR/2) + 1 \
              for (i = 1; h <= NR; i++) { \
                print comb[i], comb[h] \
                h++ } \
            }'
%
```

NEW CLOTHES FOR OLD PROCEDURES   377

■ PROCEDURE 11

```
% cat squash
# derive anagram classes
# squash, version 1.0 (C shell)
# usage: cat list | squash

awk ' $1 != prev { prev = $1; if (NR > 1) printf "\n"} \
                 { printf "%s ", $2 } \
             END { printf "\n" }'
%
```

To test the operation of these procedures, we need to set up a file of words like the following one:

```
% ap wordslist         # use ap from Section 8.6.1
parse
mode
time
spare
emit
dome
ada
spear
ctrl-d
%
```

Now try the following experiment to put all these procedures together. As a **warning,** unset time (if you have set time in your .cshrc file, then turn setting into a comment, and execute xcsh to tell the C shell the new settings.

```
% cx partition
% cx combine
% cx select
% cx squash
% cx enigma+
% enigma+ wds
ada
parse spare spear
dome mode
emit time
```

Notice that enigma+ (*and* the procedures it executes!) is not robust. The enigma+ procedure provides another good application for the isitempty procedure from Section 8.5.7.

CHALLENGE (problem 4):
Make enigma+ robust.

Because of its **noclobber** option, the C shell has a richer set of redirection options than the Bourne shell.

8.7 REDIRECTION IN THE C SHELL

The various forms of redirection in the C shell are brought together in the following table:

Redirection in the C Shell

Legend: re = (verb) redirect
         stdi = standard input
         stdo = standard output
         stde = standard error (diagnostic output)
         app stdo = append standard output

OPERATOR	MEANING	EXAMPLE
<	re stdo	% mail mozart < tylog # mails tylog
>	re stdi	% who > users
>&	re stde	% (whereis ed > place) >& errorlog
		% cat place
		/bin/ed
		% cat errlog
		find: cannot open /usr/spool/uucp
		%
>>	re stdo	% (date; who) >> users #users must exit
		% cat users
		Sat Jan 24 10:26:44 CST 1987
		mozart console Jan 24 09:12
		%
>>&	app stdo & stde	% whereis gets.c >>& errlog
		[appends standard output *and* standard error (C shell diagnostic messages) to to errlog file.]

Override noclobber if set

OPERATOR	MEANING	EXAMPLE
>!	re stdo	% date >! errlog # overwrites errlog
>&!	re stdo & stde	% grep "˜d" 'ls -l' >&! results
		[overwrites anything in results file. You may be surprised at what this command line writes to the results file.]
>>!	app stdo	% date >>! times # may create file
		[creates new times file if it does not exist.]
>>&!	app stdo & stde	% grep "˜#" 'ls' >> ! comments
		[creates new comments file if it does not exist when grep is executed.]

The last four means of redirection in the C shell override the noclobber option, if noclobber is set. The companion examples for these last four options each produce two types of results, depending on whether noclobber is set or unset. The best way to see how these examples work is to use the following method:

1. % unset noclobber
   [execute sample command lines in Table 8.?]
2. % set noclobber
   [execute sample command lines in Table 8.?]

We illustrate this idea in terms of >! and >>! in the following experiment:

☐ EXPERIMENT 12

(redirection while overriding noclobber option)

```
% set noclobber
% rm temp                                    # remove temp
rm: temp non-existent
rm: # non-existent
rm: remove non-existent
rm: temp non-existent
% (date; who) >> temp
temp: No such file or directory
```

Now override noclobber by typing

```
% (date; who) >>! temp
```

Try to redirect output from wc to temp with

```
% who | wc -l > temp
temp: File exists.
```

When you use > in terms of an existing file *and* no clobber is set, the C shell aborts any attempt to overwrite the old file. You can override noclobber with

```
% who | wc -l >! temp
% cat temp
22
%
```

The last lines of Experiment 12 bring out the advantage of leaving noclobber set most of the time. The line

```
% who | wc -l >! temp
```

obliterates what *was* in the temp file. The override redirection options force a more deliberate effort to overwrite existing files. In the case of valuable files you do not want to overwrite, the combination of setting noclobber *and* using > (redirect standard output) may someday prevent you from destroying the contents of an existing file you want to save.

The C shell also has a facility (called **noglob**) which makes it possible to tell /bin/csh to treat certain metacharacters literally in file name expansions.

8.8 GLOBBING FILENAMES

Before the C shell executes a command, it first expands any special characters you might have used (*, ?, [,], {, }, or ~) when it does filename expansions. This filename expansion process is called **globbing.** For example, you can display all the filenames in your current directory by typing

```
% echo *
allargs anagrams anagrams+ ap ap+ bell.c bin . . .
```

Before the C shell executes the echo command, it first expands the asterisk metacharacter into all the filenames in your current directory. You can turn off C shell globbing by setting the special **noglob** variable as in

```
% set noglob
% echo *              * treated literally!
*
%
```

We could accomplish the same thing by enclosing one or more metacharacters inside single quotes to tell the shell to treat these characters literally as in

```
% unset noglob
% echo '*'
*
%
```

We have seen this technique used before (in Section 8.2.2, for example). The **noglob** option is a time-saver, since it saves us the trouble of quoting metacharacters we want treated literally. Here is a more practical example of this idea in a procedure to build a lexicon containing names of files in a directory along with "grepped" information we have specified using $argv[1]:

■ PROCEDURE 12

```
% ap+ lexicon
# set up a file lexicon
# requires $argv[1] to be a search string
# usage: lexicon searchstring

set noglob
foreach name (`ls`)
  echo filename: $name
  grep $argv[1] $name
  echo " "
  end
ctrl-d
%
```

We use the lexicon procedure in various ways. For example, we can type

```
% cx lexicon
% set noglob
% lexicon file* >! temp &
```

Now temp contains entries with the following form

```
% cat temp
filename: allargs

filename: anagrams

filename: ap+
# automated file creation

filename: del+
# picking files to delete
echo 'y to remove a file'
echo 'n to save a file'
..........................................
```

By setting noglob we avoid having to enclose the lexicon argument inside quotes as in

```
% unset noglob
% lexicon 'file*' >! temp &
```

In either case, when the C shell executes this command line, it passes to grep the value of $argv[1] without expanding any metacharacters. Then grep uses the * in this example as a wild card to find all lines of all your files that contain lines with file, files, filename, filing, and so on. To see more clearly the effects of globbing, try the following experiment:

☐ EXPERIMENT 13

Note: this experiment assumes you have edited the lexicon procedure to turn **set noglob** into a comment as shown:

```
% unset noglob
% cp lexicon lexicon+
```

Now edit lexicon+ to produce

```
% cat lexicon+
# build lexicon
# lexicon, version 1.1
# usage: lexicon search-string

# set noglob
foreach name (`ls`)
   echo filename: $name
   grep $argv[1] $name
   echo " "
   end
%
```

Now try the file* argument in

```
% lexicon+ file* >! temp &
No match.
% lexicon+ 'file*' >! temp &
filename: allargs
No match.

filename: anagrams
No match.

...............................
%
```

When you enter

```
% unset noglob
% lexicon file* >! temp &
No match.
%
```

the C shell has expanded the * metacharacter in file* before it executes lexicon+. As a result, grep does not receive * as a wildcard. Instead, lexicon+ never gets off the ground because the C shell fails to find a match between file* and some files in your current directory which begin with the word 'file.' To see what the C shell does in expanding filenames, try

```
% unset noglob
% echo a*
allargs anagrams  anagrams+  ap  ap+  ...
%
```

If you use a* as a search string in Experiment 13, you should find that lexicon produces something. To see this, try

```
% unset noglob
% lexicon+ a*
filename: allargs
# usage: allargs [ zero or more arguments ]
```

grep found match from expanded form of a* in $argv[1]

Can you explain what happens in the following lines?

```
% unset noglob
% lexicon+ 'file*'
filename: allargs
No match.
        .
        .
        .
```

The lexicon procedure has some practical benefit, since it can be used in a variety of ways to glean information about all the files in your current directory. Since all C shell procedures begin with one or more explanatory comments, you can construct a procedures lexicon (dictionary that gives the "meaning" of each of your procedures) by typing

```
% set noglob
% lexicon # >! actions &
144
%
```

Once lexicon has finished executing, the actions file will have your procedure (and other file) names with accompanying comments. You can increase the usefulness of lexicon by inventing an isitaproc ("is it a procedure") command to isolate your procedure names as in Procedure 13.

■ PROCEDURE 13

```
% ap isitaproc
# return names of procedures
# isitaproc, version 1.0
# usage: isitaproc filename
```

```
grep "^#" $argv[1] >! temp
if ($status == 0) then
    exit 0
else
    exit 1
endif
```

Now we create a specialized version of the lexicon procedure that employs isitaproc to isolate names of procedures. Here is the new version of lexicon:

■ PROCEDURE 14

Note: after editing lexicon, you should have:

```
% cat lexicon
# build a lexicon
# lexicon, version 2.0
# usage: lexicon search-string

set noglob
foreach name (`ls`)
    isitaproc $name             # is it a procedure?
    if ($status == 0) then
        echo filename: $name
        grep "^$argv[1]" name
        echo " "
    endif
end
%
```

The success of this new version of lexicon depends on the use of the C shell exit statement in isitaproc. The value of $status will be 0 whenever grep succeeds in finding # at the beginning of one or more lines of a file. To see how this works, try

```
% cx isitaproc
% lexicon #
filename: allargs
# illustrate use of C shell arguments
# usage: allargs [zero or more arguments]

filename: anagrams
# find anagram classes
# usage: anagrams word-list

    .........................................
%
```

GLOBBING FILENAMES **385**

The lexicon procedure has many variations. It could be improved by introducing an options list like the following one:

Lexicon options:
-**c** output procedure name, comments in two columns as in
    allargs   # illustrate use of C shell operators
                    # usage: allargs [zero or more arguments]
    anagrams # find anagram classes
                    # usage: anagrams word-list
-**s** suppress   # in comments for procedures lexicon
-**u** only print usage-comment of each procedure
-**w** display lines of all files containing specified word

These options (and other options) can be implemented using the C shell switch statement.

CHALLENGE (problem 5):
Implement lexicon with the -[csuw] options.

8.9 SUMMARY

The C shell offers an alternative to the Bourne shell on most Unix systems. Its system name is /bin/csh. If you execute **csh** as in

```
% csh
%
```

you will be in the C shell. The % sign is its default prompt. Each line you enter in the C shell is called an *event*. Events can be command lines like

```
% set prompt = '\!% '
3% history = 12            Save up to 12 most recent events
4% vi .cshrc               Invoke vi editor
```

(to display the event number of the current line). Or events can be just a line of characters not representing a command line like the line of garbage preceding the following dialogue resulting from executing trivialP:

```
5% whoopsssssssssssssssssssssssssss
6% csh trivialP
Current version of BSD Unix? 4.2
No, 4.3 BSD Unix is the correct answer.
Inventory of C shell history mechanism? [ press del]
7%
```

The history and alias mechanisms are two pearls of the C shell. With the history mechanism you can retrieve, display, and execute with the ! operator as in

```
8% !4            Invoke 4th event
vi .cshrc
[ Begin vi editing session on .cshrc ]
```

or if you cannot remember the event number containing **vi. cshrc,** you can invoke the most recent event that *begins* with the letter 'v' by entering

```
9% !v
vi .cshrc
[ Begin editing .cshrc ]
```

For short, frequently-used command lines, the alias mechanism is a time-saver. You can start by "aliasing" the alias command itself with

```
% alias al alias
```

This is the ideal alias to start the list of aliases in your .cshrc file, which is executed each time you log in under the C shell. Then subsequent aliases, either in the .cshrc file or during a working session, can be entered like the following one for the history command:

```
% al h history
```

C shell syntax closely resembles C language syntax. It has a rich variety of arithmetic, bitwise, logical and comparison operators, and control structures. As a result, C shell procedures tend to be easy to develop, especially if you are already familiar with C itself.

The C shell shares many commands and utilities (ed, vi, sed, and awk, for example) with the Bourne shell. However, the C shell is subtly different from the Bourne shell. For example, the Bourne shell = assignment operator must always be used in conjunction with the **set** command in the C shell. In the C shell, the backslash \ must be used to escape a return when a command is continued on more than one line as in

```
% echo 'See the IEEE Trial-Use Standard for POSIX or \
Portable Operating System (based on UN)IX.'
See the IEEE Trial-Use Standard for POSIX or
Portable Operating System (based on UN)IX.
%
```

In many cases, procedures written for the Bourne shell can be adapted to the C shell by escaping continued command lines with the backslash \ *and* replacing Bourne shell control structures with appropriate C shell control structures.

8.10 REVIEW OF COMMANDS, SYMBOLS, AND KEYWORDS

In the following sections we bring together key features of the C shell for easy reference.

8.10.1 Commands

COMMAND	ACTION
alias	name a command line
/bin/csh	execute C shell
chsh	change shell
csh	execute C shell
csh [procedure]	invoke C shell to execute procedure
(control structures)	see Section 8.5.6
if	conditionally select command(s) to execute
switch	same as Bourne shell case statement with added **default** ("otherwise") feature
foreach	indexed iteration of command(s)
while	conditional iteration of command(s)
shift	assign next value in argument list to $argv[1]
goto	unconditional branch to a labelled location
break	exit from innermost loop
continue	skip remaining statements inside innermost loop and resume iteration
onintr	branches to labelled location when interrupt is detected
echo	display specified item
echo -n [item]	suppress carriage return, line feed after displaying specified item (in the Bourne shell this would be accomplished using \c)
env	display environment variables
% @	same as % env (displays environment variables)
exit (command)	return to parent shell
exit (statement)	terminate execution of procedure
exit (w/o expr)	terminate execution of procedure *and* return status of the last executed command using the **status** variable
exit expr	terminate execution of procedure *and* return value of expr (expression) using the **status** variable (see isitempty, Section 8.5.7)
gets	read character stream from keyboard
$<	same as gets
history	display previous events
printenv (BSD)	display environment variable values
set	assign string to a variable
source file	execute commands in file
source -h .hlog	(BSD Unix only) initialize history list with history commands saved in .hlog file *and* does not execute commands in .hlog
tset (BSD)	initialize terminal setup with possible mappings to alternative login terminals
unalias	deassign alias
unglob	turn off globbing (saves quoting file expansion metacharacters *, ?, [,], {, }, or ~)
unset	deassign variable
whereis (BSD)	finds specified file

8.10.2 Symbols and Special Characters

CHARACTER(S)	EXPLANATION
.	current directory
..	parent directory
~	same as $home in C shell
|	pipe
' (apostrophe)	escape meta-meaning of string of characters
* (files)	filename expansion character
* (wildcard)	regular expression metacharacter as in a* in
	`% grep a* myfile`
	to find lines in myfile containing words like a, at, anthill, antlers, apple IIe, etc.
> (redirection)	redirect standard output
> (logic)	greater than
< (redirection)	redirect standard output
< (logic)	less than
#	begins comment
%	default C shell prompt
^	history substitution operator
`	command substitution as in
	`% grep best* "ls"`
;	separates commands to be executed sequentially
?	matches any single character as in
	`% echo ap?`
	`ap+ ap- apc`
	`%`
& (and)	bitwise and (see Section 8.5.5)
& (bg process)	process in background
- (interval)	specified argument list interval as in
	`echo $argv[1-5]`
	to display first 5 arguments
- (history)	invoke n events in past with !-n
@	numerical assignment operator
>>	append standard output
!E (history)	invoke event E in history list
! (logic)	logical negation as in
	`% set x = 5`
	`% @ neg = ! $x`
	`% @ opposite = ! $neg`
	`% echo $x $neg $opposite`
	`5 0 1`
	`%`
!!	invoke previous history event (see Section 8.3 for other uses of the ! relative to history mechanism)
!=	not equal operator
\!*	alias argument for all argument list words except word 0
\!^	alias argument for word 1 in argument list

8.10.2 Symbols and Special Characters (continued)

CHARACTER(S)	EXPLANATION
>! (redirection)	override noclobber, if set
>>!	override noclobber when appending to a new file
>&!	override noclobber in redirecting any diagnostics output by shell during execution of a command
>>&!	override noclobber in appending diagnostics to a new file
\	escape any single character
$<	read input line (same as gets)
$*	all command-line arguments
$argv[*]	same as $* (see Section 8.5.1)
$argv	same as $*
$#argv	number of command-line arguments
$0	word 0 of command line
$argv[$*]	last command-line argument
$argv[$#argv]	same as $argv[$*]
$argv[n]	nth command-line argument

8.10.3 Keywords

KEYWORD(S)	EXPLANATION
.cshrc	executed automatically at login time when your default shell is /bin/csh (contains settings for variables and frequently used aliases)
.login	executed automatically at login time when your default shell is /bin/csh
.logout	executed automatically by /bin/csh when you execute **logout**
/etc/passwd	contains password entries for Unix users
/etc/termcap	contains characteristics for allowable terminals
/etc /ttytype	contains list of terminals currently in use
event	entered line of characters following %
event number	number of event relative to previous events (the current event has the highest event number in your history)
globbing	expanding filenames relative to any special characters used
ignoreeof	ignore end-of-file (control-d) variable
metacharacter	a character which has some controlling role relative to other characters being used
noclobber	prevent overwriting existing files or appending which entails creating a new file
noglob	override globbing (treat metacharacters literally)
stub	empty program structure

8.11 EXERCISES

1. How do C shell control structures differ from those in C?
2. Give a list of shells available on your system (you will find them in /bin).
3. List the entry in /etc/passwd for you. What is your default shell?
4. List your
   a. environment variables
   b. shell variables
5. What is the difference between the environment and shell variables?
6. Invent a hfiles ("hidden files") procedures which displays only all hidden files (. .. .cshrc, .login, .logout, and so on) with the following usage:

   usage: hfiles [directory-name]

   You hfiles should display the hidden files in
   a. your current directory (by default, if no directory is specified)
   b. in a specified directory. Give a sample run with (1) hfiles (2) hfiles bin (3) hfiles /etc (4) hfiles /bin.
7. Define the following aliases:
   a. dcsh ("display .cshrc file in $home")
   b. din ("display .login file in $home")
   c. dout ("display .logout file in $home")
   Give sample uses of these aliases.
8. Refine the hfiles procedure in Exercise 6 so that it has the following usage:

   usage: hfiles -[cio] [directory-name]

   where
   a. -c causes dcsh (from Exercise 7) to be executed
   b. -i causes din (from Exercise 7) to be executed
   c. -o causes dout (from Exercise 7) to be executed
   Give sample runs with (1) hfiles -c (2) hfiles -i (3) hfiles -o.
9. Give a list of terminal names available on your system.
10. Give a list of terminals currently being used on your system.
11. (for non-BSD Unix users) Replace the **whereis** alias in .cshrc file in Section 8.2.1 by a whereis procedure with the following usage:

    usage: whereis -[msS] [alternate-dirs] [filename(s)]

    Options:
    - -m Inspect manual sections only.
    - -M alternate-dirs
         Look *only* in alternate-dirs (alternate directories) for manual sections.
    - -s Look for source code (text files) only.
    - -S alternate-dirs
         Look *only* in alternate-dirs for source code.
         alternate-dirs
         Alternate directories to search for one type of file; pathname must begin with /.

    Give sample runs for each option.

12. Invent an alias called **w** which can be used in place of any of the forms of the **whereis** command (either in a BSD or in a non-BSD Unix environment). Give sample runs for each of the options specified in Exercise 11.
13. Give a sample command line illustrating the use of each of the history commands in the table in Section 8.3.
14. Give an example of a nested alias that uses
    a. h (from Section 8.2.1) to display the first three commands in your history. Call this alias trio.
    b. h (from Section 8.2.1) to display all events in your history which begin with a specified letter. Call this alias el.
    Give sample runs for trio and el.
15. Implement Experiment 4 in Section 8.4.1 with a new last10 alias (with a corresponding .last10 file) to see and save up to ten of your most recent events. Give a sample run.
16. Implement Experiment 5 in Section 8.4.1 with the last10 alias from Exercise 15. Give a sample run.
17. Implement a variation of dirz (Procedure 1, Section 8.5) so that empty files are displayed in time-order. Then implement Experiment 6 in the same section in terms of
    a. an empty file called .cmd10
    b. empty files .first, .second, first, second
    Give a sample run.
18. Refine the dirz procedure from Exercise 17 so that it also displays empty directories (ones containing *only* . and ..), and so that it has the following usage:

    Usage: dirz -[ad] [directory-name]
    Option:
     -a   Display all empty files, including subdirectories
          containing only . and ..
     -d   Display empty directories.
    default:
        Display empty non-directory files in current
        . directory

    Give a sample run with
    a. dirz
    b. dirz bin
    c. dirz -a
    d. dirz -a bin
    d. dirz -d
    e. dirz -d bin
    Note: create empty files and empty directories for sample run.
19. Use the **no** procedure (Experiment 7, Section 8.5) to list the following procedures with numbered lines:
    a. dirz (Exercise 18)
    b. whereis (Exercise 11)
20. Implement and give a sample run for dleft (Procedure 4, Section 8.5.2).
21. Refine dleft from Exercise 20 so that the calendar printed by dleft is indented to column 20. Give a sample run.
    Hint: try using awk on the output from dleft.

22. Give an allops ("all operators") procedure which illustrates *each* of the operators in the table in Section 8.5.3 and has the following usage:

    Usage: allops -[i shift-no] string string
    Option:
     -i shift-no causes >> and << to use shift-no to determine
                  how much to shift bits to right or left. The
                  default (without i-option) is to shift by 1.
     shift-no   positive integer.

    List allops procedure with numbered lines using the **no** procedure from Section 8.5. Give sample runs with
    a. allops 20 10
    b. allops 10 20

23. Implement a variation of isitempty (Procedure 6, Section 8.5.7) called isitempty+ so that this new procedure returns a status of 99 for empty files. Then implement Experiment 10 using isitempty+. Give sample runs.

24. Solve Challenge problem 1, Section 8.5.7. Then create an empty directory (call it emptydir) and verify that the new version of isitempty works. List isitempty with numbered lines.

25. Solve Challenge problem 2, Section 8.6.1. Illustrate the use of ap+.

26. Solve Challenge problem 3, Section 8.6.2. Illustrate the use of del+. List del+ with numbered lines.

27. Solve Challenge problem 4, Section 8.6.3. Illustrate the use of enigma+. List enigma+ with numbered lines.

28. Give a sample run of enigma+ (from Exercise 26) using your on-line dictionary.

29. Write a procedure called red ("redirection") which illustrates the last four noclobber override cases in the table in Section 8.7. Give sample runs of red.

30. Give the command line to create a .errlog file so that diagnostics from the find command are redirected to this file and the standard output from find is redirected to a .places file. Give sample runs.

31. Modify whereis (from Exercise 11) so that any diagnostics resulting from the execution of this command are appended to a .errlog, regardless of whether noclobber is set or not. Give sample runs.

32. Solve Challenge problem 4, Section 8.8. Give sample runs to illustrate each of the options for lexicon. List lexicon with numbered lines.

8.12 REVIEW QUIZ

Indicate whether the following statements are true or false.

1. Double quotes escape variable substitution in

   ```
   % set now = `date`; echo "$date"
   ```

2. The names of all the files in your current directory will be displayed by

   ```
   % echo '*'
   ```

3. The command lines

    ```
    % echo "*"
    ```

    and

    ```
    echo *
    ```

    do the same thing.

4. No command substitution will take place in

    ```
    % echo '`ls`'
    ```

5. The names .last10 and last10 identify the same file.
6. The @ and = operators are used in numeric assignments in the Bourne shell, but not in the C shell.
7. In the C shell, the following command line assigns the output from ls to the list variable:

    ```
    % list = `ls`
    ```

8. In the C shell, the following command lines have the same output:

    ```
    % set
    ```

    and

    ```
    % @
    ```

9. Aliases cannot be nested.
10. The command line

    ```
    % set noclobber
    ```

    activates a C shell mechanism to treat metacharacters literally.

8.13 FURTHER READING

Anderson, G. And P. Anderson. The UNIX C Shell Field Guide. Englewood Cliffs, N.J.: Prentice, 1986. See Chapter 7 on C shell programming and Chapter 8 on customizing the C shell.

Bourne, S. The UNIX Shell. The Bell System Technical Journal (now called AT&T Technical Journal), vol. 57, no. 6, part 2 (July–August, 1978), pp. 1971–90.

Joy, W. N. An Introduction to the C Shell. UNIX Programmer's Manual, 4.2 Berkeley Software Distribution, Virtual VAX-11 Version, vol. 2C. University of California, Berkeley: Computer Systems Research Group, Department of Electrical Engineering and Computer Science, August, 1980.

Joy, W. N. Foreword to Anderson and Anderson (1986).

Kernighan, B. W. and D. M. Ritchie. The C Programming Language. Englewood Cliffs, N.J.: Prentice, 1978. See p. 15 for a C program that works like gets.

Quarterman, J. S., A. Silberschatz, and J. L. Peterson. 4.2BSD and 4.3BSD as Examples of the UNIX System. ACM Computing Surveys, vol. 17, no. 4 (December, 1985), pp. 379–418.

Stroustrop, B. The C++ Programming Language. Reading, MA: Addison-Wesley, 1986. See Section 3.2 for discussion of operator precedence.

Shell Commands Handbook

I. Index to Commands

COMMAND	EXPLANATION	SECTION
.	execute command as part of current process	3.2.3
alias	name a command line	8.1
at	delayed execution of a command	3.8
awk	string-processing language	Ch. 7
break	exit from `for` or `while` loop	7.7
cal	display selected calendar	5.8.3
case	multiway selection control	4.2.5
cat	concatenates and prints files	1.4
cat *	prints files in current directory	3.4.4
cat >>f	appends standard input to file `f`	1.5.1
cat >f	redirect standard input to create (overwrite) file `f`	1.5.1
cd	change directory	1.4.3
chmod	change permission(s)	2.3.5
chsh	change shell	8.2
comm	compare files	5.8.1
cp	copy file	1.4.10
crypt	encrypt/decrypt a file	handbook
csh	execute (C shell)	8.2
cut	cut out selected field of lines in a file	3.2.6
date	prints date and time	1.3.2
df	displays number of blks free on file systems	2.5
du	determine number of free blks used by each file in .	2.5

COMMAND	EXPLANATION	SECTION
`echo`	echo argument	1.4.7
`ed`	line editor	2.2.3
`egrep`	extended pattern-matching filter	6.2.2
`env`	display environment variables	8.2
`exec`	execute command by overwriting current process	3.2.5
`exit`	causes shell to exit with a return status value	5.3
`expr`	perform arithmetic	4.5
`fgrep`	pattern matching with strings taken from a file	6.1
`file`	determines file type	1.4
`find`	finds files along specified path	2.6
`for`	indexed iteration	4.3.1
`for each`	indexed iteration in C shell	8.5.6
`grep`	search for pattern-matching lines in a file	1.6.2, 6.2.1
`hangman`	a type of game	1.4.4
`help`	ask for help	handbook
`head`	print initial lines of a specified file	2.6
`if`	test condition to select an action	4.2.1
`if`	(C shell) test condition to select an action	8.5.6
`kill`	remove process	5.4
`ln`	link file	2.7
`lpr`	t file in print queue	1.6
`ls`	list directory	1.4
`ls -i`	list i-numbers for files in .	2.3.1
`mail`	mail letter	1.3.2
`man`	list manual	1.3.2
`mesg`	permit or deny messages	1.3.2
`mkdir`	make directory	1.4.3
`mv`	move file	1.4.10
`od`	octal dump of directory or file	2.3.2
`pr`	paginate and print file	1.6
`ps`	display current processes	3.1
`pwd`	print working directory	1.4
`rm`	remove file	1.4.10
`rmdir`	remove directory	1.4.3
`sed`	stream editor	6.3
`set`	(C shell) assign string to a variable	8.2.1
`set`	display environment variables being used	3.4
`set 'x'`	set argument line variables `$1:$9` by executing `x`	3.4.7
`setenv`	set environment variables	8.2
`sh`	execute command with sh	3.2.2
`shift`	rename positional parameters	handbook
`sleep`	suspended execution	3.9
`sort`	sort lines of file	5.8.1
`source`	(C shell) execute commands in a file	8.2.1
`split`	split file	2.2.2
`stty`	set terminal (customize keyboard)	1.3.3
`tail`	output last part of a file	handbook

COMMAND	EXPLANATION	SECTION
`tee`	t-shaped pipe	2.2.1
`test`	check file type	1.4.8
`test`	test condition	4.4
`time`	display a command's elapsed, system, and user times	7.12
`tr`	translate characters	5.8.1
`trap`	detects signals and executes command sequence	3.5
`tset`	test and set terminal parameters in C shell	8.2.1
`uniq`	eliminates duplicate lines	5.8.1
`unset`	(C shell) deassign variable	8.2.3
`until`	conditional iteration of an action	4.3.2
		5.2.2
`vi`	full-screen visual editor	2.2.4
`wc`	word, character, and line count in a file	1.6.2
`whereis`	(C shell) find specified file	8.2.2
`while`	conditional iteration of an action	4.3.2
`while`	(C shell) conditional iteration of an action	8.5.6
`who`	list who is logged	1.3.3
`who am i`	display logon data about you	1.3.2
`write`	write an on-line message	1.3.2

II. Usage for Commands

COMMAND	EXPLANATION	SECTION
`. file`	Execute file as part of current process	3.2.3

EXAMPLE:
```
$ cat Firstwords
# First message from Unix
echo 'Hello, world!'
$ . Firstwords
Hello, world!
```

`alias` — Name a command line (C shell) — 8.1

USAGE:
```
alias              # print list of aliases
alias name         # print alias for name
alias name arg     # associate name with argument
```

EXAMPLES:
```
% alias
al alias
 . . . . . . . .
% alias dbug
csh -fvx
% alias whereis 'find / -name \!* -print'
```

COMMAND	EXPLANATION	SECTION
`at`	Run command at specified time	3.8

USAGE:
`at time [ day ] [ +n unit ]`
OPTIONS:
`-r jobs`	remove jobs scheduled by at
`-l [jobs]`	display job numbers of submitted jobs
`day`	month name followed by date, day of week, **today** or **tomorrow**
`n unit`	n minutes, hours, days, weeks, months or years
`time`	1–4 digits or **noon, midnight, now,** or **next**

EXAMPLE:
`$ at 5pm <Firstwords`

COMMAND	EXPLANATION	SECTION
`awk`	Pattern scanning language	Ch. 7

USAGE:
`awk [ options ] [ prog ] [ params ]`
`    [ files ]`
`stdin` read if - used or no files specified
OPTIONS:
`-f file`	use file as program
`-Fc`	field separator character is `c`
`prog`	program surrounded by single quotes (apostrophes)
`params`	in the form `x =...y=...` etc. may be passed to `awk`

FORMS:
```
awk ' pattern ' file
awk '
    pattern
    pattern
    ..........
    pattern
    ' file
awk '
    pattern { action }
    ' file
awk ' { action } ' file
awk -f prog.awk file
```

COMMAND	EXPLANATION	SECTION
`break`	Exit from enclosing `for` or `while` loop	5.3

USAGE:
`break [ n ]`
OPTION:
`n`   break n levels

USAGE FOR COMMANDS **399**

COMMAND	EXPLANATION	SECTION
`cal`	Print calendar **USAGE:** `$ cal [ month ] year` **Arguments:** `month` number between 1 and 12 `year` number between 1 and 9999	5.8.3

`case`	Selection control (Bourne shell)
	USAGE:
	`case string in`
	  `pattern-1) action;;`
	  `.........`
	  `pattern-n) action;;`
	`esac`
		4.2.5

`cat`	Concatenate and print files
	
	USAGE:
	`cat [ options ] [ files ]`
	`stdin` read if `-` or no files are specified
	OPTIONS:
	`-b` (C shell) omit line numbers on blank lines
	`-e` print `$` at end of each line (with -v option only)
	`-n` (C shell) print line number for each output line
	`-s` silent about non-existent lines
	`-t` show tabs with `^|` (with -v option only)
	`-u` unbuffered output (default: buffer output)
	`-v` make non-printing characters visible, except for tabs, newlines and form-feeds
	EXAMPLES:
	Print files in current directory with
	`$ cat *`
	Redirect standard input to create (overwrite) a file with
	`$ cat >thisfile`
	Append standard input to a file with
	`$ cat >>thisfile`
	Display files with
	`$ cat file1 file2 file3`
	Concatenate files and redirect to a file with
	`$ cat file1 file2 file3 >thisfile`
		1.4, 3.4.4, 1.5.1

`cd`	Change directory **USAGE:** `cd [ directory ]` **Default:** without an argument, shell parameter `$HOME` is used as the new working directory.	1.4.3

COMMAND	EXPLANATION	SECTION

	EXAMPLES:
	Change to your bin directory with
	`$ cd bin`
	Change back to your login directory with
	`$ cd`
	Change to root directory with
	`$ cd /`	

`chmod`	Change permission(s)
	USAGE:
	`chmod mode files`
	MODE:
	either absolute mode (an octal number) or symbolic (a letter).
	Numeric mode:
	  4000 set user ID on execution
	  2000 set group ID on execution
	  1000 **sticky bit (save text after execution)**
	  0400 read by owner
	  0200 write by owner
	  0444 read only file
	  0644 only you can write to file, which everyone can read
	  0111 executable by everybody
	Symbolic mode:
	  u user
	  g group
	  o other
	  r read
	  w write
	  x execute
	  + add permission as in `chmod o+x` file (owner can execute)
	  - remove permission: `chmod g-w` file (deny write to g)
		2.3.5
		
		see 2.3.6

`chsh`	Change login shell (BSD Unix only)
	USAGE:
	`chsh loginname [ shell ]`
	SHELL:
	`/bin/csh, /bin/sh, /bin/oldcsh,`
	  `/usr/new/csh`
		8.2

`comm`	Select or reject lines common to two sorted files **USAGE:** `comm [ -flags ] file1 file2` `stdin` read if `-` used instead of `file1` or `file2`.	5.8.1

COMMAND	EXPLANATION	SECTION

	FLAGS:
	Suppress printing of corresponding column
	`-1` suppress lines only from `file1`
	`-2` suppress lines only from `file2`
	`-3` suppress lines in both `file1` and `file2`
	EXAMPLES:
	`Print only lines common to files with`
	`  comm -12 file1 file2`
	`Print only lines in file1 but not in`
	`  file2 with comm -23 file1 file2`	

cp	Copy files
	USAGE:
	`cp oldfile newfile`
	(put copy of `oldfile` in `newfile`)
	`cp files directory`
	(put copy of `files` into specified directory)
	EXAMPLES:
	`cp thisfile temp   # temp` gets copy
	`cp thisfile bin    # bin` directory gets copy
		1.4.10

csh	C shell
	USAGE:
	`csh [ options ] [ args ]`
	OPTIONS:
	`-c cmd` execute `cmd` (command)
	`-e` exit if command fails or has non-zero exit status
	`-f` do not execute `.cshrc` to speed start of shell
	`-i` interactive mode
	`-n` parse commands without executing them
	`-s` commands read from `stdin`
	`-t` read and execute single command line, then exit
	`-v` print input lines as read (see `dbug alias`, Ch. 8)
	`-x` prints commands as executed with arguments (see `dbug alias` in Ch. 8)
	`-X` same as `-x`, but done before reading `.cshrc`
	EXAMPLE:
	`csh -fvx .cshrc`
		Chapter 8

crypt	Encrypt/decrypt `stdin` to `stdout`
	USAGE:
	`crypt [ password ]`
	EXAMPLES:
	`$ cat >message`
	`echo 'Hello, world!'`	

402   SHELL COMMANDS HANDBOOK

COMMAND	EXPLANATION	SECTION

	`ctrl-d`
	`$ crypt yes <message >secret` # encodes message
	`$ crypt yes <message` # decodes message
	`echo 'Hello, world'`
	`$`
	Note: covered only in this section	

`cut`	Cut out selected fields of each line of a file
	USAGE:
	`cut -clist [ file1 file2 ... ]`
	`cut -flist [ -dchar ] [ -s ] [ file1 file2 ... ]`
	`stdin` read if no files are specified.
	OPTIONS:
	
	`-list` a comma-separated list of integer field numbers in ascending order with optional ranges.
	`-clist` list following `-c` specifies character positions (example: `-c5-7` passes characters 5 to 7 of each line).
	`-flist` list following `-f` specifies fields.
	`-dchar` character following `-d` specifies field delimiter.
	`-s` suppresses lines with no delimiters (lines without delimiters are passed untouched, unless otherwise specified).
	EXAMPLE:
	`date ¦ cut -c5-7` # cuts out month
		3.2.6

`date`	Print and set the date and time
	USAGE:
	`date [ mmddhhmm[yy] ] [ +format ]`
	`date`
	FORMAT:
	n insert newline
	t insert tab
	m month of year (01 to 12)
	d day of month (01 to 31)
	y last two digits of year (00 to 99)
	D date as `mm/dd/yy`
	H hour as 00 to 23
	M minute as 00 to 59
	S second as 00 to 59
	T time as `HH:MM:SS`
	j day of year (001 to 366)
	w day of week (Sunday = 0)
	a abbreviated weekday (Sun to Sat)
	h abbreviated month (Jan to Dec)
	r time in `AM/PM` notation
		1.3.2

COMMAND	EXPLANATION	SECTION

EXAMPLES:
```
$ date '+DATE: %y'
DATE: 87
$ date '+ %y'
87
$ date '+date: %y%ntime: %h'
date: 87
time: 09
$ date '+date: %m/%d/%y%ntime: %H:%M:%S'
date: 02/21/87
time: 09:33:44
$ date
Sat Feb 21 09:35:10 CST 1987
```

`df` Displays number of blocks free 2.5
USAGE:
`df [ options ] [ file-system ]`
Argument:
`file-system`: list of device names
OPTIONS:
`-f` print only free list count
`-t` print total allocated blocks

`du` Summarize disk usage 2.5
USAGE:
`du [ options ] [ directories ]`
OPTIONS:
`-a` causes entry to be generated for each file (default: login directory and each of its subdirectories only)
`-r` do not remain silent about unreadable directories (default: silent about unreadable directories)
`-s` display only grand total

`echo` Echo arguments 1.4.7
USAGE:
`echo [ -n ] [ args ]`
FLAG:
`-n` (7th edition, C shell) suppress newline
`Args` (special C-like escape conventions):
   `\b` backspace
   `\c` print line without newline
   `\f` form feed
   `\n` newline
   `\r` carriage return
   `\t` tab
   `\v` vertical tab
   `\`   backslash

COMMAND	EXPLANATION	SECTION

EXAMPLES:
```
$ echo '\tHello!'
    Hello!
$ echo '\tEnter value: \c'
    Enter value:   (cursor left on this line)
```

ed Standard text editor 2.2.3

USAGE:
```
ed [ - ] [ -px ] [ file ]
```
OPTIONS:
-    suppresses printing of character counts by e, r, and w commands
- `-p P` (P stands for Prompt) specifies prompt
- `-x` edit encrypted file

egrep Extended pattern-matching filter 6.2.2

USAGE:
```
[ options ] [ expr ] [ files ]
stdin read if no files are specified
```
EXPR:
Full regular expression accepted as in **ed**, except for `\(` and `\)` as well as the following extensions:
1. A regular expression followed by a `+` matches one or more occurrences of the regular expression (RE).
2. An RE separated by `?` matches 0 or 1 occurrences of RE.
3. Two REs separated by `|` or newline match strings which are matched by either RE.
4. An RE may be enclosed by `( )` for grouping.

OPTIONS:
- `-b` precede line with block number in which it was found
- `-c` only print count of matching lines
- `-e RE` use when RE starts with a `-`
- `-f F` take expression from file F
- `-1` print only names of files with matching lines
- `-n` precede each output line with relative line number
- `-v` print all but matching lines

EXAMPLES:
```
$ egrep -c 'echo|cd' *
format: 3
insert: 7
lib: 0
$ egrep -b 'a|e|i|o|u' format
0: # construct glossary with references
. . . . . . . . . . . . . .
```

env Alter environment and execute command 8.2

USAGE:
```
env [ - ] [ name=value ] [ command args ]
```

USAGE FOR COMMANDS   **405**

COMMAND	EXPLANATION	SECTION
	OPTIONS:	
	`-` causes inherited environment to be ignored.	
	`name = value` arguments with the form name=value are merged into the inherited environment *before* command is executed.	
	`args pass` arguments to command after obtaining current environment.	
	EXAMPLE:	
	`$ env` # prints environment variables	
`exec`	Execute command	3.2.5
	USAGE:	
	`exec command`	
	Note: overwrites current process	
`exit`	causes a shell to exit with exit status	5.3
	USAGE:	
	`exit [ n ]`	
	OPTION:	
	`n` exit status value to return when a shell exits	
`expr`	Evaluate arguments as an expression	4.5
	USAGE:	
	`expr argument(s)`	
	EXAMPLES:	
	`$ this=´expr $this + 20´` # adds 20 to this	
	`$ amt=32755`	
	`$ expr $this : ´.*´` # returns number of characters in `$this`	
	`5`	
`fgrep`	Pattern matching with strings from a file	6.1
	USAGE:	
	`fgrep [ options ] [ strings ] [ files ]`	
	`stdin` read if no files are specified	
	OPTIONS:	
	`-b` precede matched line with block number	
	`-c` only print count of matching lines	
	`-e E` use if E (expression) starts with a `-`	
	`-f F` take strings from file F	
	`-l` ignore case of letters in making comparisons	
	`-n` precede each line with relative line number	
	`-v` only print lines not matching pattern	
	`-x` only lines matched in their entirety are printed	
	`strings` list of fixed strings, which must be separated by newlines and optionally enclosed inside apostrophes (single quotes)	

COMMAND	EXPLANATION	SECTION

EXAMPLE:
```
$ cat >strings
echo
yes
ctrl-d
$ fgrep -f strings *    # search through all files
Firstwords: echo 'Hello, world!'
```
....

file Classify file(s) 1.4

USAGE:
`file [ -c ] [ -f ffile ] [ -m mfile ] args`

OPTIONS:
- `-c` check magic file for format errors (no file typing is done under `-c`)
- `-f ffile` use `ffile` as a file containing names of files to be checked
- `-m mfile` instructs file to use alternate magic file (`mfile`). The default magic file is `/etc/magic` to identify files that have a "magic number," which is a numeric or string constant indicating a file type.

EXAMPLE:
```
$ file /
/:      directory
```

find Find file(s) 2.6

USAGE:
`find pathname-list Expression`

EXPRESSION:
formed with 1 or more of the following primaries:
- `-name file` true if file matches current file name
- `-perm onum` true if file permission flags exactly match the octal number `onum`
- `-type T` true if type of file matches the file `type T` which can be one of the following:
  - `b` block special file
  - `c` character special file
  - `d` directory file
  - `p` FIFO (a.k.a. named pipe)
  - `f` plain (ordinary) file
- `-links n` true if file has `n` links
- `-user uname` true if file belongs to user with user name `uname`
- `-group G` true if file belongs to group with `G` group name
- `-size n` true if file is `n` blocks long

USAGE FOR COMMANDS

COMMAND	EXPLANATION	SECTION
	`-atime n` true if file has been accessed in `n` days	
	`-ctime n` true if file has changed in `n` days	
	`-mtime n` true if file has been modified in `n` days	
	`-exec cmd` true if executed command returns `0` exit status	
	`-ok cmd` command executed if user enters y	
	`-print` causes current pathname to be printed	
	`-cpio D` write current file on device in `cpio` format (5120 byte records)	
	`-newer F` true if current file has been modified more recently that the argument file	
	`( expr )` true if parenthesized expression `(expr)` is true	

EXAMPLES:
```
find . -name dleft -print     # finds dleft
find . -name 'd*' -print      # filenames begin with d
find . -type d -print         # lists directories
```

for   Indexed iteration in Bourne shell   4.3.1

USAGE:
```
for name [ in strings ] do list done
```
EXAMPLES:
```
$ set `ls`
$ for i
>     do
>       echo Filename: $i
>       shift
>     done
Filename: 2class
Filename: 3class
........................................
$ for i in `ls`
>     do
>       echo Filename: $i
>     done
Filename: 2class
Filename: 3class
........................................
```

foreach   Indexed iteration in C shell   8.5.6

USAGE:
```
foreach item ( list ) commands end
```
EXAMPLE:
```
% foreach name ( `ls` )
?     echo Filename: $name
?     end
Filename: bin
Filename: ch8
........................................
```

COMMAND	EXPLANATION	SECTION
`grep`	Search a file for a pattern	6.2.1

    USAGE:
    `grep [ options ] expression [ files ]`
    `stdin` read when no files are specified
    EXPRESSION:
    a regular expression which specifies a pattern.
    OPTIONS:
    `-b` precede line with block number containing line
    `-c` print only a count of matching lines
    `-l` only list of names of files with matching lines
    `-n` precede each line with a relative line number
    `-s` suppress error messages
    `-v` only print lines not matching pattern

    EXAMPLES:
```
$ ls -l | grep -v '^d'      # list non-directory names
$ grep -n '#' *             # print with line numbers

Firstwords:1:# First message from Unix
. . . . . . . . . . . . . . . . . . . . . . . . . . . .
```

| `hangman` | Play hangman game | 1.4.4 |

    USAGE:
    `/usr/games/hangman`

| `head` | Display leading lines of a file | 2.6 |

    USAGE:
    `Head [ -n ] files`
    OPTION:
    `-n` display only leading `n` lines of specified files (default is 10)
    EXAMPLE:
```
$ head -2 blake terms
==> blake <==
To see a world in a Grain of Sand,
And a Heaven in a wild Flower,
==> terms <==
the         15568
of           9767
$
```

| `help` | Ask for help | |

    USAGE:
    `help [ args ]`
    EXAMPLES:
```
$ help help        # get help on help
$ help stuck       # when all else fails
```
    Note: covered only in this section

COMMAND	EXPLANATION	SECTION
`if`	Test condition to select an action	4.2.1

USAGE (Bourne shell):
```
if [ expr ] then cmds fi
if [ test expr] then cmds fi
if [ expr ] then cmds else cmds fi
if [ expr ] then cmds elif expr then cmds fi
```
USAGE (C shell):
```
if (expr) command
if (expr) then cmds endif
if (expr) then cmds else cmds endif
```

`kill`	Send signal to a process or group of processes	5.4

See `kill(2)` in your Unix manual.
USAGE:
```
kill [ -signo ] PIDs
```
OPTIONS:

`signo`	Default value is 15 (to terminate process)
`-1`	hangup
`-2`	interrupt
`-3`	quit
`-4`	illegal instruction
`-5`	trace trap
`-6`	IOT instruction
`-8`	floating point exception
`-9`	do not ignore `kill` command
`-10`	bus error
`-11`	segmentation violation
`-12`	bad system call argument
`-13`	write on unread pipe
`-14`	for alarm clock
`-15`	software termination signal (default value)
`-16`	user-defined signal 1
`-17`	user-defined signal 2
`PID`	process ID number (a 0 specifies all processes resulting from current loop)

`ln`	Make a link to a file	2.7

USAGE:
```
ln [ -f ] existing-file [ file ]
```
OPTION:
`-f` force link despite file permissions of `file`
`file` Uses `file` to create a link to an existing file
EXAMPLE:
```
$ ln Firstwords hello    # hello becomes the link
```

`lpr`	Line printer spooler	1.6

USAGE:
```
lpr [ options ] [ name ... ]
```

COMMAND	EXPLANATION	SECTION

OPTIONS:
- `-c` makes copy of file to be sent before returning to user
- `-r` removes file after sending it
- `-m` mail message when printing is done
- `-n` suppresses report of completed print job
- `-ffile` uses file as a dummy file name to report back in the mail

`ls` List contents of directories 1.4

USAGE:
`ls [ -options ] [ directories ]`
Without specified directories, `ls` lists contents of your current working directory

OPTIONS:
- `-a` list all directories, including entries which begin a `.`
- `-b` display non-graphic characters in octal (base 8)
- `-c` use time of last modification of inode instead of last modification of file for sorting (`-t`) and/or printing (`-1`)
- `-C` list directory entries in columns in order
- `-d` list only name of directory to get status of directory
- `-f` force each argument to be interpreted as a directory and list name found in each slot (this turns off options `-1`, `-t`, `-s`, and `-r` and turns on `-a`)
- `-i` for each file, print inumber in first column of report
- `-l` list in long format, giving mode, owner, group, other, number of links, group name, size *in bytes,* date, time and filename
- `-m` comma=separated list of files
- `-n` same as `-l` with GID and UID listed
- `-o` same as `-l` without group
- `-p` mark directories with a `/` (slash)
- `-q` non-graphic characters displayed with `?`
- `-r` reverse order of sort to get descending alphabetic order or ascending time-order with `-t` option
- `-R` recursively print directories, starting with `.`
- `-s` print file size in blocks
- `-t` sort by time of last modification (latest first)
- `-u` sort by time of last access instead of last modification with `-t` or `-l` option
- `-x` list in columns sorted across each row

EXAMPLES:
- `ls -rtl`   # sort in time ascent order
- `ls`   # list names in ascending order
- `ls -C bin`   # list bin in columns
- `ls -aC`   # list all files in columns

COMMAND	EXPLANATION	SECTION
`mail`	Send mail to or read mail from users	1.3.2

      USAGE:
```
mail [ -options ] [ -f file ] persons
mail [ -t ] persons
mail [ -options ] persons <filename
mail
```
      OPTIONS:

`-t`	include list of people mail sent to in message
`-e`	causes mail not to be printed; exit value is 0 if user has mail, otherwise exit value equals 1
`-p`	causes mail to be printed without prompting for disposition
`-q`	causes mail to be printed in FIFO order
`-ffile`	causes mail to use `file` instead of default `mailfile`

COMMAND	EXPLANATION	SECTION
`man`	Print entries in online manual	1.3.2

      USAGE:
```
man [ options ] [ section ] titles
```
      OPTIONS:

`-c`	causes `man` to invoke `col(1)`
`-d`	search current directory instead of `/usr/man` (you must use a full file name with `-d`)
`-s`	typeset entry in 6″x9″ (small) format
`-t`	typeset entry in 8.5″x11″ (default) format
`Tterm`	format entry using `nroff` and print it on the standard output (term is the terminal type); type `help term2` for list of recognized values of term
`-w`	print to `stdout` only pathnames of entries relative to `/usr/man` or to `.` with `-d` option
`-y`	force use of non-compacted version of macros

      EXAMPLE:
```
$ man man
```

COMMAND	EXPLANATION	SECTION
`mesg`	Permit or deny messages	1.3.2

      USAGE:
```
mesg [ n ] [ y ]
```
`mesg` by itself shows message status (`y` or `n`)

      OPTIONS:

n	forbids messages via `write`
y	reinstates `write` permission

      EXAMPLE:
```
$ mesg y
$ mesg n   # deny messages from write
```

COMMAND	EXPLANATION	SECTION
`mkdir`	Make a directory **USAGE:** `mkdir dirnames` Creates specified directory in mode 777 with standard entries `.` (for directory itself) and `..` (for parent of newly created directory) made automatically.	1.4.3

`mv`	Move files
	 USAGE:
	 `mv [ -f ] oldfile newfile`
	 `mv [ -f ] oldfile directory`
	 OPTION:
	 `-f` force move despite file permissions
		1.4.10

`od`	Octal dump of directory or file
	 USAGE:
	 `od [ options ] [ file ] [ [+]offset[.][b] ]`
	   `-b` interpret bytes in octal
	   `-c` interpret bytes in ASCII (non-graphic characters as C language escapes):
	         null = \0
	         backspace = \b
	         formfeed = \f
	         newline = \n
	         return = \r
	         tab = \t
	         others = 3 digit octal number
	   `-d` interpret words in unsigned decimal
	   `-o` interpret words in octal
	   `-s` interpret 16-bit words in signed decimal
	   `-x` interpret words in hexadecimal (base 16)
	   `file` specifies file to be dumped (`stdin` is read if no file is specified)
	   `offset` specifies where dumping is to begin argument normally interpreted in octal bytes
		2.3.2

`pr`	Print files
	 USAGE:
	 `pr [options ] [ files ]`
	 `stdin` read if `-` or no files are specified
	 OPTIONS:
	   `+k` begin printing with page k (default value of k = 1)
	   `-k` produce k column output (default is k = 1)
	   `-a` print multi-column output
	   `-d` double space the output
	   `-eck` expand input tabs to character positions k+1, 2*k+1, 3*k+1, and so on
		1.6

COMMAND	EXPLANATION	SECTION
	`-h` use next argument as header to be printed instead of the filename	
	`-ick` replace whitespace wherever possible with tabs to character positions `k+1, 2*k+1, 3*k+1`, and so on	
	`-lk` set length of page to `k` lines	
	`-ok` offset each line by `k` positions	
	`-p` pause before beginning each page if output is directed to a terminal (rings bell and waits for carriage return)	
`ps`	Report process status	3.1

USAGE:
`ps [ options ]`
OPTIONS:
- `-a`   print information about all processes, except process group leaders and processes not associated with a terminal
- `-c CF`   Use corefile `CF` instead of `/dev/mem`
- `-d`   print data about all processes except group leaders
- `-e`   print information about all processes
- `-f`   general full file listing
- `-g GL`   restrict listing to data about processes whose process groups are given in the group list `GL`
- `-l`   general long listing
- `-n NL`   argument will be taken as the name of an alternate name list `NL` (default `NL` equals `/unix`)
- `-p PL`   listing restricted to data about processes with process ID numbers given in the process list `PL`
- `-t TL`   restrict listing to data about processes associated with terminals given in terminal list `TL`

COMMAND	EXPLANATION	SECTION
`pwd`	Print working directory name	1.4

USAGE:
`pwd`

COMMAND	EXPLANATION	SECTION
`rm`	Remove file	1.4.10

USAGE:
`rm [ -options ] file`
OPTIONS:
- `-f`   forces removal of file without write permission
- `-i`   interactive file deletion mode (`rm` asks whether to delete each file)
- `-r`   recursively delete directories

EXAMPLES:
```
$ rm *.o                    # remove object modules
$ rm -i *
```

COMMAND	EXPLANATION	SECTION
| | ```
bin: bin directory
blake: ? n
brandenburg: ? y
.....................
$
``` | |
`rmdir`	Remove subdirectory **USAGE:** `rmdir directories` Except for `.` and `..`, a subdirectory must be empty before it can be deleted.	1.4.3
`sed`	Stream editor **USAGE:** `sed [ -n ] [ -e script ] [ -f sfile ]` `[ files ]` `sed [ -n ] <infile` `stdin` read if no files are specified `infile` is file to be stream-edited using specified instructions **OPTIONS:** `-n` suppresses default (unprocessed) output `-e sc` file `sc` contains commands for `sed` to execute `-f sf` cause `sed` script to be taken from `sf` file **EXAMPLES:** `$ ls -l	sed -n '/^d/pr'`    # lists subdirectories `$ sed -n '$p' blake`    # lists last line of file `$ sed -n <blake '$p'`    # lists last line of file `$ for name in 'ls'` `> do` `> echo $name` `> sed -n '/^\#/p' $name`  # create file lexicon `> done` `insert`    # insert line(s) after lines in specified file `.....................` `$`	Ch. 6

`set`	Set/unset shell flags
	USAGE:
	`set [ -options ] [ args ]`
	(sets flags)
	`set [ +options ] [args ]`
	(unsets or turns off flags)
	OPTIONS:
	`-e` exit immediately if a command exists with a non-zero exit status
		8.2.1

USAGE FOR COMMANDS
```

COMMAND	EXPLANATION	SECTION

	`-k` all keyword arguments are placed in the environment for a command, not just those that precede a command name
	`-n` read but do not execute commands
	`-t` exit after reading and executing a single command
	`-u` treat unset variables as an error when substituting
	`-x` print commands and arguments as they are executed
	`--` do not change any of the flags
	EXAMPLES:
	`$ set     # display environment variables`
	`$ set -x  # display commands being executed`	

`setenv`	Set environment variable in C shell **USAGE:** `setenv name value`	8.2

`sh`	Bourne shell command interpreter
	USAGE:
	`sh [ -options ] [ args ]`
	OPTIONS:
	`-c cmd` execute command
	`-e` exit if a command fails (with `-i`)
	`-i` sets interactive mode
	`-f` turns off wildcarding
	`-k` place all key words in environment
	`-n` read but do not execute commands
	`-r` set restricted mode (see comments on restricted shell `rsh` in `sh(1)`)
	`-s` take commands from `stdin` (standard input)
	`-t` read and execute single command (exit afterward)
	`-u` set error after substituting an unset variable
	`-v` display input lines as they are read
	`-x` display commands with arguments as executed
	EXAMPLES:
	`$ sh -i` # sets interactive mode
	`$ sh -ei what` # exit upon failure
	`what: what: cannot open`
	`$ sh -eis <Firstwords` # take command from `stdin`
	`$ $ Hello, world!`
	`$ sh -x Firstwords` # track execution by `sh`
	`+ echo Hello, world!`
	`Hello, world!`
	`$`
		3.2.2

`shift`	Rename positional parameters **USAGE:** `shift [ count ]`	

COMMAND	EXPLANATION	SECTION

COUNT:
the positional parameters from `$count + 1 ...` are
   renamed `$1 ....` (By default, n = 1)
EXAMPLE:
```
$ ls -x
2class    3class    4class    5class Firstwords  bin
.........................
$ set `ls`; echo $1; shift 5; echo $1
2class
bin
$
```

Note: covered only in this section

`sleep`   Suspend execution for an interval in seconds   3.9
USAGE:
`sleep time`
Time:
seconds
EXAMPLE:
```
$ (sleep 600; echo 'Coffee time!') &
1503
$ Coffee time!              (10 minutes later)
```

`sort`   Sort and/or merge files   5.8.1
USAGE:
```
sort [-opts] [+pos [-pos2]] ...
     [-o out][files]
```
`stdin` read if `-` or no files are specified
OPTIONS:
- `-b`   ignore leading blanks
- `-c`   check if input is in sorted order (with `-m`)
- `-d`   dictionary order (only letters, digits and blanks are significant in comparisons)
- `-f`   fold uppercase into lowercase letters
- `-i`   ignore characters outside ASCII range (040:0176) in non-numeric comparisons
- `-m`   only merge sorted files
- `-M`   sort as if field contains months
- `-n`   numeric sort with `-b`
- `-o out` place output from sort in file named by out instead of `stdout`
- `-r`   sort in descending order
- `-tx`   tab character separating fields is `x`
- `-u`   suppress occurrences of duplicate lines
- `+pos`   restricts sort key to field beginning in position `pos1` and ending just before position `pos2`. The numbers `pos1` and `pos2` have an `m.n` form where

USAGE FOR COMMANDS   **417**

COMMAND	EXPLANATION	SECTION

        m.n   specifies fields and characters to skip
        m   number of fields to skip
        n   number of characters to skip further

EXAMPLES:
(word frequencies are from Helen Gaines, *Cryptanalysis: A Study of Ciphers and their Solution*. NY: Dover, 1939, p. 226.)

```
$ cat words                  # sample file
the        15568
of          9767
and         7638
$ cat otherwds               # second sample file
where        752
me           745
been         720
$ sort -bn +2 words          # sort on second field
and         7638
of          9767
the        15568
$ sort -r otherwds           # sort in descending order
been         720
me           745
where        752
$ sort -m *2 words otherwds  # merge two files
the        15568
of          9767
and         7638
where        752
me           745
been         720
```

source   Read and execute files (C shell only)   8.2.1
USAGE:
`source [ -h ] name`
OPTION:
`-h`   place commands in history list without executing
`names` C shell executes commands in name without creating a subshell

split   Split a file into pieces   2.2.2
USAGE:
`split [ -n ] [ file [ name ] ]`
`stdin` read if - or no files are specified
OPTION:
`-n`   sets size of split files to n lines; by default, n has a value of 1000
`file` file to be split

SHELL COMMANDS HANDBOOK

COMMAND	EXPLANATION	SECTION

`name` name of first output file with `aa` appended and so
on lexicographically up to `zz` for a maximum of
676 files (name must be limited to 12 characters);
if no output name is given, then `x` is the default
name used by split

EXAMPLES:
```
$ split -100 /usr/dict/words wds    # splits dictionary
$ ls -x wds*
wdsaa   wdsab   wdsac   wdsad  ............
$ split -1 -
yes
again, yes
ctrl-d
$ ls -x x*
xaa    xab    xac    xad  ............
$
```

`stty`   Set options for a terminal   1.3.3

USAGE:
`stty [ -a ] [ -g ] [options ]`

OPTIONS:
- `-a` reports all option settings
- `-g` report current settings in a form that can be used in another `stty` command
- `0`   hang up phone line

Control:
- `[-]cread`   enable/disable (with `-`) the receiver
- `[-]clocal` enable/disable (with `-`) the modem
- `csN`   select character size with N = 5, 6, 7 or 8
- `[-]cstopb` use two/one (with `-`) stop bits per character
- `[-]parenb` enable/disable parity detection and generation
- `[-]parodd` select odd/even (with `-`) parity
- `[-]hup`   hang up data connection on last close

Input:
- `[-]ignbrk` ignore/(do not ignore) break on input
- `[-]brkin`   signal/(do not signal) INTR on break
- `[-]ignpar` ignore/(do not ignore) parity errors
- others: see `stty(1)`

EXAMPLES:
```
$ stty -a   # report current settings
$ stty -g   # report formatted settings
```

`tail`   Output last lines of a file

USAGE:
`tail[ options ] [ file ]`
`stdin` read if no file is specified

USAGE FOR COMMANDS

COMMAND	EXPLANATION	SECTION

OPTIONS:
`-f` follow growth of file rather than stop at end of file
`+n[bcl]` begin output `n` units from beginning of file with the following optional specifications:
    b blocks
    c characters
    l lines
`-n[bcl]` begin output `n` units from end of file
EXAMPLES:
(Note: the `words` *file is given with* `sort` *command*)
```
$ tail +20c words          # 20 characters from beginning
9767
and     7638
$ tail -4c words           # 4 characters from end of file
638
$ tail -21 /usr/dict/words # last 2 lines of dictionary
zucchini
Zurich
$
```
Note: covered only in this section

tee   Copy `stdin` to `stdout` and files   2.2.1
USAGE:
`tee [ -i ] [ -a ] file ] ...`
OPTIONS:
`-a` causes output to be appended to a file rather than overwrite old file
`-i` ignore interrupts
EXAMPLES:
(Note: `words` *file appears in examples for* `sort` *command*)
```
$ date | tee temp              # show what goes into temp
Sun Feb 22 08:24:41 CST 1987
$ cat words | tee -a temp      # append to temp file
the     15568
of      9767
and     7638
$ # Now temp is a time-stamped words file
$ date | tee report1 report2   # time-stamp 3 files
    report3
Sun Feb 22 08:31:23 CST 1987
$
```

test   Condition evaluation command   1.4.8
USAGE:
`test expression`
`[ expression ]`

COMMAND	EXPLANATION	SECTION

EXPRESSION:

`-b file`	true if file exists and is block special	
`-c file`	true if file exists and is character special	
`-d file`	true if file exists and is a directory	
`-f file`	true if file exists and is a regular file	
`-g file`	true if file exists and its `set-GID` bit is set	
`-k file`	true if file exists and its `sticky` bit is set	
`-n string`	true if length of string is non-zero	
`-p file`	true if file exists and is a FIFO named pipe	
`-r file`	true if file exists and is readable	
`-s file`	true if file exists and has size greater than zero	
`-t [fd]`	true if the open file with file descriptor number `fd` (by default fd = 1) is associated with a terminal device	
`-u file`	true if file exists and its `set-UID` is set	
`-w file`	true if file exists and is writable	
`-x file`	true if file exists and is executable	
`-z string`	true if size of string is zero	
`string`	true if string is not the null string	
`s1 = s2`	true if strings `s1` and `s2` are the same	
`s1 != s2`	true if strings `s1` and `s2` are not the same	
`n1 -op n2`	true if `n1 -op n2` is true where operator `-op` can be one of the following:	

```
                  -eq   =    (equality)
                  -ge   > q  (greater than or equal)
                  -gt   >    (greater than)
                  -le   <=   (less than or equal)
                  -lt   <    (less than)
```

Expressions can be combined with the following operators:

`!`	unary not operator
`-a`	binary and operator
`-o`	binary or operator
`( expr )`	use parentheses for grouping

EXAMPLES:

(Note: the `words` file appears in illustrations for `sort`)

```
$ test -d words; echo $?
1                                   [ words is not a directory ]
$ ( test -f words -a -x words ); echo $?
1                                   [ words is not executable ]
$ test -z ""; echo $?
0                                   [ string has zero length ]
$ test -z "Yes!"; echo $?
1                                   [ string has non-zero length ]
```

(Note: the following procedure illustrates the use of the `-t` option where `test -t` checks whether `stdout` goes to a terminal or is redirected to some file.)

```
$ cat >checkout                     # create test -t procedure
# check output stream
```

USAGE FOR COMMANDS **421**

COMMAND	EXPLANATION	SECTION

```
# post: test -t returns 0 if stdout goes to your screen
#       test -t returns 1 if stdout is redirected to a file
test -t
if [ $? -eq 0 ]
then
   echo stdout sent to screen with '$? = ' $?
else
   echo stdout redirected to a file with '$? = ' $?
fi
tail -1l $1               # stdout is last line of $1 file
ctrl-d
$ chmod +x checkout       # make checkout executable
$ checkout words
stdout sent to screen with $? = 0
and      7638
$ checkout words >temp    # redirect stdout
$ cat temp
stdout redirected to a file with $? = 1
and      7638
$
```

time Display a command's elapsed times 7.6
USAGE: 7.12
`time command`
EXAMPLE:
```
$ time checkout /usr/dict/words
stdout sent to screen with $? = 0
Zurich
real 2.2
user 0.1
sys 0.8
```

tset Test and set terminal parameters in C shell 8.2.1
USAGE:
`tset [ options ]`
OPTIONS:
- `-`   `stdout` is guessed output name of terminal
- `-ec` sets erase character to `c` (default erase character is backspace)
- `-i`   suppresses terminal initialization strings
- `-kc` makes `c` terminal kill character (default kill character is `ctrl-X`)
- `-m PCs` guess terminal type from PCs (port type identifier, baud rate and terminal type)
  PC-format: `'[port_id][speed]:ttytype'`
- `-n`   specify new terminal driver modes
- `-Q`   suppress `erase` and `kill` setting messages

COMMAND	EXPLANATION	SECTION
`tr`	Translate characters	5.8.1

    USAGE:
    `tr [ -options ] [ string1 [ string2 ] ]`
    OPTIONS:
      `-c` complements characters in `string1` relative to ASCII characters in 001 to 377 octal range
      `-d` deletes all input characters in `string1`
      `-s` squeezes all repeated characters in `string2` to single characters
    STRING:
      `[a-z]` string of ASCII characters in a to z range
      `[c*n]` n repetitions of character `c`
      `[\n*]` escape meaning of `n` with backslash where `n` can be 1, 2 or 3 digits as in `[\012]` for a newline
    EXAMPLES:
```
$ echo tummmmmmmmmmtytum | tr -s "m"
tumtytum
$ echo 'Washington, DC' |
        tr -cs "[A-Z][a-z]" "[\012*]
   Washington
   DC
```

`trap`	Detect signals and executes a command sequence	3.5

    USAGE:
    `trap [ commands-list ] [ signals-list ]`
    SIGNALS:
      0 shell exit
      1 hangup
      2 interrupt caused by pressing DEL (delete) key
      3 quit
      9 kill (cannot be caught or ignored)
      15 software interrupt
    EXAMPLES:
```
$ trap                        # list current values of traps
0: /usr/you/.logout
$ trap 0 2 3                  # resets traps to default values
$ trap                        # notice old trap 0 value gone
$ trap $HOME/.logout 0        # execute .logout upon exit
$ trap                        # check trap
0: /usr/you/.logout
```

`uniq`	Report repeated lines	5.8.1

    USAGE:
    `uniq [ -udc [+n] [-n] ] [ input [output] ]`
      `-c` output each line with count of number of occurrences (supersedes `-d` and `-u`)
      `-d` output one copy of repeated lines
      `-u` output lines which are not repeated

COMMAND	EXPLANATION	SECTION

	`+n` ignore first n characters of input line
	`-n` ignore first n fields plus any blanks before each field from start of input line
	EXAMPLE:
	(Note: `words` *file appears in illustrations for* `sort`*)*
	`$ uniq -c words`
	`    1 the      15568`
	`    1 of        9767`
	`    1 and       7638`
	`$`	

`unset`	Unset variables or functions **USAGE:** `unset [ names ]`	8.2.3
`until`	Conditional iteration of an action **USAGE:** `until condition do commands done`	4.3.2

`vi`	Full-screen visual editor
	USAGE:
	`vi [ +line ] [ options ] [ files ]`
	`+line` position cursor at beginning of specified line
	`-r` retrieve last saved version of file after editor and/or system crash
	`-R` read-only mode
	`-t tag` position cursor at definition of `tag` (only in a file with a tag)
	`-wn` sets default window size to `n`
	`-x` create or edit an encrypted file
		2.2.4

`wc`	Count lines, words and characters in a file
	USAGE:
	`wc [ -options ] [ names ]`
	`stdin` read if no files are specified
	OPTIONS:
	`-c` count characters
	`-l` count lines
	`-w` count words
	(Default is `wc -clw [ names ]`)
	EXAMPLE:
	`$ wc -l /usr/dict/words`
	`  23739 /usr/dict/words`
		1.6.2

`whereis`	Find specified file in C shell **USAGE:** `whereis [ options ] files` `-b` find binaries only	8.2.2

COMMAND	EXPLANATION	SECTION
	`-B alt` find binaries in `alt` (alternate directories)	
	`-m` find manual sections only	
	`-M alt` find manual sections in `alt`	
	`-s` find source code only	
	`-S` find source code in `alt`	
	`-u` find files missing binary, manual or source	
	`alt dir` pathname for an alternate directory must begin with `/`	

while   Conditional iteration   4.3.2

USAGE:
```
while condition do commands done
```
EXAMPLE:
```
$ while :
>   do
>     sleep 3600; echo tea time!
>   done &
$
```

while   Conditional iteration (C shell)   8.5.6

USAGE:
```
while (condition) commands end
```
EXAMPLE:
```
% while (1 > 0)
?   sleep 5; echo tea time!
?   end
tea time!
.....................
```

who   List users currently logged on   1.3.3

USAGE:
```
who [ -options ] [ file ]
who am i
```
OPTIONS:
- `-a`   process `/etc/utmp` or named file with all options turned on
- `-b`   indicate time and date of last reboot
- `-d`   display all processes which have expired and have not been respawned by `init`
- `-H`   print column headings for output
- `-l`   lists only those lines on which system is waiting for someone to login
- `-p`   list any process which is currently active and has been previously spawned by `init`
- `-q`   list only number of current users and user names
- `-r`   indicate current run-level of the `init` process
- `-s`   lists only name, line and time logged-in fields
- `-t`   show last change to system clock (via date) by root

USAGE FOR COMMANDS   **425**

COMMAND	EXPLANATION	SECTION
	`-T` same as `-u` option, except the state of the terminal line (whether someone else can write to that `tty`) is printed	
	`-u` list only those users who are logged on	
`write`	Write to another user interactively **USAGE:** `write username [ ttyname ]`	1.3.2

Appendixes

Appendix A: Tables

A.1 ASCII Character Set with Octal Codes

	0	20	40	60	100	120	140	160
0	nul	dle	sp	0	@	P	`	p
1	soh	dc1	!	1	A	Q	a	q
2	stx	dc2	"	2	B	R	b	r
3	etx	dc3	#	3	C	S	c	s
4	eot	dc4	$	4	D	T	d	t
5	enq	nak	%	5	E	U	e	u
6	ack	syn	&	6	F	V	f	v
7	bel	etb	'	7	G	W	g	w
10	bs	can	(	8	H	X	h	x
11	ht	em	)	9	I	Y	i	y
12	lf	sub	*	:	J	Z	j	z
13	vt	esc	+	;	K	[	k	{
14	ff	fs	,	<	L	\	l	|
15	cr	gs	-	=	M	]	m	}
16	so	rs	.	>	N	^	n	~
17	si	us	/	?	O	_	o	del

FORMULA:
column number + row number = ASCII code (in octal)

EXAMPLE:
```
140 + 1 = 141 (ASCII a) in octal
        = 1x8² + 4x8 + 1 = 97 in decimal
```

427

A.2 Unix Signals

Note: `cat /usr/include/signal.h` *to see header file which defines Unix signals.*

NAME	SIGNAL	MEANING
`sighup`	1	hangup; it is sent out when a terminal is hung up and to each process when a group leader terminates for any reason
`sigint`	2	interrupt; it is sent to every process associated with control terminal when the DEL key is pressed
`sigquit`	3	quit when ctrl-\ (default quit key) is pressed; use to get a core dump
`sigill`	4	illegal instruction (whenever hardware detects an illegal instruction)
`sigtrap`	5	trace trap; it is sent after *every* instruction when a process is run with process tracing activated with ptrace
`sigiot`	6	i/o trap sent whenever hardware fault occurs
`sigemt`	7	emulator trap sent as a result of an implementation hardware fault
`sigfpe`	8	floating point exception resulting from a floating point error
`sigkill`	9	kill absolutely! (a signal which cannot be ignored or caught)
`sigbus`	10	bus error
`sigsegv`	11	segmentation violation; happens when a process attempts to reference an address outside of its address range
`sigpipe`	13	write to `pipe` not opened for reading
`sigalrm`	14	alarm clock
`sigterm`	15	software termination
`sigusr1`	16	user-defined signal
`sigusr2`	17	user-defined signal
`sigcld`	18	when a child process dies
`sigpwr`	19	power-fail restart

A.2 C Language Escapes

Note: The following C language escapes are used in the `sh` *and* `csh` *shells as well as by* `awk`.

ESCAPE	MEANING
`\0`	null
`\b`	backspace
`\f`	formfeed
`\n`	newline
`\r`	return
`\t`	tab

Appendix B: Guide to Editing with ed

ed   Standard text editor
               USAGE:
               `ed [ - ] [ -px ] [ file ]`
               OPTIONS:

`-`		suppresses printing of character counts by `e`, `r` and `w` commands
`-p`	`P`	specifies prompt `p`
`-x`		edit encrypted file

B.1 Adding Lines to a File with ed

The following ed commands make it possible to add lines to a file:

COMMAND	INTERPRETATION
`i` (insert)	subsequent lines are inserted *before* the current line
`a` (append)	subsequent lines are inserted *after* the current line
`c` (change)	change the current line to the new line entered and follow it with additional lines
`.` (stop)	tells ed you are finished adding lines and wish to leave add-line mode

B.2 Normal Mode ed Commands

COMMAND	INTERPRETATION	
`p` (print)	print specified lines	
	Examples:	
	`1,10p`	[print lines 1 to 10]
	`1,$p`	[print all lines]
	`5,$p`	[print lines 5 to last line]
`d` (delete)	delete specified lines	
	Example:	
	`5,12d`	[delete lines 5 to 12]
`j` (join)	join specified lines together	
	Example:	
	`9,10j`	[join lines 9 and 10]

(continued on next page)

COMMAND	INTERPRETATION
m (move)	move specified lines
	Example:
	`4,7m 20` [move lines 4–7 after line 20]
r (read)	read lines from specified file and append after specified line
	Example:
	`5r temp 2` [append `temp` lines after line 2]
t (copy)	append copy of specified lines after specified line
	Example:
	`5,12t 2` [append lines 5–12 after line 2]
`w file`	write edited file to specified file
	Example:
	`w thisfile` [write `ed` file to `thisfile`]
`w`	replace original file by edited file
	Example:
	`w` [make changes permanent]
u (undo)	undo last line change that was made
q (quit)	leave ed
`!command`	execute shell command
	Example:
	`!date`
`+ lines`	advance specified number of lines
	Example:
	`+5` [advance 5 lines]
`- lines`	back up specified number of lines
`.`	prints current line
`.=`	prints current line number
`$`	go to last line
`s/string/`	search for first occurrence of string
`g/string/`	globally search for all lines containing string
`v/string/`	search for lines not containing string

B.3 Special Characters

CHARACTER	INTERPRETATION
`^`	beginning of line
`$`	end of line
`&`	copy target string back into line
`*`	match zero or more occurrences of previous character
`\ (escape)`	escape special meaning of next character
`.`	represents a single character

Appendix C: Guide to Editing with vi

vi Full-screen visual editor
USAGE:
`vi [ +line ] [ options ] [ files ]`
OPTIONS:

`+line`	position cursor at beginning of specified line
`-r`	retrieve last saved version of file after editor and/or system crash
`-R`	read-only mode
`-t tag`	position cursor at definition of `tag` (only in a file with a tag); use `ctags(1)` to make `tags` file
`-wn`	sets default window size to `n`
`-x`	create or edit an encrypted file

C.1 Cursor Movement

COMMAND	ACTION
`[n]G`	go to line `n` (G by itself moves cursor to last line)
`[n]CR`	moves cursor down n lines (a carriage return CR by itself moves the cursor down one line)
`[n]-`	moves cursor up n lines (a - by itself moves the cursor up one line)
`l`	press l key to move cursor to right
`spacebar`	same as l-key
`h`	press h key to move cursor to left
`backspace`	same as h-key
`j`	move cursor down
`ctrl-n`	same as j-key
`linefeed`	same as j-key
`k`	move cursor up
`ctrl-d`	scroll down
`ctrl-u`	scroll up
`ctrl-p`	same as k-key
`[n]$`	moves cursor to right n characters (a $ by itself moves cursor to the end of the current line)
`0`	moves cursor to beginning of current line
`^`	moves cursor left to first non-white character on current line

C.2 Special vi Commands

COMMAND	INTERPRETATION
`a` (append)	append after character where cursor is
`dd` (delete)	delete current line
`i` (insert)	insert before character where cursor is
`o` (insert)	insert after line where cursor is
`r` (replace)	replace character which cursor points to
`w` (move)	moves cursor to right a word at a time
`x` (delete)	delete character which cursor points to
`escape`	press escape key to exit from insert and append modes; this key will get you out of trouble, if forget what mode you are in (just press your escape key repeatedly until your terminal beeps).
`bksp`	remove last character entered
`ctrl-u`	restarts insertion
`ctrl-v`	removes special significance of next typed character
`ctrl-w`	move cursor back to first character of last word which was inserted
`shift ZZ`	save changes and exit from vi
`:q!`	exit from vi without saving edited file
`:x`	same as shift `ZZ`
`:w file`	write edited file to specified file
`:!cmd`	execute shell command Example: `:!date`
`:e!`	undo all previous commands since last `:w` file
`/string`	search forward for string
`?string`	search backward for string

Appendix D: C Programs

D.1

Reference: Section 7.12 awk leads to C and Procedure 3 (in Section 7.9.3)
Note: This program replaces `partition`, `select`, `cat` *and* `combine` *commands in the enigma procedure in Section 7.9.3.*

```c
#include <stdio.h>
#define WORDMAX 100

main() {
  char thisword[WORDMAX], sig[WORDMAX];
  char t;
  int i, j, k;

  while (scanf("%s", thisword) !=| EOF) {
    strcpy(sig, thisword);
    for (i = 0; i <= strlen(sig) - 1; i ++) {
      j = i;
      for (k = j + 1; k <= strlen(sig) - 1; k++)
        if (sig[k] < sig[j])
          j = k;
      t = sig[i];
      sig[i] = sig[j];
      sig[j] = t;
    }
    printf("\n%s %s\n", sig, thisword);
  }
}
```

D.2

Sample C program to read characters from the keyboard.
Note: Use this program if your system does not have **gets**.

```c
#include <stdio.h>
#define NL '\n'                                /*newline*/
main()
    {
    int ch;                                    /*char code*/

    while ((ch = getchar()) != NL && ch != EOF)
      putchar(ch);                             /*echo print*/
    putchar(NL);                               /*newline*/
    }
```

D.3

Variation of **gets** program in Appendix D.2
Method: capture **char** from **stdin** and echo char and its ASCII code
   pre: characters from stdin
   post: input character followed by ASCII code

```c
#include <stdio.h>

#define NL '\n'                              /*newline*/

main()
    {
    int ch;                                  /*char code*/

    while ((ch = getchar()) != NL && ch != EOF) {
      putchar(ch);                           /*echo print*/
      printf(" %2d\n", ch);                  /*ASCII code*/
      }
    putchar(NL);                             /*newline*/
    }
```

Appendix E: Cross-reference of Shell Procedures and Commands

PROCEDURE	COMMANDS USED	SECTION
.cshrc	alias set	8.2.1
.login	setenv set echo date	8.2.1
.logout	du echo	3.5
.logout	echo du date tee	8.2.4
.profile	date export	1.4.7
.profile	trap	3.5
0	grep	5.8.4
act0	echo ps	3.1
act20	echo sh	3.2
allargs	echo if set	8.5.2
ap	(C shell version) switch case breaksw default cat	8.6.1
ap	case ap echo	4.2.6
bee	sed	6.5
blastoff	echo exec	3.2.5
breaker	cal awk while break print END	7.7
bunch	sed	6.5
bundle	cd for name in * ckfile case bundle echo	5.7.1
bundle	for echo "cat >$name <<!"	5.7

PROCEDURE	COMMANDS USED	SECTION
capture	`awk split for printf` (with box array)	7.8
center	`echo`	5.9
check	`sleep who`	3.5
chop	`echo cut date`	3.3.2
ck	`test case $? in echo`	4.4
ckdir	`if ls wc`	4.2.1
ckfile	`set case exit case` (nested)	5.3
cksp	`tr sort uniq comm rm`	5.8.1
collect	`awk END printf`	7.9
combine	(C shell v.) `awk END print`	8.6.3
combine	`awk END print` (with arrays)	7.9.3
del	(C shell version) `echo foreach set switch case rm break`	8.6.2
del	`for i in "$@" echo read case ckfile if rm break`	5.3
dice	`while echo expr`	7.9.4
dirt	("directory for given date") `case ls grep`	5.6.2
dleft+	`set cal sed`	8.5.3
ds	`ls grep case ls echo`	5.6.1
e	`case date cut echo`	4.2.6
egg	`sleep ${1-300} echo ${2-$message}`	4.7
egg	`sleep echo`	3.9
enigma	(C shell version) `partition select cat combine sort squash`	8.6.3
enigma	`partition select cat combine sort squash`	7.9.3
exe	`chmod`	4.2.6
freq	("frequency table") `awk END print for printf while`	7.9.4
freq	`cksp sort uniq sort`	5.8.1
fromtop	`awk BEGIN END` (with arrays)	7.9
gred	`ed $2 <<!`	5.8.2
gsub	("global substitution") `ed $3 <<! g s gp w q`	4.8
hc	("house cleaning") `case $# in set while case` (nested) `ls break rm cat read`	4.3.3
hc	(refinement) `if until shift while` (nested)	4.3.3
idea	`awk BEGIN print`	7.10
isitaproc	("is it a procedure?") `grep if exit`	8.8
isitempty	("is file empty") `if echo exit test set if` (nested)	8.5.7
lexicon	`set foreach echo grep`	8.8
links	("word links (in game of doublets)") `sed -n </usr/dict/words '/^'$1'' $2''$3'$/p'`	6.6

APPENDIX E: SHELL PROCEDURES AND COMMANDS   **435**

PROCEDURE	COMMANDS USED	SECTION
loop1	`for echo`	4.3.1
loop2	`for i in * echo`	4.3.1
loop3	`for i list mail`	4.3.1
loop5	`while echo read`	4.3.2
mgram	`for name in 'cat ilist' mail`	4.3.1
mirror	`if echo mirror` (recursive call) `expr`	4.9
mole	("months left in year")	
	`case = until cal expr`	5.8.3
mototal	("monthly total storage used")	
	`ls awk END printf for` (with arrays)	7.9.1
no	("number lines of file")	
	`awk print` (C shell)	8.5
no	(refinement)	
	`if isitempty awk exit`	8.5.7
operators	`@ echo`	8.5.5
partition	("insert blank between each character")	
	(C shell version) `awk length print substr`	8.6.3
partition	(Bourne shell)	
	`awk for length printf substr`	7.8
pick	`grep ps for cut echo read case kill`	
	`break rm`	5.4
pl	`for dot in 1 2 3 4 5 6 echo $dot`	5.9
reminder	`date cut case echo`	4.2.5
response	`echo exit`	3.7
rnd	`date awk BEGIN substr sqrt int print`	7.9.4
rove	`for i in * echo expr`	4.5
samplelines	`awk print $1, $5,$NF`	7.3
savemonth	`ls awk print END`	7.10
scalp	`sed`	6.5
scan	`ls sort awk print`	7.4.3
scan2	`ls sort awk print NR, $0`	7.4.3
sd	("scan directories")	
	`cd echo ls for if sd` (recursive)	4.9
sd	(refinement)	
	`echo ls for name in $1/* do ckfile`	
	`case set sd`	5.6.3
search	`cd file grep tee wc cut if echo`	
	`cat rm`	4.2.3
seeday	`ls awk ' $6 ~ /'$1'/ && $7 ~ /'$2'/'`	7.4.4
seemonth	`ls awk print`	7.4.4
select	("selection sort")	
	`awk for` (nested)`if printf`	7.9.3
select	(C shell version)	
	`awk for if print printf`	8.6.3
show	`ls sed`	6.1
slim1	`tr -s "A-Za-z" <$1`	5.8.1
snoopy	`case $# in until sleep echo`	6.1

PROCEDURE	COMMANDS USED	SECTION
snoopy	`case $# in until who	grep $1 sleep echo`	5.2.5
snoopy	`until who	grep $1 sleep`	5.2.1
snoopy	`who egrep ''$1'|'$2''`	6.4
squash	(C shell version) `awk printf END`	8.6.3
squash	`awk printf print "\n" END`	7.9.3
stopwatch	`time $* 2>y cat awk printf rm`	7.6
strip	`sed`	6.3.3
tidy	`set 'date' ls grep`	5.8.5
tgram	("send telegram to user who logs on") `if write`	5.2.6
tylog	`cd foreach if ls echo cat`	8.5.6
window	`echo`	3.3.1
wleft	("weeks left") `set cal tee sed rm while case`	6.7
xref	`sort grep`	5.10
zap	`echo ps pick sleep`	5.4
zapln	`sed`	6.5

Selected Solutions

CHAPTER 1

3. `(date; who)|cat >rosterfile`
6. `mail you < rosterfile`
   (mail copy of rosterfile to yourself)
7. ```
   $ mail
   1 message
      1 you Thu Jul 27 10:01:32 1987

   1
   Message 1: ......

   w xerox1
   "xerox1" [ New file ] ...
   ```
17. (a) `rm t*`
    (d) `rm *bell*`

CHAPTER 2

5. ```
   $ cat >>keillor
   Garrison Keillor, Happy to be Here,
   p. 204.
   <control-d>
   $
   ```
8. ```
   $ echo "count: "; cat keillor|
   grep ing|
   tee copy|
   wc -w|
   tee count
   ```
11. `$ split -1 keillor happy`
    (creates files happyaa, happyab, and so on)

15. ```
    $ cat fc
    cd $*
    file *|grep command|
          tee -a $HOME/commands
    ```
18. ```
    $ cat phonebk|
    grep 212|
    split -1 - 212
    $
    ```
    (Creates files 212aa, 212ab, and so on. Caution: you must have a non-empty phonebk file with entries like the ones in Exercise 17.)
21. ```
    $ grep 305 phonebk |
          split -2 - 305
    ```
30. `$ find . -type f -ok wc -w {} \;`
37. ```
    $(file /usr/bin*;file bin/*) |
    grep 'commands text' |
    tee list
    ```

CHAPTER 3

1. Add

   ```
   PS1='$ '
   ```
   (Notice space after the $-sign.)

   to your .profile.
3. Add

   ```
   trap $HOME/.logout 0
   ```

   to your .profile. To test your revised .profile, try setting up a .logout file like the following one:
   ```

```
$ cat .logout
stopPID=`ps -f |
grep snoopy |
cut -c8-13`
kill $stopPID
```

To run snoopy, type

```
$ sh /usr/you/bin/snoopy &
```

Note: this assumes your snoopy file is in $HOME/bin.

10. Add

    ```
    (nice -
    10 nohup $HOME/bin/snoopy) &
    ```

    to your .profile. *Note: use $HOME/snoopy, if snoopy is in your $HOME directory.*

17. Use

    ```
    $ cd /usr/bin; pwd
    ```

26. `echo "The date" `date` "says it's winter."`

29. ```
    $ cat sv
    echo $1; shift; echo $1; shift;
    echo $1; shift; echo $1; shift;
    echo $1 $
    ```

32. ```
    $ cat clean
    cd $1; rm -i *
    $
    ```

39. ```
    $ cat zap
    at -l
    at -r $1
    echo
    at -l
    $
    ```

CHAPTER 4

1. ```
   $ cat egg
   # print a reminder later
   
   check=`expr 5 \| $1`
   message="coffee time!"
   if [ $check -ne 5 ]
   then
     (sleep $1; echo "$(2-$message)") &
   ```
   ```
   else
     (sleep $check;
       echo "$(2-$message)") &
   fi
   $
   ```

   Note: now try

   ```
   $ sh egg
   $ sh egg 2
   $ sh egg 2 "special message"
   ```

   Warning: this version of egg is still not robust. Hint: use the case statement to take care of egg-command lines with more than 2 arguments.

11. ```
    $ cat ckdir
    # modified ckdir procedure
     if (test $# -ne 2)
     then
      echo "Usage:
           ckdir dir-limit dir-name"
     else
      cd $2
      if (test `ls|wc -l` -gt $1)
      then
       echo $2" needs cleaning."
      else
       echo $2 "has more room"
      fi
     fi
    $
    ```

17. ```
    $ cat mgram
     if (test ! -s ilist)
     then
      echo "Sorry, file ilist is empty."
      exit
     fi
     for person in `cat ilist`
      do
       mail $person <message
      done
    $
    ```

32. [Solution by J.G. Seiler]

    ```
    $ cat strip
    # strips desired number of
    # characters off entered string
    ```

```
if (test $# -ne 1)
then
  echo "Usage: strip
          number-of-characters"
else
  count=$1
  echo -n "Enter a string: "; read str
  while (test "$count" -ne 0)
  do
    str=`expr $str : '.\(.*\)'`
    count=`expr $count - 1`
  done
  echo "stripped characters: " $str
fi
```

CHAPTER 5

1. ```
   $ cat snoopy
   # precondition: $1 is a user name
   # postcondition: line with $ from who
   # is printed

   (case $# in
     1) ls|grep $1
       if [ $? -eq 0 ]
       then
         until who|grep $1
         do
           sleep 600
         done
       else
         echo 'usage: $1 must be a
               user name in /user'
       fi;;
     *) echo 'Usage: snoopy user-name'
   esac) &
   ```

6. Use solution to Exercise 1.

7. Add

   ```
   ckfile $name
   ```
   to del.

11. [Solution by J.G. Seiler]

    ```
    $ cat dirs
    # case $# = 0 only (remaining cases left for exercise)

    set `date`; month=$2; day=$3;
    dir=.; flag=0
    IFS='
    '
    ```

    ```
    for name in `ls -lt $dir|
    grep -v '^t'`
    do
      tmon=`echo $name|cut -c42-44`
      tday=`echo $name|cut -c46-47`
      if [ "$tmon" != $month" -a $tday
          -ge $day ]
      then
        echo $name
      else
        flag=1
      fi
      if [ "$tmon" = "$month" -a $tday
          -ge $day ]
      then
        echo $name
      fi
      if [ "$tmon" != $month" -a $flag
          -eq 1 ]
      then
        exit
      fi
    done
    $
    ```

18. ```
    $ cat bundle
    # precondition: (1) names of files to bundle
    #               (2) name of destination file
    # postcondition: files bundled in destination file

    case $# in
      0) echo 'Usage: bundle filename(s)
    > destin-file';;
      *) for name
        do
          ckfile $name
          if [ $? -eq 2 ]
          then
            echo "cat > $name <<!"
            cat $name
            echo "!"
          fi
        done
    esac
    $
    ```

26. ```
    $ cat tally
    # precondition: file of characters
    # postcondition: tally of
    # occurrences of each word in file
    ```

440 SELECTED SOLUTIONS
    ```

```
tr -cs "[A-Z][a-z]" "[\012*]" < $1 |
tr "[A-Z]" "[a-z]" |
sort |
uniq -c |
sort -n
$
```

30. To adjust for discrepancies in changing the Julian to the Gregorian calendar, September 3 was made September 14. Do you notice anything else which is different about the 1752 calendar?

CHAPTER 6

1. Use

   ```
   grep -n . $1
   ```

6. ```
   $ cat pick
   # precondition: file to filter
   # postcondition: last "word" of each
   # line of specified file

   sed -n < $1 's/.* //g
        h
        g
        p'
   $
   ```

9. ```
   $ cat gsub
   # gsub stands for "global substitution"
   # preconditions: $1 substring to be replaced
   #                $2 new substring
   #                $3 file to scan

   ed $3 <<!
   g/$1/s//$2/gp
   w
   !echo 'edited text:'
   g/^/p
   q
   !echo 'global substitution done.'
   !
   $
   ```

12. To implement the -w option of bgrep, try

    ```
    # preconditions: $1 = bgrep option
    #                $2 = regular expression
    #                $3 = filename
    sed -n < $3 's/$//
          s/^/ /p' |
    grep " $2 "
    ```

14. (a) `grep .* *` prints every line of every file in your current directory.

16. (b) `egrep '[aeiou][aeiou][aeiou] $' /usr/dict/words | 5`

26. ```
    $ cat persons
    karen
    jim
    tammy

    $ cat showusers
    # postcondition: lines output by who
    # matching names in persons

    sed -n < persons 's/^/\//p' |
    sed -n 's/$/\/p/w list'
    who | sed -n -f list
    rm list
    $
    ```

CHAPTER 7

3. ```
   $ cat bytecount
   # precondition: nonempty current
   # directory
   # postcondition: average no. of
   # bytes per file

   ls -l . |
   awk '
     { if (NR == 1)
          total = $2
       tally = tally + $4 }
       END { printf "\nbytes/file =
              %.2f\n", tally/total }
   '
   $
   ```

10. ```
    ls -lt . |
    awk '
          $5 ~ /'$1'/ { print NR, $0 }
    '
    ```

CHAPTER 8

5. ```
   % cat hfiles
   ls -a . | sed -n '/^\./p'
   %
   ```

6. (a) `% alias dcsh 'more .csh'`
   (b) `% alias din 'cat .login'`
   (c) `% alias dout 'cat .logout'`

11. ```
    % alias w \
    'find / -name \!* -print'
    # locate file
    ```

SELECTED SOLUTIONS
    ```

Index of Symbols

/   root, 40
| pipe, 32–33
|| (or), 174
&   115–16
&&   (and), 174. *See also* **kill** command
!   (not), 174
−   33
*   27, 109
    closure operator, 244
:   174
.   (expr), 174
.   name, 25
.   command, 94–95, 107
..   parent, 40
`   (backward quote), 97, 101. *See also* Command; *substitution*
^   (up-arrow), 163
\   (case), 174

%   (C shell), 335
$ (Bourne shell), 5
$#   100–101
$$ 93. *See* Process
$*   75, 100
$!   100
$?   116–17
$0   100. *See also* Command; *verb*
$1...$9,   100, 102–3,
"$*"   100
"$@"   100, 103–4, 190
@,   10
11
?   12, 174
>   27–28
<   27–28
>>   29
<<   (here), 174

Index

A

Absolute mode, 63
Access bits, 63–64
    SGID, 64
    SUID, 64
Aho, A. V., 332
Anderson, G., 394
Anagram classes, 309–12
Arithmetic, 160. *See also* **expr**
ASCII character set, 427
at, 118–19, 399
AT&T, 332
awk, 282, 399
    applications, 307–15
    arrays, 304–7
    arithmetic, 293–95
    basic template, 284
    begin/end patterns, 288–89
    built–in functions, 301–4
    comparison with C, 318–23
    conditionals, 290
    control structures, 298–99
    features, 283
    fields, 286
    interacting with shell, 316–18
    operators, 295
    operator precedence, 295
    print, 286–87
    printf, 296–97
    records, 286
    structure, 283–86
    using shell arguments, 291
    variables, 293

B

Background processing, 115. *See also* **&**
Bailes, P. A., 332
Batch processing, 118–19
Bentley, J., 312, 332
Bin directory, 73
Babaoglu, O., 2
Bergson, H., 1, 43
Blake, W., 281
Block, 65
    block device, 65
Boehm, B. W., 235
Bolsky, M. I., 43
Boolean operator, 137
Bourne, S. R., 130, 178, 394
break, 399
BSD (Berkeley Software Distribution), 2, 31, 57
    4.2BSD, 2, 22, 65, 113
    4.3BSD, 2, 22, 113
Budgen, D., 333
Bundling software, 202–9
Hewett-Gosling method, 203, 205

444

C

C language, 2, 318
   escapes, 428
   programs, 432–34. *See also* **awk**
C shell, 334
   $history, 335
   alias, 336, 350–55, 398
   Anderson method, 347
   csh, 337
   .cshrc file, 339, 347–48
   customizing logoff, 346–47
   env, 338
   escape characters, 344
   event, 335
   history commands, 349
   procedures, 355. *See also,* **csh**
   retrieving events, 348–50
   set ignoreeof, 341
   set noclobber, 341
   setenv, 338, 340
   source, 341
   special files, 339
   tset syntax, 341
cal, 219–20, 400
   filtering output, 266–71
Calls-by-value, 110–11
   Carroll, L., 265, 281, 333
case 133, 143–44, 400
cat, 26, 400. *See also* redirection
   concatenate files, 32
   creating files, 31
cd, 19, 39, 400
chmod, 62–64, 401. *See also* Absolute mode; *permission bits*
comm, 211, 216–17, 401–2. *See also* Idiom
Command, 6, 39. *See also* **exec**
   arguments, 100
   assigned to variable, 99
   crossreference, 434–37
   lines, 6
   multiple commands, 91
   null sequence, 114
   procedure, 85, 124
   substitution, 96–99, 125
   verb, 101
   ways to execute, 88–91, 122–23
Control structure, 133–34
cp, 26, 402
crypt, 402–3

csh, 337, 402. *See also* C shell
   aliasing (*See* C shell)
   argument vector, 358
   argv, 357
   bitwise operators, 364
   chsh, 337, 401
   control structures, 367–68
   forms of exit, 370
   globbing, 381
   new clothes, 372
   numeric values, 364
   operator precedence, 363
   operators, 363
   redirection, 379
   use of **set,** 360
   variables, 360
cut command, 105–06, 403

D

date, 39, 403–04
Debugging, 112. *See also* **set**
Delete key, 110, 113–14. *See also* Interrupt
df, 77, 404
Dijkstra, E. W., 178
Directory, 14, 22. *See also* Pathname
   cd, 19
   dated entries, 200
   directory tree, 20
   entry parts, 47
   inumbers, 57, 59
   ls, 15
   ls options, 15
   mkdir, 19–20
   parts of long form, 16
   pwd, 14
   rmdir, 20–21
   searching, 141
   subdirectories, 16–19, 199
   system hierarchy, 47
Double alternative, 139. *See also* **if**
du, 66–67, 404

E

echo, 23, 404–5
Editing. *See also* Stream editing
   ed, 55–56, 146, 405, 429–30
   sed, 238, 248–81
   vi, 431–32

egrep, 245, 405. *See also* **grep**
   | (or) operator, 247
   extended regular expression, 247
   syntax, 245
elif, 142
Else, 142. *See also* **case**
env, 405–6
Equal sign, 135. *See also* String
exec, 95–96, 406
exit, 117, 134, 406
Exit status, 116, 161, 162. *See also* **$?**
Export, 110
expr, 32, 160–61, 406

F

fgrep, 406–7. *See also* **grep**
File, 14, 45. *See also* Filename; **ln**; Pathname
   access bits, 61
   command, 191
   creating files, 55–56 (*See also* **cat**; **ed**; **vi**)
   deleting, 189–91
   executable, 74
   finding files, 66–70 (*See also* **find**)
   inode, 61
   inumber, 46, 59, 61
   linking files, 47, 70–71
   number of links, 61
   permissions, 62 (*See also* **chmod**)
   separate, 74
   size, 61
   splitting files, 53–54
   ways to create, 49
File command, 65, 407
File management, 13
   commands, 13
   file, 14
Filename, 21–22, 46
   rules, 22. *See also* **ln,** Pathname
Filter, 34. *See also* **grep**; **sort**; **uniq**; **wc**
   definition, 236
Find, 67–70, 407
for command, 104, 134, 147, 205, 408
for syntax, 147
for each, 408
Fork, 3
Foxley, E., 83, 130
Fritz, T. E., 281

G

Game of doublets, 265
Global substitution, 147, 169
Gosling, J., 202
grep, 35, 73, 226, 241, 409. *See also* Regular expressions
   egrep, 237, 245, 405
   fgrep, 237, 238, 406
   grep family, 237, 240
   meaning, 237
   metacharacters, 240–41
   syntax, 240

H

hangman, 409
head, 409
help, 409
Here documents, 168–69, 203
Hewett, A., 202
HOME, 24, 106–7, 110. *See also* .profile; Search paths
Horowitz, E., 333

I

Idiom, 214
if, 133, 139–40, 410
IFS (internal field separator), 108
IEEE, 43, 87, 130, 333
Indexed iteration, 147. *See also* **for**
Inumber, 46, 59. *See also* **od**
   in hexidecimal, 60–61
   in octal, 58
Interrupt. *See* Shell; *signals*
Iteration control, 147, 151. *See also* **for**; **while**; **until**

J

Joy, B., 2, 334, 394–95
Joyce, J., 235

K

Keillor, G., 83
Kernel, 3, 45, 85
   services, 4
Kernighan, B. W., 43, 83, 130, 202, 261, 281, 333, 395
kill command, 116, 410

L

Lampson, B., 83, 235
Lindeman, J. P., 333
Lions, J., 83
ln, 47–48, 410
login, 4, 85
login shell, 85
.logout, 113. *See also* BSD, BSD4.x; **trap**
lpr, 410–11
ls, 15–19, 411–12. *See also* directory

M

man command, 75, 412
mail, 9, 11–13
   ctrl-d, 9
   delete, 9
McKusick, W. K., 83
McMahon, L. E., 281
mesg, 9, 412
Minix, 2
mkdir, 413
Mullender, S., 235
Multics, 3
mv, 26, 413

N

Next, 134
Nichols, E. A., 83

O

od, 58–61, 66, 413
Operating system, 1

P

Paradigm, 225
Pascal, 153
PATH variable, 24–25, 107
Pathname, 22
Pattern-matching rules, 163
Permission bits, 63
Peters, J. F., 83
Pike, R., 178, 202
Pipe, 32–36. *See also* |; **tee**
   filters, 34
   pipe fitting, 49
   redirection, 33

Poe, E. A., 235
Poole, P. C., 130
Pourboireki, N., 333
pr command 32, 413–14
.profile, 23–24, 107–8
Printing commands, 32
   lpr, 32–33
   pr, 32–33
Procedure, 85, 132
   Bergson design principle, 180
   crossreference, 434–37
   design, 180, 182, 187
   invariant assertions, 185
   kinds, 179–80
   postconditions, 184
   preconditions, 184
   robustness, 185
   scaffolding, 183
   stepwise refinements, 187, 198
   test data, 185
Process, 86. *See also* login shell; **ps**; **$$**
   PID, 93
   spawned, 85
   zapping, 194–95
ps command, 87, 414
PS1, 108–9
PS2, 108–9
pwd, 414

Q

Quarterman, J. S., 43, 395

R

Random numbers, 313–15
Recursive procedure, 170
Redirection, 27, 28–30. *See also* **cat**
   creating files, 31
Regular expression, 73, 240–41
   concatenated, 242
   tagged, 245
Relational operator, 135–36
Rhyming dictionary, 261
rm, 27, 414
rmdir, 415
Robust procedure, 139, 173
Rochkind, M., 2, 44, 130
Ritchie, D., 1, 44, 45, 83

S

Scanners, 210, 211, 237, 308
SCO, 44
Search paths, 24–25. *See also* **.name**
sed, 415. *See also* Stream editing
Seiler, J., 439, 440
set, 112–13, 123, 415–16
setenv, 416
sh, 4, 334, 416. *See also* Shell
Shell, 4
    Bourne shell (*See* **sh**)
    C shell, 113
    child, 124
    evaluation, 166, 168
    metacharacters, 164
    prompt, 5, 7
    script, 132 (*See also* BSD4.x; Variable)
    signals, 113
    standard i/o files, 27
    variables, 100, 103–6, 166
    variables summary, 166
    ways to evaluate, 168
Shift, 416
Silvester, M. J., 130
sleep, 119–20, 417
SNOBOL 4, 282. *See also* **awk**
sort, 35, 211, 417–18
source, 418
Spelling checker, 210
Spelling dictionary, 210
split, 53–54, 418–19
Stream editing, 248, 415
    applications, 261–271
    flow-of-control functions, 254–55
    hold-and-get functions, 257–58
    multiple line functions, 253
    sed equivalents, 259–60

sed functions, 250–51
sed syntax, 248
    substitution, 249
String, 135, 162. *See also* Relational operator
Stroustrup, B., 83, 395
stty, 9, 419

T

tail, 419
tee, 49–51, 420
    multiple files, 52
test, 25, 158–59, 420–22
Tanenbaum, A., 2. *See also* MINEX
Thompson, K., 1
Thurber, J., 281
time, 118–19, 422
Timer, 120–22
Timeshare system, 1
tr, 226, 423
trap, 113–14, 423
Truth table, 137. *See* Boolean operator
tset, 422

U

Unbundling software, 208–9
Unix, 2. *See also* BSD; Xenix
    Berkeley Unix, 57
    file, 45
    7th edition, 2
    POSIX, 2, 22
    signals, 428
    System V, 57
    time chart, 3
    Tunis, 2
uniq, 211, 423–24

unset, 424
until, 134, 153, 424
USG (Unix Support Group), 2

V

Van Wyk, C. J., 333
variable, 23–24. *See also* PATH variable; PS1; PS2; IFS
    $-sign prefix, 23
    command line, 101
    default values, 110
    shell, 100
    special, 100
    standard shell, 106–7
vi, 56–57, 424
Vick, C. R., 235
vt100, 11

W

Walton, I., 130
wc, 35, 424
whereis, 424–25
while, 134, 151, 425
who, 425–26
Wildcards, 25–26
write, 7, 226, 426
    write session, 8
who, 5, 7
    who am i, 5
    -q option, 6
    -t option, 5

X

Xenix, 2
    MS Xenix, 2
    Xenix-3, 2

Table of Special Bourne Shell Command Arguments

argument	value
`$#`	Number of command line positional parameters
`$0`	Command line verb
`$1`	First command line argument (if there is one)
`$2 , , $9`	Command line arguments 2 through 9
`$*`	All command line arguments (uninterpreted)
`"$*"`	All command line arguments interpreted as one word (equivalent to " $1 $2 $3 …")
`"$@"`	All command line arguments but not joined together (equivalent to "—1" "—2" "—3" …)
`$-`	Shell options as in
	`$ echo $-`
	`s`
	`$ set -x` # turn on echoing commands
	`$ echo $-`
	`+ echo xs`
	`xs`
	`$`
`$?`	Value returned by last command executed
`$$`	Process id of current shell
`$!`	Process id of last command started with &
`$HOME`	Default argument for cd command
`$IFS`	Characters that separate words in arguments
`$MAIL`	Name of mail file
`$MAILCHECK`	Check mailfiles for mail every n seconds (default value of n = 600)
`$PATH`	List of directories in search path
`$PS1`	Primary prompt string (default is —)
`$PS2`	Secondary prompt string (default is >)

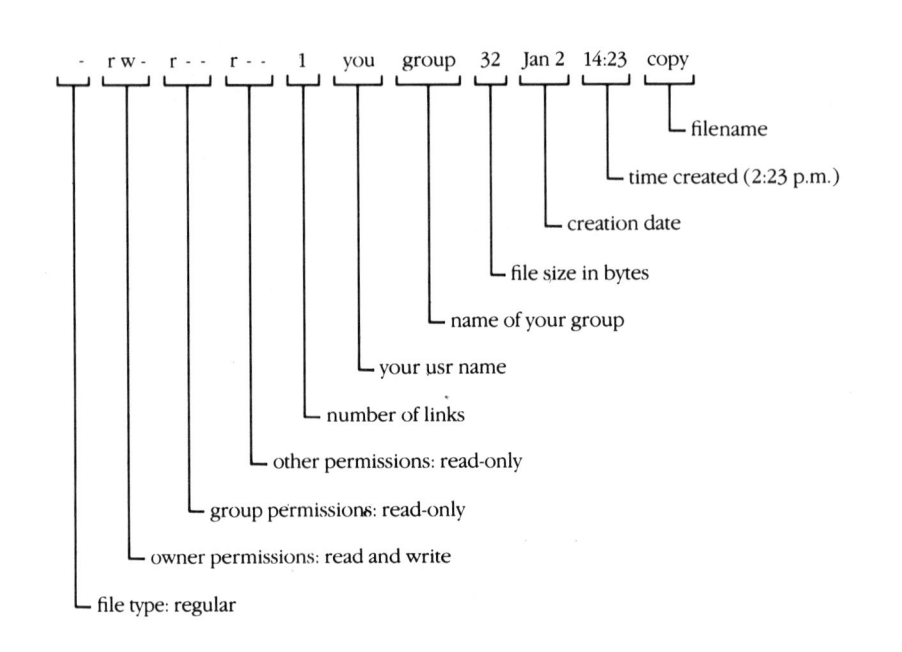

```
- rw- r-- r-- 1 you group 32 Jan 2 14:23 copy
│  │   │   │  │   │    │    │     │    │
│  │   │   │  │   │    │    │     │    └─ filename
│  │   │   │  │   │    │    │     └─ time created (2:23 p.m.)
│  │   │   │  │   │    │    └─ creation date
│  │   │   │  │   │    └─ file size in bytes
│  │   │   │  │   └─ name of your group
│  │   │   │  └─ your usr name
│  │   │   └─ number of links
│  │   └─ other permissions: read-only
│  └─ group permissions: read-only
└─ owner permissions: read and write
└─ file type: regular
```